Lecture Notes in Computer Science 1022
Edited by G. Goos, J. Hartmanis and J. van Leeuwen

Springer
Berlin
Heidelberg
New York
Barcelona
Budapest
Hong Kong
London
Milan
Paris
Santa Clara
Singapore
Tokyo

Pieter H. Hartel Rinus Plasmeijer (Eds.)

Funtional Programming Languages in Education

First International Symposium, FPLE '95
Nijmegen, The Netherlands, December 4-6, 1995
Proceedings

Springer

Volume Editors

Pieter H. Hartel
University of Amsterdam, Faculty of Mathematics and Computer Science
Kruislaan 403, 1098 SJ Amsterdam, The Netherlands

Rinus Plasmeijer
University of Nijmegen, Computing Science Institute
Toernooiveld 1, 6525 ED Nijmegen, The Netherlands

Cataloging-in-Publication data applied for

Die Deutsche Bibliothek - CIP-Einheitsaufnahme

Functional programming languages in education : first international symposium ; proceedings / FPLE '95, Nijmegen, The Netherlands, December 4 - 6, 1995. Pieter H. Hartel ; Rinus Plasmeijer (ed.). - Berlin ; Heidelberg ; New York ; Barcelona ; Budapest ; Hong Kong ; London ; Milan ; Paris ; Tokyo : Springer, 1995
(Lecture notes in computer science ; Vol. 1022)
ISBN 3-540-60675-0
NE: Hartel, Pieter H. [Hrsg.]; FPLE <1, 1995, Nijmegen>; GT

CR Subject Classification (1991): D.1.1, F.3.1, K.3.2

ISBN 3-540-60675-0 Springer-Verlag Berlin Heidelberg New York

Printed in Germany

Typesetting: Camera-ready by author
SPIN 10512326 06/3142 - 5 4 3 2 1 0 Printed on acid-free paper

Preface

This volume contains the papers accepted for presentation at the first international symposium on *Functional Programming Languages in Education*, held near Nijmegen, The Netherlands, December 4–6, 1995. These proceedings represent current trends in using functional languages to support computer science education. Functional languages are to be understood here in a broad sense; lazy and strict functional languages, languages with a powerful functional subset, and algebraic specification formalisms.

Functional languages are increasingly used for teaching in a number of important areas such as algorithms and data structures, compiler construction, computer architecture, computer graphics, mathematics, problem solving, and the semantics of programming languages. Experience gained in these areas is represented in this volume.

Functional languages are gathering momentum in education because they facilitate the expression of concepts and structures at a high level of abstraction. This makes it possible to cover more ground than when using a more traditional approach to teaching. This claim is substantiated by many of the authors who have contributed to this volume.

The first paper is an invited paper by one of the pioneers of functional programming: Professor David Turner. His paper on strong functional programming represents an exciting avenue that should have important implications for our teaching practice.

The next four papers describe the use of functional languages at the very beginning of the curriculum. The subjects include teaching the principles of programming and problem solving (Keravnou), programming in C as a second language (Davison), an introduction to computer science for science students (Jacquot and Guyard), and data structures (Núñez et al).

The next two papers consider the use of functional programming in a more advanced context. Thompson and Hill offer a broad perspective on functional programming in undergraduate teaching of computer architecture, computer graphics and the semantics of programming languages. Jarvis et al. discuss teaching functional programming at graduate level in the context of a large research project.

The support of functional programming for teaching in areas of mathematics is explored in the next set of four papers. The papers by Karczmarczuk and Fokker discuss algebraic and other mathematical structures in connection with type and constructor classes. The use of powerful type systems offered by modern functional languages has been found to be helpful in gaining an understanding of complex mathematical structures. Karczmarczuk is critical of the facilities offered by Gofer and Haskell. Further research in this area is needed to develop even more powerful type systems.

The paper by Lester and Mintchev, and the paper by Burton address the important concepts of induction and recursion. Lester and Mintchev describe the use of a theorem prover to help students with the development of inductive proofs; Burton offers a taxonomy of recursive structures to guide the students through a myriad of choices.

Broadly speaking the subjects of the first ten regular papers are mainly to do with programming and with mathematics. The connection with functional programming is immediate, as functional programming is intimately associated both with mathematics and with programming. Not so obvious, but very exciting, is the connection between functional programming and the subjects of the next two papers: computer architecture and databases.

O'Donnell discusses a course in circuit design and computer architecture on the basis of a functional language. Koopman and Zweije present an introduction to databases using a functional language. In both papers the high level of abstraction afforded by the use of a functional language makes it possible to discuss all levels of abstraction that are relevant to the course.

The next two papers describe the use of functional languages in compiler design. Kluge et al. describe the use of an interactive reduction system to support the teaching of abstract machine concepts and compilation. Hilsdale et al. describe the construction of a realistic compiler in a limited amount of time.

In most of the first 14 regular papers of this volume, teaching experience is discussed in some detail. However, the emphasis is generally on technical issues. The last two papers specifically look at teaching experience. Hartel et al. consider the (lack of) basic proof skills of computer science students and investigate the relation between teaching a functional language and the level of proof skills. Clack and Myers discuss in detail the sort of mistakes that students can make when they are learning functional programming. They give valuable advice to teachers on how to avoid common problems.

The papers in this volume represent the current state of the art in using functional languages in education. However, many of the courses that are described in this volume are only taught at a few institutions. There is a need for text books covering new approaches to teaching on the basis of a functional language. Several of the authors who have contributed to this volume are indeed writing new text books. The appearance of such texts will undoubtedly stimulate others to take up the new teaching methods that are being developed today.

We look forward to a period wherein these approaches are consolidated and a wider dissemination of these approaches is achieved. We also hope that functional languages may be found useful in teaching other subject areas. It is clear to us that functional languages do have their role to play in education, as do imperative, object oriented, and logic languages.

On behalf of the programme committee we thank all those who submitted papers. We thank the referees for their careful work in the reviewing and selection process. Jacqueline Parijs has done most of the local organisation, which is gratefully acknowledged.

Pieter H. Hartel, Amsterdam
Rinus Plasmeijer, Nijmegen
September 1995

Programme committee

Hugh Glaser	University of Southampton, UK
Pieter Hartel	University of Amsterdam, The Netherlands
Paul Hudak	Yale University, USA
John Hughes	Chalmers University, Sweden
Herbert Kuchen	University of Aachen, Germany
Peter Lee	Carnegie-Mellon University, USA
Nick Mansurov	Moscow State University, Russia
Daniel Le Métayer	IRISA/INRIA Rennes, France
John O'Donnell	University of Glasgow, UK
Rinus Plasmeijer	University of Nijmegen, The Netherlands

Referees

Marcel Beemster	Pieter Hartel	Jon Mountjoy
Mark van den Brand	Paul Hudak	Henk Muller
Chih-Ping Chen	John Hughes	Jacques Noye
Dinesh	Herbert Kuchen	John O'Donnell
Rémi Douence	Dominique Lavenier	Rinus Plasmeijer
Annie Foret	Peter Lee	Olivier Ridoux
Pascal Fradet	Gilles Lesventes	Mark Tullsen
Hugh Glaser	Nikolai Mansurov	Susan Üsküdarlı
Anne Grazon	Daniel Le Métayer	Eelco Visser

The FPLE '95 symposium was organised in cooperation with IFIP WG 2.8

Table of contents

Elementary Strong Functional Programming

D. A. Turner

University of Kent
Canterbury CT2 7NF, England

Abstract. Functional programming is a good idea, but we haven't got it quite right yet. What we have been doing up to now is weak (or partial) functional programming. What we should be doing is strong (or total) functional programming - in which all computations terminate. We propose an elementary discipline of strong functional programming. A key feature of the discipline is that we introduce a type distinction between *data*, which is known to be finite, and *codata*, which is (potentially) infinite.

1. What is Functional Programming?

It is widely agreed that functional programming languages make excellent introductory teaching vehicles for the basic concepts of computing. The wide range of topics covered in this symposium is evidence for that. But what is functional programming?

Well, it is programming with functions, that much seems clear. But this really is not specific enough. The methods of denotational semantics show us how almost any programming language construction, no matter how opaque and side-effect ridden, can be construed functionally if we are willing to introduce complicated enough spaces for the functions to work on.

It is somewhat difficult to pin down with complete precision, but what we conventionally mean by functional programming involves the idea that the functions are transparent in the notation we actually write, rather than having to be teased out by some complex process of interpretation. For example if I write, in Miranda[1] or Haskell (actually neither language has `nat` as a distinct type, but that's an oversight)

```
>       fac :: nat->nat
>       fac 0 = 1
>       fac (n+1) = (n+1)*fac n
```

then the semantics I intend has that `fac` really is a function from natural numbers to natural numbers, not something else, such as a function from `nat×store` to `nat×store`, as I would have to say in a language with side effects, or a transformation over `nat`-demanding continuations, which is what I would have to say in a language with jumps as well as side effects.

Further, the equations which I have written as the definition of `fac` are actually true, and are everything I need to know about it. From them I can infer not only, e.g.

```
        fac 3 = 6
```

but also more general properties of `fac`, by using induction principles and algebraic reasoning.

In a functional language things are what we say they are, not something much more complicated in disguise. This is particularly apparent in the notational style represented by such languages as Miranda [9], Haskell [4], and the functional subset of Standard ML [3]. We have

(i) strong typing: the domain and codomain of each function is either stated in or inferable from the program text, and there is a syntactic discipline which prevents a function from being applied to an inappropriate argument.

(ii) functions are defined by equations - typically involving case analysis by pattern matching - and we can do equational reasoning in a familiar algebraic way.

(iii) expressions can be evaluated by treating the program equations as rewrite rules, so computation is a special case of equational reasoning - and the final result will be independent of the order in which the rewrite rules are applied.

(iv) there are simple induction rules associated with the various (non-function) data types - and new types are introduced in a way that enables a corresponding induction principle to be readily inferred.

We can sum this up by saying that functional programming is programming with functions in a style that supports equational reasoning and proof by induction.

Those of us who have become converted are convinced that this is an excellent way to teach programming.

THE BAD NEWS. Unfortunately, none of the properties I have ascribed to functional languages above is actually quite true of any of our present languages. There is a pathology, connected with the possibility of run-time errors and non-terminating computations, which runs right through everything, and messes up all the details.

For a discussion of the complexities that can arise in reasoning about Miranda programs see Thompson [7]. Similar complications arise for any of the functional languages in current use, the details depending on such matters as whether the language is strict or lazy.

The thesis of this paper is as follows. Functional programming is a very good idea, but we haven't got it quite right yet. What we have been doing up to now is *weak* functional programming. What we should be doing is *strong* functional programming.

The remaining sections of the paper are organised as follows. Section 2 introduces the idea of strong functional programming. In section 3 we outline an elementary language for strong functional programming over finite data. In section 4 we show how the concept of codata can be added, to bring back the possibility of programming with infinite streams etc. In section 5 we make some closing remarks.

2. Strong Functional Programming.

Conventional functional programming may be called *weak*. What is the difference between weak and strong?

In a weak functional language if we have an expression, say

```
e :: int
```

we know that if evaluation of e terminates successfully, the result will be an integer - but evaluation of e might fail to terminate, or might result in an error condition.

In a strong functional language, if we have an expression

```
e :: int
```

we know that evaluation of e will terminate successfully with an integer result . In strong functional programming there are no non-terminating computations, and no run-time errors.

In the semantics of weak functional programming each type T contains an extra element $\perp_T$ to denote errors and non-terminations.

In strong functional programming $\perp$ does not exist. The data types are those of standard mathematics.

What are the advantages of strong functional programming? There are three principle ones:

1) The proof theory is much more straightforward.
2) The implementor has greater freedom of action.
3) Language design issues are greatly simplified (no strict versus non-strict).

2.1 Simpler Proof Theory.

One of the things we say about functional programming is that it's easy to prove things, because there are no side effects. But in Miranda or Haskell - or indeed SML - the rules are not those of standard mathematics. For example if e is of type nat, we cannot assume

```
e - e = 0
```

because e might have for its value $\perp_{nat}$.

Similarly we cannot rely on usual principle of induction for nats

$$\frac{\begin{array}{l}P(0)\\ \forall n.P(n) \Rightarrow P(n+1)\end{array}}{\forall n.P(n)}$$

without taking precautions to deal with the case $n = \perp$

These problems arise, in different ways, in both strict and lazy languages. In strong functional programming these problems go away because there is no $\perp$ to worry about. We are back in the familiar world of sets.

2.2 Flexibility of Implementation.

In strong functional programming reduction is *strongly Church-Rosser.* Note the distinction between

(A) Church-Rosser Property:

If E can be reduced in two different ways, then if they both produce normal forms, these will be the same

(B) Strong Church-Rosser Property:

Every reduction sequence leads to a normal form, and normal forms are unique.

The ordinary Church-Rosser property gives a form of confluence, with strong Church-Rosser we have this plus strong normalisability - so we can evaluate in any order. This gives much greater freedom for implementor to choose an efficient strategy, perhaps to improve space behaviour, or to get more parallelism. The choice of eager or lazy evaluation becomes a matter for the implementor, and cannot affect the semantics.

2.3 Simpler Language Design.

In weak functional programming languages we have many extra design decisions to make, because of strict versus non-strict. Consider for example the & operation on `bool`, defined by

```
True & True = True
True & False = False
False & True = False
False & False = False
```

but there are more cases to consider:

```
⊥ & y = ?
x & ⊥ = ?
```

considering the possible values for these (which are constrained by monotonicity) gives us a total of four different possible kinds of &, namely

(i) doubly strict &
(ii) left-strict &
(iii) right-strict &
(iv) doubly non-strict (parallel) &

Should we provide them all? Only one? How shall we decide?

In strong functional programming these semantic choices go away. Only one & operation exists, and it is defined by its actions on `True`, `False` alone.

2.4 Disadvantages.

What are the disadvantages of strong functional programming? There are two obvious ones

1) Programming language is no longer Turing complete!
2) If all programs terminate, how do we write an operating system?

Can we live with 1? We will return to this in the closing section, so let us postpone discussion for now.

The answer to 2 is that we need *codata* as well as data. (But unlike in weak functional programming, the two will be kept separate. We will have finite data and infinite codata, but no partial data.)

There already exists a theory of strong functional programming which has been extensively studied. This is the constructive type theory of Per Martin-Löf (of which there are several different versions). This is a very complex theory which includes:

- Dependent types (types indexed over values)
- Second order types
- An isomorphism between types and propositions, that enables programs to encode proof information.

This is a powerful and interesting theory, but it not suitable as a vehicle for first year teaching - it seems unlikely to replace PASCAL as the introductory programming language.

We need something simpler.

3. Elementary strong Functional Programming?

What I propose is something much more modest than constructive type theory, namely an *elementary* discipline of strong functional programming.

Elementary here means

1) Type structure no more complicated than Hindley/Milner, or one of its simple variants. So we will have types like int→int, and polymorphic types like $\alpha \to \alpha$, but nothing worse.

2) Programs and proofs will be kept separate, as in conventional programming. What we are looking for is essentially a strongly terminating subset of Miranda or Haskell (or for that matter SML, since the difference between strict and lazy goes away in a strong functional language)

First, we must be able to define data types.

```
>  data day = Mon | Tue | Wed | Thur | Fri | Sat | Sun

>  data nat = Zero | Suc nat

>  data list α = Nil | Cons α (list α)

>  data tree = Nilt | Node nat tree tree

>  data array α = Array (nat→α)
```

As is usual some types - `nat`, `list` for example - will be built in, with special syntax, for convenience. So we can write e.g. 3 instead of `Suc(Suc(Suc Zero))`.

There are three essential restrictions.

RULE 1) All primitive operations must be total. This will involve a some non-standard decisions - for example we will have

$$0/0=0$$

Runciman [6] gives a useful and interesting discussion of how to make natural arithmetic closed. He argues that the basic arithmetic type in a functional language should be `nat` and not `int`, and I am persuaded by his arguments.

Making all basic operations total of course requires some attention at types other than `nat` - for example we have to decide what to do about `hd[]`. There are various possible solutions - making `hd` return an element of a disjoint union, or giving it an extra argument, which is the value to be returned on `[]`, are the two obvious possibilities. It will require a period of experiment to find the best style. Notice that because hd is polymorphic we cannot simply assign a conventional value to hd [ ], for with the abolition of ⊥ we no longer have any values of type α.

RULE 2) Type recursion must be *covariant*. That is type recursion through the left hand side of → is not permitted. For example

```
>  data silly = Silly (silly→nat)      ||not allowed!
```

Contravariant types like silly allow ⊥ to sneak back in, and are therefore banned.

Finally, it should be clear that we also need some restriction on recursive function definitions. Allowing unrestricted general recursion would bring back ⊥.

First note that to define functions we introduce the usual style of equational definition, using pattern matching over data types. Eg

```
>  size :: tree α → nat
>  size Nilt = 0
>  size (Node n x y) = n + size x + size y
```

To avoid non-termination, we must restrict ourselves to *well-founded recursion*. How should we do this? If we were to allow arbitrary well-founded recursion, we would have to submit a proof that each recursive call descends on some well-founded ordering, which the compiler would have to check. We might also have to supply a proof that the ordering in question really is well-founded, if it is not a standard one.

This contradicts our requirement for an *elementary* language, in which programs and proofs can be kept separate. We need a purely syntactic criterion, by which the compiler can enforce well-foundedness. I propose the following rule

RULE 3) Each recursive function call must be on a syntactic subcomponent of its formal parameter (the exact rule is slightly more elaborate, to take account of pattern matching over several arguments simultaneously - this is so as to allow "nested" structural recursion, as in Ackermann's function - the extension adds no power, because what it does can be desugared using higher order functions, but is syntactically convenient).

The classic example of what this allows is recursion of the form

```
>  f :: nat→thing
>  f 0 = something
>  f (n+1) = ...f n...
```

except that we generalise the paradigm to multiple arguments and to syntactic descent on the constructors of any data type, not just nat.

The rule effectively restricts us to primitive recursion, which is guaranteed to terminate. But isn't primitive recursion quite weak? For example is it not the case that Ackermann's function fails to be primitive recursive? NO, that's a first order result - it does not apply to a language with higher order functions.

IMPORTANT FACT: we are here working in a higher order language, so what we actually have are the primitive recursive functionals of finite type, as studied by Gödel [2] in his System T.

These are known to include every recursive function whose totality can be proved in first order logic (starting from the usual axioms for the elementary data types, eg the Peano axioms for nat). So Ackermann is there, and much, much else. Indeed, we have more than system T, because we can define data structures with functional components, giving us infinitarily branching trees. Depending on the exact rules for typechecking polymorphic functions, it is possible to enlarge the set of definable functions to all those which can be proved total in *second order* arithmetic.

So it seems the restriction to primitive recursion does not deprive us of any functions that we need, BUT we may have to code things in an unfamiliar way - and it is an open question whether it gives us all the *algorithms* we need (this is a different issue, as it relates to complexity and not just computability). I have been studying various examples, and find the discipline surprisingly convenient.

An example.

Quicksort is not primitive recursive. However Treesort is primitive recursive (we descend on the subtrees) and for each version of Quicksort there is a Treesort which performs exactly the same comparisons and has the same complexity, so we haven't lost anything.

Another example - fast exponentiation.

```
>  pow :: nat->nat->nat
>  pow x n   =  1,                         if n == 0
>            =  x × pow (x × x) (n/2),     if odd n
>            =  pow (x × x) (n/2),         otherwise
```

(An aside - note that the last guard of a guard set must be otherwise.) This definition is not primitive recursive - it descends from n to n/2. Primitive recursion on nats descends from (n+1) to n.

However, we can recode by introducing an intermediate data type [bit], (i.e. list-of-bit), and assuming a built in function that gives us access to the binary representation of a number.

```
>  data bit = On | Off

>  bits :: nat->[bit]           ||built in

>  pow x n = pow1 x (bits n)
>  pow1 x Nil = 1
>  pow1 x (On : y) = x × pow1 (x × x) y
>  pow1 x (Off : y) = pow1 (x × x) y
```

Summary of programming situation:

Expressive power - we can write any function which can be proved total in the first order theory of the (relevant) data types. (FACT, DUE TO GÖDEL)

Efficiency - I find that around 80% of the algorithms we ordinarily write are already primitive recursive. Many of the others can be reexpressed as primitive recursive, with same computational complexity, by introducing an intermediate data structure. (MY CONJECTURE: with more practice we will find this is always true.)

I believe it would not be at all difficult to learn to program in this discipline, but you do have to make some changes to your programming style. More research is needed (for example Euclid's algorithm for `gcd` is difficult to express in a natural way).

It is worth remarking that there is a sledge-hammer approach that can be used to rewrite as primitive recursive any algorithm for which we can compute an upper bound on its complexity. We add an additional parameter, which is a natural number initialised to the complexity bound, and count down on that argument while recursing. This wins no prizes for elegance, but it is an existence proof that makes more plausible my conjecture above.

3.1 PROOFS

Proving things about programs written in this discipline is very straightforward. Equational reasoning, starting from the program equations as axioms about the functions they define.

For each data type we have a principle of structural induction, which can be read off from the type definition, eg

```
>       data nat = Zero | Suc nat
```

this gives us, for any property `P` over `nat`

$$\frac{P(\text{Zero}) \qquad \forall n.P(n) \rightarrow P(\text{Suc } n)}{\forall n.P(n)}$$

We have no $\bot$ and no domain theory to worry about. We are in standard (set theoretic) mathematics.

4. CODATA

What we have sketched so far would make a nice teaching language but is not enough for production programming. Let us return to the issue of writing an operating system.

An operating system can be considered as a function from a stream of requests to a stream of responses. To program things like this functionally we need infinite lists - or something equivalent to infinite lists.

In making everything well-founded and terminating we have seemingly removed the possibility of defining infinite data structures. To get them back we introduce *codata type definitions*:

```
>  codata colist a = Conil | a ♦ colist a
```

`Codata` definitions are equations over types that produce final algebras, instead of the initial algebras we get for `data` definitions. So the type `colist` contains all the infinite lists as well as finite ones - to get the infinite ones alone we would omit the `Conil` alternative. Note that infix ♦ is the coconstructor for colists.

The rule for coprimitive corecursion on codata is the dual to that for primitive recursion on data. Instead of descending on the argument, we ascend on the result. Like this

```
>  f :: something→colist nat          ||example
>  f args = RHS (f args')
```

where the leading operator of `RHS` *must be a coconstructor*. There is no constraint on the form of `args'`.

Notice that corecursion *creates* (potentially infinite) codata, whereas ordinary recursion *analyses* (necessarily finite) data. Ordinary recursion is not legal over codata, because it might not terminate. Conversely corecursion is not legal if the result type is data, because data must be finite.

Now we can define infinite structures, such as

```
>  ones :: colist nat
>  ones = 1 ♦ ones

>  fibs :: colist nat
>  fibs  =   f 0 1
>            where
>            f a b = a ♦ f b (a+b)
```

and many other examples which every Miranda or Haskell programmer knows and loves.

NOTE THAT ALL OUR INFINITE STRUCTURES ARE TOTAL

As in the case of primitive recursion over data, the rule for coprimitive corecursion over codata requires us to rewrite some of our algorithms, to adhere to the discipline of strong functional programming. This is sometimes quite hard - for example rewriting the well known sieve of Eratosthenes program in this discipline involves coding in some bound on the distance from one prime to the next.

There is a (very nice) principle of coinduction, which we use to prove infinite structures equal. It can be read off from the definition of the codata type. We discuss this in the next subsection.

A question. Does the introduction of codata destroy the strong Church-Rosser property? No! (But you have to have the right definition of normal form. Every expression whose principle operator is a coconstructor is in normal form.)

4.1 Coinduction

First we give the definition of bisimilarity (on colists). We can characterise ≈ the bisimilarity relation as follows

```
    x ≈ y   ⇒ hd x = hd y  &   tl x ≈ tl y
```

Actually this is itself a corecursive definition! To avoid a meaningless regress what one actually says is that anything obeying the above is a *bisimulation*, and by bisimilarity we mean the largest such relation. For a fuller discussion see Pitt [5]. Taking as read this background understanding of how to avoid logical regress, we say that in general two pieces of codata are bisimilar if:

- their finite parts are equal, and
- their infinite parts are bisimilar.

The principle of coinduction may now be stated as follows: *Bisimilar objects are equal.*

One way to understand this principle is to take it as the definition of equality on infinite objects

We can package the definition of bisimilarity and the principle that bisimilar objects are equal in the following method of proof: *When proving the equality of two infinite structures we may assume the equality of recursive substructures of the same form.*

For colists we get - to prove

$$g\ x_1\ \ldots\ x_n \ = \ h\ x_1\ \ldots\ x_n$$

It is sufficient to show

$$g\ x_1\ \ldots\ x_n \ = \ e \blacklozenge g\ a_1\ \ldots\ a_n$$
$$h\ x_1\ \ldots\ x_n \ = \ e \blacklozenge h\ a_1\ \ldots\ a_n$$

There is a similar rule for each codata type

A trivial example

```
>          x  =  1 ♦ x
>          y  =  1 ♦ y
```

How do we prove that x = y?

<u>Theorem</u> x = y
<u>Proof</u> by coinduction

```
          x
          =   1 ♦ x                   {x}
          =   1 ♦ y                   {ex hypothesi}
          =   y                       {y}
```

<u>QED</u>

Example: reflection on infinite trees

```
>  codata inftree = T nat inftree inftree
>  refl :: inftree → inftree
>  refl (T a x y) = T a (refl y)(refl x)
```

Theorem `refl (refl x) = x`
Proof by coinduction

```
refl (refl (T a y z)
   = refl (T a (refl z) (refl y))          {refl}
   = T a (refl (refl y)) (refl (refl z))   {refl}
   = T a y z                               {ex hypothesi}
```

QED

Example: the (co)map-iterate theorem

The following example is taken due to Bird & Wadler (see [1], page 184). We have changed the name of map to `comap` because for us they are different functions.

```
>        iterate f x = x ♦ iterate f (f x)
>        comap f (a ♦ x) = f a ♦ comap f x
```

Theorem `iterate f (f x) = comap f (iterate f x)`
Proof by coinduction

```
iterate f (f x)
   = f x ♦ iterate f (f (f x))           {iterate}
   = f x ♦ comap f (iterate f (f x))     {ex hyp}
   = comap f (x ♦ iterate f (f x))       {comap}
   = comap f (iterate f x)               {iterate}
```

QED

The proof given in [1] uses the `take`-lemma - it is longer than that given above and requires an auxiliary construction, involving the application of a `take` function to both sides of the equation, and an induction on the length of the take.

Summary

The "strong coinduction" principle illustrated here seems to give shorter proofs of equations over infinite lists than either of the proof methods for this which have been developed in the theory of weak functional programming - namely partial object induction (Turner [8]) and the `take`-lemma (Bird [1]).

The framework seems simpler than previous accounts of coinduction - see for example Pitt [5], because we are not working with domain theory and partial objects, but with the simpler world of total objects.

Moral: Getting rid of partial objects seems to be an unmitigated blessing - not only when reasoning about finite data, but also, perhaps even more so, in the case of infinite data.

5. Observations and Concluding Remarks

I have outlined an elementary discipline of strong (or total) functional programming, in which we have both finite data and (potentially) infinite codata, which we keep separate from each other by a minor variant of the Hindley Milner type discipline. There are syntactic restrictions on recursion and corecursion which ensure well-foundation for the former, and finite progress for the latter, and simple proof rules for both data and codata.

Although the particular syntactic discipline proposed may be too restrictive (particularly in the forms of corecursion it permits - further research is required here) I would like to argue that the distinction between data and codata is very helpful to a clean discipline of functional programming, and gives us a better teaching vehicle, and perhaps a better vehicle for production programming also (because of the greater freedom of choice for the implementor).

A question we postponed from section 2 is whether we ought to be willing to give up Turing completeness. Anyone who has taken a course in theory of computation will be familiar with the following result, which is a corollary of the Halting Theorem.

Theorem: For any language in which all programs terminate, there are always-terminating programs which cannot be written in it - among these are the interpreter for the language itself.

So if we call our proposed language for strong functional programming, L, an interpreter for L in L cannot be written. Does this really matter? I can see two arguments which suggest this might in fact be something to which we could accommodate ourselves quite easily

1) We will have a hierarchy of languages, of ascending power, each of which can express the interpreters of those below it. For example if our language L has a first order type system, we can easily add some second order features to get a language L_2, in which we can write the interpreter for L, and so on up. Constructive type theory, with its hierarchy of universes, is like this, for example.

2) There is no such theoretical obstacle to our writing a compiler for L in L, which is of far greater practical importance.

Summary: There is a dichotomy in language design, because of the halting problem. For our programming discipline we are forced to choose between

A) Security - a language in which all programs are known to terminate.

B) Universality - a language in which we can write
 (i) all terminating programs
 (ii) silly programs which fail to terminate
 and, given an arbitrary program we cannot in general say if it is (i) or (ii).

Four decades ago, at the beginning of electronic computing, we chose (B). It may be time to reconsider this decision.

Acknowledgements. An earlier version of this paper was presented at the A. J. Perlis Memorial Symposium, on the Future of Programming Languages, at Yale University in April 1993. I am grateful to the audience at that symposium for a number of comments.

References

1. R. S. Bird, P. Wadler "Introduction to Functional Programming", Prentice Hall, 1988.
2. K. Gödel "On a hitherto unutilized extension of the finitary standpoint", Dialectica 12, pp 280-287 (1958).
3. R. Harper, D. MacQueen, R. Milner "Standard ML", University of Edinburgh LFCS Report 86-2, 1986.
4. Paul Hudak *et al.* "Report on the Programming Language Haskell", SIGPLAN Notices, vol 27, no 5 (May 1992).
5. A. M. Pitt "A Co-induction Principle for Recursively Defined Domains", Theoretical Computer Science, vol 124, 1994.
6. Colin Runciman "What about the Natural Numbers", Computer Languages vol 14, no 3, pp 181-191, 1989.
7. S. J. Thompson "A Logic for Miranda", Formal Aspects of Computing, vol 1, no 4, pp 339-365, 1989.
8. D. A. Turner "Functional Programming and Proofs of Program Correctness" in Tools and Notions for Program Construction, pp 187-209, Cambridge University Press, 1982 (ed. Néel).
9. D. A. Turner "Miranda: A non-strict functional language with polymorphic types" Proceedings IFIP International Conference on Functional Programming Languages and Computer Architecture, Nancy, France, September 1985 (LNCS, vol 201).

[1]Note: Miranda is a trademark of Research Software Limited

Introducing Computer Science Undergraduates to Principles of Programming Through a Functional Language

E. T. Keravnou

Department of Computer Science, University of Cyprus
P.O.Box 537, CY-1678 Nicosia, Cyprus
email: elpida@turing.cs.ucy.ac.cy

Abstract. The paper discusses experience, over a three year period, at the Department of Computer Science of the University of Cyprus, in introducing undergraduate students in Computer Science to principles of programming (modularity, abstraction, genericity) through a functional language, and more specifically the language Miranda. The viability of this approach as well as the consequences for other courses in the curriculum, as evidenced in practice, are analysed.

1 Introduction

The Department of Computer Science of the University of Cyprus admitted its first undergraduate students in September 1992, for a 4 year programme of studies leading to the acquisition of a degree in Computer Science. The curriculum consists of: mandatory courses, constrained electives, free electives, and courses in a foreign language. The mandatory courses and the constrained electives are classified into the areas: theoretical foundations, problem solving, computing systems, and applications. The various courses teaching principles of programming or specific programming paradigms are classified under problem solving since the emphasis is on teaching students how to solve problems algorithmically, rather than on teaching the syntax and semantics of a number of programming languages. A main objective is to teach students principles of programming independently of programming languages and paradigms, and to enable them to acquire substantial experience in modular and structured programming primarily through imperative languages (Modula-2, C, C++). Another objective of the problem solving area is to acquaint students with the principal paradigms of programming, namely functional, imperative, object-oriented, logic and concurrent, their similarities and differences as well as the distinction between the declarative and procedural approaches.

The students are introduced to principles of programming through a functional language, namely Miranda. The paper attempts to answer two questions: (a) Does a functional language provide a better vehicle over the more traditional languages in introducing undergraduate Computer Science students to the principles of programming? and (b) What consequences does this approach have on other courses in the curriculum? The answers are placed in the context of our curriculum and are based on a three year experience.

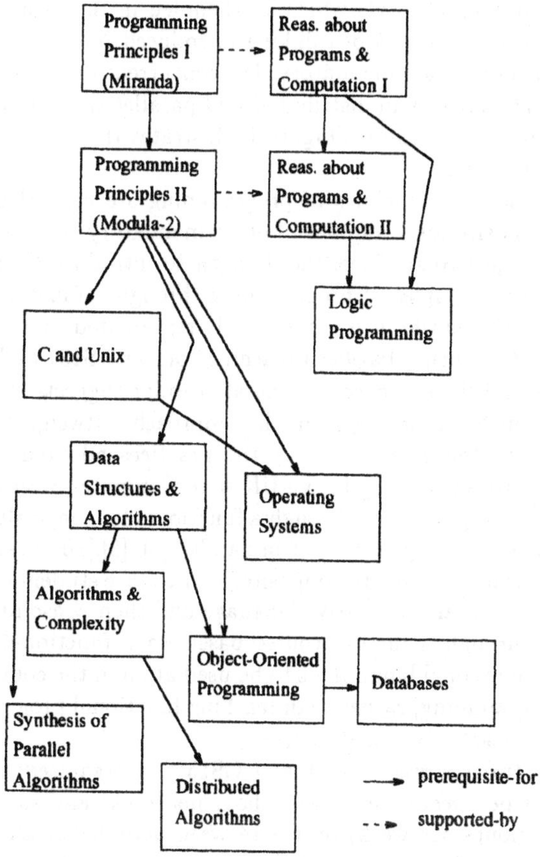

Fig. 1. Course Dependencies

1.1 Placing the Programming Principles Courses in the Curriculum

In the first semester of their studies, students are introduced to fundamental principles of programming through the functional language Miranda (course CS131). These principles are further consolidated and enhanced in the second semester through a further course on principles of programming which is based on the imperative language Modula-2 (course CS132). Course CS131 is the prerequisite for course CS132. Course CS132 is a prerequisite for a number of other courses in the curriculum such as Data Structures and Algorithms (CS231), C and Unix (CS230), Operating Systems (CS222), Object-oriented Programming (CS233), etc. A course on Reasoning about Programs and Computation (CS111), which runs in parallel with course CS131, provides support to the latter at a theoretical level (eg through formal proof methods for the correctness of programs). A course on Logic Programming (CS234) which is scheduled in the fifth semester builds further on the declarative way of thinking introduced in course CS131. All the courses mentioned above are mandatory. The concurrent programming paradigm is covered through electives in distributed and parallel algorithms which are offered in the final year of studies. Figure 1 illustrates the relations between the above mentioned courses.

The two courses on principles of programming are critical courses; course CS132 is a prerequisite for a number of other mandatory courses and the route to CS132 is through CS131. Thus the decision to introduce Computer Science undergraduates to principles of programming through a functional language is a critical one and this is why it is continuously reevaluated to ensure that it is a correct decision. The author has been teaching courses CS131 and CS132 for the past three years and the evidence accumulated so far suggests that the decision is correct; the benefits accruing from this approach outweigh the limitations. Indirect support to this is also lent by the practices adopted by many other European Universities primarily in the UK were Computer Science students are also introduced to programming through a functional language although in some cases an imperative language is taught in parallel [6], [8],[10]. It should be noted that we have not contemplated the opposite, ie introduce students to principles of programming through an imperative language and then consolidate and extent this knowledge through a further course based on a functional language. We believe that if a functional language is to be used at all in the context of teaching principles of programming, rather than teaching functional programming per se, then it should be used in the first course.

Each of the two courses, CS131 and CS132, is organised on the basis of lectures (3 hours per week), tutorials (1 hour per week) and supervised laboratory sessions (6 hours per week) over a 14 week period. For all its courses the University of Cyprus has adopted the system of continuous assessment. Each of the above courses is assessed on the basis of programming assignments, a midsemester examination, and a final examination, with relative weights 3, 1 and 6 respectively. The programming assignments are of two types: tutorial exercises, consisting of a large number of relatively small exercises, and practicals which usually consist of a single extensive problem to be solved. Practicals are the only assignments that count towards the course assessment. The 4-5 practicals assigned during the run of each course are increasingly more demanding requiring substantial design and programming effort. The details for course CS131 are collectively listed below:

1. **Short title:** CS131 Programming Principles I
2. **Aims:** The acquisition of fundamental skills in problem solving and the fermentation of algorithmic thinking; the grounding of central principles of programming (modularity, abstraction, genericity), algorithmic techniques and program structures; and the acquisition of some competence in the use

of a high level programming language.
3. **Audience:** Computer Science undergraduates.
4. **Year of study:** First year (spring semester).
5. **Prerequisites:** None.
6. **Text books:** The main text books for the course during the first three years of its running were the ones by Bird and Wadler [2] and Holyer [7]. However, for the fourth year of its running the course will be mainly supported by the books by Broda et al [4] and Clack et al [5].
7. **Duration of course:** 14 weeks.

	number of times per week	*duration per session*	*total duration per week*
lecture hours	2	1.5 *hours*	3 *hours*
tutorials	1	1 *hour*	1 *hour*
laboratories	2	3 *hours*	6 *hours*

8. **Student assessment.** The students are continuously being assessed through a number of examinations and laboratory assignments. The overall course result depends on a final examination (60%), a midsemester examination (10%) and a subset of the laboratory assignments (30%).

2 Principles of Programming and Functional Languages

The main aim of course CS131 is to introduce students to central principles of programming; teaching functional programming per se is definitely not an aim. We chose Miranda as the functional language to use because of its simplicity in syntax and the availability of good text books based on it [2],[4],[5],[7]. The fundamental principles of programming we wish to instil in students are *modularity* and *structuredness* (problem decomposition), *abstraction*, and *genericity*. Programming is seen as problem solving and this is why successive practicals are increasingly more demanding in analysis and design. As side-effects, students are introduced to *declarative* style of thinking and list processing. Below we analyse each of the above principles in turn, indicating how well they are supported by a functional language and whether a functional language constitutes an appropriate medium for communicating such principles to newcomers to Computer Science. This covers the first of the two questions that we set out to answer.

2.1 Modularity and Structuredness

Abstraction, modularity and genericity are closely related concepts in algorithmic problem solving and hence programming. An algorithmic solution is *modular* if it is divided into a number of distinct components (modules). A modular solution is *structured* if the modules comprising it are organised in some explicit (hierarchical) structure where modules are explicitly specified as residing within other modules. Thus the structure is defined through the *locality* relations between the different modules. If no locality relations are specified then all the modules are at the same level (global) and the algorithmic design exhibits a flat structure. A good algorithmic design should be both modular and structured.

Using a functional language forces one to break a problem into subproblems which are modelled through one or more functions. A *function* is a primitive form of a processing entity or module. The students are introduced to the notion of converting the given input (values) to the required output (values), by applying appropriate transformations, chained together through the functional composition operator (.). The notion of functional decomposition is also covered in the context of course CS121 Digital Systems. In order to make the connection more explicit, and thus the generality of the principle of modularity more apparent, the first programming assignments deal with binary arithmetic and converting numbers from one base into another.

Viewing functions as black boxes, ie separating the *what* from the *how*, is a principle well supported by functional languages, with the absence of side-effects. A complex system can be built by integrating together a number of such boxes in an incremental fashion. A system can therefore be analysed (for correctness) at the level of functionalities and component interfaces, without any reference to the actual implementations of primitive functions. A good, structured, design has multiple levels, where each level and the primitive, non-decomposable, functions residing at the lowest level are immediately understandable. The notion of locality in modules (local functions) is naturally introduced in the context of functional languages: a function is a black box; if we look inside it we see that it consists of a number of smaller black boxes connected together in some fashion, etc (thus expressing some functionality at multiple levels of abstraction where finer and finer modules are introduced in a recursive fashion).

Students are required to apply the principle of modularity throughout the two courses on principles of programming. The relatively primitive forms of modularity illustrated in the context of functional programming (function, local function) are substantially enhanced in the context of imperative programming. Below we illustrate how the students get into grips with the notion of modularity by briefly discussing two practical assignments used in course CS131. Both assignments require much usage of functional decomposition and composition. In addition each assignment is planned in two parts, where the code produced in the first part is 'imported' in the script for the second part, in order to introduce students to the idea of building large software systems by logically and physically breaking the problem solution into separate modules. The themes of the two assignments are text processing and picture drawing respectively.

In the first part of the text processing 'package', students are asked to write functions for converting some text (sequence of characters) into its word sequence, and for joining words to form text of specified line length, both for left-justified and not left-justified text. The second part requires the conversion of some text into a two column format for specified page length and width, where the title is centralised, footers and headers can be optionally used, and columns can be optionally left-justified.

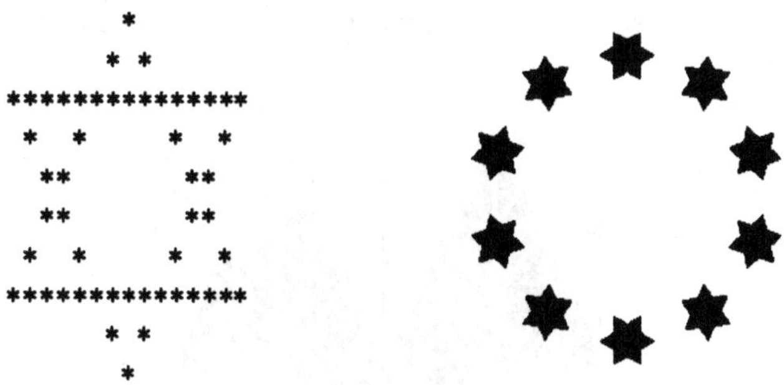

Fig. 2. Raster printing of a hollow star and graphical printing of a circular arrangement of 10 filled stars

The picture drawing 'package' is used in two versions, dealing with raster pictures [3],[11] and graphics pictures [10] respectively. Under either version a picture is a sequence of lines where for a raster picture a line consists of a sequence of characters and it is always horizontal, while for a graphics picture a line is a pair of points denoting the beginning and ending of the line; thus a line can have any direction. The first part of the picture drawing package requires the creation of primitive pictures such as squares, triangles, circles, ellipses, etc, both 'hollow' (only the boundary showing) and filled/shaded pictures (see figure 2). The second part requires the composition of pictures to build more complex pictures. In the case of raster pictures primitive compositions involve placing pictures row-wise, column-wise, and diagonally, or overlaying pictures. In the case of graphics pictures, compositions are based on applying various transformations on pictures such as rotating, shifting, scaling, reflecting, etc [10]. The end result is to produce a christmas card or the logo of the University of Cyprus (see figure 3). Students seem to enjoy especially the picture drawing assignment and the graphics version is particulary appealing due to the visual effects. The results of their efforts are quite impressive and the use of the principle of modularity is clearly evident.

It should be noted that the list processing facilities provided by functional languages considerably ease the solution for both the above problems. In comparison, the relevant machinery provided by imperative languages is much more primitive. If the first course on principles of programming were based on an imperative language it is doubtful as to whether students would have been able to tackle problems of the same complexity in the same time period, as is the case now. Functional languages provide a higher level of abstraction in comparison with imperative languages which is definitely a plus in the context of an introductory course on principles of programming. This point is elaborated in the following section.

Fig. 3. University of Cyprus Logo

2.2 Abstraction

The notion of abstraction is central in Computer Science. Abstraction is directly related to modularity; applying the principle of abstraction in problem solving results in the construction of modular solutions. Abstracting means being able to identify what is the essence and what is detail in some context, and therefore to focus on the essential aspects, and temporarily ignore the detail which can be incorporated at a later stage in an incremental fashion. Furthermore abstracting means creating understandable, conceptual models of reality that leave out irrelevant detail. Abstraction applies both to processing entities (programs) and data [1]. Both ***program abstraction*** and ***data abstraction*** are well supported in functional languages. To start with, as indicated above, functional languages provide a much higher level of abstraction in relation to imperative languages since the computation models used in functional languages are very distant from the computation model (fetch-execute cycle) employed by a physical machine, while the sequential computation models used in imperative languages are quite close to this model. The absence of the notions of state, store, address, pointer, etc and the provision of high level list processing facilities are clear evidence of the enhanced abstraction provided by functional languages. Functional languages aim to provide more abstract virtual machines.

The function is the main device for program abstraction (as well as modularity) in a functional context, just like the procedure is the main device for program abstraction in an imperative context. The declarativeness of functional languages which facilitates the separation between what a function does and how it does it, is a necessary ingredient for program abstraction. Higher order functions and partial parameterisation (currying) also add to program abstraction as well as to genericity (see next section).

With regard to data abstraction, functional languages provide list processing abstraction since the list is a built-in data structure and a rich collection of list processing functions are provided. Furthermore functional languages support the creation of new data types (eg algebraic types in Miranda) and most importantly they support Abstract Data Types (ADTs). ADTs is the last topic covered in course CS131 and is based on typical examples such as a stack of any type of items and a queue of any type of items:

```
abstype stack * with
  create_stack :: stack *
  empty_stack  :: stack * -> bool
  full_stack   :: stack * -> bool
  pop          :: stack * -> stack *
  push         :: * -> stack * -> stack *
  top          :: stack * -> *

stack * == [*]
.........

abstype queue * with
  create_queue :: queue *
  empty_queue  :: queue * -> bool
  full_queue   :: queue * -> bool
  join_queue   :: * -> queue * -> queue *
  leave_queue  :: queue * -> queue *
  next         :: queue * -> *

queue * == ([*],[*])
.......
```

Other examples of ADTs used in the course include sets and rational numbers. The simplicity of ADTs in functional languages such as Miranda (which in the case of the above examples is facilitated by the built-in list processing) is a strong point in favour of using such languages for introducing students to this very important concept. Undoubtedly the concept of an ADT is a difficult one to convey, more difficult than the concept of recursion which students seem to grasp relatively easily (another tribute to the use of a functional language). The objective is to give students a flavour of ADTs in this first course and to elaborate further in the second course. Once again the concept is introduced from the perspective of separating the functionality (what is this new type all about) and the implementation of the functionality, which draws a distinction between the *public* part of some entity (module) and its *private* part. The important thing is for the students to appreciate the reasons behind this separation. Most students appreciate the essence of this separation. For example it is evident that they appreciate the fact that the public part of a module provides its interface to the 'outside world' which must therefore be immediately understandable and relatively narrow, while the private part is of no interest to other modules and can be altered independently of such external modules. Altering the public part however may have repercussions on such external modules, unless the alterations are just the addition of new access functions. These points are illustrated by discussing different potential implementations (their pros and cons) for the private parts of various ADTs, eg implementing a queue either as a list or as a pair of lists. Thus students do seem to take on board the generic principle that a module's usage (integration) is based on its functionality and not on its implementation. Through ADTs students are introduced to the important concept of *information hiding* and through abstraction in general they are introduced to the concept of *genericity* and *reusability* which are elaborated in the next section. On a more subtle issue the use of ADTs is compared and contrasted against the use of type synonyms for creating new data types such as rational numbers [12]. As mentioned above the discussion on ADTs continues in course CS132, this time in the context of imperative programming, and the overall objective is to use ADTs as the preamble to object-orientation.

2.3 Genericity

Genericity is closely related, and equally important, to modularity and abstraction, in problem solving. The genericity of a problem solving method, a processing element (function), or a data type depends on its range of applicability in different problems/contexts. The higher the genericity of something the higher its reusability potential.

The three aspects that justify top ranking for functional languages on the scale of genericity support are *polymorphism*, *higher order functions* and *partial parameterisation*. More importantly all these aspects are provided in a very simple way.

List processing deserves a mention in the context of genericity as well. The list is a polymorphic structure and the built-in functions for list processing are generic. This provision enormously facilitates the construction of programs. The operations of *mapping*, *filtering* and *folding* are important, generic, problem solving methods [7].

The principle of genericity is illustrated through examples of generic functions, generic data types and generic problem solving methods. Typical examples of generic functions are sort functions which are so simple to define in functional languages due to the provision of polymorphism and higher order functions, eg:

```
bubble_sort :: (* -> * -> bool) -> [*] -> [*]
bubble_sort p
= until (sorted p) (swap p)
    where
      sorted p [] = True
      sorted p (x:xs) = and (zipwith p (init (x:xs), xs))
```

```
        swap p [] = []
        swap p [x] = [x]
        swap p (x:x':xs)
        = x:(swap p (x':xs)), if p x x'
        = x':(swap p (x:xs)), otherwise

quick_sort :: (* -> * -> bool) -> [*] -> [*]
quick_sort p [] = []
quick_sort p (x:xs)
= (quick_sort p bs) ++ [x] ++ (quick_sort p as)
     where bs = [y | y <- xs ; p y x]
           as = xs -- bs
```

Typical examples of generic (abstract) data types are the stack and the queue. The reusability of the stack data type is demonstrated through a number of examples. One such example is the evaluation of simple arithmetic expressions, where a stack is used in two contexts, the conversion of the expression from infix to postfix form by applying the reverse polish algorithm, and the evaluation of the postfix expression. In the first context stacks of tokens are used while in the second context a stack of numbers is used:

```
%include "stack"

aexp == [char]
token ::= OB | CB | Num num | Op aop
aop ::= Power | Times | Div | Plus | Minus

eval_aexp :: aexp -> num
eval_aexp
= postorder_eval . reverse_polish . tokenise

tokenise :: aexp -> [token]
tokenise [] = []
tokenise (c:cs) = ......

reverse_polish :: [token] -> [token]
reverse_polish tks
=  reverse_aux tks create_stack create_stack

reverse_aux :: [token] -> (stack token)
               -> (stack token) -> [token]

reverse_aux [] res_st op_st
= create_token_list res_st, if empty_stack op_st
= reverse_aux [] (push (top op_st) res_st)
              (pop op_st), otherwise
```

```
reverse_aux ((Num n):ts) res_st op_st
= reverse_aux ts (push (Num n) res_st) op_st

......

postorder_eval :: [token] -> num
postorder_eval ps = post_aux ps create_stack

post_aux :: [token] -> (stack num) -> num
post_aux [] st = top st
post_aux ((Num n):t) st
= post_aux t (push n st)
post_aux ((Op o):t) st
= post_aux t (push (apply o op1 op2) st'')
    where op2 = top st
          st' = pop st
          op1 = top st'
          st'' = pop st'
          apply_op Power = (^)
          apply_op Times = (*)
          ........
```

With regard to generic problem solving methods, the ones used in CS131 are *depth search* and *breadth search* which respectively use a stack and a queue:

```
%include "stack"

search :: * -> (* -> bool) -> (* -> [*]) -> *
search sol term expand
= depth_search (push sol create_stack) term expand

depth_search :: (stack *) -> (* -> bool)
                -> (* -> [*]) -> *
depth_search st p exp
= error "no solution", if empty_stack st
= tp, if p tp
= depth_search new_st p exp, otherwise
    where
      tp = top st
      new_st = foldr push (pop st) (exp tp)
```

or

```
%include "queue"
```

```
search :: * -> (* -> bool) -> (* -> [*]) -> *
search sol term expand
= breadth_search (join_queue sol create_queue)
                 term expand

breadth_search :: (queue *) -> (* -> bool)
                  -> (* -> [*]) -> *
breadth_search qu p exp
= error "no solution", if empty_queue qu
= nt, if p nt
= breadth_search new_qu p exp, otherwise
   where
    nt = next qu
    new_qu = foldr join_queue (leave_queue qu) (exp tp)
```

The students are gradually coached towards inducing these methods through a number of problems and discussions on the similarities and differences between their respective solutions, culminating on how such seemingly different, at the outset, solutions can be generalised into a single solution. Once the generic methods are explicated, students are asked to explicitly apply them on new problems. Examples of problems used for this part of the course are [9]:

1. *Farmer, goat, cabbage and wolf problem.* A farmer wishes to safely transport himself, a goat, a cabbage and a wolf across a river. Only the farmer can row the available boat whose capacity is 2. The situations we need to safeguard against are the wolf left alone with the goat, or the goat left alone with the cabbage. The problem is to determine a sequence of crossings leading to a safe transportation of everyone on the other side of the river.
2. *Finding a path between two cities.* A directed graph representing a road map is modelled in terms of association lists. The problem is to find any path between a source and a destination which naturally triggers a discussion on finding an optimal (shortest) path, subsequently discussed in the context of breadth search.
3. *Treasure hunt.* This is a variant of the above problem. A robot is placed in some room where there are barriers positioned vertically or horizontally. The robot can move in steps of one unit in the directions left, right, up, or down. The problem is to discover a hidden treasure in the room by directing the robot to move around the room avoiding barriers and never passing over the same point again because it will be automatically detonated.
4. *k-puzzle.* There is a unique 9-digit natural number, N, where each of its initial segments of length k = 1,2, ..., 9, is divisible by k. What is this number?
5. *The stamps problem.* Given that there can be t types of different value stamps and that the number of stamps that can be used on some letter can not exceed s, what should the different types of stamps be in order to cover the greatest possible number of consecutive postage costs starting from unit cost?

6. *Sliding puzzle.* Three black and three white blocks, where the elements of each set are numbered from 1 to 3, are placed in a box whose capacity is 7 such blocks in a horizontal arrangement; thus there is a vacant position. Starting from some configuration of the six blocks what is a potential sequence of moves for transferring this to another configuration? The permitted moves are either for a block to slide into the vacant position, or for a block to jump, over at most two other blocks, into the vacant position (see figure 4).

For some of the above problems pictorial representation of the different problem states is required. For illustration we give the code for the k-puzzle and the sliding puzzle problems.

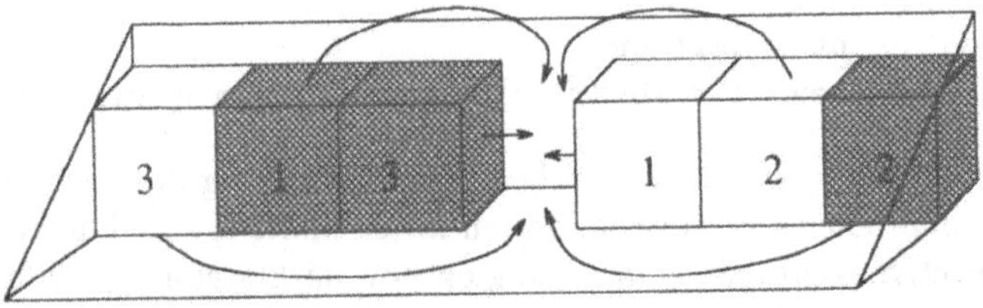

Fig. 4. Sliding Puzzle

k-puzzle, where the number is returned as a list of digits:

```
%include "search"

unique
= hd (search [] ((= 9).(#)) expand)
  where
   expand x
   = [x ++ [d] | d <- ([1..9] -- x); possible(x ++ [d])]
   possible x
   = n mod k = 0
       where n = foldl1 addDigit x
             k = #x
             addDigit x y = x * 10 + y
```

Sliding puzzle, where the required configuration of blocks is expressed through a predicate:

```
%include "search"

block ::= E | B | W
state == [(block,num)]

|| determining the vacant position
empty_pos :: state -> num
```

```
empty_pos ((E,n):bs) = 0
empty_pos ((b,n):bs) = 1 + (empty_pos bs)

moves :: state -> [state]
moves st
= [swap st e i | i <- [(e - 3) .. (e + 3)];
                 i >= 0; i <= 6; i ~= e]
   where
     e = empty_pos st
     swap st i j
     = swap_aux st 0 (st ! j) (st ! i)

        where
          swap_aux [] c ej ei = []
          swap_aux (b:bs) c ej ei
          = ej:(swap_aux bs (c+1) ej ei), if c = i
          = ei:(swap_aux bs (c+1) ej ei), if c = j
          = b:(swap_aux bs (c+1) ej ei), otherwise

slide_puzzle :: (state -> bool) -> state -> [state]
slide_puzzle term st
= reverse
   (search [st] (term.hd) exp)
      where exp (h:t)
            = [h':h:t | h' <- moves h;
                        ~(member (h:t) h')]
```

The students appreciate the genericity of the particular problem solving methods and at the same time they start appreciating computability issues in a practical sense, especially when the breadth search method is used.

In summary, the level of abstraction provided by functional languages, the built-in list processing, and the support towards modularity and genericity, enable newcomers to Computer Science to write smaller, more elegant, and more understandable, algorithmic solutions to substantial problems in a relatively short period of time.

2.4 Benefits and Limitations

It is often the case that students learn more in a course than they can initially appreciate. This is very much so with course CS131. The benefits of this course are not immediately apparent to most students but the value of what they have learned is appreciated in the context of other courses especially course CS132. The benefits to students through course CS131 are perceived to be the following:

- Understanding of the notion of problem decomposition.
- Familiarity with the concept of a computational entity (function), ie a black box accepting information, doing some computation, and returning results.

- Thus appreciation of the difference between what some functionality is and how it is implemented and hence an appreciation of declarative thinking.
- Understanding of the important algorithmic structures of choice (analysis of cases), recursion (the distinction between stack and tail recursion), a form of iteration (list comprehension) and functional composition.
- Appreciation of the notion of strong typing.
- Appreciation of list processing and overall,
- A sound understanding of the general principles of (structured) modularity, abstraction (both for processing entities and data types), and genericity (appreciation of polymorphism, higher order functions, and general problem solving methods).

However, there are some limitations associated with this approach. Firstly, interactive programs are not naturally modelled in functional languages. The modelling of interaction through lazy evaluation is not an easy concept to communicate to newcomers and therefore a discussion on it is completely left out of course CS131. Lazy evaluation and infinite lists are mentioned only in passing since the aim of the course is to teach principles of programming and not concepts specific to functional programming per se. Secondly, functional languages do not provide an adequate forum for discussing issues on testing and debugging since the notions of store and state are missing. Thus extensive discussions on this important aspect of programming are left until course CS132. Thirdly, many students encounter difficulties, at least initially, with the declarative style of thinking especially those with some experience in imperative programming. For example to those already familiar with the notion of executing commands which result in altering the state of a program, the notion of evaluating expressions does seem a bit foreign at the outset. Through practice this conceptual difficulty is overcome by most students. To give an example, the first practical assignment this year required the definition of a function, shiftL, that applied a circular shift of one position to the left, to the digits of some natural number, and shiftNL, that applied a circular shift of n positions to the left, again to the digits of some natural number. Out of a group of 35 students only 2 gave the following declarative answer for shiftNL, while the rest of the students gave answers based on the use of operators **mod** and **div** which in fact did not cover all cases:

```
shiftNL :: num -> num -> num
shiftNL n x
= x, if n = 0
= shiftNL (n-1) (shiftL x), otherwise
```

In the same assignment, they were asked to define a predicate, prime_no, that returns True for numbers which are prime, and function nth_prime, that returns the nth prime number. Again most students gave 'procedural' answers for prime_no and only a few attempted a definition for nth_prime. When they were presented with the following solutions at a tutorial class most of them expressed pleasant surprise at their simplicity:

```
prime_no :: num -> bool
prime_no n
= False, if n < 2
= prime_aux n 2, otherwise
   where prime_aux n x
         = True, if (x * x) > n
         = False, if (n mod x) = 0
         = prime_aux n (x+1), otherwise

nth_prime :: num -> num
nth_prime 1 = 2
nth_prime (n+2)
= next_from (nth_prime (n+1))
    where next_from p
          = (p+1), if prime_no (p+1)
          = next_from (p+1), otherwise
```

Gradually, however, most students become quite declarative in their thinking.

Amongst the 35 or so students taking course CS131 each year, the success rate is about 75% which is comparable to the generally expected success rates for introductory courses in programming, irrespective of whether they are based on a functional or a procedural language. Thus the failure rate is in no way alarming to justify a drastic change of approach and since overall the benefits accruing from the use of a functional language outweigh the limitations, for the time being we intend to continue this way. Much more ground can be covered and more concepts introduced and integrated in a simple fashion than would have been possible had we started the students on an imperative language. Thus our experience so far suggests that functional languages do provide better vehicles over the traditional languages in introducing Computer Science undergraduates to principles of programming. Functional languages enable a global and comprehensive coverage of fundamental issues. Next we explore the issue of whether the consequences of this approach for other courses in the curriculum, directly or indirectly related to course CS131, are equally positive, or whether some negative overtones arise.

3 Consequences for Other Courses

First we consider the consequences of our approach for the successor course (CS132) on principles of programming and then we consider the consequences for other courses; the former are the immediate consequences and the latter are indirect consequences.

3.1 Immediate Consequences

Courses CS131 and CS132 are seen as an integral whole, whose collective objective is to ferment algorithmic thinking and language independent principles of programming, in the context of problem solving. The fact that so far it has been possible for both courses to be taught by the same person further adds to their integral association. We repeat that it is not an aim of courses CS131 and CS132 to teach the functional and procedural paradigms of programming; if that were so, the two courses would have been taught as two separate entities. Thus whether our decision to use a functional language as the basis for course CS131 is overall a valid one, really depends on how well the collective objective is met. The benefits resulting from course CS131, as explained above, take us a long step in the direction of achieving this joint goal. The pair of courses CS131 and CS132 are quite crucial in our curriculum since the success of a number of other courses depends on how well the joint goal of these two courses is attained.

The specific aims of course CS132 are to consolidate further and extend the principles of modularity, abstraction and genericity, in the context of imperative programming, to analyse the significance of the concepts of information-hiding and reusability from the perspective of building large software systems, and to discuss testing and debugging strategies. The programming language used in course CS132, for the past three years, is Modula-2 which was primarily chosen for its pedagogical nature. Modula-2's syntax is more complicated than Miranda's but still relatively simple. In spite of this students have said that the syntax would have been an obstacle had they started with Modula-2 instead of Miranda. Course CS132 starts by briefly pointing out the distinct features of imperative languages with regard to functional languages, namely the distinction in the notion of a variable between the two paradigms, and the distinction between an expression and a command, which introduce the notions of storage and address. Fundamental algorithmic structures apply both to expressions and commands and since students are already well conversant with choice, recursion, etc, one week is sufficient time to discuss all algorithmic structures relevant to a command-based context [3]: memory (assignment), sequence, choice (simple and multiple), iteration (enumerative, indefinite), recursion, procedure. Thus the knowledge and experience gained through CS131 enable us to cover much ground in a short period of time, so that from the third week onwards in the life of course CS132 we can concentrate on the essence of the course which is problem solving. The above statement is in fact a comment made by the students every year, which reflects the point raised earlier, ie the benefits of course CS131 become apparent to them through course CS132. The significance of the list processing facilities of Miranda and in general its higher level of abstraction are much appreciated when pointers and dynamic data structures are covered in Modula-2. Deliberately students are asked to tackle some of the same problems in CS132 in order to draw their own comparisons between the two approaches and also to appreciate the generality of the principles underlying their solutions.

Modula-2 supports well modularity, information hiding, and reusability, but the absence of polymorphism, partial parameterisation, and dynamic arrays , weakens substantially its support to genericity in comparison with Miranda. It is very encouraging to see that students reach this conclusion themselves without any direct prompting. The simple explanation is that, through course CS131, they acquired the habit of aiming to create as general, and thus as reusable, solutions to problems and hence in many occasions they were coming to the conclusion that Modula-2 was unreasonably constraining them in this respect. In a sense two educational philosophies are, either to start the students by giving them a global taste of the true range of possibilities and then to let them critique situations where what is actually supplied is very constraining in some respects, or to start them with a more constrained, and usually specific, set of possibilities and gradually to relax this set by introducing new avenues. What we in fact apply is a combination of these two philosophies. Through Miranda we instil in the minds of students a more realistic picture of what is possible, at a high level, and cultivate critical thinking by gleaning out the relative limitations of Modula-2. However not all possibilities can be covered through Miranda, eg dynamic arrays, interaction, or sequential processing cannot be discussed. Once introduced to the notions of store, assignment, and sequential processing, the majority of students express the feeling that they find the procedural style of thinking much more natural to them over the declarative style. They appreciate that functional compositions are a type of sequence but they find sequences of commands more appealing to use. Even if students never use a functional language or declarative thinking after the CS131 course, this does not defeat our purpose since that was never our objective. The objective as specified above is still met and hence course CS131 adequately serves its purpose. The application of the principles of programming introduced in CS131, is clearly evident in CS132; the immediate consequences of using a functional language are therefore considered positive.

3.2 Indirect Consequences

Directly or indirectly, the pair of courses CS131 and CS132, affect most other courses in the curriculum. If through these courses students become good algorithmic problem solvers then the consequences for other courses can only be positive. This inference is mostly true but not quite. In this section we only concentrate on those courses which are more directly affected by courses CS131 and CS132. These are the courses on C and Unix, Data Structures and Algorithms, Operating Systems, Object-Oriented Programming, Logic Programming, and Theory and Practice of Compilers. The course on C and Unix is facilitated by the courses in discussion since students are already familiar with imperative programming. Similarly for the courses on Data Structures and Algorithms, and Operating Systems since the language used in both these courses for the practical assignments is Modula-2. Due to the positive effects of course CS131, it is possible to devote a large part of course CS132 on data structures, both static and dynamic, and ADTs, and this is a very positive consequence for the Data Structures and Algorithms course. The course on Logic Programming benefits from the declarative style of thinking introduced in CS131. However, with regard to the courses on Object-Oriented Programming, and Theory and Practice of Compilers, a limitation arises. Both courses require students to be very conversant in the C language, but most students are not competent C programmers by the time they take these courses. Since the objective of courses CS131 and CS132 is to help students master algorithmic problem solving and principles of programming rather than to master the intricacies of a specific programming language, the above limitation cannot be attributed to the use of a functional language in the initial course. Mastering of a programming language does not necessarily imply mastering of principles of programming and problem solving while the latter should be a necessary precondition for the former (the mastering of a language must be done within the appropriate foundational context). In our department we are especially conscious of this fact. This is why when we teach ancillary programming courses in Fortran or C for the students of other departments we ensure that the particular language is taught within the relevant background of programming principles. Presently we are discussing possible solutions to the above limitation, which do not in fact affect the CS131 course. One possibility is to base the CS132 course on the language C++ rather than Modula-2, a practice adopted by many Universities in the UK, or to change the nature of the course on C and Unix. The latter course is a prerequisite for the courses on object-orientation and compilers. Thus, overall, the consequences for other courses in the curriculum, of our decision to use a functional language to introduce Computer Science undergraduates to principles of programming, are positive.

4 Conclusions

Since the mid eighties many departments of Computer Science, especially at UK Universities, have radically changed their approach to teaching programming at the undergraduate level. Since then, the traditional approach was to teach students structured programming through a procedural language which in most cases was Pascal. The new approach is to start students on a functional language and then to switch onto a procedural language. Initially the Scheme dialect of Lisp was used for the functional language but soon other, pure functional languages, such as Miranda, SML, etc took over this role. The fact that this practice is growing stronger over the years, and is expanding to other parts of Europe, constitutes considerable evidence in favour of this approach.

The paper discusses experience at the Department of Computer Science of the relatively newly established University of Cyprus in introducing Computer Science undergraduates to principles of programming through the functional language Miranda and analyses the consequences of this approach for other courses in the curriculum. Our objective is to instil in the minds of newcomers to Computer Science the fundamental principles of (structured) modularity, abstraction, and genericity. The evidence accumulated over the past three years suggests that a functional language provides a better medium over an imperative language in initially teaching such principles and that an imperative language is best utilised afterwards for further consolidation and extension. The consequences for other courses in the curriculum are equally positive and one limitation encountered (inadequate level of competence in C programming) is not in fact attributed to the initial use of Miranda.

Acknowledgements

I would like to thank the 100 or so students that have so far gone through courses CS131 and CS132 for the many illuminating discussions I have had with them which resulted in various refinements for the two courses. Also I would like to thank my colleagues at the University of Cyprus and my ex-colleagues at University College London, in particular John Washbrook and Paul Samet, for many interactions concerning the teaching of principles of programming.

References

1. H. Abelson, G.J. Sussman, and J. Sussman, *Structure and Interpretation of Computer Programs,* The MIT Press, 1985.
2. R. Bird, and P. Wadler, *Introduction to Functional Programming,* Prentice Hall, 1988.
3. R. Bornat, *Programming from First Principles,* Prentice Hall, 1987.
4. K. Broda, S. Eisenbach, H. Khoshnevisan, and S. Vickers, *Reasoned Programming,* Prentice Hall, 1994.
5. C. Clack, C. Myers, and E. Poon, *Programming with Miranda,* Prentice Hall, 1995.
6. R. Harrison, "The use of functional languages in teaching computer science," *J. Functional Programming,* Vol. 3, pp. 67-75, 1993.
7. I. Holyer, *Functional Programming with Miranda,* UCL Press, 1991.
8. S. Joosten, K. van der Berg, and G. van der Hoeven, "Teaching functional programming to first-year students," *J. Functional Programming,* Vol. 3, pp. 49-65, 1993.
9. E. T. Keravnou, "Lecture Notes, Tutorials and Practicals for Programming Principles I & II (1992-95)" (in Greek).
10. T. Lambert, P. Lindsay, and K. Robinson, "Using Miranda as a first programming language" *J. Functional Programming,* Vol. 3, pp. 5-34, 1993.
11. C. Reade, *Elements of Functional Programming,* Addison Wesley, 1989.
12. D. A. Watt, *Programming Language Concepts and Paradigms,* Prentice Hall, 1990.

Teaching C after Miranda

Andrew Davison

Department of Computer Science
University of Melbourne
Parkville, Victoria 3052, Australia
Email: ad@cs.mu.oz.au

Abstract. The first year of our computer science degree begins with a subject based around the lazy functional language Miranda, and is followed by a subject using ANSI C.
We discuss the C subject, and how Miranda has been utilised within it. In particular, Miranda is used as a specification language for Abstract Data Types (ADTs), which demonstrates the utility of its high level features for developing reusable code. C versions of these ADTs are also developed, which allows a comparison of the two languages and their programming paradigms.

1 Introduction

The initial motivation for this work was a change in the first year syllabus in the Computer Science (CS) Department at Melbourne University: Pascal was dropped as the language for the first and second CS subjects. In its place, we are using the lazy Functional Programming (FP) language Miranda to teach problem solving and program design in the first subject [2, 5, 1], while the second subject also emphasises problem solving and program design, but in the context of ANSI C [9, 4].

In section 2 we review our reasons for using Miranda as the programming language in the first CS subject. In section 3, we similarly justify the use of C in the second subject. Section 4 examines the C subject in more detail, looking at its objectives, the topics covered, and the contribution of Miranda. Section 5 concerns the topic where Miranda and C come together the most – the development of Abstract Data Types (ADTs). In section 6, we discuss two questionnaires given to the students in 1994 and 1995. The final section summarises the advantages and disadvantages of the utilisation of Miranda in the C subject, and proposes a few changes. It also includes a brief subject summary.

2 Why Miranda?

The main aim of the first CS subject is to teach the students good problem solving skills, with an emphasis on the specification and design of algorithms [3]. By the end of the subject, we hope that a successful student will have a grasp of the benefits of abstraction, functional decomposition, ways of composing programs from existing units, and be able to reason about their programs in a rudimentary way.

The FP paradigm is an ideal basis for a first programming language because of its simple evaluation model, the fact that everything is an expression, and because of referential transparency ("equals can be replaced by equals") [6]. The absence of side effects in FP means that functions are more modular, easier to compose together, and more structured. Typically they have less bugs, and are easier to reason about.

Many of the features of Miranda actively contribute to the abstraction, functional decomposition, and composition principles that our first CS subject is promoting. Pattern matching clarifies the links between data structures and function definitions, and makes formal proofs simpler by encouraging structural decomposition. Polymorphism permits functions to be more general, increasing their modularity and the possibilities for reuse. Higher order functions allow abstraction away from recursion, to algorithms which subsume a 'family' of related recursive functions. Currying and lambda abstractions encourage the partial definition of functions, and the hiding of selected components of an operation. Lazy evaluation promotes modularity, permitting a problem to be separated into distinct generate and test phases. Laziness also allows the encoding of infinite data structures and networks of deterministic processes [7]. Miranda supports powerful algebraic types, type synonyms and an ADT notation.

The syntax of Miranda is considerably simpler than Pascal, letting it be taught more quickly. Syntax was a significant problem with the Pascal-based subject, where the algorithmic aims tended to become secondary to the task of teaching Pascal's notation.

A minor point is that FP and Miranda are unknown to our students. They all start with the same lack of knowledge, a fact that pleases many students, who feel that Pascal gives other students, who learnt it at school, an unfair advantage. An 'unusual' language also pleases the more advanced students, who enjoy the challenge of mastering it.

3 Why C?

The second CS subject has the same broad aims as the Miranda subject, but in the context of ANSI C (hereafter referred to as C).

C was chosen for pragmatic reasons – it is widely used in other subjects, and outside the university, which means that a student should know how to program with it at an early stage. This was also why Pascal was dropped: it is a waste of time to teach Pascal first and C later.

There are a number of good introductory C texts available [4, 8], and cheap implementations of C for PCs. These points are important because we try to encourage students to study for themselves.

C offers a more realistic programming experience than (standard) Pascal, which is under-powered in a number of areas, such as I/O, file manipulation, separate compilation, libraries, and memory management.

C is a fairer first imperative language than Pascal, in the sense that few students have encountered it at school. This means that there is less chance of a student having developed poor programming habits, and less chance of a student being bored by familiarity.

C's close links to UNIX allow some basic operating system issues to be taught, and the utility of libraries can be introduced.

There are some major problems with C as a first imperative language, but the problems due to the underlying programming paradigm should be separated from those due to the language.

A major criticism of the imperative style is that it is based on a low level operational model, which is too closely linked to the memory of the underlying hardware. It is certainly low level, but it is also a simple operational model to explain (at least informally). In addition, it permits the introduction of machine level concepts (addressing, loading, storing, etc) which must be taught eventually.

The main problem with C was summarised by Brian Reid: *"Power Tools Can Kill"*. The complex syntax and semantics of C is a formidable hurdle for first year students. Some specific problems are: the vague evaluation order for expressions, the lack of basic types, the confusing type syntax, and the complex representation of dynamic data structures such as lists and trees. This complexity is due to the lack of recursive data structures in C, and their emulation with pointers.

Our approach to the 'power tool' problem is to strongly emphasise safety. By utilising ANSI C, many of the main criticisms of the original C language are addressed [10]. Also, we discourage the use of C's poor features, and concentrate on good programming strategies. These include procedural and data abstraction, information hiding, and generalisation.

The other language considered as a replacement for Pascal was Ada. It is popular because of its object-based features, such as modules and generics, and also its concurrent capabilities. Typically, Ada is taught in stages, leaving the more advanced features for later year subjects. Our main reason for not changing to Ada was the reliance on C by many of our later year subjects (e.g. subjects concerned with networking and operating systems).

One final reason for teaching C was as a stepping stone to C++, which is introduced in 2nd year when object oriented programming is taught. Also, C++ is used quite extensively in the software engineering stream of one of our degrees.

4 The C Subject

The aim of this section is to outline the objectives of the C subject, to give an outline of the topics taught, and to highlight the contributions of Miranda. A brief subject summary can be found at the end of section 7.

4.1 The Objectives of the Subject

There are six main objectives:

1. To teach C to an intermediate level, so that the students will have an understanding of C up to and including pointers and their use for building dynamic data structures.
2. To introduce ADTs, which are used later as a motivation for object oriented ideas in 2nd year, and as a general design principle in other subjects.
3. To give an overview of some computer science topics aside from C programming. This aim is included because a minority of our students take the Miranda and C subjects as the sole computing part of another degree course.
4. To use Miranda as an ADT specification language.
5. To compare C with Miranda.
6. To use Miranda beyond the scope of the Miranda subject. The intention is to overcome the belief of some students that Miranda is of no further use after the first CS subject.

These last three points will be developed and expanded upon in the following sections.

4.2 Outline of the Topics

The subject, which is called 433-142 Computing Fundamentals B, runs for a single semester of 13 weeks, and consist of 3 one hour lectures per week. Each student attends a two hour laboratory session and a one hour tutorial class per week. The lab session is for carrying out programming exercises and completing project assignments. Project work should take about 30 hours to complete, and is usually divided between two or three C coding assignments. The tutorial class (an average size of 20) allows the students to raise questions in an informal setting; the lecture class size is about 170.

The first lab class is given over to a review of Miranda and UNIX, which is especially necessary for the small number of students who enter the subject without having done the preceding Miranda subject (433-141 Computing Fundamentals A). Also available on-line are an extensive set of self-review exercises (with answers) on Miranda and UNIX.

The first seven (or so) weeks of the subject follows a traditional introduction to C format, closely aligned to the text *C: How to Program* (2nd edition) [4]. This book is liked by the students and also contains several chapters on C++ which are utilised by a 2nd year subject.

The subject begins with some simple C programs which allow the ideas of variables, types, assignment and loops to be introduced. A 'box' picture of variables is used when assignment is discussed, and special emphasis is placed on the destructive nature of assignment in C as compared to Miranda. A 'box' is simply a visual representation of a variable's memory location. It is useful for explaining how destructive assignment works, and can aid the discussion of arrays, structs and pointers. Less time is spent on the type concept, an idea which the students are already very familiar with from Miranda. Iteration is accompanied by numerous examples because of its novelty to Miranda programmers.

Functions are introduced next, along with some discussion of header files and libraries. Some time is also spent talking about pseudo-code, program decomposition, and debugging techniques. Generally, functional decomposition can be taught much more quickly than normally because of its coverage in the Miranda subject. Some care is taken at this stage *not* to mention the difference between strict and non-strict functions, which might lead to confusion about when arguments are evaluated in C.

Several introductory C texts leave recursion until later, but because of our student's familiarity with the notion, it has been brought forward. This allows an early discussion of the connections between iteration and recursion, illustrated by some simple functions (e.g. factorial, summing inputs) coded both ways.

Arrays are discussed with reference to Miranda lists, and the notions of constant time access and update with arrays are compared to the linear search of lists and the creation of a new list by (partial) copying in Miranda. Structures are compared to Miranda tuples.

Several weeks are spent on pointers, using a visual approach based on the 'boxes' idea for variables, and the creation/deletion of such boxes as functions are called and return. Strings are discussed, followed by pointers to structures and arrays.

The last chapter of *Deitel and Deitel* used is on file processing.

At week 8, Abstract Data Types (ADTs) are introduced, and used as the guiding concept for the development of list and tree data structures and their associated functions. This material typically occupies three weeks, and is the main place in the subject where Miranda and C are brought together. In the following week, searching and sorting are described, again using Miranda and C. Half way through this period, a special lunch time tutorial is offered on Miranda, which acts as a refresher class for some students. This is especially liked by engineering students who usually learn C six months after the end of the Miranda subject.

The final two weeks are spent on a brief overview of some computing concepts, such as machine architectures, human factors, software engineering, and the future of computing. Some of this material is in the form of articles which the students are expected to read outside of class.

4.3 The Contribution of Miranda

As seen from the discussion above, Miranda is only used briefly during the first seven weeks of the subject, as a reference point when types, recursion, functions, arrays and structures are introduced. This is intentional since the students may otherwise confuse Miranda with C while they are learning C.

The two main areas where Miranda appears are in ADTs and searching/sorting. The former is the topic of the next section, but Miranda's role in the latter is briefly discussed below.

The C coding used for searching and sorting is based on arrays of integers, with an emphasis placed on different algorithms and their complexities. Linear search and divide and conquer are discussed first, using iteration and recursion.

The four sorting algorithms described are: selection, insertion, bubble and quick sort.

Normally, after the iterative and recursive C functions for an algorithm have been explained, it is reexpressed in Miranda. Many interesting points of similarity and difference appear. Firstly, the C type is less general since it is not polymorphic. However, the array mechanism wins in terms of efficiency because it can be accessed and updated in constant time compared to Miranda lists. Recursion in Miranda is very similar to C, but there is no way of achieving the efficiency of an iterative algorithm. However, C does not include a mechanism like list comprehensions which makes an algorithm like quicksort extremely easy to express.

An alternative approach would be to present the Miranda code first, and use it as a high level specification for a recursive C solution. One drawback of that strategy is that the Miranda list data structure does not map directly to an array solution in C.

5 ADTs

The ADT concept is introduced to the students first, followed by how Miranda and C ADT's can be written. Once these ADTs have been developed, Miranda's utility as a specification language for ADTs is examined. Also, it becomes clear that Miranda ADT functions can be painlessly translated into C ADT functions. In addition, the ADT topic allows a general comparison of Miranda and C to be carried out.

The following sections elaborate on these themes.

5.1 How ADTs are Introduced

ADTs are explained by reference to *clients* and *manufacturers*. Manufacturers develop collections of ADTs which clients use as required. Since a client does not want to be concerned with the implementation details of the ADT he or she is using, the ADT should possess a clear user interface which is quite separate from its implementation details. This also has benefits for the manufacturer since he or she can alter the implementation of the ADT with impunity so long as the interface stays the same. For instance, this means that the implementation can use less efficient algorithms, data structures, or even less efficient programming languages initially.

A vital design aim of ADTs is that they act as good building blocks for larger programs. In practice this means that a client should be able to mix and match the data types and operations of an ADT without concern about hidden side effects or the implementation quirks of the ADT.

5.2 ADTs in Miranda and C

List and tree ADTs are taught in the subject, a choice based on their importance in our second year subject on advanced algorithms in C. However, from a Miranda viewpoint, the list is not a particularly good choice, since some students find it difficult to understand why a list ADT needs to be developed in Miranda when the language already supports the data structure.

Due to space limitations, the following description will concentrate on how the list ADT is presented, but a similar approach is used for the tree ADT.

Initially, the ADT is described without reference to any programming language, and a set of basic operations are collected under the general headings of *constructor*, *selector*, *testing* and *destructor* operations. For the list ADT, the two constructor operations are 'create an empty list' and 'add (`cons`) an element onto the front of an existing list'. A typical selector operation is 'return the head element of a list without altering the list'. A tail returning operation is considered to be a selector if it does not alter the list supplied as input. However, if the operation deletes the head element to produce the tail then it would be classed as a destructor. A typical test operation is to check whether a list is empty.

A Miranda type for the ADT and its associated functions are developed next:

```
list * ::=  Nil  |  Cons * (list *)
```

Rather than develop the list ADT operations using this type, the 'built-in' list type (which uses a `[..]` notation) is utilised. One reason for this choice is the student's familiarity with this kind of list. It also directly raises the question of why an ADT has to be developed at all when there are already list capabilities in Miranda.

One advantage of using the ADT is that the implementation is hidden and so can be easily changed. For instance, storing a list as several separate sub-lists might be a useful implementation strategy if the total list is going to be very long, and search and update has to be fast. This could be achieved by searching each sub-list in parallel.

Another advantage of the ADT is that code which uses it is more portable. For example, the `concat` and `insert` functions developed below do not use Miranda's list pattern matching capabilities. This makes it easier to port them to other systems (as long as those systems supports a list ADT). This point is made again when `concat` and `insert` are coded using the C list ADT, and are seen to be very like their Miranda counterparts.

Two typical selector functions are:

```
head :: [*] -> *        || return head
head (x:xs) = x

tail :: [*] -> [*]   || return tail
tail (x:xs) = xs
```

Functions of a similar complexity are developed for `mkempty`, `cons`, and `isempty`.

The list ADT is finally identified as consisting of the `[*]` list type and the operations `head`, `tail`, `mkempty`, `cons` and `isempty`. An important point is that the ADT contains no destructor operations because of Miranda's single assignment property. Instead, a list must be changed by creating a new list. More is made of this when the C version of the ADT is developed.

Once the ADT is available, more 'complex' operations, such as `length`, `member`, `insert` and `concat`, are written. For instance, `insert` and `concat` are:

```
|| insert element in ascending order
insert :: * -> [*] -> [*]
insert c xs
  = cons c mkempty, if isempty xs
insert c xs
  = cons c xs, if c < x
  = cons x (insert c (tail xs)),otherwise
    where x = head xs

concat :: [*] -> [*] -> [*]
concat xs ys
  = ys, if isempty xs
  = cons (head xs)
         (concat (tail xs) ys), otherwise
```

A key point is that the client will be writing these functions, not the manufacturer. Thus, the ADT operations being used should hide the list type implementation.

Several interesting points can be made about the list type, namely that it is recursive and polymorphic. In addition, the empty and non-empty alternatives for a list strongly suggest a case-based style of function development.

Most of the students will be reluctant to code the 'complex' functions in this way, because pattern matching is much simpler. For instance, the typical way of writing `concat` is:

```
concat :: [*] -> [*] -> [*]
concat [] ys = ys
concat (x:xs) ys = x : (concat xs ys)
```

The drawback is that pattern matching reintroduces the list type implementation into the client's code. This illustrates the tension between pattern matching and information hiding.

A final point is that the Miranda `tail` operation is a selector since the original list is unaltered. Of course, it is not possible to implement destructors in Miranda because of the lack of memory manipulation and destructive assignment. However, the students should realise that this does not restrict the functionality of the resulting ADT.

The next major stage is to code the ADT in C. An array encoding of the list type is briefly considered but rejected due to the limitations on its size. The final type uses the standard pointer structure:

```
typedef struct listnode {
   int data;
   struct listnode *nextptr;
} LISTNODE;
typedef LISTNODE *LIST;
```

The typedef is described as one of C's information hiding mechanisms, since it allows the pointer/struct implementation to be renamed. An interesting comparison of this type with the Miranda list type can now be carried out. The listnode struct is closest to the second part of the Miranda type:

```
list *   ::=   Cons * (list *)
```

The * field of Cons corresponds to the data field of listnode, while the list * part is represented in C by a pointer to the struct. However, there seems to be no correspondence in the C code for:

```
list *   ::=   Nil
```

A more general C version of the Miranda type would make listnode a union type, consisting of separate types for non-empty and empty lists. Fortunately, we can spare ourselves this complexity by employing the usual trick of representing an 'empty' dynamic data structure by a NULL pointer. The students are reminded that this coding decision is *not* part of the type (as it really should be), but is simply a coding style. This makes it harder to understand the purpose of the type, since the use of NULL in the various list operations cannot be justified by looking at the type. This is another reason for hiding the type and the implementation of its operations from the client.

The basic functions are coded in the normal way. Two functions of interest are cons() and tail():

```
LIST cons(int x, LIST xs)
{
   LIST temp;
   temp = (LIST) malloc(sizeof(LISTNODE));
   temp->data = x;
   temp->nextptr = xs;
   return temp;
}

LIST tail(LIST xs)
{
   return xs->nextptr;
}
```

The C cons() function is more complicated than the Miranda version since C forces the programmer to explicitly create memory at run time, a feature that should probably be hidden in a high level language.

In the Miranda ADT type, destructor operations are not possible, but this is not so in C. For instance, a function called des_tail() can be coded:

```
LIST des_tail(LIST xs)
/* Destructively remove the
   head element from the list */
{
  LIST temp;
  temp = xs;
  xs = xs->nextptr;
  free(temp);
  return xs;
}
```

The usefulness of this function should be unclear to the students. It performs the same task as tail() but the side effects upon its input makes it a much poorer building block. In other words, there are drawbacks to using destructive assignment for coding ADT operations.

The single advantage of functions like des_tail() is for maintaining space efficiency, but it can be a crucial advantage when memory is scarce. The Miranda programming style means that a list update is accomplished by creating a new list, and the old list *may* never be used again. Consequently, it may be using up memory needlessly and should be garbage collected. This can be carried out explicitly in C by using free(), but the problem is that the programmer can have a difficult time deciding when a list is no longer required by anything, and so can be safely discarded. The overly hasty free-ing of dynamic data structures is one of the main sources of errors in programs, and it can be argued that such a delicate operation should be managed by the run-time system. In other words, garbage collection should not be available at the programming language level, but should be utilised by the run-time system.

When completed, the C list ADT consists of the LIST type and the functions head(), tail(), mkempty(), cons() and isempty(). It is no surprise that this corresponds closely to the Miranda list ADT. The C ADT could also include destructor functions, such as des_tail(), but we have chosen to avoid them due to their unpleasant side effects.

Once the ADT is available, more 'complex' list operations such as length, member, insert and concat can be written. For instance, insert() and concat() are:

```
LIST insert(int c, LIST xs)
{
  int x;
  if (isempty(xs))
    return cons(c, mkempty());
  x = head(xs);    /* where decl */
  if (c < x)
    return cons(c, xs);
  else
    return cons(x, insert(c,tail(xs)));
}
```

```
LIST concat(LIST xs, LIST ys)
{
  if (isempty(xs))
    return ys;
  else
    return cons(head(xs),
                concat(tail(xs),ys));
}
```

Of course, it is no coincidence that these operations have been chosen, since they offer an opportunity to compare how a client may use a C list ADT as opposed to a Miranda version.

There is a close correspondence between the Miranda and C functions, although it is somewhat obscured by the differences in the syntax of the two languages. A natural question is why C programmers do not code in this style? Part of the reason is that C does not support ADTs as part of the language and also that functions like `insert()` are quite inefficient.

A close look at the execution strategy of `insert()` shows that its inefficiency stems from the fact that it *copies* elements into a new list until the search reaches the insertion point.

A more typical C insertion function is:

```
/* Destructively insert */
void insertD(int c, LIST *sptr)
{
   LIST newptr, prevptr, currptr;

   newptr = (LIST) malloc(sizeof(LISTNODE));
   newptr->data = c;
   newptr->nextptr = NULL;

   prevptr = NULL; currptr = *sptr;
   while (currptr != NULL && c > currptr->data) {
     prevptr = currptr;
     currptr = currptr->nextptr;
   }

   if (prevptr == NULL) {
     newptr->nextptr = *sptr;
     *sptr = newptr;
   }
   else {
     prevptr->nextptr = newptr;
     newptr->nextptr = currptr;
   }
}
```

The students are hopefully less than impressed by this code which is more complex than `insert()` and negates its usefulness as a building block for other operations by altering its input. Also, the client programmer needs to manipulate the list type. Its only advantage is efficiency, and this may be marginal if insertion with `insert()` is usually near the front of the list.

All of the other functions which build new lists from existing ones can be rephrased to destructively update the lists rather than to (selectively) copy them; `concat()` is one such operation. However, the same trade-offs as for `insert()` must be considered.

5.3 Why is Miranda Good for Writing ADTs?

The students are now in a position to draw some conclusions about the usefulness of Miranda for writing ADTs. The recursive and polymorphic types in Miranda mean that functions are easier to write and are more general purpose. The functions are generally small and easy to understand, partly because of the brief syntax of Miranda, but also because of the absence of destructive assignment and explicit memory manipulation. Single assignment is the central reason why the Miranda ADT functions are good building blocks.

These points carry more weight because of the availability of the C code. C is also a high level language, but without the advantages of Miranda in these areas.

Miranda has some problems also. One is that the natural Miranda programming style, pattern matching on the data type, conflicts with the information hiding idea of ADTs. The other problem is one of efficiency, which is made clear when the corresponding C versions of the Miranda functions are examined.

5.4 Why Use C for Writing ADTs?

The inefficiency problem with Miranda is one reason why C might be used to write ADTs. Since destructive assignment and low level memory manipulation are available, it is possible to fine-tune an algorithm for speed and efficient memory usage.

The danger with C is that in the process of fine-tuning a set of ADT operations, their utility is lost because of the introduction of side-effects.

The preceding sections indicate that Miranda has a role as a ADT prototyping tool, whose code can be replaced by C if efficiency is required. Furthermore, once a C version of the ADT has been developed, the client's ADT functions coded in Miranda (e.g. `insert`, `concat`) can be readily translated into C. In fact, the translation is so simple it could be automated.

5.5 Comparing Miranda and C

The comparison points between Miranda and C have been outlined in the previous sections, but we summarise them again here.

Miranda and C types have many interesting similarities and differences, especially in the areas of recursive type definition and polymorphism. Single and destructive assignment can be compared, which leads to the realisation that algorithm design is not a precise art, there being a trade-off between efficiency and abstraction. The utilisation of the languages for a single topic allows their different features to be compared in a very concrete way, by looking at functions which perform similar tasks.

6 Student Feedback

This subject has been taught twice: once in semester 1 of 1994, once in semester 1 of 1995. At the end of each semester, the students were invited to fill in an anonymous questionnaire which asked them about all aspects of the subject (e.g. the usefulness of the text book, the availability of lab assistance). The questionnaire included two questions related to Miranda:

1. How did Miranda help your understanding of C?
2. How did Miranda hinder your understanding of C?

6.1 Student Responses Summarised

In 1994, 68 questionnaires were returned from a class total of 120, while in 1995, 90 responses were obtained from a class size of 170. This low number was partly due to student resistance to filling out questionnaires, and also partly due to poor class turnout on the day. Of the responses returned, the Miranda questions were sometimes left unanswered. Bearing all this in mind, there is no statistical significance to what follows, but the answers do provide an interesting insight into this approach. One point to consider is that a small proportion of both classes had not done the Miranda subject, and so were probably more likely to give negative responses about the usefulness of Miranda. One difference between 1994 and 1995 was the introduction of self-review exercises into the 1995 subject, along with more time spent on Miranda in tutorial and lab time.

In 1994, 38 people thought that Miranda had helped them. 8 students mentioned that it had helped them understand lists and trees, while 8 said that it improved their understanding of algorithms. 8 cited it as a good way of thinking, or as an aid to understanding; 4 thought that it taught a useful coding style; 4 thought Miranda made recursion easier to understand.

As regards Miranda hindering the understanding of C, 10 people thought that Miranda and C were very different which made it hard to understand C. Among the range of other answers, a few said that C was too complex, and too low level.

In 1995, 48 people thought Miranda had helped them. 16 people thought it had helped them understand trees and lists; 8 mentioned that recursion was clearer; 7 thought algorithms were easier to understand.

As regards Miranda hindering the understanding of C, 4 people thought that Miranda and C were not well matched. Among the other comments was a dislike of Miranda since it could not be 'hacked'.

7 Summary of this Approach

We begin by outlining some of the advantages of this approach, then some of the disadvantages, followed by a few proposals for changes. The final subsection summarises the structure of the subject.

7.1 Advantages

The main advantage of using Miranda in our C subject is that it is a powerful tool for developing ADTs. The code developed can be readily used as a high level specification of the C version of the ADT.

Another important point is that by using Miranda and C to solve the same problems it is possible to compare the two languages (and their programming paradigms) by looking at examples.

The third main advantage is that this approach reinforces the functional style of problem solving in the student's mind, and connects it to C, which is the average student's idea of a 'real world' programming tool.

7.2 Disadvantages

The main disadvantage of this approach is that the student has to learn a lot of material in one semester. Not only is C taught to quite an advanced level, but Miranda is reintroduced. This is especially hard for the small number of students each year who have not done the Miranda subject.

There is a danger that Miranda may become confused with C, especially in the areas of pattern matching and recursive data types. In addition, a student may become uncertain about basic imperative features like destructive assignment, pointer manipulation, and iteration. This is the reason why Miranda is not used extensively until the eighth week of the subject.

Another concern is whether the right ADTs are being taught. The list type is 'built' into Miranda, and so developing the list ADT in Miranda may seem a waste of time to the students.

A final concern is whether enough Miranda is being used. For instance, lazy evaluation is ignored, as are higher order functions. In fact, a strict functional language could be used as the functional component of this subject.

7.3 Proposed Changes

After the C material has been completed, the last two weeks of the subject are spent on an overview of some computer science topics. We shall try to use Miranda in these topics, thereby increasing its exposure while avoiding a reduction in the C material. In particular, we currently use a machine code simulator written in C, but this could be recoded in Miranda.

A small group of students still cannot see the relevance of Miranda to their computing career. This could be remedied by increasing the use of Miranda in other subjects in our degree. At present it only appears in any significant amount in one 2nd year subject on the comparison of programming paradigms.

7.4 Subject Summary

1. *Short title of the subject:*
   433-142 Computing Fundamentals B

2. *Aims of the subject:*
   To teach C to an intermediate level (i.e. up to and including pointers); to introduce ADTs using C and Miranda; to survey some additional CS topics; to compare C and Miranda. See section 4.1 for more details.

3. *For what kinds of students is the subject intended?*
   First year computer science students, first year science students, second year engineering students, and a small mix of students from other disciplines.

4. *For what year of study is the subject intended?*
   First and second year.

5. *What are the prerequisites for the subject?*
   433-141 Computing Fundamentals A, where problem solving using Miranda is taught.

6. *What text book is used?*
   C: How to Program (2nd edition), H.M. Deitel and P.J. Deitel [4].

7. Duration of the subject in weeks: 13

   Per week the following details:

	number of times per week		duration per session (hours)		total duration per week (hours)
lecture hours	3	x	1	=	3
tutorials	1	x	1	=	1
labs	1	x	2	=	2
project work	–	x	–	=	about 2.5

   The tutorials and labs start in the second week. The project work consists of two or three C programming assignments which should take a total of about 30 hours to complete. They are typically handed out in weeks 3, 7, and 10.

8. *How are the students assessed?*
   Two or three C programming projects (worth up to 30% of the final mark) and one 3 hour written examination (worth up to 70%).

Acknowledgements

I thank Roy Johnston and the FPLE'95 referees for many helpful comments.

References

1. Bird, R., Wadler, P.: *Introduction to Functional Programming*, (1988), Prentice Hall Int.
2. Clack, C., Myers, C., Poon, E.: *Programming with Miranda*, (1995), Prentice Hall Int.
3. Curmi, J., Johnston, R., Moffat, A., Naish, L., Sonenberg, L.: *433-141 Computing Fundamentals A, Notes and Exercises*, (1994), Dept. of Computer Science, Univ. of Melbourne, Australia
4. Deitel, H.M., Deitel, P.J.: *C: How To Program*, 2nd Edition, (1994), Prentice Hall Int.
5. Holyer, I.: *Functional Programming With Miranda*, (1991), Pitman
6. Hudak, P.: Conception, Evolution, and Application of Functional Programming Languages, *Computing Surveys*, 21(3), September, (1989), 359–411
7. Hughes, J.: Why Functional Programming Matters, *The Computer Journal*, Vol. 32, No. 2, (1989), 98–107
8. Kelley, A., Pohl, I.: *A Book on C*, 3rd Edition, (1995), Benjamin Cummings
9. Kernighan, B.W., Ritchie, D.M.: *The C Programming Language*, 2nd Edition, (1988), Prentice Hall Int.
10. Pohl, I., Edelson, D.: A To Z: C Language Shortcomings, *Computer Language*, Vol. 13, No. 2, (1988), 51–64.

Requirements for an Ideal First Language

J.-P. Jacquot and J. Guyard

Université Henri Poincaré — Nancy 1
CNRS — CRIN — INRIA-Lorraine
B.P. 239
54506 Vandœuvre-lès-Nancy Cedex
France

tel: (+33) 83 59 20 16
fax: (+33) 83 41 30 70
e-mail: {jacquot, guyard}@loria.fr

Abstract. Five years ago, we have introduced functional languages in the introductory computer science course at our University. This experience taught us there is still room for improvement in support languages for beginners. This is summarized in the form of six requirements for languages in such a context: conceptual neatness, consistency with common usage, language extensibility, tools for probing and profiling, enforcement of good habits, and observability of mechanisms. Our experience, observations, and requirements are discussed and justified.

1 Introduction

The idea to use a functional language as a first language to learn is quite an old one: it dates back to LOGO [8]. Abelson and Sussman [1] have made it a viable solution for university level education. They have also shown that we can move away from heart-warming, but rather limited, pedagogic experiments to a mature use in mass-teaching. However, as pedagogical user of such languages, we still look for a better language than what is on the market.

Five years ago, we seized the opportunity of a general reform in our university to bust out PASCAL from the introductory informatics courses. Instead we chosed ISetl [3] and Scheme [1]. Since then, nearly 2000 students have enjoyed (or suffered for some of them) either languages. This year, we have made a new move to Caml [4]. Change for change's sake is not a good idea, particularly in an educational environment. Both times, we were prompted by a great insatisfaction, not with the languages, but with the concepts we could not teach with the languages. Both times, we have accompanied the change with a deep reflection on the aim, on the organization, and on the foundation of our teaching.

Our major aim is to educate scientists, not to train in computer use or to raise computer programmers. Thus, we need languages which put forward certain key concepts. We moved from PASCAL because we have observed how it gets in the way between concepts such as functions and their actual realizations. We moved to Caml after observing how difficult it is to introduce the concept of type with languages which do not make this notion visible. He also feel that Caml will help us to make a clean treatment of the passage from functional to imperative computation model.

Reforms have at least one very positive effect: they increase our knowledge! In particular, the evaluation of the differences between the different states gives us a good starting point to deepen our understanding of students' and instructors' needs for introductory courses. It also allows us to propose a set of requirements for the next best introductory language. To sum up, our requirements are derived from four strong ideas:

1. languages and their environment *are* important,
2. conceptual neatness is necessary, but *not* sufficient,
3. adherence to common usages, user-friendliness, and student-proofness *are* necessary, and
4. the needs of learners are *not* the same as the needs of programmers: the language and its environment must reflect this.

The paper is organized as follows. First, we will briefly present the context of our teaching and our aims. Then, we will discuss some observations made during the last five years. Last, we will elaborate on requirements for the language we would like to use in the future.

2 Goals of our teaching

As a pedagogical tool, as opposed to a field topic of their own, functional languages are best used to introduce computer science and programming. We use them during the first two university years for the introductory informatics courses. Although students have not yet chosen their specific major, these years are organized around "channels" (mathematics, physics and chemistry, geology, engineering, sciences of life) which are "preferred ways" leading to specialized curricula. We have worked in the first three channels. The course is a mandatory one.

Students entering university come straight from *lycées* (i.e., high-schools). Between 10% and 20% of our entering students have had an exposure to computer usage (baring games) or programming. This means that we can start from a "clean slate". On the one hand, we find this situation rather good: correcting bad habits or, worse, bad concepts, is hard! On the other hand, this gives us the special responsibility in motivating students to consider computer science as a necessary topic to study: all subsequent curricula include some informatics courses.

An introductory course at this level is hard to define in a positive way: we certainly know what we *do not* want, but we are still feeling a bit fuzzy about what we *do* want. Our choice has been to make this course a *scientific introduction to a field.* That is, to present a discipline with its own basic principles, concepts, and vocabulary, as well as its own mathematical approach. This view is strongly opposed to the teaching of programming *per se*, of one programming language, of software tools and manipulation, or of computing as a service discipline for others. These last approaches are legitimate—they are in fact used in other channels of the University— although we do not find them appropriate for our students. The main implication of our philosophy is that programming and programming languages are a *necessary support for learning,* but not an end to teach.

The introductory informatics course is rather short: 60 to 90 class-hours per student. This has led us to define a syllabus focused on the study of very few concepts:

- naming and abstracting,
- computation mechanisms (either through naive β-reduction or memory box-drawings, depending on the language used),
- functions, both as modeling tools and computational abstractions,
- data types, from basics (provided by the language) to module-like used in modeling,
- algorithm schemas, mostly recursive, and
- formal language:
  - grammars,
  - syntax and syntactic analysis,
  - semantics (actual computation of denotations for simple cases like predicates), and
  - run-time and actual computations.

We have kept this syllabus voluntarily short for two reasons. First, we want students to build a correct conceptual frame for these concepts and their relation: this takes time. Second, we insist that they work on concrete problems emphasizing the concepts: this is done in controlled lab-sessions included in the hours allotted to the course.

We must emphasize that our courses are not intended for future computer science students, quite the contrary! Most of our students will proceed in mathematics, physics and chemistry. In each of those curricula, they will have to follow a computing course, more oriented toward numerical computation in physics and chemistry, or toward algorithms and operational research in mathematics. Our courses are then the only pure informatics courses for most of our students.

Last, but not least, many students have not yet chosen their professional future. Then, we have a certain responsibility to attract able students to the software oriented curricula. Software curricula are reputed for being very demanding on students. So, students know that, if they enroll, their part of the contract will be tough. Our part is to show that investments will be worthwhile, that there is a scientific content, and that the discipline is intellectually challenging.

The interested reader will find the synthetic description of the course in the annex.

3 Languages and strategies

From 90 to 94, the mathematical channel and the physics-chemistry channel had different courses for numerous reasons, one being that we wanted to experiment with different pedagogic strategies, a second being that we wanted to adapt our pedagogy to students with a priori different motivations.

In the mathematical channel, we used ISetl [11]. Although not a functional language, strictly speaking (the execution model is imperative), ISetl has most of the features traditionally associated with functional languages. In particular, functions are first-class citizens defined by a form homologous to λ-abstractions. Moreover, association lists or lists are treated syntactically and semantically as true functions. The major difference with traditional functional languages is the very rich set (pun intended) of basic data-types. This led us to follow an original strategy.

The first semester (1/3 of the total course) was devoted to mathematical modeling and a global approach to computing. We used the fact that students have a little knowledge about logic and set theory to introduce the use of those "tools" in modeling problems and programming. Since ISetl allows us to execute specifications, we were able to present three major ideas: 1) a rigorous approach to solving problems with computers, 2) a proper view of computing as building complex objects (as opposed to fiddling with simple values), and 3) a set of intellectually challenging and reasonably concrete problems.

The second semester was devoted to an analytical study of a few selected concepts. First, we introduced the notion of data-types and we used it as a systematic analysis grid of ISetl itself (or, more precisely, of its semantic domain). Type-checking was seen in its dynamic flavor. Second, we studied functions and recursion (both theoretically with induction and practically with memory management). Last, we studied what is in a language by programming a complete compiler/interpreter. This last theme was done in six weeks; the trick was to provide students with large pieces of code they had to complete.

In the physics-chemistry channel, the strategy was slightly different. The cleaner computing model of Scheme allowed us to begin by the notion of reduction, immediately followed by the study of recursion. The somewhat poor set of basic types induced us to look for examples and exercises in the domain of numerical methods. The second semester was devoted to data-types. First a short study of type-constructors (pairs and lists) was done, then extended to the use of data-types as modeling tools.

A very fruitful innovation in this course was to engage teaching assistants from the physics and chemistry departments. The role of these young colleagues is to make a link between the informatics course and the other scientific courses. They have already introduced several problem themes and they have actively participated in their pedagogical elaboration in a computer science perspective. As a result, we have now a course still speaking of real computer science, but well rooted in a concrete domain. Additionally, these assistants participate in the computing service courses in their own discipline, where they can efficiently build on what students know.

4 Observations from the trenches

From running in parallel during four years those courses, many observations have been made. A first comment consists in blowing away a strongly rooted idea: that programming language is secondary, it is the concepts that count. Yes, indeed, but:

- beginners have a need to make ideas concrete, or, to put it bluntly: no syntax, no concept! Our most prominent problem has been with the notion of type. Although several lectures and exercises were dedicated to this concept, too few students did get it correctly. On the other hand, a priori difficult concepts, like higher-order functions, did not pose many difficulties since they are supported by the syntax and the computation model.
- the application languages have had a strong influence on the overall strategy of the courses. For instance, modeling could be introduced at first in the ISetl-based channel because mathematical formulae transl(iter)ate directly in ISetl, while modeling in the Scheme-based channel had to wait until recursive data-structures were introduced. Albeit not a problem in itself, this point must be fully acknowledged.

The second comment is that concepts do count! Too often, students pretend that they do not know the syntax to write this or that. Generally, the answer "just write it in math, or in French," results in the same white page. The point is that we should not give our students the feeling their lame excuse is correct. Syntax and computational model must be simple, tailored to students' knowledge, and adapted to students' capabilities to abstract.

The third comment concerns the absolute necessity of simple environments. Students must be able to program and see the results in the most easy way. We see two reasons to that. First, there should be no magic, or, more exactly, the magic must be in the power of solving problems by programming. Many students are rebuffed by learning esoteric manipulations by rote; afterall, they are no different from us who refuse to use the majority of functionalities of our telephones for the same reason [7]! Second, we have no time to spend on learning to use a computer. The lack of time sounds like an easy excuse, but actually, there is a deeper reason. We strongly feel that "teaching to use a computer" (a service course) and "teaching computer science" are totally different topics. In fact, mixing both is detrimental to students: they feel confused about what they are doing and what is our purpose. Furthermore, there is still the need to impose to certain colleagues the idea that informatics is a scientific discipline of its own.

The last comment is that difficulties were not always where we expected them. Three examples illustrate this comment: recursion, higher-order functions, and numbers. Recursion has been introduced either upfront (in the Scheme-based channel) or after iterations (in the ISetl-based channel). In both channels, we did not notice any particular difficulty. Of course, some students did not get it, but they did not get either what functions or computations are. We attribute this to two major factors. First, we introduce recursion by capitalizing on the knowledge of recursive sequences that students have studied in math; second, we provide them with a precise syntax—actually, a function skeleton. This year, the type constructors of Caml allowed us to present, with some success, recursive data-structures (trees representing formulae) during the first lecture; the trick was to built on the knowledge of computation of derivatives from the calculus course. Initially, we feared that higher-order functions would be a stumbling block: we were wrong. Using functions as parameters is straightforward; returning functions as results takes students a little more time to feel confident with the idea. Again, we attribute this to the fact that there is no "syntactic cost" in using higher-order functions. On the other hand, the type rigidity of Caml introduced a lot of problems to many students when manipulating numbers. The need to differentiate between the integer 2 and the floating 2.0, or between the integer addition + and the floating one +. is very confusing to many students. This was shown by haphazard uses of type-converters or wrong syntactic generalization like postfixing variable names with a dot to indicate a floating type, for instance.

These comments are the major lessons that students taught us. In the next section, we will see how we can exploit them to define an ideal language.

5 Requirements for the next generation language

Designing new languages is a pet activity of computer scientists. The following requirements are not an essay in introducing new programming paradigms or computational models. Our aim is to suggest improvements in a particular use of a language: mass-teaching in introductory informatics.

5.1 Conceptual neatness

The requirement of conceptual neatness is probably the most important of all, albeit it leaves open many different realizations. In a sense, we, as teachers, do not mind the actual concepts used so long as we can explain clearly to students a simple and correct model of what is going on. For beginners, our role is to help them build a solid base frame which further education will expand and refine by introducing more complexity. We are deeply convinced that an early introduction of details and exceptions results in confused minds and warped concepts. Actually, this philosophy is followed in scientific courses where simplified abstractions are presented first: massive point in mechanics, perfect-gas law in thermodynamics, stoechiometric equations in chemistry, etc. Simplification and approximation are important tools for scientists in general, and computer scientists in particular.

Two corollaries follow from the requirement.

The first is that there should be a one-to-one mapping between concepts and syntactic expressions. Whatever we think about the importance beginners attribute to syntax, we must acknowledge this fact. On the one hand, too many ways of expressing the same computation place students in the uncomfortable position where they must make a choice, but they have no rationale for it.

Notions like convenience, efficiency, or implementation optimization require a certain amount of experience as well as a good understanding of the basics. On the other hand, giving totally different, context-dependent meaning to the same tokens or syntactic constructs induces major difficulties for many beginners. In this respect, the **var** keyword of PASCAL (variable declaration, or parameter passing method) or the = token of Caml (name binding, or equality predicates) are typical examples. From our point of view, the problem comes from the fact that two different concepts collide and mix in an unpredictable way.

The second corollary is that students must be able to do *all* their work in only one language: problem modeling, algorithm design, programming, debugging, everything! This means that the language must be simple and straightforward enough to allow beginners to think directly *in* it. In particular, implementation-dependent constraints, like the order of declarations for instance, should be hidden at the beginner level. Of course, some language philosophies may be in contradiction with this idea, the ML family requires a strict order for its type-inference mechanism to work for instance. We are convinced that programming-environment technologies can provide adequate answers to this apparent mismatch.

5.2 Consistency with common usage

When students enter our introductory computer science course, they already have a serious history of manipulating formal and symbolic languages. They have written many systems of equations and many functions; they have computed with many complex objects: natural numbers, real numbers, complex numbers, vectors, functions (in calculus), sequences, sets, etc. To perform these activities, students have been taught notations and computation rules with which they are fluent. We think that a first programming language *must* be consistent with these time-honored notations. Three reasons justify this requirement.

A minor reason is the pedagogic bonus we get each time we can say: "Look, this is not different from what you wrote in your last math course!" The trick here is the ability to convince students that we are not teaching them something totally new, instead, we are seeing a new facet of a known concept. We have found such discourse to be reassuring—The ground is chartered—and also to be a good attention-getter—Are we saying the truth?

Another minor reason is that we want students to focus on the essentials, not on the details. In that respect, each deviance from common usage must be explained, justified, and then looks like an important issue. We must also stress that common usage now includes hand-held powerful calculators.

The major reason is the philosophy of our approach. We think we have a role to play in the scientific formation of our students. One of our main objectives is to provide students with a knowledge they can reuse in their favorite discipline. The introductory computer science course is a unique place where concepts as functions, symbolic expressions, and modeling can be studied and deepened. But to do so, we need tools which support an easy transfer between disciplines.

Among the different sources of deviances, the treatment of numbers is probably the worst offender. Common usage relies heavily on the fact that a natural number is an integer, which is a rational, which is a real, which is a complex, ... It also relies on the facts that numbers can be quite large and that $x < x+1$ is always true. Our experience with languages which conform to this usage (Scheme and ISetl have infinite integers, rational arithmetic, implicit type conversions) and with languages which do not (Caml has a strict type enforcement policy and 32bits integers) clearly favors the formers. An important reason lies in the kind of problems we propose to beginners: mainly numerical computations. This choice is the only one compatible with the idea that students must work on one concept at a time, hence problems must come from a world they know. When learning the notion of algorithms and computation, students must not be distracted by number representation. While this last notion is certainly very important for computer scientists, we would prefer to introduce it much later in the curriculum; we will say more on this subject later.

A second important offender is the use of parenthesis, particularly with function applications. The absence of parenthesis in Caml is as disturbing as the unusual syntax of Scheme. This issue, strongly related to the need for nice notation emphasized in [5], is certainly more complex than it looks.

5.3 Incremental language

Along with the idea of learning one concept at a time, is the idea of smooth pedagogic progression. This means that language constructs are introduced gradually; in a sense, the language should grow at the same pace than students learn the concepts. While this is certainly more of a concern to the educator rather than to the language implementor, we would appreciate if languages supported this requirement.

We certainly understand that our requirement is at odds with the legitimate and necessary desire of language designers to achieve the largest power of expression. Actually, what we would like is simply a mechanism which would allow us to hide and make inaccessible certain features of the language. For instance, at the very beginning with Caml we would hide the imperative constructs (references), the iterative constructs (loops), and the tuple type.

Very practical reasons justify this requirement. First, it would eliminate the tiring traditional argument which runs: "–It's not what I wanted –But, it works! –Yes, but I said to use recursion—But, it works..." Second, it would greatly simplify on-the-fly debugging of students' programs during lab-sessions. Rules enforced by the machine are so much easier to handle by everybody!

Another, deeper, reason is that, during lab sessions, we encourage students to discuss and share their solutions. With our supervision and the natural honesty of students, this strategy works quite well. However, we regularly face the case where one advanced student finds a solution which relies on not-yet-taught concepts. We are then forced to improvise untimely explanations. Whether this situation is detrimental is certainly an open question; personally, we fear so. At the least, it distracts "slow" students from the particular concept they have to understand.

5.4 Profiling and probing

Caml [12] shows that a neat integration of imperative constructs in a functional framework can be achieved. [11] shows that a language (namely, the full Setl) can usefully be complemented with implementation hints for data-structures. Reusing this idea in the simpler case of numbers would greatly ease the problems we have discussed in the preceding section. For instance, we could begin with a "number" type, very general but slow, then move to 32bits integer and floats, efficient but more complex to use. However, to get the full benefit of such ideas, we need a comprehensive set of tools, fully integrated into the run-time engine to probe, to time, and to measure memory usage during executions.

An interesting rationale for this requirement is our observation that, with the years, we wrote less and less programs, but more and more specifications. Actually, this is not surprising when we consider what concepts we want to teach. The real advantage of functional programming languages is that specifications can be executed. But to stay at this level is frustrating: efficiency is also a fundamental concept of our discipline. In fact, an introductory course should go up to the point where techniques like object representation (of numbers at least) and imperative programming are introduced and, crucially, justified.

The main pedagogic reason justifying this requirement is to show the motto "first make it right, then make it fast" at work. In other words, we want to be able to introduce the notion of computation complexity. Since students do not have the necessary mathematical background at this level of education, we must rely on a concrete, experimental, approach to introduce this concept in a clean way.

We have discovered, through many discussions and interrogations, that a fair number of students have a genuine interest about the notion of efficiency of computations. This is certainly the kind of curiosity we must encourage and nurture.

5.5 Enforcement of good habits

Introductory courses should promote an important message: programs are less for machines than for humans. Unfortunately, such message can only be understood once one has accumulated a certain amount of experience and has worked on dirty code. However, we have noted that good style is something which lasts when learnt early. While it is certainly the duty of educators to set good examples and to correct bad style, we think language designers have a part to play. The use of a language must lead naturally to simple and elegant expressions.

The first, and most important, notion of elegance is in the intuitive semantic model used by the language. For that reason, we greatly appreciated programming with sets and first-order logic formulae in ISetl. In Caml and Scheme, the power of functions and the referential transparency possess this flavor of elegance.

The challenge is to keep this feeling even in dirty areas such as input-output for instance.

The second notion of elegance lies in the bijective relation between concepts and means of expression. In our view, diversity, options, or shortcuts are not good things at the beginner level. For instance, Caml proposes three different, nearly equivalent (but not exactly), notations to define a function. This led us to a dilemma: either we presented the three notations, but without being able to give rationales for the choice of one for one particular problem, or we stuck to one notation, but with the recurrent problem of explaining to bemused students why their "erroneous" text was accepted by the interpreter. Both cases are equally bad since they make students ask themselves irrelevant questions. While the idea of unique expression may sound restrictive, it is coherent with our principle that a concept must be mastered before its variants can be studied. Actually, a mechanism which would allow us to introduce gradually more and more freedom would suit us perfectly.

The last notion of elegance is the presentation of program texts. Typography is important. Technologies, such as pretty-printing or syntax-directed edition are now sufficiently well known to be included in the front-end of any pedagogic language.

5.6 Observability of the execution mechanism

One of the most frustrating points of our course is that we explain what are computations, parsing, stacks, name binding environments, but that we are unable to observe those concepts on the tool we use. By analogy, we are in the situation of an electrical engineering professor who would show and explain a radio-receiver but who would forbid students to open it and look inside.

This requirement is motivated by the observation that too many students are unable to explain on paper a computation or to correct their programs although they have been given a model and notations, they have been lectured about it, and we have proposed and corrected several exercises. Seeing the paper model actually working, i.e., making it concrete, would certainly be of great help for these students. We also hypothesize that many students would be more confident in the writing of recursive functions after they have seen how the system practically computes with them.

A particularly needed observation tool concerns the name bindings. We were slightly baffled by the difficulties we noted in the student's misuse of local names, until we realized that we were very explicit about this notion, but used implicitly a global name space for functions. We are now much more careful, but the special status of the top-level name space presents a real difficulty.

How it is possible to provide beginners with observation tools they can understand is yet an open problem. Some ideas have already been explored ([13] for instance) but, apparently did not catch up in modern languages. Ideas could also be gained from the research done in algorithm animation and from the huge experience with practical debugging tools.

6 Conclusion

We would like to conclude this paper by commenting on its paradoxical tone: we use the teaching of concepts as a rationale for requiring mainly surface features!

The importance of surface features is certainly something we would not have admitted a few years ago. The structured-programming stream promoted ideas like pseudo-code or even dual languages: one for algorithm design (the real thing), and one for programming (the contingent thing) [6]. While these views are certainly adequate for professional programmers, they are far off the mark for beginners. We are now deeply convinced that beginners need concreteness to build concepts. Philosophically, this idea is nothing more than Poincaré's hypothesis [10] which places the root of mathematics in our perceptive capabilities[1]. In our case, this means external features like syntax, tools enforcing styles, or direct observations. If we do not provide students with the adequate concrete paraphernalia, we run the major risk that they will try to find their own (unfortunately often the idiosyncrasies of the language or computer system). We also run the minor risk that students will simply ignore us!

Our insistence on surface can be rightly interpreted as a sign of quality for the languages we use. Current incarnations of concepts are reasonably well done! However, there is still an unsolved problem: modularity. Lack of this notion is the most important blocking factor we feel at present. Be they objects, signatures, abstract-data type, or whatever, modules are a concept that can be taught to beginners. The reason is that they are a straightforward extension of the notion of types which can be introduced naturally with the idea of modeling physical systems. Again, the important issue for our purpose is to have a clear syntax and a simple intuitive model. The approach followed in SML [9] is certainly very promising, particularly due to its neatness. However, there is certainly a need to develop simplified versions of this idea. Proposing a nice solution to the modularity problem is certainly the point we are the most eager to see in the future.

And please, please, all you implementors, allow your system to run on PCs, Macintosches and Unix systems. All with less than 4 MB memory!

Acknowledgements

The courses presented in the paper are the result of the work of teams. Over the year, many people have contributed to the construction of the courses, and so, to the elaboration of our ideas. To all, we address our heartful thanks, with a special note to N. Lévy and F. Alexandre who have had major influences. We have been impressed by the tremendous job done by the anonymous referees: many thanks, the final paper form owes much to you.

[1] Poincaré argued the idea that the genesis of mathematical theories comes from perceptual experiences and a notion of choice of theory based on the criteria of "most convenient." It is close to intuitionistic theories.

Annex: Synthetic description of the course

We present here the current incarnation of our course.
Name: *Tronc commun d'Informatique*

Aims: This course presents a scientific introduction to the field of informatics. Students will learn the basic concepts and vocabulary of the discipline.

Years: technically spread on the first two years.

Prerequisite: none.

Textbooks: When using Scheme, we recommended the French translation of [1]. At present, we recommend [2].

Duration: 14 cycles, on two semesters. Practical constraints (we run among 12 to 17 groups of 40 students per semester)! A cycle is either a week or two weeks. The following breakdown is in cycle:

	# of times per cycle	duration per session	total per cycle
hall lectures	1	2	2
classes	1	2	2
laboratories	1	2	2
homework		none required	

Assessment: Two written examinations, two laboratories examinations.

References

1. H. Abelson and G. Sussman. *Structure and Interpretation of Computer Programs.* MacGraw Hill, 1985.
2. Th. Accart-Hardin and V. Donzeau-Gouge Viguié. *Concepts et outils de programmation.* InterÉdition, Paris, 1992.
3. N. baxter, E. Dubinsky, and G. Levin. *Learning Discrete Mathematics with ISETL.* Springer-Verlag, New York, 1989.
4. G. Cousineau and G. Huet. The Caml primer. Technical Report 122, INRIA, Roquencourt — France, 1990.
5. E.W. Dijsktra and C.S. Scholten. *Predicate Calculus and Program Semantics.* Springer-Verlag, New York, 1990.
6. A. Ducrin. *Programmation.* Dunod, Paris, 1984.
7. D. Norman. *Things that Make us Smart.* Addison-Wesley, 1993.

8. S. Papert. *Jaillissement de l'esprit.* Flammarion, translation from *Mindstorm, Children, and Powerful Ideas* Basic Books Inc., New-York edition, 1981.
9. L. Paulson. *ML for the Working Programmer.* Cambridge University Press, 1991.
10. H. Poincaré. *La Science et l'hypothèse.* Collection Champs. Flammarion, Paris, paper-back (reprint) edition, 1902.
11. J.T. Schwartz, R.B.K. Dewar, E. Dubinsky, and E. Schonberg. *Programming with Sets: An Introduction to SETL.* Springer-Verlag, New-York, 1986.
12. P. Weiss and X. Leroy. *Le langage Caml.* InterÉdition, Paris, 1993.
13. H. Wertz. *Intelligence artificielle, application à l'analyse des programmes.* Masson, Paris, 1985.

A Second Year Course on Data Structures Based on Functional Programming*

Manuel Núñez, Pedro Palao and Ricardo Peña

Dept. de Informática y Automática
Universidad Complutense de Madrid, Spain
e-mail: {manuelnu,ecceso,ricardo}@dia.ucm.es

Abstract. In this paper, we make a proposal for a second year course on advanced programming, based on the functional paradigm. It assumes the existence of a first course on programming, also based on functional languages. Its main subject is *data structures*.
We claim that advanced data structures and algorithms can be better taught at the functional paradigm than at the imperative one, and that this can be done without losing efficiency. We also claim that, as a consequence of the higher level of abstraction of functional languages, more subjects can be covered in the given amount of time.
In the paper, numerous examples of unusual data structures and algorithms are presented illustrating the contents and the philosophy of the proposed course.

1 Introduction

The controversy about the use of a functional language as the first programming language is still alive. Several proposals have been made on a first programming course based on the functional paradigm or on a mixture of the functional and imperative ones. Some of them have been actually implemented in practice [11, 14].

Many teachers feel that the functional paradigm is better suited than the imperative one to introduce students to the design of algorithms, and we do not want to repeat here the numerous arguments given for this. However, one of the obstacles to put these ideas into practice is the feeling that there is not a clear continuation for this first course. There are plenty of textbooks well suited for advanced programming, including in this category texts on formal verification, data structures and algorithms, and modular programming. But all of them assume the imperative paradigm. Perhaps, most of the people assume that advanced programming (meaning the optimal use of the computer) can only be done with imperative languages.

In this paper, we propose the objectives and contents of a second year course. Its main subject is *data structures*. We claim that advanced data structures and algorithms can be better taught at the functional paradigm than at the imperative one. We also claim that this can be done in the same spirit of using

* In the next page, a short description of the course is given.

Short title: Data Structures.
Aims of the course: At the end of the course students should be able:

1. To formally specify an abstract data type (ADT) from an informal description of it.
2. To choose an efficient functional implementation of a formally specified ADT. In order to do that, students should use one of the data structures taught along the course.
3. To show the correctness of the implementation chosen for the ADT.

Kind of students: Computer Science students.
Year: Second year.
Prerequisites: A first course on functional programming and some imperative notions such as arrays, iteration, ...
Text books: A combination of texts on functional programming and conventional texts on data structures. For instance [1, 4, 7].
Duration of the course: 30 weeks.

	sessions per week		duration per session		duration per week
lecture hours	2	×	1h	=	2h
tutorials	2	×	1h	=	2h
laboratories	1	×	3h	=	3h
private tuition				=	6h

The laboratory is a separated subject with its own evaluation. Small programs, written in Gofer, should be assigned as home work. The tuition hours given in the table correspond to the time dedicated by the teacher to solve students questions in his/her office.
Assessment: The laboratory will be evaluated by means of a medium sized program developed by a team of 2–3 students. The theory will be evaluated by a written examination covering the above stated aims.

Fig. 1. Course Description

the computer resources in the most possible efficient way. A third claim is that, as a consequence of the higher level of abstraction of functional languages, more subjects can be covered in the given amount of time. We can exhibit, as a proof of these assertions, our experience in teaching data structures and algorithms in the imperative paradigm, and a limited experiment conducted by us, putting some of the ideas below into practice in a one semester course on functional programming for graduates having no previous experience on programming.

The philosophy of the course is not just to translate to the functional paradigm the data structures and algorithms developed in the imperative field. In many cases —for instance when dealing with trees— this is appropriate, but in many others —the algorithms based on heaps are an example— it is not. In some of these cases there exist alternative functional structures that can do the job with the same efficiency as their imperative counterparts. Several examples of this are given in the paper. When there is not such an alternative, it seems unavoidable the use of arrays updated in place. For this reason, we include a last part of the course based on mutable arrays. There are now enough proposals to have this feature in a functional language without losing transparential referency. We give in the paper some examples of their use.

We are assuming that a first course on programming based on functional languages has already been implemented, and so students know how to design small/medium sized functional programs, mainly based on lists. They are also supposed to know the use of induction to reason about the correctness of recursive programs, and the use of higher order functions to avoid recursion. On the other hand, they must have enough notions on imperative programming — received, for instance, at the end of the course on functional programming or in a separate course including computer architecture issues—, such as arrays, iteration and the relation between tail recursive programs and iteration. These notions are needed to allow a detailed discussion on the efficiency of some algorithms.

The language used in the following is Haskell. After this introduction, the rest of the paper is organized as follows: in Sect. 2 we briefly explain our current second year course on advanced programming. Section 3 contains a proposal for a new second year course based on the functional paradigm. Sections 4, 5 and 6 explain in detail the most original parts of the proposal and provide numerous examples illustrating the spirit of the new course. Finally, in Sect. 7 we present our conclusions.

2 A Second Year Course on Imperative Programming

Just to compare how things are being done at present, in this section we are sketching the objectives and contents of the second year course on programming currently being taught at our institution. The course follows to a conventional first course on imperative programming where students learn how to program in the small, having Pascal as the base language. The data structures of this first course are limited to arrays, records and sequential files. The methodological aspects provided by the course are those derivated of the stepwise refinement technique, together with some abstract program schemes for traversing a sequence or searching an element in a sequence.

The objectives selected for the second course are mainly two:

1. At the end of the course, the student should be able to specify and implement efficient and correct small programs.
2. The student should also be able to formally specify the external behavior of an abstract data type, and to choose an efficient implementation of this behavior.

As it can be observed, the main emphasis is done in formal specification and verification issues but, to satisfy the second part of objective 2, also a sufficient number of data structures must be covered. Then, the course is naturally divided into two parts: the first one dedicated to formal techniques for analyzing, specifying, deriving, transforming and verifying small programs, and the second one covering the most important data structures. This second part begins with an introduction to the theory of abstract data types and their algebraic specification techniques. Then, every data structure is first presented as an abstract data type and specified as such. Once the external behavior is clear, several implementations are proposed. For each one, the cost in space of the representation and the cost in time of the operations are studied. A scheme of the contents of this second year course follows:

1. Efficiency analysis of algorithms.
2. Specification of algorithms by using predicate logic.
3. Recursive design and formal verification of recursive programs. Divide and conquer algorithms. Quicksort.
4. Program transformation techniques.
5. Iterative design and verification. Formal derivation of iterative programs.
6. Abstract data types: concept, algebraic specification techniques and underlying model of a specification.
7. Linear data structures: stacks, queues, and lists. Array-based and linked-based implementations.
8. Trees: binary trees, n-ary trees, search trees, threaded trees, AVL-trees, 2-3 trees. Algorithms for inserting and deleting an element. Disjoint sets structure for the *union-find* problem. Implementation by using an array.
9. Priority queues. Implementation by means of a heap (in turn implemented by an array). Heapsort.
10. Lookup tables and sets. Implementation by means of balanced trees. Implementation by hash tables.
11. Graphs. Implementation by using an adjacency matrix and by adjacency lists. Important algorithms for graphs: Dijkstra, Floyd, Prim and Kruskal.

As it can be observed, the course is rather dense and a little bit hard to follow. However, our students seem to tolerate well the flood of formal concepts. In fact, with respect to programming methodology, this course is the central one of the curriculum. It is followed by a third year course on programming where students learn more sophisticated algorithms (dynamic programming, branch and bound, probabilistic algorithms, etc.). But the formal basis required to analyze the cost and correctness of these algorithms is supposed to be acquired in the second year course.

To complement the theory, there is a separate course on laboratory assignments where students begin developing small modules representing abstract data types and end with a medium sized program composed of several modules. For this last assignment, students are grouped in teams of two or three people. The programming language is Modula-2 on MS/DOS. In total, students receive 4 hours per week of formal lectures and tutorials, and spend 3 supervised hours in the laboratory. The course duration is about 30 weeks. It is assumed some home work and the use of non supervised hours in the laboratory.

3 A New Proposal for this Course

We are detailing here the objectives and contents of our proposal for a second year course. In order to establish the objectives, we assume students already have acquired, in their first year, the skills enumerated in the introduction of this paper.

We propose as the main objective the second one mentioned in the description of the imperative course given in Sect. 2, that is, at the end of the course:

> *The student should be able to formally specify the external behavior of an abstract data type, and to choose an efficient implementation of this behavior.*

That is, the main wonderings of the course are ***abstraction*** and ***efficiency***. The reasons for this choice are the same as in the imperative case: a first advanced programming course must put the emphasis more in fundamental concepts and techniques than in broading the programmer catalog of available algorithms. Next courses can play this role.

As one of the main concerns is efficiency, the first subject of the course must obviously be the efficiency analysis of functional programs. The usual way to teach cost analysis is by studying the worst case and by using recurrences. These recurrences can be easily established and solved assuming applicative order of evaluation, i.e. eager languages. However, lazy languages offer better opportunities for teaching as they allow a more abstract style of programming [10]. Unfortunately, cost analysis of lazy functional programs is not developed enough (see [19] for a recent approach) to be taught at a second year course. So, we propose to analyze the cost assuming eager evaluation, and to use the result as an upper bound for lazily evaluated programs. Of course, this approach is only applicable to programs terminating under eager evaluation.

The course is divided into three parts:

1. Abstract data types.
2. Efficient functional data structures not assuming mutable arrays.
3. Efficient functional data structures relying on mutable arrays.

The first part follows the same approach as the corresponding part of the imperative course described in Sect. 2, but it now includes precise techniques to show the correctness of an abstract data type implementation. This kind of proofs are very hard to carry out when the implementing language is imperative, but much easier to do when it is functional. This part of the program is explained in detail in Sect. 4. In the remaining lectures of the course, each time an implementation is proposed, its correctness with respect to the algebraic specification of the data type will be shown. It is expected that students will acquire this ability.

The second part presents data structures —and algorithms to manipulate them— achieving the same efficiency, up to a multiplicative constant, than their imperative counterparts. So, the advantages of using a functional language are kept, and nothing is lost with respect to the efficient use of the computer. We present structures not very common, such as the functional versions of leftist trees [7] and Braun trees [6], which can elegantly replace their imperative equivalent ones whose efficiency is based on the constant access time of arrays. Some implementations may even use arrays (purely functional languages such as Haskell [9] provide this structure as primitive), but in a read-only way. So, they do not rely on complex techniques or smart compilers to guarantee that arrays are not copied. More details are given in Sect. 5.

The third part shows that all efficient imperative implementations based on arrays (the typical example is a hash table) can be translated into a functional language having arrays, provided that some method is used to guarantee that arrays are updated in place. A more detailed discussion and some examples are given in Sect. 6.

The table of contents of the course follows:

Part I: Fundamentals

1. Efficiency analysis of functional algorithms.
2. Abstract data types: concept, algebraic specification techniques and underlying model of a specification.
3. Reasoning about data types: Using the ADT specification to reason about the correctness of a program external to the ADT. Correctness proof of an implementation.

Part II: Functional Data Structures

4. Linear data structures: stacks, queues and double queues. Direct definitions and implementation of queues by using a pair of lists.
5. Trees: binary trees, n-ary trees, search trees, AVL-trees, 2-3 trees, red-black trees, splay trees. Algorithms for inserting and deleting an element.
6. Priority queues. Implementation by using a list. Implementation by means of a heap, in turn implemented by a leftist tree.
7. Lookup tables, arrays and sets. Implementation by using an anonymous function. Implementation by a list. Implementation by balanced trees. Primitive arrays. Implementation of flexible arrays by means of Braun trees.
8. Graphs. Implementation by using an adjacency matrix and by adjacency lists. Prim's algorithm to compute an optimal spanning tree.

Part III: Translation of Imperative Data Structures

9. Mutable arrays. Techniques to ensure updating in place.
10. Implementation of queues and heaps by using mutable arrays.
11. Hash tables. Implementation of lookup tables and sets by means of hash tables.
12. Graphs revisited. Traversals. Disjoint sets structure. Kruskal's algorithm for optimal spanning tree. Other algorithms for graphs: Dijkstra's algorithm and Floyd's algorithm to compute shortest paths.

4 Reasoning about Abstract Data Types

Perhaps the main methodological aspect a second year course must stress is that the programming activity consists of continuously repeating the sequence: *first* specify, *then* implement, *then* show the correctness.

Algebraic specifications of abstract data types have been around for many years, and there exists a consensus that they are an appropriate mean to inform a potential user about the external behavior of a data type, without revealing implementation details. For instance, if we wish to specify the behavior of a FIFO queue, then the following signature and equations will do the job:

```
abstype Queue a
  emptyQueue   :: Queue a
  enqueue      :: Queue a -> a -> Queue a
  dequeue      :: Queue a -> Queue a
  firstQueue   :: Queue a -> a
  isEmptyQueue :: Queue a -> Bool
  dequeue (enqueue emptyQueue x) = emptyQueue
  isEmptyQueue q = False =>
      dequeue (enqueue q x) = enqueue (dequeue q) x
  firstQueue (enqueue emptyQueue x) = x
  isEmptyQueue q = False =>
      firstQueue (enqueue q x) = firstQueue q
  isEmptyQueue emptyQueue = True
  isEmptyQueue (enqueue q x) = False
```

Just to facilitate further reasoning, we have adopted a syntax as close as possible to that of functional languages. However, the symbol = has here a slightly different meaning: `t1 = t2` establishes a congruence between pairs of terms obtained instantiating `t1` and `t2` in all possible ways. In particular, we have adopted a variant of algebraic specifications in which operations can be partial, equations can be conditional, and the symbol = is interpreted as existential equality. An equation `s = s' => t = t'` specifies that, if (an instance of) `s` is well defined and (the corresponding instance of) `s'` is congruent to `s`, then (the corresponding instances of) `t` and `t'` are well defined and they are congruent (see [2, 17] for details).

A consequence of the theory underlying this style of specification is that terms not explicitly mentioned in the conclusion of an equation are undefined by default. For instance, in the above example, `(firstQueue emptyQueue)` and `(dequeue emptyQueue)` are undefined.

The algebraic specification of a data type has two main uses:

- It allows to reason about the correctness of functions external to the data type.
- It serves as a requirement that any valid implementation of the data type must satisfy.

The first use is rather familiar to functional programmers, as it simply consists of equational reasoning. An equation of the data type may be used as a rewriting rule, in either direction, as long as terms are well defined and the premises of the equation are satisfied. For instance, if **dequeue (enqueue q x)** is a subexpression of **e**, then we can safely replace in **e** that subexpression by the expression **enqueue (dequeue q) x**, provided that **q** is well defined and is not empty.

Properties satisfied by a specification are not limited to equations themselves. Any other property derived from them by equational reasoning or by inductive proofs could also be used. For instance, it is very easy to prove the following inductive theorem from the above specification:

```
isEmptyQueue q => q = emptyQueue
```

The second use of a specification is to prove the correctness of an implementation. Let us assume we implement a queue by a pair of lists in such a way that the first element of the queue is the head of the left list, and the last element of the queue is the head of the right one. In this way, all the operations can be executed in amortized constant time as the implementation below shows:

```
data Queue a = Queue [a] [a]
emptyQueue   = Queue [] []
enqueue (Queue [] _)  x  = Queue [x] []
enqueue (Queue fs ls) x  = Queue fs (x:ls)
dequeue (Queue (_:fs@(_:_)) ls)  = Queue fs ls
dequeue (Queue [_]          ls)  = Queue (reverse ls) []
firstQueue (Queue (x:_) _ )  = x
isEmptyQueue (Queue fs _)  = null fs
```

In the worst case, **dequeue** has linear time complexity, but this cost is compensated by the previous constant time insertions. This can be easily proved by using normal amortized cost analysis techniques. By the way, this implementation illustrates well the objective we are attempting at in this course: to suggest functional implementations not having counterparts in the imperative field, but achieving somehow the same efficiency.

To prove this implementation correct, the programmer must provide two additional pieces of information:

- The *invariant* of the representation. This is a predicate satisfied by all term generated values of the type.
- The *equality function* **(==):: a -> a -> Bool**, telling us when two legally generated values of the type represent the same abstract value.

In our example, these predicate and function, respectively, are:

$$Inv \stackrel{\text{def}}{=} \forall\,(\texttt{Queue fs ls})\,.\,\texttt{null fs} \Rightarrow \texttt{null ls}$$

$$(\texttt{Queue fs ls}) == (\texttt{Queue fs' ls'}) \stackrel{\text{def}}{=}$$
$$\texttt{fs ++ reverse ls == fs' ++ reverse ls'}$$

The last step consists of showing that every equation of the specification is satisfied by the implementation, modulo the equality function. In essence, this amounts to replace in the equation the abstract values and operations by their concrete versions, to assume that the invariant holds for all the concrete values, and to show that both parts of the equation lead to equal values, where the equality function == is the one corresponding to the equation type.

For instance, to prove the second equation of our specification, we write:

```
isEmptyQueue (Queue fs ls) == False ⇒
dequeue (enqueue (Queue fs ls) x) ==
    enqueue (dequeue (Queue fs ls)) x
```

By applying the definition of **isEmptyQueue**, the premise of the equation can be simplified to **null fs == False** and, by algebraic properties of lists, this amounts to say that **fs** matches the pattern **f:fs'**, then we can rewrite the conclusion of the equation as:

```
dequeue (enqueue (Queue (f:fs') ls) x) ==
enqueue (dequeue (Queue (f:fs') ls)) x
```

After applying the definitions of **enqueue** and **dequeue** we find two possible cases. If **fs'** is not the empty list, we obtain:

```
Queue fs' (x:ls) == Queue fs' (x:ls)
```

which is obviously true. If **fs'** is the empty list, we obtain:

```
Queue (reverse (x:ls)) [] == Queue (reverse ls)  [x]
```

which is true by the definition of the equality function for queues, that is

```
reverse (x:ls) ++ [] == reverse ls ++ [x]
```

The kind of reasoning suggested in this section is easy to do when the underlying language is functional, but it is totally unpractical when the language is imperative. So, we are including these techniques, and the needed theory, in the first part of the course. Then, we use them to show the correctness of most of the implementations appearing in the rest of the course.

5 Functional Data Structures

In this section we study ADT's whose implementing type is an algebraic one, i.e. a freely generated type. Sometimes, the implemented type (e.g. binary trees) is also a freely generated type, and then there is no distinction between the specification and the implementation. In these cases we allow constructors to be visible, in order to allow pattern matching over them.

5.1 Linear Data Structures

The first ADT's studied in the course are *stacks* and *queues*. Stack is a freely generated type, so the ADT generating operations are transformed into algebraic constructors, and the specification equations, once adequately oriented as rewriting rules, give a functional implementation of the rest of the operations.

We suggest implementing queues by using three different algebraic types. The first implementation is performed using the constructor **Enqueue**:

```
data Queue a = EmptyQueue | Enqueue (Queue a) a
```

The time complexities of **firstQueue** and **dequeue** are linear in the length of the queue. In the second representation, the constructor adds elements at the front of the queue, so **enqueue** is linear:

```
data Queue a = EmptyQueue | ConsQueue a (Queue a)
```

After making a stand to the students on the apparently unavoidable linear complexity of these implementations, the amortized constant time implementation given in Sect. 4 is presented. More advanced queue implementations could be covered later in the course using, for example, the material in [16].

Lists are considered primitive types. Students have extensively worked with lists in their first course. In contrast with the imperative course, we lose some implementations: circular lists, two-way linked lists, etc. We think this is not a handicap for students (see the conclusion section).

5.2 Trees

Trees are a fundamental data structure in the curriculum of any computer science student. Algebraic types and recursion are two characteristics of functional languages which strongly facilitate the presentation of this data structure and the algorithms manipulating it.

The most basic ones are binary trees with elements at the nodes:

```
data Tree a = Empty | Node (Tree a) a (Tree a)
```

Using recursion and pattern matching, a great variety of functions over trees can be easily and clearly presented: height of the tree, traversals, balance conditions, etc. Anyway, most of the times recursion can be avoided using the corresponding versions of *fold* and *map* for trees (see [4, 5]).

Binary search trees, general trees, and their operations are the next topics. Their definitions follow:

```
data Ord a => SearchTree a =
    Empty
  | Node (SearchTree a) a (SearchTree a)

data Tree a   = Node a (Forest a)
     Forest a = [Tree a]
```

where we have overloaded the tree constructors.

The most important topic is the presentation of balancing techniques such as AVL trees, splay trees and 2-3 trees. Fortunately, the algorithms for insertion and deletion result so concise that they can be completely developed in a single lecture. A good reference for 2-3 trees in a functional setting is [18]. Just to show how compact the algorithms result, we are presenting here our version of AVL-trees:

```
data Ord a => AVLTree a =
     Empty
   | Node Int (AVLTree a) a (AVLTree a)
```

The `Node` constructor has as its first argument the height of the tree. This allows an easier implementation than the one using a balance factor (-1,0,1). The key of this implementation is the function `joinAVL`, which joins two AVL trees. If `x = (joinAVL l a r)`, then `inorder x = inorder l ++ [a] ++ inorder r`.

```
joinAVL l a r
  | abs (ld-rd) <= 1  = sJoinAVL l a r
  | ld == rd+2        = lJoinAVL l a r
  | ld+2 == rd        = rJoinAVL l a r
  | ld > rd+2         = joinAVL ll la (joinAVL lr a r)
  | ld+2 < rd         = joinAVL (joinAVL l a rl) ra rr
    where ld = depth l
          rd = depth r
          (Node _ ll la lr) = l
          (Node _ rl ra rr) = r

lJoinAVL l a r
  | lld >= lrd  = sJoinAVL ll la (sJoinAVL lr a r)
  | otherwise   = sJoinAVL (sJoinAVL ll la lrl) lra
                           (sJoinAVL lrr a r)
    where (Node ld ll la lr) = l
          lld = depth ll
          lrd = depth lr
          (Node _ lrl lra lrr) = lr

rJoinAVL l a r
  | rrd <= rld  = sJoinAVL (sJoinAVL l a rl) b rr
  | otherwise   = sJoinAVL (sJoinAVL l a rll) rla
                           (sJoinAVL rlr ra r)
    where (Node rd rl ra rr) = r
          rrd = depth rr
          rld = depth rl
          (Node _ rll rla rlr) = rl

sJoinAVL l a r  = Node (1+max (depth l) (depth r)) l a r
```

```
depth Empty              = 0
depth (Node d _ _ _)     = d
```

From joinAVL, functions for insertion and deletion in AVL trees can be trivially defined, just adapting those for binary search trees by replacing the occurrences of the constructor Node by the function joinAVL.

Even though we can present tree-like data structures in more detail than using an imperative language, we lose some ideas. For instance, threaded trees cannot be easily represented, because the threads generate a graph.

5.3 Priority Queues

The first proposal for the implementation of this data structure is a list where elements are inserted at the beginning. We need to go through the list in order to find the best element (we suppose that this element is the smallest one)

```
data Ord a => PriQueue a = PriQueue [a]
```

This implementation is efficient enough if there are few elements, so it can be used in practice. But its linear complexity makes it inefficient if there are many elements. Other simple implementations, such as ordered lists, do not improve the situation.

The *heap* data structure gets logarithmic complexity for insertion and deletion, and constant time for consulting the minimum, because in imperative programming heaps are implemented by arrays. There exist other *imperative* data structures, more general and with very good complexities, such as *skew heaps* [20], but they cannot be easily translated to the functional framework. Fortunately, there exist data structures adequate for its implementation in a functional language: binomial queues [12] and leftist trees [7]. Here, we show the last one because it is simpler:

```
data Ord a => Leftist a =
     Empty
   | Node Int (Leftist a) a (Leftist a)
```

These trees have the same invariant property as heaps: the element at the root is always less than or equal to the rest of the elements. But now, the condition that heaps are almost-complete trees is replaced by the condition that the shortest path from any node to a leaf is the rightmost one. The length of this path is kept in the first field of Node. As a consequence of this condition, joining two leftist trees by simultaneously descending through the rightmost path of both trees, takes time in $O(\log n)$.

```
join Empty llt = llt
join llt Empty = llt
join l@(Node n ll a lr) r@(Node m rl b rr)
  | a < b   = cons ll a (join lr r)
```

```
  | a >= b  = cons rl b (join rr l)
cons Empty a r = Node 1 r a Empty
cons l@(Node n _ _ _) a r@(Node m _ _ _) =
  | n >= m = Node (m+1) l a r
  | n < m  = Node (n+1) r a l
```

Using `join`, the operations of the *min priority queue* ADT can be implemented as:

```
emptyQueue = Empty
enqueue q a = join q (Node 1 Empty a Empty)
firstQueue (Node _ _ a _) = a
dequeue (Node _ l _ r) = join l r
remQueue q = (firstQueue q, dequeue q)
```

Similarly, *min-max priority queues* can be as easily defined as *min priority queues*. These constitute examples of data structures that would not be presented in an imperative course.

5.4 Lookup Tables, Arrays and Sets

Lookup tables (and by extension *sets*) are a fundamental data structure for practical programming. Usually, tables represent partial functions going from a *domain* type to a *range* type. This point of view leads to the first implementation, in which a memoized function is used:

```
data Eq a => Table a b = Table (a -> b)
emptyTable = Table \a -> error "No association."
lookup (Table f) a = f a
update (Table f) a b = Table \a' -> if a' == a then b else f a'
```

This implementation is an interesting example of the use of a function inside a data structure, and this should be remarked to the students. Other naïve implementation of tables consists of using a list of pairs (*key, value*).

As a first step in the presentation of arrays, we present implementations for general tables separately from those whose domain type is `Int`, or in general any index type. Then, we go on with implementations for tables based on search trees using some of the balancing techniques, as it is usual in the imperative course. Once again, for tables indexed by integers there exists a tree-like data structure easier than the general balanced trees: Braun trees [6]

```
data Braun a = Empty | Node a (Braun a) (Braun a)
```

The elements are inserted in the tree using a very ingenuous technique: the value associated with index 0 is stored at the root, odd indexes are stored in the left subtree, while even indexes are stored in the right subtree. Then, the lookup and update operations are:

```
lookup (Node a odds evens) n
  | n == 0   = a
  | odd n    = lookup odds ((n-1)/2)
  | even n   = lookup evens ((n/2)-1)

update (Node a odds evens) n b
  | n == 0   = Node b odds evens
  | odd n    = Node a (update odds ((n-1)/2) b) evens
  | even n   = Node a odds (update evens ((n/2)-1) b)
```

where the **update** operation receive an index belonging to those stored in the tree. Thus, a function creating an array with n elements is needed:

```
mkIdxTable n b
  | n == 0   = Empty
  | n > 0    = Node b (mkIdxTable odd b)
                      (mkIdxTable (n-odd-1) b)
                 where odd = n/2
```

where nodes are initiated with the same fix value **b**.

Let us note that Braun trees are more versatile than usual arrays, because *flexible arrays* can be implemented using these trees (i.e. arrays where indexes may be added or removed). Below, we present functions to add an index to any of the array ends (functions for removing an index are symmetric).

```
lowExtend Empty a =  Node a Empty Empty
lowExtend (Node a odds evens) b =
    Node b (lowExtend evens a) odds
highExtend tree b =  extend tree (cardinality tree) b
extend Empty n b =  Node b Empty Empty
extend (Node a odds evens) n b
  | even n      =  Node a odds (extend evens (n/2-1) b)
  | otherwise   =  Node a (extend odds (n/2) b) evens
```

We would let the students note that insertion, deletion and extension take logarithmic time. As an exercise for students, the implementation of flexible arrays where the low limit of the range it is not forced to be equal to 0 can be proposed.

Now, we would briefly introduce *primitive arrays*. Arrays in functional languages have constant time complexity for the lookup operation, and they are primitive in Haskell. In order to get constant time complexity for the update operation, they must be updated in place.

5.5 Graphs

Graphs are a *strange* data structure from the ADT point of view. Although they can be specified with all the needed operations in order to be manipulated hiding the internal representation, the efficiency of many algorithms is conditioned to having direct access to this representation. After specifying the ADT, in this part of the course we study several alternative representations: adjacency matrix, adjacency lists, list of arcs, etc. In some cases, these representations can be implemented using lists instead of arrays without losing efficiency. One example is Prim's algorithm for the computation of the minimal spanning tree of a weighted graph, representing its adjacency matrix by a list of lists:

```
data Graph = [[Float]]
```

Assuming that the resulting spanning tree is represented by a list of edges, Prim's algorithm can be computed by:

```
prim :: Graph -> [(Int,Int)]
prim g = prim' (length g - 1) (zip [1,1..] (g !! 1))
  where prim' 0     l  = []
        prim' (n+1) l  = (i,j) : prim' n (improve i l (g !! i))
          where (j,d) = foldr1 minPar l
                   i = pos (j,d) l
        improve i = zipWith
            (\(j,d) d' -> if d <= d' then (j,d) else (i,d'))
        minPar (j,d) (j',d') = if d<=d' then (j,d) else (j',d')
```

As in the imperative case, the complexity of this algorithm is $O(n^2)$.

In general, there is no problem in using primitive arrays, because most algorithms for graphs access to the representation but they do not modify it. Unfortunately, the efficient implementation of the usual algorithms for graphs need auxiliary data structures using arrays updated in place. These algorithms will be seen in the last part of the course.

6 Translation of Imperative Data Structures

Our aim in this section is to show that imperative techniques can be easily adapted to the functional framework.

In the previous section, we did not cover two fundamental data structures: hash tables and disjoint sets. Also, the well known algorithms on graphs by Kruskal, Dijkstra, Floyd, and those using depth-first search were skipped. The efficient implementations of these data structures and algorithms need arrays with constant time lookup and update operations. Functional arrays implemented consecutively in memory have constant access time to their components, but when a modification is performed, a new copy of the array may be generated. Then the cost would be linear. If the original array is not further needed, in place modification could be done, getting a constant cost. Thus, the programmer must take care of the fact that if an array is modified, then the old one cannot be used. This property is usually referred to as single-threaded updating. By abstract interpretation, a compiler may realize, in some cases, that structures are used in a single-threaded way, and in this case does not generate unneeded copies. Because the problem is undecidable, some programming techniques have been proposed to help the compiler in this task. Recently, two solutions, allowing a great expressive power and with a low number of restrictions, have been given: monadic data structures [15] and uniqueness types [3]. They allow to simultaneously have several data structures treated in a single-threaded way.

In the presentation of the algorithms to the students, we recommend to use a style asumming that the compiler will deduce the single-threaded flows. The reason for this is that students must not be constrained to a particular technique. This is a research field that may produce more expressive techniques in the forthcoming years.

6.1 Queues, Heaps and Hash Tables

With the objective of introducing functional arrays to the students, two classical implementations would be presented: queues and heaps. Here, we show a queue implemented by means of a circular array:

```
data Queue a = Queue Int              --Capacity
                     Int              --First element
                     Int              --Number of elements
                    (Array Int a)     --Circular array

mkQueue c = Queue c 0 0 (array (0,c-1) [])
enqueue (Queue c f n a) e =
    if n < c then Queue c f (n+1) (a // [((f+n) `mod` c,e)])
    else error "Full queue"
dequeue (Queue c f n a) =
    if 0 < n then Queue c ((f+1) `mod` c) (n-1) a
    else error "Empty queue"
firstQueue (Queue c f n a) =
    if 0 < n then (a!f)  else error "Empty queue"
```

As we have shown in this example, the translation of imperative implementations using arrays does not present special problems. As well as for queues, the corresponding translations of imperative heaps and hash tables are simple.

6.2 Graphs Revisited

The recent work [13] is a good example showing how modern functional languages and the use of mutable arrays (monadically implemented) can be applied to the implementation of algorithms on graphs. It contains very valuable material to be used in this part of the course.

In addition to these ones, we include the shortest path algorithms by Dijkstra and by Floyd, and Kruskal's minimal spanning tree algorithm (Prim's one has already been studied). We give below the implementation of Kruskal's algorithm using the disjoint sets ADT. Due to lack of space, we just write the signature of this ADT (there exist efficient implementations based on arrays):

```
data DisSet
mkDisSet :: Int -> DisSet
find :: Int -> DisSet -> (Int,DisSet)
union :: Int -> Int -> DisSet -> DisSet
```

The first operation generates the sets $\{1\}, \{2\}, \ldots, \{n\}$. Given an integer and a disjoint set, **find** returns a set label (**Int**) and a disjoint set equivalent to the one given as argument, but reorganized in order to increase the efficiency of later consults. Given two labels, **union** joins the corresponding sets.

If the graph is represented by a list of weighted arcs, we have:

```
data Edge = Edge Int Int Float
(Edge _ _ p1) < (Edge _ _ p2) = p1 < p2
data Graph = Graph [Edge]
```

then Kruskal's algorithm is

```
kruskal :: Graph -> Graph
kruskal (Graph es)  =
    Graph (kruskal' (n, h, mkDisSet n))
  where n = numNodes (Graph es)
        h = foldr (flip enqueue) emptyQueue es
        kruskal' :: (Int, PriQueue Edge, DisSet) -> [Edge]
        kruskal' (n, h, p)
          | (n==0) || isEmptyQueue h = []
          | li==lj     = kruskal' (n,h1,p2)
          | otherwise = e : kruskal' (n-1, h1, union li lj p2)
             where (e,h1) = remQueue h
                   (Edge i j _) = e
                   (li, p1) = find i p
                   (lj, p2) = find j p1
```

Let us note, that not only the disjoint set is used in a single-threaded way, but also the priority queue.

6.3 Guaranteing Single-Threaded Use of Arrays

Just to show that the transformations needed to guarantee the single-threaded use of mutable types are not so big, we present two implementations of queues respectively using monadic data structures and uniqueness types. To shortern the presentation, we omit error detection. Below we give the monadic implementation:

```
data Queue s a = Queue Int (MutVar s Int) (MutVar s Int)
                           (MutArr s Int a)

--mkQueue :: Int -> ST s (Queue s a)
mkQueue n =
    newVar 0             'thenST' \f ->
    newVar 0             'thenST' \t ->
    arr (0,n-1) []       'thenST' \a ->
    returnST (CirQueue n f t a)
--enqueue :: Queue s a -> a -> ST s ()
```

```
enqueue (CirQueue n f t a) e =
    readVar t                    'thenST' \tv ->
    readVar f                    'thenST' \fv ->
    writeArr a ((fv+tv)'mod'n) e 'thenST_'
    writeVar t (tv+1)
--dequeue :: Queue s a -> ST s ()
dequeue (CirQueue n f t a) =
    readVar t                     'thenST' \tv ->
    readVar f                     'thenST' \fv ->
    writeVar f ((fv+1) 'mod' n) 'thenST_'
    writeVar t (tv - 1)
--firstQueue :: Queue s a -> ST s a
firstQueue (CirQueue n f t a) =
    readVar f                     'thenST' \fv ->
    readArr a fv
```

The implementation with uniqueness types would be:

```
data Queue a  = Queue Int Int Int *(Array Int a)

mkQueue :: Int -> *(Queue a)
mkQueue n  = Queue n 0 0 (array (0,n-1) [])
enqueue :: *(Queue a) -> a -> *(Queue a)
enqueue (Queue max f t a) e =
    Queue max f (t+1) (a // [(f+t)'mod'max := e])
dequeue :: *(Queue a) -> *(Queue a)
dequeue (Queue max f t a) = Queue max ((f+1)'mod'max) (t-1) a
firstQueue :: *(Queue a) -> (a,*(Queue a))
firstQueue (Queue max f t a) = let! e = a ! f
                               in (e, Queue max f t a)
```

Let us note that, in contrast to the implementation given in Sect. 6.1, there are differences between the type of the operations given in the specification and that of the implementation. These kind of problems also appear in the imperative implementation of data types. For monadic data structures, there exist techniques which mechanically relate the monadic and non monadic implementations of a given type (see [8]). For uniqueness types, the conversion techniques are very easy because there is only a trivial change in the signature, and the compiler can infer the uniqueness types.

7 Conclusion

We have presented a proposal for a course on data structures based on the functional paradigm. One of the claims made at the begining of the paper about this proposal was that, compared to an equivalent course based on imperative programming, more material can be covered. To prove this claim, we note that both more ADT's, and more implementations, are taught in the course:

- The *priority queue* ADT is enriched with a new *join* operation, merging two priority queues into one.
- The *array* ADT is enriched with operations to make it flexible.
- More balanced trees are covered —*splay trees, red-black trees*— and, perhaps more important than this, they are covered in full detail: the imperative versions of *delete* operations are usually too cumbersome to be taught in detail. This is not the case with the functional ones.
- Leftist trees and Braun trees are usually not covered in an imperative course on data structures.

Another improvement is that —due to the proximity between the functional paradigm and the algebraic specification formalism— to show the correctness of an ADT implementation is now a feasible task. In many situations (for instance, dealing with search trees algorithms), the algebraic equations can be directly transformed into functional definitions. There is the hope that, after teaching this course several times, many algorithms could be derived by transforming the ADT specification. This would lead to a *derivation* approach to correctness, as an improvement of the more traditional *verification* approach.

Compared to the imperative course, there are some topics not covered by the functional one: queue implementation by using a simply-linked list and two pointers, circular lists, doubly-linked lists and threaded trees. These implementations correspond to ADT's with special operations. For instance, doubly-linked lists is a good implementation of a *sequence-with-memory* ADT, which "remembers" the cursor position and provides operations to move the cursor forward and backward. A functional alternative to these implementations is always possible. For instance, the *sequence-with-memory* ADT could be implemented by a pair of lists used in a rather similar way that those of the queue implementation of Sect. 4. We believe that nothing essential is missed if the student does not learn these pointer-based implementations. These topics are useful when looking at the machine at a very low level, for instance in physical organizations of data bases, or in some operating systems data structures. Then, these low level structures would be better covered in the corresponding matters using them.

As we said in the introduction, the course has not been fully implemented yet. An important drawback of it, when integrated with the normal student curriculum, is that no provision is made to translate the structures and the algorithms covered by the course, to the imperative paradigm. We have claimed in this paper that these topics are better taught using a functional language, but we are *not* proposing that the imperative implementations should not be taught at all. In their professional lives, students will surely have to program in imperative languages. So, some functional to imperative translation techniques should be provided somewhere. To cover them, we suggest to arrange a separated short module running in parallel with the last part of the course (perhaps as part of the laboratory topics). In essence, the module would include techniques to implement recursive types by means of linked structures, to appropriately translate the corresponding algorithms, and to transform recursive algorithms into iterative ones.

Acknowledgments

We would like to thank the anonymous referees for the careful reading, and for pointing out some mistakes, of the previous version of this paper.

References

1. Harold Abelson and Gerald J. Sussman. *Structure and Interpretation of Computer Programs.* MIT Press, 1985.
2. E. Astesiano and M. Cerioli. On the existence of initial models for partial (higher order) conditional specifications. In *Proceedings of TAPSOFT'89. LNCS 351*, 1989.
3. E. Barendsen and J.E.W. Smetsers. Conventional and uniqueness typing in graph rewrite systems. In *Proceedings of the 13th FST & TCS. LNCS 761*, 1993.
4. R. Bird and P. Wadler. *Introduction to Functional Programming.* Prentice-Hall, 1988.
5. L. A. Galán, M. Núñez, C. Pareja, and R. Peña. Non homomorphic reductions of data structures. *GULP-PRODE*, 2:393–407, 1994.
6. R. R. Hoogerwood. A logarithmic implementation of flexible arrays. In *Proceedings of the 2th Conference on the Mathematics of Program Construction. LNCS 699*, 1992.
7. E. Horowitz and S. Sahni. *Fundamentals of Data Structures in PASCAL.* Computer Science Press, 4th. edition, 1994.
8. P. Hudak. Mutable abstract datatypes or How to have your state and munge it too. Technical Report YALEU/DCS/RR-914, Yale University, 1993.
9. P. Hudak, S. Peyton-Jones, and P. Wadler. Report on the Functional Programming Language Haskell. *SIGPLAN Notices*, 27(5), 1992.
10. J. Hughes. *Why Functional Programming Matters*, pages 17–43. Research Topics in Functional Programming. (Ed.) D. A. Turner. Addison-Wesley, 1990.
11. S. Joosten, K. van den Berg, and G. van der Hoeven. Teaching functional programming to first-year students. *Journal of Functional Programming*, 3:49–65, 1993.
12. D. J. King. Functional binomial queues. In *Proceedings of the Glasgow Workshop on Functional Programming*, 1994.
13. D. J. King and H. Launchbury. Structuring depth-first search algorithms in Haskell. In *Proceedings of POPL'95*, 1995.
14. T. Lambert, P. Lindsay, and K. Robinson. Using Miranda as a first programming language. *Journal of Functional Programming*, 3:5–34, 1993.
15. J. Launchbury and S. L. Peyton Jones. Lazy functional state threads. In *Proceedings of the ACM Conference on Programming Languages Design and Implementation*, 1994.
16. C. Okasaki. Simple and efficient purely functional queues and deques. *Journal of Functional Programming*, 1994. To appear.
17. R. Peña. *Diseño de Programas: Formalismo y Abstracción.* Prentice Hall, 1993. In Spanish.
18. C. M. P. Reade. Balanced trees with removals: an exercise in rewriting and proof. *Science of Computer Programming*, 18:181–204, 1992.
19. D. Sands. A Naïve Time Analysis and its Theory of Cost Equivalence. *The Journal of Logic and Computation*, 1994. To appear.
20. D. D. Sleator and R. E. Tarjan. Self-adjusting heaps. *SIAM Journal of Computing*, 15(1):52–69, 1986.

Functional programming through the curriculum

Simon Thompson and Steve Hill

Computing Laboratory
University of Kent at Canterbury, U.K.
{S.J.Thompson,S.A.Hill}@ukc.ac.uk

Abstract. This paper discusses our experience in using a functional language in topics across the computer science curriculum. After examining the arguments for taking a functional approach, we look in detail at four case studies from different areas: programming language semantics, machine architectures, graphics and formal languages.

1 Introduction

We first explore our reasons for using a functional programming language, Miranda, as a vehicle for teaching a number of topics across the computer science curriculum. Figure 1 gives an overview of the courses we look at. We then give an overview of the paper itself.

Why?

We see five major reasons for using a functional language in a variety of components of a computer science course.

A common language First, a functional language provides a common medium in which we can express many of the ideas which come into a variety of courses. For example,

- rules in operational semantics;
- functions in a denotational semantics;
- sets and other data structures (which appear in many situations, such as non-deterministic automata (NFAs) and executable versions of model-based specifications);
- hardware description, and abstract machines of various sorts;
- geometric transformations and their composition, which appear in courses on computer graphics.

This language is familiar, so that the student can concentrate on any new ideas being expressed, rather than the particular way in which they are written down. There is anecdotal evidence for this from one of the author's experience: in covering a simple imperative language and its structured operational semantics

Degree programme	Computer Science and related subjects, which in the English system take three years to complete.
Students	Students are specialists, who have suitable qualifications in mathematics, or are taught the equivalent material in the first year of their programme.
Courses:	
Introductory programming	Year 1: 25 1 hour lectures + 20 classes.
Formal languages	Year 2: 8-10 lectures[1] + assessment work.
Machine architectures	Year 2: 10 lectures[1] + assessment work.
Formal Semantics	Final year: 10 lectures[1] + assessment work.
Computer Graphics	Final year: 5 lectures[1] + assessment work.

For each course assessment is by means of a mixture of continuous assessment (typically allocated 25% of the marks) and written examination.

Fig. 1. Summary of the degree programme and courses

the students preferred the (rather more cluttered) Miranda rendering to the rules written out in a natural deduction style.

It is easy for teachers to forget the overhead of learning another formal notation; our students are perhaps happier learning programming languages, which all follow the same ground rules, rather than more mathematical sorts of notation.

Of course there is a trade-off here; in restricting ourselves to a single (meta-) language in our studies we may limit some applications. One example might be denotational semantics, where our meta-language would be sequential.

High-level language The common language we have chosen is high-level; we gain advantages from this. In particular, the conciseness of the functional descriptions should help rather than overwhelm students.

For project work, the language supports rapid and accurate program development which is essential if students are to be able to perform substantial tasks with limited time available.

Static checking Our third reason is that the language is syntax- and type-checked: the descriptions we (or our students) write can be checked for syntactic correctness, and more importantly for type correctness. We use the types of the

[1] These lectures occur as parts of larger courses, typically taking 30 hours; the figures given here show the part allocated to the functional material discussed here.

language, particularly in giving semantic descriptions of programming languages; this point is discussed in more detail in Section 3.

Executable The fourth justification is that the language is executable. We gain, therefore

- executable semantic descriptions;
- prototypes of model-based specifications;
- machines and hardware which are directly executable.

Moreover, it is possible for students to test their solutions to exercises, as well as to embark upon larger-scale experiments.

Reinforcement Finally, using functional languages through the curriculum reinforces an initial exposure to functional programming. The ideas of lazy functional programming are subtle, and it would be naive of us to think that a first exposure would be sufficient for most students. In treating regular expressions and NFAs, for example, we find non-trivial instances of

- polymorphism: we use sets of various types of element;
- type abstraction: sets are a prime example;
- modularisation;
- higher-order functions: parsing regular expressions.

In first teaching Miranda we make links with imperative programming; these links can be strengthened as we continue to use the language.

Other issues In the longer term, we see the mathematical elegance of functional languages as affording opportunities for formal proof in a variety of areas, such as machine simulation and compiling. This is one area into which we hope to move in the future.

Finally, a rather more negative justification is that an isolated course in functional programming which is not followed up has a strong implicit negative message: "we teach you this stuff because we feel we ought to, but we don't use it ourselves"!

Overview of the paper

In the remainder of the paper we give a description of how we use functional programming in a number of areas, evaluating our approach as we go along. After giving a short description of how we introduce programming, we discuss in turn how we use a functional approach in covering the topics of programming language semantics, machine architectures, computer graphics and formal languages, before concluding the paper.

Some of the materials mentioned are available over the World Wide Web or by FTP; we detail this in the appropriate sections.

2 Learning to program

Functional programming has strong support at our institution, and we are able to draw on the expertise of some six lecturers and similar numbers of postgraduates and research staff. The topic is introduced in the first year with 25 lectures of basic material supported by a similar number of practical classes. The material is taught in parallel with 30 lectures and classes on the imperative language Modula-3.

In teaching functional programming we are mindful that our students also write imperative programs. We see the two approaches as complementary, with functional programming providing a valuable perspective on the imperative in a number of ways.

- A functional language is a useful *design* language for imperative programs, especially those which manipulate dynamic data structures. We can give functional list-processing programs which can be translated into an imperative language by adding the appropriate memory manipulating code.
- The different approach of functional programming can make plain what is happening in an imperative language: the different notions of 'variable' come to mind, for instance.
- A functional approach can also illuminate deficiencies in imperative languages, or alternative approaches which are unfamiliar to a more traditional programmer.

3 Semantics of Programming Languages

Since the inception of computing there has been interest in explaining in a clear and comprehensible way the behaviour of programs, that is giving a semantics to programming languages. The *denotational* school of Scott and Strachey, [5], aimed to give a mathematical model of (sequential, imperative) programs as functions from machine state to machine state. In order to find the appropriate structures to model these states and functions *domain theory* [8] was developed.

In retrospect, if not at the time, it is clear that the denotational semantics of a programming language can be factored into two parts.

- A functional model of the language is built, using an existing functional programming language — in this paper we shall use Miranda. Under this approach, the meaning of a command, for instance, is a function of the appropriate type: `stores -> stores`.
  In other words, the functional programming language is used as a semantic *meta*-language.
- The functional programming language itself is given a domain-theoretic semantics.

This separation makes clear the two quite different processes underlying the semantic description of the language.

- Using the basic notions of value, type, function and recursion we give a model of the more complex structures of an imperative language. These include
  - commands (as state transformers);
  - expression evaluation, which will in general have side-effects;
  - styles of parameter passing, with their corresponding styles of variable declaration ([6]);
  - different forms of binding: sequential or 'parallel', static or dynamic, and so forth.
- In the second stage, analyses of type, function and recursion have themselves to be given. It is only at this stage that the more technical aspects of domain theory need to be apparent.

This split shows that much can be gained by a student who only follows the first of these phases; s/he is able to see how the complex behaviour of a modern imperative language is rendered in simple (and hopefully familiar) terms.

The second phase, which involves further technicality, is optional. If it is examined, the first phase gives motivation for a closer examination of recursion in the definition of both functions and data, and so gives a clear reason for domains to appear. If the two phases are merged, it has been our experience that students find it more difficult to grasp what is going on; this is simply the lesson of 'divide and conquer' in the context of semantic descriptions rather than program development.

In the rest of this section we give an overview of our material on semantics in Miranda. This consists of descriptions of various aspects of a Pascal-like programming language together with an examination of its operational semantics, in the style of Plotkin. We discuss potential exercises and projects for students as we go along, and conclude with an evaluation of the approach advocated here, as well as looking at other advantages of the treatment.

The Miranda code and a reference document for the material can be found on the World Wide Web using the 'Further material' section given under the URL

`http://www.ukc.ac.uk/computer_science/Miranda_craft/`

or via anonymous FTP from the directory

`ftp://ftp.ukc.ac.uk/pub/sjt/Craft/`

Basic semantics

In writing the semantics we identify three stages. First we look at the base types we shall need to consider, then clarify the types of the major semantic functions, and finally we write the definitions of these functions.

Types First we have to establish how we model the programs themselves; we can use algebraic (or concrete) types to specify the structure of each syntactic category (commands, expressions and so on). The Miranda definition of `command` in Figure 2 shows how commands can be specified; note how the algebraic type

```
command ::= Skip |
            If_Then_Else b_expr command command |
            While_Do b_expr command |
            Sequence [command] |
            Assignment ident expr

values == num
lookup :: ident -> stores -> values
update :: stores -> ident -> values -> stores
```

```
command_value :: command -> stores -> stores
expr_value    :: expr -> stores -> values
nop_value     :: nop -> values -> values -> values
```

```
command_value Skip st = st

command_value (If_Then_Else e c1 c2) st
        = command_value c1 st , if  b_expr_value e st
        = command_value c2 st , otherwise

command_value (While_Do e c) st
        = command_value (While_Do e c) (command_value c st)
                , if b_expr_value e st
        = st    , otherwise

command_value (Sequence []) st = st
command_value (Sequence (c:cs)) st
        = command_value (Sequence cs) (command_value c st)

command_value (Assignment i e) st
        = update st i (expr_value e st)
```

Fig. 2. Basic denotational semantics

corresponds to a BNF-style syntax definition, and also that the type of commands is defined in terms of the types expressions **expr** and boolean expressions, **b_expr**.

Programs are to be modelled as functions from stores to stores, taking the machine state before executing the command to the state after the command terminates. We therefore need a type to model the store; at this level of the semantics we simply specify the signature required of the **stores** type, as is done in Figure 2; various implementations exist.

Typing the semantic functions Central to our approach is how we model commands; each command is seen as a function from `stores` to `stores`. The function interpreting commands, `command_value`, will therefore have type

```
command -> stores -> stores
```

The other declarations in the second part of Figure 2 show the value of typing the semantic functions in a separate phase, since these type declarations contain important information about the interpretation of various parts of the language. For example, we see that to give expressions a value we need a store (to interpret any variables in the expression), whilst to interpret a binary numerical operator (an object of type `nop`) no store is needed – operators have fixed values.

Were we to adapt the semantics to model a language with side-effects, this would be apparent in the type of `expr_value`; instead of returning an object of type `values` alone, the result would be of type `(values,stores)` in which the second component gives the state of execution after the expression evaluation has terminated.

Defining the semantic functions The definition of the functions themselves is straightforward; for commands we exhibit the definition in the final part of Figure 2. At this point it becomes clear that recursion is used in the modelling: a structural recursion runs along a `Sequence` of commands, while a potentially non-terminating recursion is used to interpret the `While_Do` loop.

Assessment In teaching this material we ask students to write definitions for themselves. It is instructive to look at `repeat` and `for` loops, as well as 'parallel assignment', `x,y:=e,f`. One obvious advantage for the student is that they can *check* their solutions for syntax and type errors using the Miranda system, and then for correctness by *executing* against example programs.

A second assessment building on the basic semantics is to add side-effects, which we do with the expression

```
Do_Return c e
```

whose effect is to execute the command `c` before evaluating the expression `e`. This requires students to think of changes to the types of the semantic functions before re-examining their definitions. Particularly instructive in this case is the parallel assignment command.

Extending the semantics

We have built a number of extensions of the basic semantics which illustrate various aspects of programming languages.

The definition mechanism An *environment* is used to keep track of the definitions in scope at any point during execution; this structure is quite separate

```
def_value     :: def -> env -> stores -> env
command_value :: command -> env -> stores -> stores
expr_value    :: expr -> env -> stores -> values
```

Fig. 3. Extending the denotational semantics

```
config ::= Inter command stores | Final stores

step :: config -> config

step (Inter (If_Then_Else e c1 c2) st)
  = (Inter c1 st)          , if b_expr_value e st
  = (Inter c2 st)          , otherwise
step (Inter (While_Do e c) st)
  = (Inter (If_Then_Else e (Sequence [c,While_Do e c]) Skip) st)
step (Inter (Assignment i e) st)
  = Final (update st i (expr_value e st))
```

Fig. 4. Basic operational semantics

from the store, which models the effect of commands on the machine state. The types of the main semantic functions are illustrated in Figure 3.

Abstraction: procedures and functions. There is considerable room for experimentation here.
- We treat different forms of parameter passing: value and reference as in Pascal, but with the possibility of adding others.
- We illustrate the difference between static and dynamic binding.
- We model recursive and non-recursive procedures.

Jumps We show the difficulty of interpreting languages with **goto** by extending the basic language with labels and jumps; the example illustrates the fact that modularity breaks down, with the interpretation function becoming a mutual-recursion involving the meanings of all the labels in the program.

In each of these cases there is room for students to experiment with the material, modifying or extending it and gaining feedback about the syntactic correctness of their work before executing it.

Operational semantics

An alternative semantic view is operational: we see the effect of a command as a series of execution steps for an abstract machine. Part of an operational model for our basic language is illustrated in Figure 4. The `configuration` of a machine is either

`Final st` : the machine has terminated in state `st`, or,
`Inter c st` : the command `c` is to be executed, starting at state `st`.

One `step` of execution takes one `config` to the next, and various cases of `step` are given in the figure.

On teaching this material, the rules were presented in functional form as well as more traditional 'deduction rule'; it became apparent that although the latter form was more abstract (and to us easier to read) the students preferred the Miranda version because the syntax was familiar, and so they were able to concentrate on the ideas, rather than on the surface syntax.

Conclusion

This section shows how a functional language is adequate for the functional description of many aspects of modern programming languages. Further details of this work are to be found in [7].

The advantages of this approach are threefold

- The semantics are presented in a language which is executable. In doing assessment work, students are able to check the syntax and typing of their work, before executing their solutions.
- The semantics are presented in a familiar language. Even if definitions are somewhat less elegant, readers can concentrate on the ideas rather than the syntax.
- The two phases of the semantics — going to a functional language; interpreting that language — are explicit here, and we have found this avoids some of the confusions of other expositions.

4 Machine Architectures

The work in this area arose from the need to provide a platform for the simulation of microprocessor architectures suitable for undergraduate students of the core computer science course. The problem was this: in the second year of our undergraduate programme, two groups of students study a digital systems course. The first group study Computer Systems Engineering which is oriented more towards electronics than the second group who are reading a Computer Science degree. Originally, the digital systems course contained a laboratory experiment which involved a fair amount of practical electronics. We decided that it was an unreasonable requirement that the mainstream computer scientists, especially those from largely mathematical or computing backgrounds, should have to perform this experiment. It was proposed, therefore, that these students be offered a software-based project as an alternative.

This provided an ideal opportunity for an experiment in using a functional platform, which we wanted to do for reasons discussed in the Introduction: in particular we wanted a concise yet precise description of machines, as well as a platform upon which to build project work.

We chose to provide simulations for two architectural styles - a register machine and a stack machine. Both machines share a common core which is extended to provide their peculiar instruction sets. The simulations are constructed in three levels.

- The core machine provides the basic architecture described by means of primitive transitions of machine state.
- The micro-code provides a specialisation of the core machine by implementing an instruction set in terms of the basic transitions.
- The assembly language interface is implemented by an assembler and loader which together construct an initial machine state. This is then run until the machine halts.

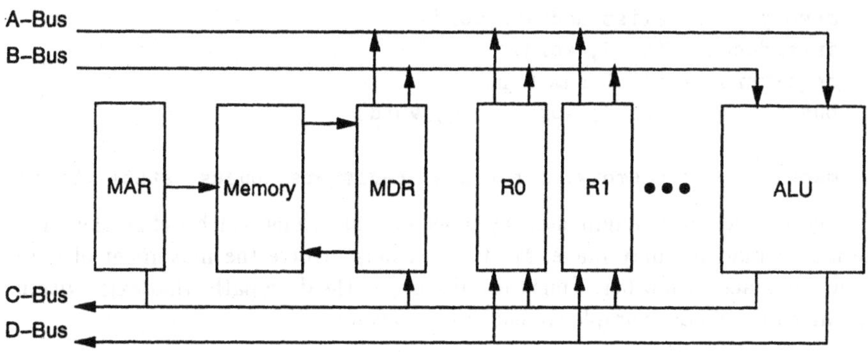

Fig. 5. Architecture of the Core Machine

Implementation

The core machine, depicted in Figure 5, provides a characterisation of a generic machine architecture. It comprises a type of "machine state" along with a set of permitted state transitions. These transitions are the only ones allowed. The style is similar to that adopted by Peyton Jones and Lester [3] for the description of abstract machines for the implementation of functional languages.

Ideally, the type of machine state would have been made abstract, but it is not possible to cover abstract datatypes in sufficient detail in the first-year functional programming course to allow this.

The machine was decomposed into the following parts:

- Memory - the memory is modelled as an association list between address and contents.

- Memory Interface - the memory interface comprises two special purpose registers - the memory address register (MAR) and the memory data register (MDR).
- Register File - the registers are modelled as an association list between register number and register contents. The core machine thus makes no commitments as to the number of registers available.
- Buses - the machine has four internal buses or data highways.
- Statistics - the statistics field is used to accumulate measures of the machine's performance.
- Halt Flag - this indicates if the machine has halted.

These components are conveniently represented in Miranda as a tuple.

```
address   == num
word      == num

memory    == alist address word
interface == (word, word)
registers == alist num word
buses     == (word, word, word, word)

machine   == (memory, interface, registers, buses, stats, bool)
```

The core machine is augmented by a set of transitions which define the valid actions a machine may make. Most transitions involve the movement of data from one place to another. Thus they also define the data paths that exist within the machine. Some example transitions are given:

```
transition == machine -> machine

regToAbus :: num -> transition

regToAbus n (m, i, r, (a, b, c, d), s, h)
          = (m, i, r, (a1, b, c, d), s, h)
            where a1 = aLookup n r

mdrToAbus :: transition

mdrToAbus (m, (mar, mdr), r, (a, b, c, d), s, h)
        = (m, (mar, mdr), r, (mdr, b, c, d), s, h)
```

The primitive transitions are combined via a small set of combinators. The most important comma is a version of function composition:

```
comma :: transition -> transition -> transition
```

```
(t1 $comma t2) m = t2 (t1 m)
```

and is used to construct the derived combinator:

```
do :: [transition] -> transition

do []     = id
do (t:ts) = t $comma do ts
```

The `switch` transition is more specialised. It allows a transition to be selected from a table according to the contents of a register. Its role mimics the operation of the mapping PROM in a micro-code engine. Similarly, it is often the case that a section of micro-code is parametrised on a register value and the function `passReg` is provided for this purpose.

```
switch  :: num -> alist num transition -> transition
passReg :: num -> (num -> transition) -> transition
```

We are now in a position to be able to define transitions which correspond more closely to the register transfer style. The first allows the contents of one register to be copied to another and might be written as:

$$R_s \rightarrow R_d$$

```
regToReg :: num -> num -> transition

regToReg rs rd
 = do [ regToAbus rs,
        aluCycle AluA,
        cbusToReg rd ]
```

Finally, some compound transitions for combining registers via the ALU are provided. These might be written in the register transfer style thus:

$$\ominus R_n \rightarrow R_d$$
$$R_n \oplus R_m \rightarrow R_d$$

The second of these transitions is presented:

```
op2 :: num -> aluOp -> num -> num -> transition

op2 rn op rm rd
 = do [ regToAbus rn,
        regToBbus rm,
        aluCycle,
        cbusToReg rd ]
```

Combinations of transitions are used to implement a fetch-execute cycle where each instruction is coded as a compound of basic or derived transitions.

The final stage of the simulation was to provide an assembly language, loader and functions to run programs to completion (*ie.* until the halt flag is set) and to print out statistics. Using a functional programming environment here was of great benefit. Programs were represented simply as lists of instructions which were themselves elements of an algebraic datatype. There was no need to have a concrete syntax for assembly language programs, nor parsing/unparsing functions. Instead, the syntax of lists and constructors is used directly, and the compiler provides adequate checking and error messages.

For simplicity, labels were not implemented, although in retrospect this was probably a mistake. Many of the errors that students encountered in their test data were due to incorrect jumps.

Assessment

Students perform a single sixteen-hour assessment based on the simulation. Their tasks include the following:

- Read the core machine definition and produce a schematic diagram similar to Figure 5.
- Implement the instruction sets of two similar machines and perform some optimisations on these machines.
- Write test programs for the machines, and collate performance statistics.

The first task provides a useful revision of Miranda syntax, this being the first functional programming that the students encounter after their first year course. It provides a useful revision exercise, as well as getting them to think about the machine architecture. The transitions are named such that a detailed understanding of their operation is not required.

Conclusion

The core definitions can be regarded as defining a meta-language or micro-code for the core machine. For the purposes of the simulation exercise, the students need only be proficient in a small subset of the Miranda language, namely the syntax of lists, function application and definition. Experience would suggest that the approach is successful. When students have problems with the work, it is most often to do with the implementation of their machine, rather than the details of functional programming.

However, we must be somewhat cautious. The groups that attempt this assessment are self-selecting. Any student who struggled with functional programming in the first year is unlikely to want to attempt this work. Between a half and a third of the CS cohort opt for the alternative hardware-based experiment each year.

From the point of view of the implementer, the simulator has been a great success. During the three years of its use, we have identified only a few minor bugs which were fixed in a matter of minutes. One was due to a typographical error and a couple of others were introduced when the simulation was modified to emulate a new architecture. Performance was not a problem for us since the students' test programs were quite small. Further details of this implementation can be found in [2].

5 Computer Graphics

In their text, Salmon and Slater [4] use a notation based on Standard ML to describe many features of higher-level graphics libraries. The reason for using a functional notation which they cite is conciseness. In particular the expression of values of simple datatypes is uncluttered and requires no explicit memory allocation.

Similar motivations lead to our use of Miranda in a final year course on computer graphics. We have found it to be a convenient language for the description of geometric transformations and building upon this hierarchical geometric models.

The first stage of this part of the course introduces the following notions:

- the abstract concept of a geometric transformation
- an implementation based on homogeneous transformation matrices where composition is achieved via matrix product
- an implementation based on functions where composition is achieved via functional composition

In the Miranda implementation, the homogeneous matrices are treated as an abstract data type with given implementations of the common transformations and matrix product. The function-based implementation is typified by definitions such as:

```
translate :: point2 -> point2 -> point2
translate (tx, ty) (x, y)
    = (x + tx, y + ty)

rotate :: num -> point2 -> point2
rotate t (x, y)
    = (x * cos t - y * sin t,
       x * sin t + y * cos t)
```

Such transformations can be combined naturally with function composition, but for consistency with the matrix notation (which uses row vectors for points), we chose a variant with the arguments reversed giving a natural left-to-right reading.

```
(t1 $o t2) p = t2 (t1 p)
```

The next stage in the course introduces the notion of a symbol (sometimes called a structure). Symbols are essentially parametrised (over transformation and possibly a graphics environment) graphical objects. We describe two approaches for representing symbols:

- a symbol is a function taking a transformation to a sequence of graphical commands, or
- a symbol is a list of graphical commands. An instance of the symbol is obtained by applying a transformation to each of the commands to obtain a sequence of graphical commands.

The final step is to construct hierarchical geometric models from the symbols. Again, we present two techniques.

- A hierarchy is constructed using functions parametrised on a (global) transformation. The transformation is applied to all graphical operations at this level. All children are invoked with augmented transformations which are the composition of the global transformation and any local transformations required to position them correctly within the model. For example:

  ```
  robot t p m =
    base m ++
    arm1 (a1 $o m) ++
    arm2 (a2 $o m)
    where
    a1 = rotate t $o
         translate 0 l1
    a2 = rotate p $o
         translate 0 l2 $o
         a1
  ```

  where `arm1`, `leg1` and `base` are the symbols which constitute the relevant parts of the robot.
- A hierarchy is constructed as a tree. Each node contains a symbol, a local transformation and a list (possibly empty) of children. A function is provided to instance a tree. It visits each node maintaining a current transformation which is the composition of any global transformation and all the local transformations on the path from the root to the current position in the tree.

  ```
  tree ::= Node symbol trans [tree]

  figure m =
    Node body m [
       Node arm arm1 [],
       Node arm arm2 [],
       Node leg leg1 [],
       Node leg leg2 [],
       Node head head1 []]
  ```

```
matches :: reg -> string -> bool

matches (Or r1 r2) st
  = matches r1 st \/ matches r2 st
matches (Then r1 r2) st
  = or [ matches r1 s1 & matches r2 s2 | (s1,s2)<-splits ]
    where
    splits = [ (take n st,drop n st) | n <- [0..#st] ]
```

Fig. 6. Regular expression matching

```
draw_tree m1 (Node sym m2 l) =
  sym m3 ++
  concat (map (draw_tree m3) l)
  where
  m3 = m2 $o m1
```

Here `arm`, `leg` and `head` are symbols, and `arm1` *etc.* are the local transformations which position these symbols within the model.

Conclusion

As with Salmon and Slater, we found the major advantage of the use of Miranda to be conciseness. The ease with which new datatypes can be defined and values of these types can be expressed makes the presentation of material of this nature much easier. Many imperative languages have a baroque syntax for literal values of anything but the predefined datatypes and this is both distracting and wasteful of space. When lists or trees are involved the notation becomes unwieldy and often impractical to present on, say, a single OHP slide. Miranda has a concise notation for the values of all algebraic datatypes, with a particularly concise notation for lists.

In their text, Salmon and Slater also use Pascal. They state that one should regard the Pascal as an implementation of the higher-level ML presentation. This is precisely one of the messages we try to give in our first year courses.

6 Formal Languages

In a short module on the processing of formal languages we cover regular expressions, and the different sorts of automaton used to recognise them, as described in [1], Chapter 3. We use Miranda as a description and implementation language for various of the ideas here. This material is also available through the URL
`http://www.ukc.ac.uk/computer_science/Miranda_craft/`

Matching

After describing regular expressions as a Miranda type, we are able to give a Miranda definition of when a string matches an expression, the function `matches` of Figure 6. The description is short, and more importantly *unambiguous*. In this context we are using Miranda as a formal specification language.

The system

In our system we give implementations of

- A type of NFAs, and a simulation of NFAs;
- a function transforming a regular expression into an NFA;
- a function making an NFA into a deterministic machine, a DFA;
- a function optimising a DFA by minimising its state set.

Much of the code can be re-used; we discuss a particular case in the next section.

Sets

The automata used to recognise matches are built from sets; we exploit the Miranda `abstype` mechanism to hide the particular implementation of the sets. Moreover, in different parts of the implementation we need to consider sets of different type: in the simple non-deterministic automaton we consider sets of numbers, in building a deterministic version we use sets of sets of numbers; polymorphism supports this sort of re-use.

Programming the system

Using a programming language forces us to consider both the details of the system and how it is built from its constituent parts. A functional language is sufficiently high-level that the details do not engulf the wider picture; for example, we need do no explicit memory management in a functional description. The Miranda language also has a module system, and this is most helpful in putting together the complete implementation.

As in earlier sections, the twin advantages of type/syntax checking and executability give us assurance that what we have written is sensible, as well as allowing students to experiment with the systems and their assessment work.

7 Conclusions

In the introduction to this paper we argued that there were considerable advantages to using a functional language as a teaching vehicle in a computer science degree. We illustrated our arguments with examples from four areas: semantics, architecture, graphics and formal languages. We believe that there are other parts of the degree in which a functional approach will be equally useful, specification animation and program verification being two obvious examples, and we hope to explore these and other topics in the years to come.

References

1. Alfred V. Aho, Ravi Sethi, and Jeffrey D. Ullman. *Compilers: Principles, Techniques and Tools.* Addison-Wesley, 1985.
2. Steve Hill. The functional simulation of a simple microprocessor. Technical Report 17-94, UKC Computing Laboratory, 1994. Available by ftp from `unix.hensa.ac.uk` in the directory `pub/misc/ukc.reports/comp.sci/reports` as the file `17-94.ps.Z`.
3. Simon L. Peyton Jones. *Implementing Functional Languages.* Prentice-Hall, 1992.
4. Rod Salmon and Mel Slater. *Computer Graphics - Systems and Concepts.* Addison-Wesley, 1987.
5. Joseph E. Stoy. *Denotational Semantics: The Scott-Strachey approach to programming language theory.* MIT Press, 1977.
6. Robert D. Tennent. *Principles of Programming Languages.* Prentice Hall, 1979.
7. Simon Thompson. Programming language semantics using Miranda. Technical Report 9-95, Computing Laboratory, University of Kent at Canterbury, 1995.
8. Glynn Winskel. *The Formal Semantics of Programming Languages.* MIT Press, 1993.

Understanding LOLITA: Experiences in Teaching Large Scale Functional Programming

Stephen A. Jarvis[1], Sanjay Poria[2] and Rick G. Morgan[2]

[1] Oxford University Computing Laboratory, Wolfson Building, Parks Road, Oxford, England.
Stephen.Jarvis@comlab.ox.ac.uk

[2] Dept of Computer Science, Durham University, South Road, Durham, England.
Sanjay.Poria@durham.ac.uk
R.G.Morgan@durham.ac.uk

Abstract. LOLITA is a large scale natural processing system written in the functional language Haskell. It consists of over 47,000 lines of code written over 180 different modules. There are currently 20 people working on the system, most of whom are Ph.D. students. The majority of research projects involve the development of an application which is written around a semantic network; the knowledge representation structure at the core of the system. Because of the type of various applications, developers often join the team with little or no functional programming experience. For this reason the task of teaching these developers to the level required to implement their respective applications, requires teaching at various levels of abstraction. The strategy chosen means that each researcher only needs to be taught at the particular level of abstraction at which they work. These abstractions give rise to the notion of a domain specific sublanguage; that is a programming style in which a different language is created for each desired level of abstraction. In this paper we show how functional languages provide the necessary framework to enable these sublanguages to be created.

1 Introduction

The LOLITA (Large-scale Object-based Linguistic Interactor Translator and Analyser) system [2] is a state of the art natural language processing system, able to grammatically parse, semantically and pragmatically analyse, reason about, and answer queries on complex texts, such as articles from the financial pages of quality newspapers. Written in the pure, lazy functional programming language Haskell [5], it consists of over 47,000 lines of source code [3] (excluding comments).

The semantic network, which is the system's central data structure, contains over 90,000 nodes, allowing more than 100,000 inflected word forms. Begun in 1986, when the language Miranda[3] was used, the system is being developed by the Laboratory for Natural Language Engineering at the University of Durham,

[3] Miranda is a trademark of Research Software Ltd.

currently involving a team of approximately twenty developers. In June 1993 the LOLITA system was demonstrated to the Royal Society in London.

LOLITA is an example of a large system which has been developed in a *lazy* functional language purely because it was felt that this was the most suitable type of language to use. It is important to note the distinction between this development, where the choice of lazy functional languages is incidental, and projects which are either initiated as *experiments* in lazy functional languages or have a vested interest in the use of lazy functional languages. There are many examples of the latter, the FLARE project [14], the Glasgow [11], and Chalmers [3] compilers; there are substantial examples of the former, the LOLITA project is one of the larger of these developments [3].

2 The LOLITA Natural Language Processing System

Many Natural Language Processing (NLP) systems have been built to solve specific problems. These systems are restricted, either in the particular task they perform or the domain in which they work. The aim with LOLITA is to produce a general, domain-independent knowledge representation and reasoning system.

LOLITA's core consists of a language independent representation for natural language in the form of an inheritance based *Sem*antic *Net*work; SemNet (see [8] for a more in-depth discussion). Statements are represented as a collection of nodes and arcs, signifying concepts and relationships respectively. This representation provides a rich and expressive formalism for any natural language sentence.

The core system can parse complex text, conduct semantic and pragmatic analyses of the resulting parse graphs/trees and add the relevant conclusions to SemNet. The system can also answer natural language (NL) interrogations about the knowledge held in the network by generating natural language from SemNet.

Built around this core are the various applications shown in Figure 1. An example of one of the applications is template generation. This involves the identification of relevant information contained within ordinary text such as newspaper articles. The relevant information is presented using a template. The template contains various slots which act as field headings, whose bodies are filled in according to the content of the original text. For example a suitable template for *meetings* might contain the slots: *participants*, *when* and *where*. LOLITA identifies the information to fill these slots.

3 Teaching Functional Languages

Most of the applications of the LOLITA system are Ph.D. research projects, and are built around the core system. The types of project are extremely diverse ranging from Chinese language tutoring to the generation of causal explanations

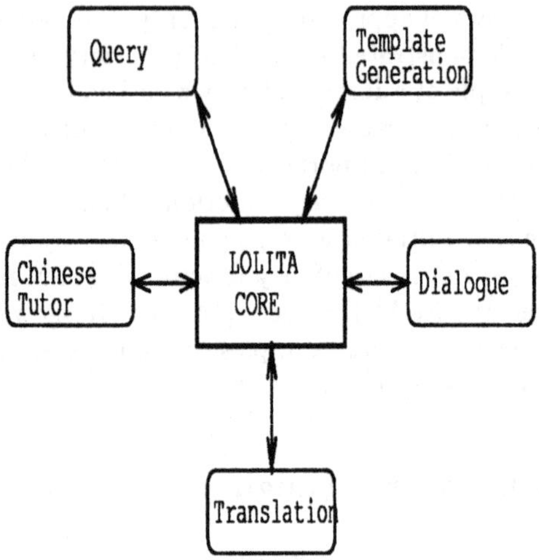

Fig. 1. A diagram showing the various applications built around the LOLITA core.

by abduction from the network. Consequently the backgrounds of researchers in the team varies greatly, from linguistics and mathematics to computer science and economics.

As expected, the programming experience of people coming into the team varies greatly from those who have no programming experience, people who have experience of imperative languages to those who are proficient functional programmers. In addition some developers have no experience of simple mathematical notions.

Since most projects in the team involve implementing some application it is important to teach functional programming such that each person is adequately equipped to implement their component.

One possibility is that, all developers on the project are brought up to the same level of functional programming expertise. This would require teaching all aspects of functional languages. On a project this scale, such an approach has proved to be infeasible because of the problems caused by varying backgrounds and abilities of the various developers.

Instead the approach taken is to try and minimise the amount of teaching that needs to be done by teaching functional programming at various abstract levels. It will be shown that functional programming languages provide features which enable these levels of abstraction to be created.

3.1 Problems of Teaching Functional Programming

LOLITA is an example of an Artificial Intelligence system. Speed of response to the required queries is of importance. The production of efficient code is hence essential. This provides a difficulty since the traditional paradigm of functional languages (also of logic based languages), is that the user declaratively describes *what* the function does but now *how* the function computes. Put in other words they try to abstract away from the more concrete representation of the various structures required to compute the result, to a more abstract notion of computation.

The problem which arises in teaching the various personnel is to find a balance between teaching a minimal amount such that the particular person may implement their application and teaching an adequate amount such that the implementation is efficient. Whereas there is a temptation to teach as little as possible and at a level of abstraction that the person will be working at, it is offset with the need to teach low level issues such as compiler details and models of reduction, to understand where inefficiencies typically occur. It is essential that the teaching must find the correct balance between the two on a large project. Consequently tools have been developed to enable this. One example of such a tool is a profiling tool [9] [7] which enables users working at the subsequent levels of abstraction to monitor the time efficiency of the code easily without requiring an in depth knowledge of other parts of LOLITA and Haskell system.

4 A Development Hierarchy for Functional Programmers

From our experience the natural solution to finding a balance between teaching at the right level of abstraction and detail of efficient implementation is to develop a hierarchy of programmers. This hierarchy has naturally developed into the levels shown in Figure 2.

The figure shows abstractions created by developers at various levels in the hierarchy, together with typical levels of expertise. People at each level will provide support to those higher up (either by creating abstractions or providing tools). An abstraction at the lower level in the hierarchy may hide developers from primitive I/O operations and access to other parts of the system implemented in C or C++.

In the rest of this paper we explain why certain features of functional languages are particularly suited to the creation of these levels of abstraction.

5 Suitability of Functional Languages

We use particular examples as a case studies, but stress that this abstraction approach can also be applied more generally. This section looks more specifically at aspects of functional languages which provide us with the desirable features mentioned above.

Consider the case of a typical level 2 to level 3 abstraction in our scheme (where level 1 is the lowest level in the table i.e. the Haskell language level). A developer at level 3 may be working on the parsing/grammar of natural language; that is, they are interested in the resulting parse graphs produced by variation of the grammar rules. A developer at this level is less interested in a specific

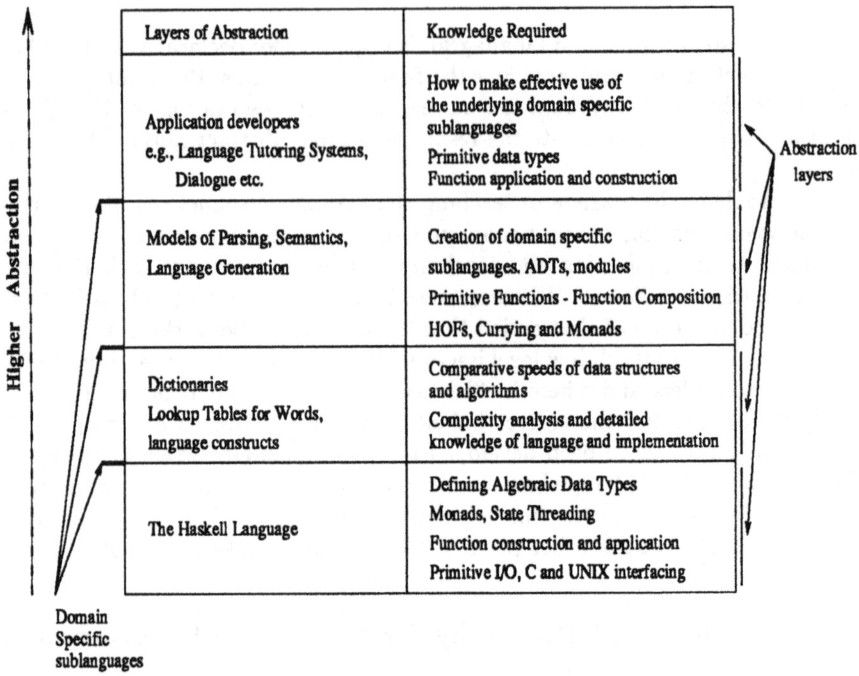

Layers of Abstraction
Knowledge Required
Application developers
e.g., Language Tutoring Systems,
Dialogue etc.
How to make effective use of
the underlying domain specific
sublanguages
Primitive data types
Function application and construction
Models of Parsing, Semantics,
Language Generation
Creation of domain specific
sublanguages. ADTs, modules
Primitive Functions - Function Composition
HOFs, Currying and Monads
Dictionaries
Lookup Tables for Words,
language constructs
Comparative speeds of data structures
and algorithms
Complexity analysis and detailed
knowledge of language and implementation
The Haskell Language
Defining Algebraic Data Types
Monads, State Threading
Function construction and application
Primitive I/O, C and UNIX interfacing
Higher Abstraction
Abstraction
layers
Domain
Specific
sublanguages

Fig. 2. A diagram showing the various levels of abstraction that exist. The column on the left shows the layers of abstraction, based on the Haskell language, at which applications are developed. People developing at lower layers support those at higher layers by providing tools and/or creating a level of abstraction. The second columns shows the knowledge that those working at each level require. Each level of abstraction can be bridged by the use of a DSS. The real power of Functional Languages lies in the way in which the boundaries between these levels of abstraction can be drawn.

types of detail (e.g. efficiency or how the grammar is used to actually produce a parse) but they are concerned with the effects of these grammar rule variations. For such a person we wish to create a different type of abstraction to a person who is working at the level of the natural language dictionary where efficient word lookup is paramount for the effective working on the system.

5.1 Domain Specific Sublanguages

Most people would accept that the choice of an ideal programming language for some task would greatly depend upon that task. That is, there is no notion of a universal programming language which is well suited to all programming tasks. We might therefore be left with a choice between designing and implementing a new language which is well suited to the particular domain in which we wish to work, or using a language which does not allow us to express ourselves directly in terms of this domain, and has already been designed and implemented with wider goals in mind.

A solution which lies somewhere between these two extremes is provided by the use of what we call *Domain Specific Sublanguages* (DSS). We build such languages as collections of Haskell types, operators and functions, and so in a sense they are not a new language at all. However, they are designed in such a way that the programs written using them, not only look unlike "normal" haskell programs, but correspond closely to the important concepts in the domain in which our problem lies. So for example we provide a domain specific sublanguage for writing grammars which hides any details of how the grammar might be used to actually parse sentences.

We will illustrate with case studies that if well defined, a domain specific sublanguage can appear to the programmer to be a new language specially tailored to the required level of abstraction. We also try to show that lazy functional programming languages are ideal candidates to enable the creation of these sublanguages.

5.2 Case Study 1: The LOLITA Grammar

Perhaps the best example of a DSS currently in the LOLITA system is the NL grammar. This may be because DSS's are particularly suited to domains which rely on large numbers of rules which have similar structure. An example of one such grammar rule is shown in Figure 3.

```
> reported_sentence :: Parser
> reported_sentence
>       = prephrases
>         +++
>         sentence &? excl_mark       >> exclamN
>         +++
>         sentence & ques_mark        >> questN
```

Fig. 3. An example of one of LOLITA's grammar rules. `exclamN` and `questN` specify the labels to be placed on the resulting parse tree nodes, as well as the feature aspects (such as number and tense).

Although this rule is Haskell code it has a close correspondence with the standard formalisms for describing grammars. For example Figure 4 shows the grammar rule shown in Figure 3 in a more traditional BNF (Backus Naur Form).

As can be seen there exists a natural mapping of operators between the two formalisms.

```
reported_sentence
     =  prephrases |
        sentence ?excl_mark |
        sentence ques_mark
```

Fig. 4. The grammar rule in 3 in BNF form.

This example fully exploits the powerful abstraction mechanisms provided by functional languages by providing a DSS. The example above is a particularly good case because:

- The mapping from original BNF grammar to the domain specific language is particularly natural.
- The domain is totally enclosed. The user of such a language has not been given any opportunity to revert to the full complexity of Haskell.
- We have moved away from Haskell specific details like how to combine and apply functions to totally syntactic issues of how to combine terminal and non-terminal symbols. Combining such symbols requires only a simplified view of complex functional programming aspects such as the type system (see Section 8).

5.3 Case Study 2: The Semantic Parser

The semantic parser is a central feature of the LOLITA system (see Figure 5).

The input to the semantic parser is a syntactic parse tree built at a previous phase in the system. The output from the semantic parser is the corresponding semantic network structure. The fundamental task therefore is the transformation from the parse tree structure to the semantic network data type. Consider for example the parse tree representing the sentence "Roberto owns a motorbike", and its conversion to the corresponding piece of semantic network, shown in Figure 6.

Each node in the parse tree is labelled with its grammatical construct. For instance the root node of the parse tree is labelled with **sen**, representing the complete sentence structure. Each of these labels has a corresponding semantic rule which transforms the parse tree structure into the semantic network structure. Rather than coding these rules directly, we have defined a language which is used to specify these rules in an abstract way. This language has been modified as our comprehension of what is required by semantic analysis has changed and developed.

Two types of semantic rule are used, one for parse tree leaves and the other for branches. The parse tree leaf rules are represented by the abstract data type (ADT) 'leaf_rule' and are given as part of the definition of a function **meta_leaf** which maps parse tree labels onto the corresponding leaf rule. In a similar way

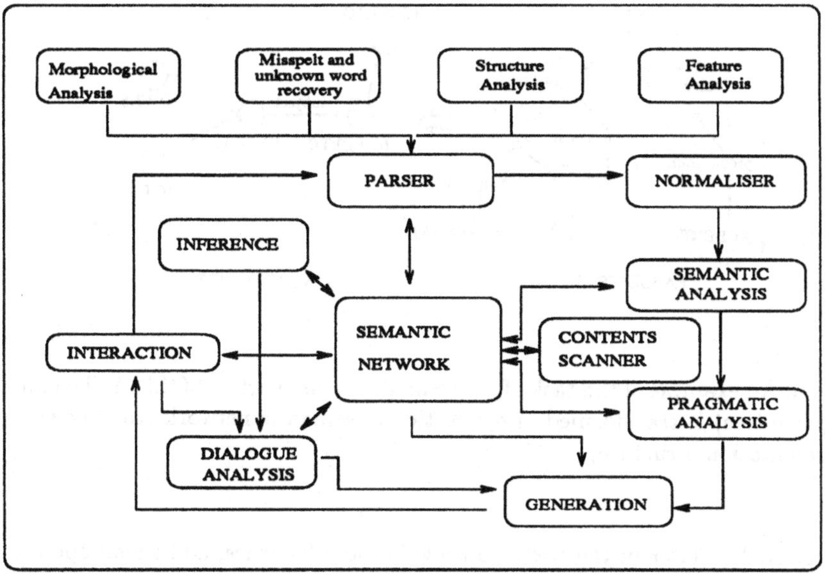

Fig. 5. A diagram showing the components of the LOLITA core.

the parse tree branch rules are represented by the ADT 'branch_rule' and are given as part of the definition of a function **meta_branch**.

```
meta_leaf :: ParseTreeLabel -> LeafRule
meta_branch :: ParseTreeLabel -> BranchRule
```

The semantic representation of a binary node in the parse tree is mainly determined compositionally according to its label and the semantics of the subtrees below it. Taking the **transvp** node of Figure 6 as an example, the left subtree produces the concept of ownership and the right subtree produces the concept of a particular (but unspecified) motorbike. The fact that these are linked by a **transvp** branch means that the 'ownership' must be an action and the motorbike must be an object. This rule is specified as follows:

```
> meta_branch "transvp"
>   = labelboth Act Obj
```

Although the rule for **transvp** can define the semantic representation for a node entirely in terms of the semantic representation of the subtrees, other rules must take into account contextual information such as the set of referents[4] that are available. It must also be possible to mark points in the parse tree which may correspond to new nodes in the semantic network as well as points which may

[4] Nodes which may be referred to in later pieces of text by pronouns (e.g. 'he' or 'it')

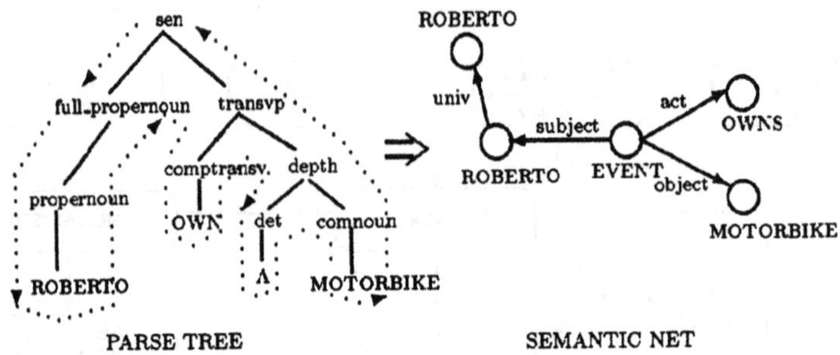

Fig. 6. An example of the task of the semantic parser part of LOLITA. The input (a parse tree) is transformed into a section of semantic network (the knowledge representation structure).

be referred to later in the text. To provide these facilities, additional operators and functions are provided.

The operator **compose** combines two rules and applies the first rule to the result obtained from the application of the second (it is the semantic rule equivalent of function composition). The following example creates a branch-rule for proper nouns by combining three smaller rules: **labelLeft**, **newnode** and **addref**.

```
> meta_branch "full_propernoun"
>   = addref              'compose'
>     newnode object      'compose'
>     labelLeft Univ
```

This rule specifies the semantics for **full_propernoun** as a unique new object node related to the semantics of the left subtree by the universal link (as indicated in Figure 6, **full_propernoun** branches contain no right subtree). It also ensures that this new node is available as a referent (this would be used in the sentence "Roberto owns a motorbike and *he* cleans it almost every day"). The new node is necessary here to distinguish between the unique 'ROBERTO' being talked about in the example and the universal concept of 'ROBERTO'.

This short example illustrates how we use domain specific sublanguages to create a level of abstraction.

The developer who is working on transforming parse trees to corresponding semantic network fragments need not have internal knowledge of the representation of **BranchRule**'s and **LeafRule**'s and how they are further used to actually build the fragment of semantic network (this is hidden in an ADT). The person is actually working at a conceptual *meta-level.* The developer only needs to worry about *what* the rules at each level in the parse tree should be. Also note that although `BranchRule` and `LeafRule` are implemented as functions, the semantic rule writer, need have no knowledge of the higher order aspects of Haskell needed to implement `'compose'`.

Abstract types therefore provide a framework for creating domain specific sublanguages and as we see in this example, there may be one or many abstract types needed to implement a domain specific sublanguage.

6 Supporting Domain Specific Sublanguages

Although declarative languages provide an abstraction away from the machine representation this is precisely what is needed for some tasks in a diverse system such as LOLITA which has many components.

The user is shielded from the complexity of the solution. For example, for a long time it was thought that the grammar of the system was adequately written. However, it was not until we obtained a graphical tool to display parse graphs (a graph of all possible parse trees of a sentence) that it was realised that parsing contributed a significant amount to the space problem that was being encountered. It was later found to be a problem caused by the way in which the rules had been written.

It was soon realised that people were required to support the development of the system at the lowest level indicated in the hierarchy. This has lead to the development of debugging[4] and profiling tools [9] as Ph.D. projects. These developers need to be aware of all the details of functional languages including graph reduction techniques, program optimisations and transformations carried out by the compiler. Part of their object is to shield people who develop components higher up in the programming hierarchy from implementation issues, and also to present debugging and profiling information at the required level of abstraction, (rather then at lower levels). Without these techniques it is not possible to monitor the complexity behaviour of the programs at higher levels of abstraction without detailed knowledge, hence defeating the object of creating DSS's. These projects are looked at in more detail.

6.1 Debugging Domain Specific Sublanguages

Since each developer works at a particular level of abstraction and is not expected to know details of the mechanism underlying the particular DSS, aspects such as debugging code can present a problem. In the case of an error one of two possible cases has occured:

1. Either, the error has occured at the abstract level at which the developer is working (e.g. a DSS function applied to illegal arguments), or,
2. the error has occured at some lower level.

What needs to be determined is which of these two cases has occured. To aid in this search a debugging tool has been developed [4].

A class of run-time error which was found to be occurring frequently in developers code was the *exception error* type. An exception error is one which results in termination of the program and the printing of an error message. Examples of this type of error in Haskell are

```
Fail: head{PreludeList}: head []
```

which results from passing the list head function an empty list and

```
Fail: (!!){PreludeList}: index too large
```

which occurs when the list indexing operator is passed a subscript which is outside the bounds of the list. These exception errors give the applications programmer no indication of whereabouts in the program the error occurred. In particular the errors are displayed with reference to the lowest level in the system; the list function defined in the standard prelude.

This is a problem as functions such as **head** and the list indexing operator are used many times in many different parts of LOLITA. Previously, this problem had been approached by providing a customised version of each function capable of generating an exception error for each module. This new version of the function would report the name of the module when it generated an exception error. However simply knowing the name of the module in which the exception was generated is not sufficient—the error causing the exception error to be generated may be in a function which called the exception-generating one, or even some way back in a chain of functions each calling the other with the exception-generating function at the very end of the chain. Reporting errors in this way is of no use in the determination of errors at the level of a domain specific sublanguage.

The *distinguished path debugging tool* allows the display of chains of functions, termed *distinguished paths.* The path displayed is the route taken through the dependency graph of the functions in the program. The tool works by transforming each function to take an extra parameter, a representation of the distinguished path, which is built up from one function call to the next. When an exception error is encountered, the value of this extra parameter is displayed. Unlike the previous method of debugging such errors, which involved altering the source code by hand, the tool works automatically by transforming each source module.

Using such a tool it is possible to display the cause of errors at a higher level in the programming hierarchy. Though the error may have been caused by a list index out of range, this is of little help to a developer working on spell checking input text. However, it may be more useful if they are able to see that one of their functions (case 1 above) caused such an index out of range, (in which case it is the developers job to investigate the error) or the error is further down the chain, below the DSS (a case 2 error). In this latter case the developer may have to consult the person who works at this lower level so it can be fixed.

6.2 Profiling Domain Specific Sublanguages

During the development of the LOLITA system attention has been paid to the efficiency of the code. A large amount of time has been spent profiling the system with both the Glasgow cost centre profiler [10], part of GHC, and also the York heap profiler [12] [13], supplied with the Chalmers haskell compiler. Improvements to the overall system achieved through the use of the profilers have been in the order of 35%.

The profiling task requires the parts of the code that the programmer is interested in to be identified. This process can take place automatically, the compiler will select functions, modules or constructors to profile at compile time, or alternatively this selection can be made by hand, by annotating the code.

Using hand annotated code to identify functions for profiling it is possible to profile the functions of the domain specific sublanguage abstract data types. Perhaps more importantly it is possible for the applications programmer to shield themselves from the lower level functions in the system by profiling just the modules in which they program.

The analysis of the profiling results may be limited if the programmer is unaware of precise details relating to the functional language. For instance they may not understand why a space leak manifests itself or why functions are not evaluated lazily when this is the aim. However, the profiling results do allow them to compare and contrast different implementations of their application functions and to see which appears to be more efficient.

Work has been done at Durham to develop a profiling tool which provides the programmer with detailed profiling information in an interactive post-processing environment[5]. A modified version of the Glasgow Haskell Compiler produces profiling results based on *stacks* of functions. These stacks are used to recreate the function call-graph. The programmer can interact with functions in this call-graph to gather costs at different levels in the program. Since the profiling costs are recorded in this stack form, the inheritance of costs to high levels in the call-graph is accurate; no statistical averaging is used for shared functions.

6.3 Optimising Domain Specific Sublanguages

One of the drawbacks with the domain specific sublanguage approach is the lack of any facilities to provide off-line processing of the sublanguage. Such a scheme would become particularly important in situations where the code in which the domain specific sublanguage is written could be optimised and transformed at compile time. The development of the grammatical analysis offers a typical example of where this would have been useful.

In order to achieve efficient parsing of natural language, a number of transformations were performed on the original grammar to make it largely deterministic [1]. The grammar was originally coded in its deterministic form but this was found to destroy the structure of the grammar and it became difficult to

[5] The *cost-centre stack* profiler, [9].

maintain. It was therefore decided that the transformations should be applied to the grammar.

The transformations were were performed by a three stage process. First, the original Haskell form of the grammar was parsed, secondly the transformations were applied, and finally the results of the transformations were built using the parsing ADT with additional deterministic constructs contained within it. Using the ADT to code the source of the grammar meant that the grammar could be tested without having to wait for the transformations to be applied. Given that the transformations typically took three hours, this made the maintenance of the grammar far more practical. The efficiency of the untransformed grammar meant that it could not be applied to long and complex sentences; however it could be applied to sufficiently small sub-parts.

The current situation could be considerably improved if the compiler were able to provide a mechanism to perform the stages of grammar transformations as part of the compilation process. The grammar operators could then be implemented as constructors which would build a data structure representing the grammar (this contrasts with the present implementation in which grammar operators are functions). Supposing this was represented by the type NewParser:

```
> data NewParser = NewParser :+++ NewParser |
>     NewParser :>> ParserName |

etc.
```

The **parse** function which actually performs the parsing would then have the type:

```
> parse:: NewParser -> Input -> Output
```

and would be implemented as

```
> parse p i = (transformGrammar p) i
```

The function `transformGrammar` would produce the actual parsing function, and would be evaluated at compile time.

This type of facility would then ensure that such off-line preprocessing could be performed more easily than at present, preventing the need to parse the original Haskell code and generate and compile new Haskell code. It is interesting to note that many Prolog implementations provide a facility to transform the source code as it is loaded or compiled into the Prolog system. Although this facility can be used to perform the type of off-line transformations discussed here, it has the disadvantage that it can change the semantics of the initial source program. Using compile time evaluation would provide a means of performing such off-line transformations, but without changing the semantics of the program.

7 Support for the Construction of Domain Specific Sublanguages

It is certainly possible to use this domain specific sublanguage approach in other languages. Most modern languages provide facilities for the creation of abstraction data types – these are essential to the use of DSS's as they prevent the user of the sublanguage from accessing the implementation of the types used in the sublanguage directly. The ability to define operators with specified precedence and associativity is also provided in other languages.

However, certain features of functional languages make them particularly suitable for the implementation of DSS's. These are:

Higher-Order Functions. In the use of domain specific sublanguages, the programmer will often apply a function to a value without realising that these values are also functions. For example in Figure 3, +++ and >> are thus higher order functions as they take values of type `Parser` as parameters. The result of using this form of representation is to make functions written using these abstract types easier to write and clearer to read. They enable a more natural mapping between the original rules the user may wish to enter and the form that Haskell the created Haskell sublanguage will accept.

Lazy Evaluation. Once an abstraction into a DSS is created it needs to be interfaced to the rest of the system. Lazy evaluation provides an essential mechanism that enables this integration [6]. For example, consider the conditional function `cond` taken from the Generator DSS of LOLITA

```
> cond :: GenCond -> Gen -> Gen -> Gen
> sayEvent
>    = cond hasObject
>           sayObject
>           sayNothing
```

The function `cond` evaluates either its second or third argument depending upon the value of the first. In a strict language an interface to this function is not practical because it requires the evaluation of both the *then* and *else* parts of the conditional.
Another example can be found in the parser. A typical piece of grammar will look like:

```
> paragraph = sentence & (empty +++ paragraph)   >> parLabel
```

If the operators `+++`, `&` and `>>` are all strict in both arguments, any attempt to evaluate `paragraph` leads to non termination (or a "black hole" error) since it requires an evaluation of `paragraph` to return a result. This in practise is avoided because the operator `+++` is non strict in its second argument.

8 Teaching and Domain Specific Sublanguages

We have presented a methodology for the development of large scale functional systems. This consists of:

- The various Domain Specific Sublanguages which make up the system; the case studies presented show examples of these.
- Tools which make these abstractions practical. These include the profiling, debugging and potentially the optimisation of domain specific sublanguages.

Consequently, this presents a structured paradigm for teaching of functional programming. Developers are taught an application specific DSS, Typically this means teaching a greatly simplified functional language typically consisting of the functions available at the application specific DSS (with relevant types), together with:

1. basic function definitions: (un)guarded expressions...,
2. associated typing rules: (`f::t`, simplified view of type system excluding aspects such as currying,
3. function application,
4. simple module interfaces - **`module X`** ($f_1 \ldots f_n$) **`where import...`**

This avoids teaching advanced aspects of functional programming such as algebraic data types, higher order functions, monads and interfacing to other languages....

Also we gain the normal benefits given by abstract data types. Common functional programming ideas such as list comprehension and currying can be hidden from the application programmer. The amount of actual Haskell that needs to be taught is therefore only a small subset of the actual language.

At an optimal level in the system a developer need only know the functions of the supporting domain specific sublanguage and Haskell operations such as function application which enables them to combine these functions for their own development. Even powerful ideas like higher order functions can be hidden from the programmer because they are explicitly built into the domain specific sublanguage.

It must be stressed that although the strategy is to teach a minimal amount (i.e. the DSS and those constructs listed above only), often developers will teach themselves a greater range of features. However, examples where developers have only learned the provided sublanguage do exist.

9 Conclusion

In this paper we have presented a different paradigm for the teaching of functional programming for large scale systems such as LOLITA. That is the creation of problem dependent abstraction levels via sublanguages where required. This paradigm of development has advantages over other development processes, where the full complexity of the language is used at all levels in the code. Hence our developers do not have to show proficiency at all levels in programming techniques. Although it may seem desirable to have all developers showing proficiency in programming techniques at all levels of functional languages, it has been found to be infeasible in large project such as the ours. This arises mainly as a result of the scale of the project, tight time constraints on teaching, and the varying abilities and backgrounds of the members joining the team.

In choosing our own natural syntax and hiding levels of detail in an ADT we are able to create a domain specific sublanguage for a particular task. The approach we have developed has a number of well established traits:

- **Flexibility** — By using a sublanguage of Haskell, the syntax and semantics of the language may be changed simply. This is something that has frequently occurred within the development of the LOLITA system.
- **Power** — These domain specific sublanguages are extremely useful when we can find an appropriate set of constructions that cover all of rules we want to describe without becoming overly complex. However, we do find in a substantial rule set that there are often some rules which need special treatment. In our approach it is easy to revert to the full power of Haskell (and lose some abstraction at isolated points). In the external language approach, this would be far more difficult to achieve, and either requires the special construction of "one off" primitives, or some facility to interface with a more powerful language.
- **Scale** — The overheads in setting up new language tools mean that the external approach is really only feasible for substantial rule sets. The internal approach has a very small overhead and is thus applicable to much smaller rule sets.

The development of the LOLITA system over a number of years, by a number of people with mixed programming experience, has given us a large amount of functional programming experience. The significance of this work highlights not only how, features of functional languages alleviate the burden of teaching a wide spectrum of functional techniques to developers of large-scale real world system, but also, with the need for developing advanced programming tools, where such a scheme fails.

Acknowledgements

Our thanks to Dave Nettleton and Paul Callaghan for reading earlier drafts of this paper.

References

1. N. Ellis, R. Garigliano, and R. Morgan. A new transformation into deterministically parsableform for natural language grammars. In *Proceedings of 3rd International Workshop on Parsing Technologies*, Tilburg, Netherlands, 1993.

2. R. Garigliano. LOLITA: Progress report 1. Technical Report 12/92, School of Engineering and Computer Science, University of Durham, 1992.
3. A. Gill and P. Wadler. Real world applications of functional programs. http://www.dcs.gla.ac.uk/fp/realworld.html.
4. J. Hazan and R. Morgan. The location of errors in functional programs. *Lecture Notes in Computer Science*, 749:135–152, 1993.
5. P. Hudak, S. Peyton Jones, P. Wadler, et al. *Report on the Programming Language Haskell Version 1.2*, 1992.
6. J. Hughes. Why fuctional programming matters. *The Computer Journal*, 32, 1989.
7. S. Jarvis. Profiling large-scale lazy functional programs. PhD thesis, Durham University, *forthcoming*.
8. D. Long and R. Garigliano. *Reasoning by Analogy and Causality: A model and application.* Artificial Intelligence. Ellis Horwood, 1994.
9. R. G. Morgan and S. A. Jarvis. Profiling large-scale lazy functional programs. In *Proceedings of the Conference on High Performance Functional Computing*, Denver, USA., April 1995.
10. S. L. Peyton Jones. Implementing lazy functional programs on stock hardware: the spineless tagless g-machine. *Journal of Functional Programming*, 2:127–202, 1992.
11. S. L. Peyton Jones et al. The Glasgow Haskell Compiler: a technical overview. In *Framework for Information Technology Technical Conference*, Keele, 1993.
12. C. Runciman and D. Wakeling. Heap profiling of a lazy functional compiler. In J. Launchbury and P. Sansom, editors, *Functional Programming.* Springer-Verlag, 1992.
13. C. Runciman and D. Wakeling. Heap profiling for lazy functional programs. *Journal of Functional Programming*, 3, April 1993.
14. C. Runciman and D. Wakeling. *Applications of Functional Programming.* UCL Press, 1995.

Functional Programming and Mathematical Objects

Jerzy Karczmarczuk

Dept. of Computer Science, University of Caen, France

Abstract. We discuss the application of the Haskell/Gofer type classes and constructor classes to the implementation and teaching of the manipulation techniques in the domain of formal mathematical expressions. We show also how the lazy evaluation paradigms simplify the construction and the presentation of several algorithms dealing with iterative data types, such as power series or formal Padé expansion. We show the application of higher order functions to algebra and geometry, and specifically — to the construction of parametric surfaces.

1 Introduction

Formal manipulation of algebraic and geometric objects seems *à priori* to be a wonderful training ground for mathematically oriented students who want to learn the design and the implementation of complex algorithms and heterogeneous data structures. It is not very often exploited, though. While it is standard at quite elementary level, to teach formal differentiation of algebraic tree structures, or the arithmetic of compound data structures such as complex numbers or rationals, it is not very easy to leave the *syntactic* approach to the modelling of the mathematical objects, and to make use of the *structure* (in the mathematical, rather than programming) sense of the underlying domain.

The students learn easily how to operate on fractions and polynomials, but the algebra of rational functions has usually to be implemented again, without code reusing. Standard list or term manipulation languages, as Lisp or Prolog lack the inheritance concept. But the classical object-oriented systems, such as Smalltalk or Common Lisp Object System are too heavy, and they exploit intensely the *data inheritance*, which might not be very useful if we just need to assert that both polynomials and matrices belong to a Ring category, and that from a Ring and some additional properties we can construct effectively the field of quotients, with the same (in principle) algorithms in the case of rational numbers and ratios of polynomials.

The necessity to formulate the computer algebra algorithms and data structures in a mathematically structured way was recognized many years ago. The system Axiom was built explicitly upon this principle, and the Maple package is distributed now with the public library Gauss[1] – an "object-oriented" sublanguage which heavily uses inheritance. Their learning curves are unfortunately quite steep, and their pedagogical influence is rather weak, as too many details are hidden in "black boxes".

This paper is devoted to some aspects of teaching of programming to students of Mathematics and Computer Science. We decided to look at the problem mentioned above from the perspective of modern, typed lazy functional programming. The relation between types – as realized in the language Haskell[2] – and the mathematical domains, will be discussed in the section 3. With lazy streams it is easy to create potentially infinite data structures such as series, continuous fractions, etc. But there are more arguments as well: thanks to the deferred evaluation and higher order functions it is easier to formulate the algorithms in a static, declarative manner, without polluting them with countless **for/while** loops and other imperative constructs, which hide sometimes the clarity of the underlying strategy. We have chosen Gofer[3], a popular dialect of Haskell, which permits the redefinition of the *standard prelude* where the properties of the standard operators are specified.

We wanted to bridge the gap between formal descriptions of the properties of mathematical operations, and their *practical* implementation, and also to show the students *how* this is done. So, we have designed a simplified, but quite elaborate mathematical hierarchy of classes in Gofer, and we have applied it to numerous, small, but not always trivial examples of algorithms, some of which one might not easily find in standard textbooks. This talk presents partially the work done. We have consciously omitted all computer algebra "classics" such as the algebra of symbolic extensions. The presentation below is not self-contained, we assume some knowledge of Haskell, and of standard algebra. Our aim was threefold:

- To popularize advanced functional techniques among experienced students too conditioned by the object-oriented paradigms, or "handicapped" a little by imperative programming languages.
- To show how a practical, effective programming language can be used as a tool to construct quite abstract mathematics.
- To analyse the possible traps and inadequacies of the current polymorphic functional languages, in order to propose one day a more powerful machinery.

Several structure definitions and algorithms have been reconstructed together with the students, and it was a real pleasure seeing how fast they could recover from all possible bugs and pitfalls thanks to the clarity of the language used.

2 Pedagogical Context

This paper is *not* based on *one* homogeneous course. The techniques presented here have been taught to 4th year (Maîtrise) students of Mathematics and Mathematical Engineering during a one-semester course on Functional Programming, and offered also to students of Computer Science, (4th year) as a complementary material for the course on Image Synthesis. Some of the techniques discussed below have been presented on a seminar attended by the students of DEA (Diplôme d'Études Approfondies; 5th year) on Computer Science, and have been applied to graphic modelling on a DEA stage. The 4th year courses were accompanied by practical exercices (3 hours per week) and were assessed by a written examination, and by one or two programming projects demanding a few weeks of work.

So, the audience was rather advanced. All students were acquainted with the essentials of list processing, and heard about lazy evaluation semantics (realized in Scheme). Unfortunately, for historical reasons, Gofer could not be used as a principal programming language, the course on Functional Programming was essentially based on CAML. The implementation of algorithms in Gofer was proposed informally. Nothing was really enforced, and the success of the project could be estimated by the enthusiasm of the best students, who did not restrict themselves to obligatory topics.

Thus, neither our teaching of the lazy techniques and hierarchical polymorphism, nor this paper stress upon the strictly pedagogical issues, but — as mentioned above — concentrates on a methodology of construction of mathematical objects. We used the implementations of Gofer and CAML running on Sparc stations, and in DOS boxes under MS-Windows.

3 Modified Classes of Types in Gofer

One of the powerful mechanisms in the programming language Haskell is the concept of *type classes* whose aim is to control selectively the operator overloading. Such overloading is an old concept. Everybody knows that the mathematical sign `+` is used to represent the addition of integer and real numbers in almost all popular programming languages. Sometimes the same symbol denotes the concatenation of character strings. However, in order to add two matrices by writing just `A + B` one needs an extensible language, such as the powerful object-oriented machinery of C++. For any new type of objects, one has to implement the new addition operation completely ad hoc, and it not easy to ensure some uniformity of the generalized arithmetic domain.

The creators of Haskell decided to base the polymorphism on the existence of common operational properties of a *class* of different, possibly heterogeneous data types. For example, the class `Ord a` declares the relation of order `<=`, and specifies that for all objects belonging to the type `a`, and only for them, such relation exists. Later we declare that some type, for example the field of rational fractions: pairs `(Num,Den)` is an *instance* of the class `Ord`, and we define explicitly an appropriate order relation. If, as it is usual – the class `Ord` is a subclass of the class `Eq` which encompasses all data types with the equivalence relation defined, there is no need for other order relations, all can be derived from `<=` by inversion and/or composition with the inequality.

It was exactly what we needed — to be able to define abstract mathematical operations such as additions, independently of the data structures representing the added objects. We found it methodologically harmful that our students engraved too deeply in their memories that a complex number is essentially a record with two real fields, and other similar "truths".

But the arithmetic operators in standard Haskell are essentially numeric, and their genericity is restricted to integers, floats, etc. There are definitions of rational fractions and complex numbers in the standard preludes, but the possibility of introducing more general data categories in this context is largely unexploited. The question has been posed already several times: why not provide a more general class, say, `AdditiveGroup` where the operation `(+)` would be declared, another class `SemiGroup` defining the multiplication, etc. There are some theoretical problems, for example the `AdditiveGroup` is also a `SemiGroup`, so it should somehow inherit something from it, but it cannot: the system of type classes in Haskell states that a given operation *exists*, and not that it *has some properties*. We cannot declare within the `SemiGroup` *one* neutral element for both arithmetic operations. In order to do this, we would have to declare the operations `(+)` and`(*)` as having polymorphic types belonging to two instances of the same class and that would need a system of functional meta-classes which is currently not implemented in any known functional language.

Moreover, the standard Haskell system is too rigid. For example, one cannot specify that a given type belongs to a `VectorSpace`, as this would imply the engagement of at least two usually distinct types: the additive group of vectors and the field of scalars, and this demanded a multi-parameter class. But this was exactly our aim: to take a standard textbook on algebra and to show to our students that not only polynomials are implementable, but the Galois fields, or Rings as well.

Fortunately the Haskell-like language Gofer is more flexible, although according to its author, the multi-parameter classes are a can of worms for the type-checking system. But for pedagogical purposes this constructive approach to mathematics is very fruitful, and the question of the kind "why is this definition ambiguous?" is not only a code debugging exercise, but provides an insight into the coherence of the defined mathematical structure. So, we have chosen Gofer as our battle horse, and we have reconstructed the algebraic layer of its automatically loaded *standard prelude*.

The above mentioned dilemma with having two different group structures in a `Ring` could not be solved satisfactorily, so we defined independently the additive and the multiplicative group. In order not to multiply the number of rarely used classes, we started already with semi-groups with unity. Here is the beginning of the hierarchy, we assume that the reader is acquainted with the syntax of Haskell:

```
class Monoid a where
  groupOne :: a;      (*) :: a -> a -> a
  powerInt, (^) :: a -> Int -> a  -- Pos. expt.
  negExp :: a -> Int -> a

  x `powerInt` n = itbin (*) x n groupOne
  negExp _ _ = error "Ring: negative exponent"
  x ^ n | n >= 0 = x `powerInt` n
        | otherwise = negExp x (-n)
```

```
class Monoid a => Group a where
  (/) :: a -> a -> a
  recip :: a -> a

  recip x = groupOne / x
  x/y = x * recip y        -- Beware! Cyclic defs!

class AddGroup a where
  addgroupZero :: a;
  (+), (-), subtract :: a -> a -> a
  negate, double :: a -> a
  (#) :: Int -> a -> a    -- Mult. by integer

  negate x = addgroupZero - x
  x - y = x + negate y    -- Beware! cyclic!
  subtract = flip (-)
  n # x | n<0 = negate ((-n) # x)
        | otherwise = iterbin (+) x n addgroupZero
```

The idea was to choose the minimal set of objects which characterized these structures, but also to deduce some secondary operations existing by default, such as the multiplication by integer if the addition was defined. The essential point – not always understood – is that all the *definitions* above are effective pieces of program, not just specifications. They are *default* definitions which hold for any type, unless overrided by the instances. Later on, when we defined the data type `Zp` of modular integers, which for prime p is a field, everybody recognized easily that the most evident implementation of the division x/y was the multiplication of x by the inverse of y. It suffices thus to define the latter. On the other hand, the reciprocal of a power series is just a particular case of the division, so we define the division as presented in the next section, and we keep the default for the function `recip`. Obviously, the operation `n # x` for `x` belonging to integers was reimplemented through hardware primitives. We introduced also some standard and less standard polymorphic combinators such as `flip` which switches the order of the arguments of a given function, or `iterbin` which iterates an associative binary operation, and we have shown that they provide the necessary implementation "glue". The students were supposed to discover the analogy between the integer power as the iterated multiplication, and the multiplication by an integer as an iterated addition, and to propose an abstract iterator which used the binary splitting of the integer:

```
iterbin op = g where
   g x 1 = op x
   g x 0 = id
   g x n | even n     = p
         | otherwise = p . (op x)
           where p = g (op x x) (n `div` 2)
```

The construction of Ring was a small non-trivial discovery: having at our disposal both the *unity* and the *zero*, we could construct an abstract conversion function `fromInteger` which mapped ℕ to *any* Ring. It suffices to define `fromInteger n` as `n # groupOne`.

We have discovered also a dilemma: how to define x^n for *any* integer n? The problem is that for a positive n it is just an iterated multiplication, so it should be defined within the `Monoid`, but for a negative n the base x should belong to a Group in order to compute its inverse. We cannot *redefine* the operation `(^)` inside the `Monoid` subclasses, the inheritance mechanism in Haskell is really different from the classical object-oriented paradigms. But we can define the appropriate `negExp` function within the *instances* of `Monoid`, For all the fields such as Floats or Rationals this function returns $(1/x)^{(-n)}$, but for integers etc. we leave the default. This example shows a visible limitation of the type classes for our purposes.

The next steps of our creation of the mathematical world were quite straightforward. We have defined some *ordered* structures necessary to establish the existence of such functions as the predicate `negative` or the function `abs`. Later on, when we made the `Module` and `LinearSpace` the students were asked to define the absolute value of a vector, and they obviously had a little surprise, which helped them to assess the status of the concept of *norm*, and proved that our progression is not linear, that we should go back and take into account that even such simple structures as `AdditiveGroups` are already `Modules` over integers, etc.

We continued with the definition of the `DivisionRing` with such operations as `div`, `mod`, or `gcd`, and we have constructed all the typical numerical instances of our abstract classes, such as `Floats, Integers, RationalFractions`, complex numbers, etc. with all the appropriate operations. This part of the work was rather trivial, it was mainly straightforward coding of mathematical formulae, something a little optimised, see for example the book of Knuth[4]. Still, it was interesting to see how the system protects itself from an attempt of making fractions of *anything/anything*, demanding that a specific algebraic context of *anything* be respected. There is almost nothing interesting in the definition of the data structure representing a fraction `num :% den`:

```
data DivisionRing a => Ratio a = a :% a
type Rat = Ratio Int    -- classics
```

apart from the fact that the type of the numerator and the denominator is *statically* restricted. The students did appreciate the fact that an attempt to operate on "fractions" composed of floats or strings did not result in some execution error, but such "fractions" could not be constructed, were statically rejected, being mathematically ill-defined structures. When we try to define the addition of two generic fractions declaring that the type `Ratio a` belongs to an additive group, we have to provide a detailed algebraic context for the type `a`:

```
instance (AddGroup a, Monoid a, DivisionRing a) =>
  AddGroup (Ratio a) where
```

```
addgroupZero = addgroupZero :% groupOne
(n1:%d1)+(n2:%d2) =
let g1 = gcd d1 d2 in
 if g1==ringOne
  then (n1*d2+d1*n2) :% (d1*d2)
  else let t = n1*(d2 'div' g1)+n2*(d1 'div' g1)
           g2 = gcd t g1
       in  (t 'div' g2) :%
           ((d1 'div' g1)*(d2 'div' g2))
```

The detailed code of the addition is irrelevant here, this is the optimized algorithm presented in the book of Knuth. What is interesting, is the genericity of the construction. The operation above will add *any* two fractions, not necessarily rational numbers. The definition of the addgroupZero is not cyclic, but recursive along the chain of types.

3.1 A Non-standard Example: the Peano-Church Arithmetic

Construction of "concrete", known, composite numbers, such as the rational fractions or complex numbers is interesting and useful, but does not teach anything new in the field of sophisticated functional programming. We have constructed and played with the ring of univariate polynomials, and the field of modular integers. We have then constructed the Galois field as the class of polynomials on the modular integers and the quotient field of the rational functions. Of course each such construction ended with a comprehensive set of examples. These packages which are quite short, are available from the author.

Paradoxically, a much more primitive model gives a more fruitful insight into the structure of functional computations. We have played with the Peano-Church numerals, a minimalistic construction of the integer arithmetic. The model is frequently used to present some applications of the abstract lambda calculus, but then one usually neglects the problems of polymorphic typing.

The model is based on the following premises. There are two abstract objects, a "dummy" constant *zero* which can be really anything, and an abstract endomorphism, the *successor*, which can be applied to objects of the same type as *zero*. The number N is represented by the *Church numeral* $\mathcal{N}$. This is a function which applies N times the *successor* to *zero*. We declare thus the types of the *successor* and of the Church numerals as:

```
type Succ a = a -> a
type Chnum a = Succ a -> a -> a
```

We will name the first Church numerals ch0, ch1 etc. The object ch0 is a function which does nothing to its argument *zero* and returns it: ch0 s z = z. The Church ch1 applies the *successor* once: ch1 s z = s z. After having introduced some combinatoric shortcuts, and exploiting the standard combinator (f . g) x = f (g x) it is easy to prove the validity of the following instance definitions:

```
instance AddGroup (Chnum a) where
  addgroupZero = flip const
  (n1 + n2) s = n1 s . n2 s
instance Monoid (Chnum a) where
  groupOne = id
  (*) = (.)
```

The arithmetic operations are based on the following observation: if one applies $n1$ times the *successor* to *zero*, and then more $n2$ times to the previous result, one gets the above definition for `(n1 + n2)`. The multiplication is even simpler, since the partial application `n s` is a function which applied n times the *successor* `s` to something, so `(n1 * n2) s z = n1 (n2 s) z`.

Some ambitious students ask the obvious question about the subtraction, and usually they cannot find themselves the solution. The problem is that even if the successor operation in the domain of Church numerals (which should not be confound with the abstract successor which is the *argument* of the Church numeral; the present author used intensely the coloured chalk, but it was not always fully appreciated...) is straightforward: `succ n s = n s . s`, the predecessor is not so easy to derive, and Church himself had some doubts.

We define a special successor which acts on pairs of objects according to the rule `sp s (x,any) = (s x,x)`. This successor applied N times to $(zero, zero)$ gives obviously something like $(N, N-1)$ and we may recover the predecessor, from which we construct the subtraction. Of course, the complexity of subtraction is simply horrible, but the evaluation of this complexity is an interesting didactic exercise:

```
pred n s z = pr where
  (_,pr) = n sp (z,z)
  sp (x,_) = (s x,x)
```

All this can be done without algebraic type classes, with specific operations names such as `add` or `mult` substituted for `(+)` and `(*)`. It is possible to define the exponentiation, whose simplicity is shocking:

```
n1^n2 = n2 n1
```

The explanation how it works takes some time, but the students have a splendid occasion to realise that the Set theory expression B^A for the set of all applications from A to B is *not* just a symbolic notation! Moreover, after three years of studies they have seen plenty of recursion examples, from factorial to the Ackerman function, but this was the first time they found the recursion hidden in a functional combinator without the classical recursive structure, terminal clause, etc., and yet conceptually rather simple.

As our primary concern here was to show the application of the functional combinators, and not the structuring of the polymorphism, this example was elaborated in CAML, not in Gofer. With the system classes there are some interesting problems. One *cannot* define abstract, polymorphic numerals represented by concrete objects, for example:

```
ch0 = addgroupZero :: Chnum a
```

because all top level definitions must be resolved, and the system complains that `addgroupZero` is still ambiguous. Of course we can restrict our domain to, say `Chnum String` where the *zero* is the empty string, and the *successor* simply concatenates `"*"` with its argument. But then we had other problems, which are addressed in the Conclusions.

4 Infinite Data Types

4.1 Lazy Manipulation of Power Series

All textbooks on lazy programming, and the packages distributed with Haskell present many lazy streams such as the list of all positive integers, the Fibonacci sequence, or all the primes constructed with the aid of the Eratosthenes sieve. The construction of cyclic data structures has been also discussed in the literature ([5]). We found thus a useful and a little less worked domain of lazy infinite power series.

An *effective and simple* coding of an algorithm dealing with such series is not entirely trivial. The algorithms are usually dominated by the administration of the truncation trivia. In fact, if one implements the algorithms discussed in [4], one sees mainly summing loops and the evaluation of the bounds of these loops, which becomes quite boring. In our approach an univariate power series $u_0 + u_1 x + u_2 x^2 + u_3 x^3 \ldots$ will be represented by the sequence:

```
u0 :> u1 :> u2 :> u3    ...
```

where `:>` is an infix, right associative constructor:

```
data Series a = a :> (Series a)
-- No termination clause!!
```

We could use normal lists, but we have introduced a specific datatype for the following reasons:

- The above definition precludes all attempts to construct explicit *finite* objects. This is a useful debugging aid and a challenge for those students whose first reaction is: "this perversion will never work!".
- We didn't want to overload normal lists with too specific algebraic structure. As we wanted to use the classical comprehension notation, we declared the constructor `:>` as an instance of the `Functor` class, so that we could use such functionals as `map`. We have also overloaded such functionals as `fold` and `zip`.

Our main idea was to show that infinite lazy lists treated as "normal" data, as "first class citizens" simplify enormously the algorithms. The class system served here uniquely for bookkeeping and syntax simplification.

Addition (or subtraction) of series is defined within the `AddGroup` class as `u + v = zipWith (+) u v` where in our case the series fusion might be defined as:

```
zipWith op (u0:>uq) (v0:>vq) = (u0 `op` v0) :> zipWith op uq vq
```

The multiplication is defined recursively. If the series $U = U_0 + x \cdot \overline{U}$, $V = V_0 + x \cdot \overline{V}$, then we find that $U \cdot V = U_0 \cdot V_0 + x \cdot (U \cdot \overline{V} + V_0 \cdot \overline{U})$. The Gofer translation is trivial. The head of the solution is given immediately, and in order to get the tail we need only the head of the recursive application. We see immediately that the series form an algebra: the definition above is placed in the class `Monoid`, as all internal multiplications, but its context demands that a series be also an instance of the `Module`. So we have a nice cross-referencing structure:

```
instance Monoid a => Module a (Series a) where
   x #* s = map (x *) s

instance (Monoid a, AddGroup (Series a),
          Module a (Series a)) =>
  Monoid (Series a) where
   u@(u0:>uq)*(v0:>vq) = u0*v0 :> (v0 #* uq) + vq*u
```

The division uses the same principle, if $W = U/V$, then $U = V \cdot W$, or $U_0 + x \cdot \overline{U} = V_0 \cdot W_0 + x \cdot (W_0 \cdot \overline{V} + V \cdot \overline{W}$, which after rearranging gives us:

```
instance (Group a) => Group (Series a) where
   (u0:>uq)/v@(v0:>vq) = w0 :> (uq - w0 #* vq)/v
                         where w0 = u0/v0
```

where we see that we don't even need a procedure to divide a series by a coefficient. This example shows once more some mild limitations of the system used. If the scalars of a given Module belong to a Group, and thus to a Field, the Module is a Linear Space. We can declare it explicitly together with the default division as:

```
class (Group a, Module a b) => LinSpace a b where
  (/#) :: b -> a -> b
  x /# y = recip y #* x
```

but nobody will deduce for us that a declared series belongs to a Linear Space, provided that the coefficients admit the division. We must do it by hand, although the instance declaration is empty – we use only the inferred defaults.

Other operations on power series are equally easy to code (compare with [4]). If $W = U^\alpha$, then after the differentiation of both sides we get $W' = \alpha \cdot U^{\alpha-1}U'$, or $W = \alpha \int W \cdot U'/U$. It is the lazy integration which gives sense to this propagating recursion:

```
integ :: (Group a, Ring a) => a -> (Series a) -> (Series a)
integ c0 u = c0 :> zipWith comp2 u intS
  where   comp2 x y = x / (fromInteger y)
          intS = intSeq 1 where intSeq n = n :> intSeq (n+1)
```

It takes some time to master this technique and to appreciate the fact that the definition: $W = \text{Const} + \int f(W)$ is not just a specification, or an equation, but an *algorithm*. It suffices to know the Const to be able to generate the next term and the whole series. The definition above is equivalent to the obvious identity for any series f: $f_n = \frac{f'_{n-1}}{n}$.

Other elementary functions are coded in the same way, for example $W = \exp(U) = \int W \cdot U'$, etc.

If the series fulfills a more complicated, non-linear equation, the lazy approach influences also the construction of the Newton algorithm. Again, instead of coding a loop broken by some convergence criteria, we construct shamelessly an infinite list of infinite iterants. For example, if $W = \sqrt{U}$, then we get $[W^{(0)}, W^{(1)}, \ldots, W^{(n)} \ldots]$, where $W^{(n+1)} = \frac{1}{2}\left(W^{(n)} + U/W^{(n)}\right)$. The construction of this stream is quite simple, the standard prelude function:

```
iterate f x = x : iterate f (f x)
```

does the job, for example to get a square root of y in the domain of rational series, we define:

```
sqRS y = iterate (\x->(1%2)#*(x + y/x))
                 (fromInteger 1) :: [RatSeries]
```

The convergence in this case means obviously the increasing number of correct terms. How to present the final answer to the "end user" of this algorithm? At this moment most students fall into their bad habits, and claim that we must give explicitly the number of terms wanted. So, we restate our religious credo: no, you should generate *one* stream, where the number of correct terms is *exactly* equal to the number of terms looked at. The final solution is based on the observation that the number of correct terms doubles with every iteration $W^{(n)}$. So, we neglect the zeroth (initial) iterant, extract one term from the first series, two terms from the second (after having skipped the first), next four terms from the third after having skipped three, then eight, etc. This exercise is a little impure, as it requires finite lists, their concatenation and reconversion into series, but it is still quite elegant and coded in two lines. The infinite list which convolutes all the stream of series `strS` is given by:

```
convit 1 (tail strS) where
  convit n (x:q) = take n (drop (n-1) x ++ convit (2*n) q
```

The composition and reversal of series is usually considered to be a serious programming challenge. But laziness is a virtue here, and the final codes are again three-liners. Let $U(x) = U_0 + U_1 x + U_2 x^2 + \ldots$, and $V(x) = V_1 x + V_2 x^2 + \ldots$, as usual. The free term must be absent from V. We want to find $W = U(V)$. The solution is nothing more than the ordinary, but infinite Horner scheme:

$$U(V) = U_0 + x(V_1 + V_2 x + \ldots) \times (U_1 + x(V_1 + V_2 x + \ldots) \times (U2 + x(\ldots))) \quad (1)$$

or, horribly enough

```
sercomp u (must_be_zero:>vq) = cmv u where
        cmv (u0:>uq) = u0:>(vq * cmv uq)
```

The reverse of a given series is the solution of the following problem. Given

$$z = t + V_2t^2 + V_3t^3 + \ldots, \qquad \text{find} \quad t = z + W_2z^2 + W_3z^3 + \ldots \tag{2}$$

The suggestion that might be offered to students is to reduce this problem to a composition of series. This is readily done if we note that an auxiliary series p defined by $t = z(1 - zp)$ fulfills the identity:

$$p = (1 - zp)^2 \left(V_2 + V_3z(1 - zp) + V_4z^2(1 - zp)^2 + \ldots\right) \tag{3}$$

```
serinverse (_zero :> _one :> vt) = t  where
   t = fromInteger 0 :> m
   m = fromInteger 1 :> negate (m*m) * sercomp vt t
```

The approach presented above is easily generalized; one might try to find the reciprocal, or solve polynomial equation in the series domain using the approach of Kung and Traub[6]. It is extremely easy to construct formal Padé approximants applying the continuous fraction expansion to the field of series, and reconstructing the rational form. It is possible also to apply lazy streams to the generation of graphs from their partition function[7], but this is a topic too distant from the aim of this conference.

4.2 Partition Generating Function

Another interesting example of the extrapolating recursion is the generation of the *number of partitions of a given integer N* the number of inequivalent non-negative integer solutions of the equation $\sum_{k=1}^{N} x_k = N$ (known also as the number of Ferrer graphs, or Young diagrams for a given N). For example:

$$5 = 4+1 = 3+2 = 3+1+1 = 2+2+1 = 2+1+1+1 = 1+1+1+1+1 \tag{4}$$

i.e. 7 solutions. The generating function for these numbers is well known, but not very easy to handle:

$$Z(x) = \prod_{n=1}^{\infty} \frac{1}{1 - x^n}. \tag{5}$$

Computing a finite approximation to it by standard iterative methods and getting the list
$[1, 1, 2, 3, 5, 7, 11, 15, 22, 30, 42, 56, 77, \ldots]$ is simply unwieldy. But we can rewrite this as an open recurrence:

$$Z(x) = Z_1(x), \qquad \text{where} \quad Z_m(x) = \frac{1}{1 - x^m} Z_{m+1}(x). \tag{6}$$

After rewriting Z_m as $Z_m(x) = Z_{m+1}(x) + x^n Z_m(x)$ and after introducing $B_m(x)$ such that $Z_m(x) = 1 + x^m B_m(x)$, we have the final receipt:

$$B_m(x) = 1 + x\left(B_{m+1} + x^{m-1} B_m(x)\right), \tag{7}$$

which gives us the following efficient program:

```
partgen :: IntSeries
partgen = one :> w one where
  one = ringOne
  w n = one :> w (n+1) + byxn ringZero (n-1) (w n)
```

where byxn is a function which multiplies a series by x^n (adds n zeros at the beginning).

5 Some Geometry

5.1 Concrete and Abstract Vectors

Defining vectors as triplets (x, y, z), or some tagged data structures is not very interesting, even if with our type class system it is nice to have a syntactically simple way of adding vectors or multiplying them by scalars. We have discussed already some issues related to the construction of the multi-parametric class `LinSpace a b`, where `a` is the type of scalars, and `b` – vectors.

We may play some time with vectors, define scalar `(*.)` and vector `(/\)` products, and even introduce some simplistic tensors. But our main purpose was to show how to use the functional formalism to generate some graphic object, and more specifically – some three-dimensional surfaces created by generalized sweeps or extrusions. We began by restricting our vectors to the type `Vec` which was just the type of floating triplets, and then we have shown how to extend the standard operations to functional objects which described parametrized displacements of vectors:

```
type Path = Float -> Vec    -- The Float means "time"
instance AddGroup Path where
  (f + g) s = f s + g s
  (f - g) s = f s - g s
instance (Module Float) Path where
  (a #* g) s = a #* g s
```

etc. A generalized sweep is an operation which consists in taking a curve, thus a `Path` object, and to transform it by a parametrized transformation, such as rotations or translations, or combinations thereof. It was thus natural to define:

```
type Vtransf = Vec -> Vec
instance Monoid Vtransf where
   groupOne = id
   f * g = f . g
```

Given a transformation `f` of a vector, it is extended to a path by a simple convolution: `trf f g s = f (g s)`, or `trf = (.)`. If this transformation is additionally parametrized, if the function acting upon a vector has a form `f t`, then the induced transformation of paths has a form:

```
transf f t g s = f t (g s)
```

which can be reduced to a combinator `trfpath f = (.) . f`, a form truly detested by most students. So, they are demanded to construct some simple paths, such as a horizontal unit circle, or any parametrized straight line $\mathbf{x} = \mathbf{x}_0 + \mathbf{u}t$:

```
circ ang = (cos ang, sin ang, 0.0)
strline x0 u t = x0 + t#*u
```

We pass then to transformations, for example a parametrized (by a scalar) translation along a given vector **u**:

```
transl u = (+) . (#* u)
```

or, if you prefer, `transl u t x = t#*u + x`. Note that we are doing everything not to use any concrete coordinate representation, when it is possible. So when we define a rotation, we do not care about its general matrix form, but try to reason relative to objects defining our "scene". This is coherent with our main didactic philosophy, that the functional abstractions should be based always on concretes. We define thus a rotation around a normalized axis **n** by an angle ϕ by splitting a vector into its parallel and perpendicular components, and performing the 2-dimensional rotation:

```
rotv n phi x = let parl = (n *. x) #* n
                   perp = x-parl;  tr3 = x/\n
               in parl + cos phi #* perp
                       - sin phi #* tr3
```

5.2 Construction of Parametric Surfaces

We are now ready for a more complex manipulation of vector objects, for example, if we wish to apply two parametrized transformations `f1` and then `f2` at the same time, such as a translation combined with a rotation, we combine it:

```
ovrlap f2 f1 t = f2 t . f1 t
```

Finally we construct our sweeping surface:

```
sweepsurf trf g s t = trf t g s
```

whose combinatoric form `sweepsurf = (flip .) . flip` should be reserved to amateurs.

The remaining task is to take some curve, to design our favourite transformation, and to produce the surface. But the standard versions of Gofer have no graphical output, so we seize the opportunity to convey to our students sometimes forgotten information that modern, multitasking, windowed environments encourage the cooperation between heterogeneous applications. We choose two lists – intervals of the parameters s and t: `intervT` and `intervS`, and we make a grid:

```
grid intervS intervT surf =
  [[surf s t | s <- intervS] | t <- intervT]
```

This grid is lazy, so it may be quite large. It is transformed then into a many-line output string, and piped into Gnuplot or any other drawing program, or saved in a file and processed off-line. For example if we rotate an oblique straight line around the z axis, and if we add to this rotation an oscillating variation of scale, we have to program the following:

```
scale phi v = (1.0 + 0.3*sin(8.0*phi))#*v
mytransf = trfpath (ovrlap scale (rotv (0.0,0.0,1.0)))
line t = strline (1.0,1.0,0.0) normalize (1.0,0.0,1.0) t
mysurf s = sweepsurf mytransf line s
```

and the result is presented on Fig. 1.

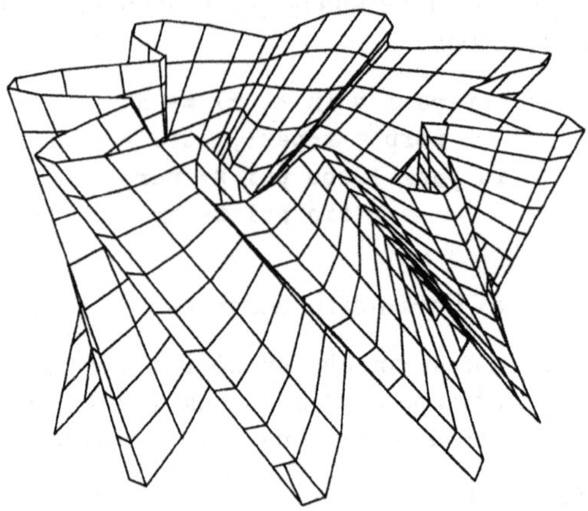

Fig. 1. An example of a parametric surface

Another type of sweep surfaces are *tubes*, constructed by a translation of the generating curve along a trajectory together with a rotation which keeps the original alignment of the generator with respect to the tangent vector of the trajectory. Of course we can compose this translation and rotation with some other transformations. The size of this paper makes it impossible to include more beautiful and very complicated 3D drawings produced by very short programs.

This exercise touches the problem of computing the tangent vector to a path, and permits to develop another branch of our functional mathematics – the construction of differential structures, which cannot be discussed here.

6 Conclusions

We tried to demonstrate that modern polymorphic functional languages may be sensibly used to model and implement quite abstract mathematical structures in a way which is transparent enough to be accepted by mathematically oriented undergraduate students.

Programs in functional languages such as Haskell or Miranda, thanks to their lack of syntactic overhead are coded fast. Higher order functions and lazy evaluation are capable to produce little programming miracles. The inheritance and genericity offered by Haskell seem to be more adequate for that kind of mathematical programming than the approaches based on object-oriented languages, although we would like very much to compare them with, say, the C++ or CLOS protagonists.

We found that the type classes system may be used to define statically the hierarchy of mathematical domains, but that there are some flaws therein. We missed some meta-class system which would permit, for example, the simultaneous construction of several Galois fields parametrized by different characteristics and order; we had problems with the Church numerals: if their polymorphic type is restricted, one cannot attribute any sensible type to the exponentiation operator, as the objects are self-applicable. We had problems with ambiguous types while trying to define metric (or normed) vector spaces: the type of a perfectly reasonable function which normalized a vector dividing it by its norm, did not fit into the class system.

Such observations are addressed rather to readers interested in the programming tool building, and not only in the pedagogical process, but they seem important. The typed, lazy programming languages are excellent tools to teach the constructive approach to mathematics. But the type classes are *not* mathematical domains. Our plans for the future include the construction of a different class system, perhaps better adapted to the construction of abstract mathematics.

References

1. D. Guntz, M. Monagan, *Introduction to Gauss*, Sigsam Bulletin **28**, no. 2, (1994), pp 3 – 19.
2. P. Hudak, S. Peyton Jones, P. Wadler et al., *Report on the programming language Haskell, (Version 1.3)*, Technical report Yale University/Glasgow University, (1995).
3. Mark P. Jones, *Gofer, Functional Programming Environment*, (1991).
4. Donald E. Knuth, *The Art of Computer Programming, Vol 2 / Seminumerical Algorithms*, Addison-Wesley, Reading, (1981).
5. Lloyd Allison, *Circular Programs and Self-referential Structures*, Software — Practice and Experience, Vol. **19**(2), (1989), pp. 99 – 109.

6. H. T. Kung, J. F. Traub, JACM **25** (1978), pp. 245–260.
7. Jerzy Karczmarczuk, *Lazy Functional Programming and Manipulation of Perturbation Series*, Proc. III International Workshop on Software Engineering for High Energy Physics, (1993), pp. 571–581.

Explaining algebraic theory with functional programs

Jeroen Fokker

Dept. of Computer Science, Utrecht University
P.O.Box 80.089, 3508 TB Utrecht, The Netherlands
jeroen@cs.ruu.nl, http://www.cs.ruu.nl/people/jeroen

Abstract. A hierarchy of six important structures from abstract algebra (groups, rings, fields etc.) is introduced as Gofer class definitions and laws about them. Many instance declarations are provided, explaining the algebraic construction of integers, quotients, adding i, function spaces, polynomials, and matrices. The definitions include generalized implementations of polynomial division and matrix inversion. Monadic parsers are provided for all constructs discussed. As an application, a one-line program is given for calculating the eigenvalue equation of a matrix.

1 Introduction

Mathematicians are said to have recognized the importance of software reuse long before the advent of computers. Large 'libraries' of theorems are available, which can be applied to prove new theorems. A generally accepted quality criterion for mathematical theorems is that applicability should be limited by as few constraints as possible. The quest for simple, universally applicable theorems resembles the construction of general purpose software libraries.

In programming languages, a lot of notations and concepts were borrowed from mathematics: from the use of arithmetic expressions in Fortran, through the notions of sums and products of datatypes in Algol and C, to the exploitation of category theory to build graphical user interfaces in Haskell. But, being an engineering discipline, programming has developed its own notations for managing the complexity of large programs. Evolution has led us from a simple notion of modules in Simula and Modula to class hierarchies and inheritance in today's object oriented languages. Typed functional programming languages contributed the idea of polymorphic data types.

It is time that programming pays back mathematics with some of these notations for structuring information. The concept of classes in Haskell and Gofer for overloading operators on polymorphic, parameterized data structures is very suitable for making explicit the assumptions for various concepts and algorithms in an algebra course.

In this article we introduce the notions of (among others) group, ring and field as being 'classes' in section 2. Examples of these classes (integers, polynomials etc.)

are constructed as algebraic (!) data types, and made instance of the applicable classes in section 3. As an added benefit, the manipulation of sequences (e.g. in the case of polynomials and matrices) is eased by the use of well known standard functions on lists, available in the programming language [BW88, Jon94, Fok92]. In section 4, conversion to and from string representation is defined for the examples in section 3. Applications of the definitions are given in section 5, both in the form of new types as a special case, and in the form of concrete calculations.

Most of the examples were taken from a textbook on linear algebra [Lan70]. We believe that using a notation which appeals to the programmer's intuition eases the comprehension of abstract ideas, especially in the case of computer science students. In fact, the material presented in this paper is covered, with some more explanation, as a case study in the first year course on functional programming for computer science students in Utrecht. Available time (10 weeks for the whole course, with no former knowledge of programming) and scope of that course prohibit us to treat all details in the course, but it should be enough to convince the students that mathematical algorithms can be presented quite elegantly using a functional programming language.

All courses on functional programming in Utrecht are summarized in appendix A. The code that is described in this article is avialable from the WWW address given below the title.

2 Classes

2.1 The algebraic hierarchy

One of the simplest algebraic structures one can imagine is that of a *monoid*. A set forms a monoid if it is closed under an associative binary operator, that has a neutral element. Using a class definition we can declare the types of the operator and its neutral element:

```
class Eq a => Monoid a  where
      (<+>)    :: a->a->a
      zzero    :: a
```

The laws that the `<+>` operator and the `zzero` constant have to obey are:

```
--      x <+> (y<+>z)   ==  (x<+>y) <+> z
--      zzero <+> y     ==  y
--      x <+> zzero     ==  x
```

The laws are written in a comment to the class definition. Gofer, Haskell and most other functional languages do not allow laws to be defined in the language. This is a pity, because even if the implementation wouldn't check the validity of the laws, at least they could be type checked.

Because in the laws the notion of equality is used, we have made the `Monoid` class a subclass of `Eq`, that is all instances of `Monoid` must also be instance of `Eq`, by providing a definition for the equality operator `==`. This is not strictly necessary, because it might be argued that the equality in the laws is only needed on a meta-level.

The next class in the algebraic hierarchy is a *group*. Instances of this class provide a function neg, which for each value gives its inverse under addition:

```
class Monoid a => Group a where
      neg      :: a->a
--    x <+> neg x  ==  zzero
--    neg x <+> x  ==  zzero
--    x <+> y      ==  y <+> x
```

We also specified that in a group, addition should be commutative. Some authors do not include this law, and speak of a 'commutative' or 'Abelian' group when commutativity holds. We do not introduce a separate class here, as no new operators are introduced.

If a type supports an associative operator which distributes over addition, it is said to form a *rng*. Usually, this operator is called 'multiplication':

```
class Group a => Rng a where
      (<*>)    :: a->a->a
--    x <*> (y<*>z)  ==  (x<*>y) <*> z
--    x <*> (y<+>z)  ==  x<*>y <+> x<*>z
--    (x<+>y) <*> z  ==  x<*>z <+> y<*>z
```

The multiplication operator does not need to have a neutral element. If it has, the structure is called a *ring*:

```
class Rng a => Ring a where
      one      :: a
--    one <*> x  == x
--    x <*> one  == x
```

The word *rng* is chosen for the previous class because it is a ring which lacks an unity – symbolized by dropping the letter 'i'.

If it is possible to divide with remainder, a structure is called an *Euclidean space.* The remainder of a division should be less than the denominator in some sense. In which sense 'being smaller' should be understood, is specified by the degree function:

```
class Ring a => Euclid a where
      degree  :: a->Int
      divide  :: a->a->a
      modulo  :: a->a->a
      x `modulo` y  |  y/=zzero  =  x <+> neg((x `divide` y) <*> y)
--    y/=zzero  |  degree (x `modulo` y) < degree y
--                 || x `modulo` y == zzero
--    y/=zzero  |  degree x <= degree (x<*>y)
```

One of the laws for Euclidian spaces, which states that multiplying the quotient by the denominator again and adding the remainder yields the numerator, is given as a default definition for modulo in the class definition.

The richest structure in the hierarchy is a *field.* In a field, every element but zero is required to have an exact inverse under multiplication:

```
class Ring a => Field a where
      inv      :: a->a
--    x/=zzero | x <*> inv x == one
```

The definition of the Field class is independent from the Euclid class. Nevertheless, the classes introduced (Monoid, Group, Rng, Ring, Euclid and Field) can be thought of as a linear hierarchy, as every field can be made into an Euclidean space in a trivial way:

```
instance  Field a => Euclid a  where
   degree x      =  0
   x `divide` y =  x <*> inv y
```

2.2 Derived operators

Operators that are defined in terms of the operators in the class hierarchy are automatically overloaded for instances of the classes involved. We will give an example of this for all six classes in the hierarchy.

The well known sum function, which adds all element of a list starting with zero, can be generalized to an arbitrary Monoid:

```
summ :: Monoid a => [a] -> a
summ = foldr (<+>) zzero
```

In a group, we can use the notion of subtraction, which is defined as adding the negation:

```
(<->) :: Group a => a->a->a
x <-> y = x <+> neg y
```

When a multiplication is available (i.e., in a Rng), the square of a value is that value multiplied by itself:

```
square :: Rng a => a->a
square x = x <*> x
```

In a ring with unity, raising a value to a natural power can be defined. The type Nat of naturla numbers will be defined in section 3.2.

```
(<^>) :: Ring a => a -> Nat -> a
x <^> Zer      = one
x <^> Suc n    = x <*>  x <^> n
```

The Euclidean algorithm for determining the greatest common divisor can be applied not only to integers, but also to arbitrary instances of an Euclidean space:

```
gcDiv  ::  Euclid a => a->a->a
gcDiv x y  |  degree y<=0 =  x
           |  otherwise   =  gcDiv y (x `modulo` y)
```

Finally, in a field we can define a shorthand notation for division:

```
(</>) :: Field a => a->a->a
x </> y = x <*> inv y
```

Useful priorities for all operators defined are given by:

```
infixl 8  <^>
infix  7  <*>, </>
infix  7  `divide`, `modulo`, `gcDiv`
infixl 6  <+>, <->
```

2.3 Additional classes

In section 3 a lot of types will be made instance of the six classes in the hierarchy. For the easy manipulation of values, we will use a string representation for most of them. Parse and unparse functions are provided by making a type instance of Repr:

```
class Repr a  where
      parse  :: Parser a
      unpars :: a -> ShowS
```

Here, Parser is the type of backtracking parsers:

```
type Parser a = String -> [(a,String)]
```

and ShowS is the type of functions that prepend some string to their argument:

```
type ShowS = String -> String
```

Finally, a class Finite will be used in section 3.6. Instances are finite types of which all members can be enumerated in a list:

```
class Finite a  where
      members :: [a]
```

3 Instances

3.1 Primitives

The numeric built-in type Int can be made a Group and a Ring in a trivial way, by using the built-in addition and multiplication functions.

```
instance Monoid Int where
   zzero  = 0
   (<+>)  = (+)
instance Group Int where
   neg    = negate
instance Rng Int where
   (<*>)  = (*)
instance Ring Int where
   one    = 1
```

Similarly, the type Float can be made a Group and a Ring. The integers form an Euclidean space. The degree function is taken to be the absolute value, so that degree (x 'modulo' y) < degree y as required, even if y is negative.

```
instance Euclid Int where
   degree  =  abs
   divide  =  div
   modulo  =  mod
```

Floating point values, as an approximation of real numbers, form a field:

```
instance  Field Float  where
   inv    =  (1.0/)
```

By the generic definition of section 2.2, they also form an Euclidean space in a trivial way.

3.2 Natural numbers

Without using built-in features, natural numbers can be defined as being either zero or the successor of another natural number.

```
data Nat = Zer
         | Suc Nat
```

The Peano axioms for the natural numbers (no confusion, ability to do induction) are implicit in the semantics of a `data` declaration. We can abstract from induction over natural numbers by a 'fold' over natural numbers:

```
foldNat :: a -> (a->a) -> Nat -> a
foldNat e f Zer     = e
foldNat e f (Suc x) = f (foldNat e f x)
```

Equality and ordering of natural numbers is expressed by:

```
instance  Eq Nat  where
   Zer   == Zer    =  True
   Suc x == Suc y  =  x==y
   _     == _      =  False
instance  Ord Nat  where
   Zer   <= _      =  True
   Suc _ <= Zer    =  False
   Suc x <= Suc y  =  x <= y
```

Natural numbers are enumerable. Also, they form a monoid, because an associative addition operator with zero as identity can be defined.

```
instance  Enum Nat  where
   enumFrom n   =  n : enumFrom (Suc n)
instance  Monoid Nat  where
   zzero        =  Zer
   Zer   <+> y  =  y
   Suc x <+> y  =  Suc (x<+>y)
```

Natural numbers do not form a group, because the set is not closed under negation. The function `natMin` is a partial minus function, using the `Maybe` datatype to indicate failure.

```
data Maybe a = No | Yes a

natMin :: Nat -> Nat -> Maybe Nat
natMin x       Zer     =  Yes x
natMin Zer     _       =  No
natMin (Suc x) (Suc y) =  natMin x y
```

A total multiplication function can be defined. Nevertheless, natural numbers do not form a ring, as this requires that they form a group, too. Similarly, a division function can be defined, but this does not make the natural numbers an Euclidean space.

```
natMul :: Nat -> Nat -> Nat
natMul Zer     _  =  Zer
natMul (Suc x) y  =  y <+> natMul x y

natDiv :: Nat -> Nat -> Nat
natDiv x y  = case natMin x y
                of No    -> Zer
                   Yes d -> Suc (natDiv d y)
```

3.3 Integers

We will define integers as either negative or positive natural numbers. This gives us two representations for zero. For symmetry, we add a third representation for zero explicitly, and assume that **Neg** and **Pos** are never applied to the natural number **Zer**.

```
data Integ = Neg Nat
           | Zero
           | Pos Nat
```

Integers can be compared and ordered:

```
instance  Eq Integ  where
   Neg x == Neg y   =  x==y
   Zero  == Zero    =  True
   Pos x == Pos y   =  x==y
   _     == _       =  False
instance  Ord Integ  where
   Neg x <= Neg y   =  x>=y
   Neg _ <= _       =  True
   Zero  <= Neg _   =  False
   Zero  <= _       =  True
   Pos x <= Pos y   =  x<=y
   Pos _ <= _       =  False
```

For addition of integers with the same sign, addition of the natural number after the sign can be used. If the signs differ, we make use of the fact that the sign constructors are applied to non-zero natural numbers only.

```
instance  Monoid Integ  where
   zzero            =  Zero
   Zero  <+> y      =  y
   Neg x <+> Neg y  =  Neg (x<+>y)
   Pos x <+> Pos y  =  Pos (x<+>y)
   Neg (Suc Zer) <+> Pos (Suc Zer)  =  Zero
   Neg (Suc Zer) <+> Pos (Suc y)    =  Pos y
   Neg (Suc x)   <+> Pos (Suc Zer)  =  Neg x
   Neg (Suc x)   <+> Pos (Suc y)    =  Neg x <+> Pos y
   x             <+> y              =  y <+> x
```

Integers are a group, with negation just changing the sign. In the definition of multiplication, multiplication of natural numbers is augmented with the sign rule. Once we have defined a one, we can define enumeration as repeatedly adding one.

```
instance  Group Integ  where
   neg Zero         =  Zero
   neg (Neg x)      =  Pos x
   neg (Pos x)      =  Neg x
instance  Rng Integ  where
   Zero  <*> y      =  y
   Neg x <*> Neg y  =  Pos (natMul x y)
   Pos x <*> Pos y  =  Pos (natMul x y)
   Neg x <*> Pos y  =  Neg (natMul x y)
```

```
   x      <*> y       =  y <*> x
instance  Ring Integ  where
   one                =  Pos (Suc Zer)
instance  Enum Integ  where
   enumFrom n         =  n : enumFrom (n<+>one)
```

Finally, integers form an Euclidean space. Integer division is natural division augmented with a sign rule; the degree function is the absolute value, defined by a fold over the natural number following the sign. The modulo function was already defined with a default definition in section 2.

```
instance  Euclid Integ  where
   degree Zero     =  0
   degree (Pos n)  =  foldNat 0 (+1) n
   degree (Neg n)  =  foldNat 0 (+1) n
   divide Zero     y         =  Zero
   divide (Pos x) (Pos y)    =  Pos (natDiv x y)
   divide (Pos x) (Neg y)    =  Neg (natDiv x y)
   divide (Neg x) (Pos y)    =  Neg (natDiv x y)
   divide (Neg x) (Neg y)    =  Pos (natDiv x y)
```

3.4 Quotients

From the integers, rational numbers can be constructed by taking pairs modulo an equivalence relation. The rational numbers form a field. A generalization of this is the construction of the quotient field over an arbitrary ring a.

```
data Quot a = Quot (a,a)
```

We will assume that the second part of the tuples are not zero. Two quotients are equivalent, and thus denote the same fraction, if cross multiplication yields equal results:

```
instance Rng a => Eq (Quot a) where
   Quot (a,b) == Quot (c,d)   =   a<*>d == c<*>b
```

For being able to multiply, we need the base type to be a ring, although this ring needs not to have a 'one'. If the base ring can be ordered, then so can be quotients:

```
instance (Ord a,Rng a) => Ord (Quot a) where
   Quot (a,b) <= Quot (c,d)   =   a<*>d <= c<*>b
```

An associative addition can be defined for quotients, by making a common denominator:

```
instance Ring a => Monoid (Quot a) where
   zzero = Quot (zzero, one)
   Quot (a,b) <+> Quot (c,d)   =   Quot (a<*>d <+> c<*>b, b<*>d)
```

For the zero element, we need a non-zero denominator. The `one` of the base ring is the only element guaranteed to be non-zero, so we need the base ring to have a unit for making quotients to be a monoid. The type information given is sufficient to deduce that by `zzero`, `one`, `<+>` and `<*>` on the right hand side of the definitions, the operations of the base ring are denoted.

Finally, quotients can easily be made into a ring and a field:

```
instance Ring a => Rng (Quot a) where
   Quot (a,b) <*> Quot (c,d)  =  Quot (a<*>c, b<*>d)
instance Ring a => Ring (Quot a) where
   one                        =  Quot (one, one)
instance Ring a => Field (Quot a) where
   inv (Quot (a,b))           =  Quot (b,a)
```

3.5 Addition of i

Complex numbers can be constructed from real numbers by considering formal sums $a + b * i$, where i has the property $i * i = -1$. An generalization of this are formal sums $a + b * i$ over an arbitrary base type. The closure of adding i can be made to belong to the same class (monoid, group, rng, ring or field) as the base type. This is formalized in the following instance declarations, in which the rules for manipulating complex numbers can be recognized.

```
data Iadd a = Iadd (a,a)

instance Eq a => Eq (Iadd a) where
   Iadd (a,b) == Iadd (c,d)  =  a==c && b==d
instance Monoid a => Monoid (Iadd a) where
   zzero                     =  Iadd (zzero, zzero)
   Iadd (a,b) <+> Iadd (c,d) =  Iadd (a<+>c, b<+>d)
instance Group a => Group (Iadd a) where
   neg (Iadd (a,b))          =  Iadd (neg a, neg b)
instance Rng a => Rng (Iadd a) where
   Iadd (a,b) <*> Iadd (c,d) =  Iadd (a<*>c <-> b<*>d, a<*>d <+> b<*>c)
instance Ring a => Ring (Iadd a) where
   one                       =  Iadd (one, zzero)
instance Field a => Field (Iadd a) where
   inv (Iadd (c,d))          =  Iadd (c</>e, neg d</>e)
                          where  e =  square c <+> square d
```

3.6 Function spaces

Function spaces form a monoid, with function composition as 'addition' and the identity function as 'zero'.

```
instance  Monoid  (a->a)  where
   zzero = id
   (<+>) = (.)
```

Function spaces in general do not form a group, as negation should be function inversion. For some special cases, inversion can be defined. A well-known example is invertible real functions, of which the inverse can be computed by Newton's method (adapted here from Bird and Wadler [BW88]):

```
instance  Group (Float->Float)  where
   neg g a = until satisfied improve 1.0
      where satisfied b  =  f b ~= 0.0
            improve b    =  b - f b / f' b
```

```
f x     =  g x - a
a~=b    =  a-b<h  &&  b-a<h
f' x    =  (f (x+h) - f x) / h
h       =  0.00001
```

Also, functions on a finite domain are invertible, by trying all elements, and thus form a group:

```
instance  (Eq a,Finite a) => Group (a->a)  where
   neg g a = head [ x | x<-members, g x==a ]
```

To provide some finite types, we define some instances of the `Finite` class: booleans, characters, pairs of finite types, and function spaces between finite types:

```
instance  Finite Bool  where
   members  =  [False, True]
instance  Finite Char  where
   members  =  map chr [0..127]
instance  (Finite a, Finite b) => Finite (a,b)  where
   members  =  [ (x,y) | x<-members, y<-members ]
instance  (Eq a, Finite a, Finite b) => Finite (a->b)  where
   members  =  funspace members members
funspace :: Eq a => [a] -> [b] -> [a->b]
funspace [x] ys      =  map const ys
funspace (x:xs) ys   =  [ \p->if p==x then y else f p
                        | y <- ys
                        , f <- funspace xs ys
                        ]
```

As a condition for forming a monoid and group, we need a type to be instance of `Eq`. For function spaces this is a problem: it can only be done constructively for finite domains, using the Leibnitz property that functions are equal if they are equal for all arguments:

```
instance  (Finite a, Eq b) => Eq (a->b)  where
   f == g  =  and [ f x==g x | x<-members ]
```

Because these definitions are applied recursively, we are now capable of e.g. verifying De Morgan's law by evaluating

```
(\x y -> not(x&&y)) == (\x y->not x|| not y)
```

Equality is only required for the monoid and group classes for being able to formulate laws; it is not used in computations. If we are only interested in computing, and not in mechanically checking laws, we may give a dummy implementation for function equality.

3.7 Matrices

Matrices are blocks of values. Often, the values of a matrix are taken to be real or complex numbers, but here we will allow for matrices over an arbitrary type. Depending on the class of the base type, matrices can be made an instance of the same class. Matrices are represented as lists of their rows:

```
data Matrix a  =  Mat [[a]]
```

We will assume some constraints on the size of matrices. Firstly, all rows should have the same length. In the class `Monoid`, for addition of two matrices, they should have the same size. In the class `Ring`, for multiplication of matrices, the number of rows of the first operand should be equal to the number of columns of the second. In the class `Field`, for inverting matrices, we consider only square invertible matrices.

For some operations on matrices, a function is applied to all its elements. For this, we make auxiliary functions which are a 2-dimensional analogue to `map` and `zipWith`:

```
mapp     :: (a->b)    -> [[a]] -> [[b]]
zippWith :: (a->b->c) -> [[a]] -> [[b]] -> [[c]]
mapp     =  map     . map
zippWith =  zipWith . zipWith

pointwise1 f  (Mat xss)           = Mat (mapp f xss)
pointwise2 op (Mat xss) (Mat yss) = Mat (zippWith op xss yss)
```

For example, scaling a matrix by a constant value, the multiplication is applied to all its elements, and equality of matrices is the conjunction of equality of all respective elements:

```
scalemat :: Rng a => a -> Matrix a -> Matrix a
scalemat x  = pointwise1 (x<*>)
instance  Eq a => Eq (Matrix a)  where
    Mat xss == Mat yss  =  all and (zippWith (==) xss yss)
```

Matrices can be added by adding their elements pointwise. As a zero element, we take an infinite matrix of zeroes, which can be added or compared to a matrix of arbitrary size:

```
instance Monoid a => Monoid (Matrix a) where
   zzero = Mat (repeat (repeat zzero))
   (<+>) = pointwise2 (<+>)
instance Group a => Group (Matrix a) where
   neg   = pointwise1 neg
```

In textbooks, multiplication of matrices is often described using a notation with indices. Indices are however seldomly necessary in a functional program, and indeed matrix multiplication can be described using standard list operations:

```
instance Rng a => Rng (Matrix a) where
   Mat xss <*> Mat yss  =  Mat (map f xss)
                     where  f a = map (inprod a) (transpose yss)
                            inprod xs ys = summ (zipWith (<*>) xs ys)
```

If `transpose` were not defined in the prelude, here is a nice definition:

```
transpose  =  foldr (zipWith (:)) (repeat [])
```

The unit matrix is a matrix with ones on its diagonal and zeroes elsewhere.

$$\begin{pmatrix} 1 & 0 & 0 & 0 & \cdots \\ 0 & 1 & 0 & 0 & \\ 0 & 0 & 1 & 0 & \\ 0 & 0 & 0 & 1 & \\ \vdots & & & & \ddots \end{pmatrix}$$

As in the case of the zero matrix, we make it an infinite matrix, which will size down to the right size when multiplied by another matrix:

```
instance Ring a => Ring (Matrix a) where
   one  =  Mat (iterate (zzero:) (one:repeat zzero))
```

An important notion for matrices is its *determinant*, which can be computed if the base type is a ring. The determinant can be computed recursively by multiplying the elements of the first row with sub-matrices that are obtained by deleting the first row and the corresponding column, and adding the products with alternating signs. For example, in the 3×3 case:

$$\det\begin{pmatrix} a & b & c \\ d & e & f \\ g & h & i \end{pmatrix} = \begin{array}{l} +a \times \det\begin{pmatrix} e & f \\ h & i \end{pmatrix} \\ -b \times \det\begin{pmatrix} d & f \\ g & i \end{pmatrix} \\ +c \times \det\begin{pmatrix} d & e \\ g & h \end{pmatrix} \end{array}$$

This is formalized in the following definition:

```
det  ::  Ring a  =>  Matrix a -> a
det (Mat [[x]])    =  x
det (Mat (xs:xss)) =  ( altsum
                      . zipWith (<*>) xs
                      . map (det.Mat)
                      . gaps
                      . transpose
                      ) xss
```

The auxiliary function gaps deletes one element from a list in all possible ways, and the function `altsum` calculates a sum with alternating signs:

```
gaps          ::  [a] -> [[a]]
gaps []        =  [ ]
gaps (x:xs)    =  xs  :  map (x:) (gaps xs)

altlist  :: Ring a  => [a]
altlist  =  one : neg one : altlist
altsum   :: Ring a  =>  [a] -> a
altsum   =  summ . zipWith (<*>) altlist
```

For square matrices with non-zero determinant, an inverse can be calculated by Cramer's rule. For calculating an element of the inverse matrix, its row and column should be deleted form the transpose of the original matrix, its determinant calculated, and divided by the determinant of the entire original matrix. Again, the signs should be taken alternatingly. See figure 1 for a 3×3 example. It is easier to express this rather awkward description using a function composition:

$$\operatorname{inv}\begin{pmatrix} a & b & c \\ d & e & f \\ g & h & i \end{pmatrix} = \frac{\begin{pmatrix} +\det\begin{pmatrix} \cancel{a} & \cancel{d} & \cancel{g} \\ \cancel{b} & e & h \\ \cancel{c} & f & i \end{pmatrix} & -\det\begin{pmatrix} \cancel{a} & d & g \\ \cancel{b} & \cancel{e} & \cancel{h} \\ \cancel{c} & f & i \end{pmatrix} & +\det\begin{pmatrix} \cancel{a} & d & g \\ \cancel{b} & e & h \\ \cancel{c} & \cancel{f} & \cancel{i} \end{pmatrix} \\ -\det\begin{pmatrix} \cancel{a} & \cancel{d} & \cancel{g} \\ b & \cancel{e} & h \\ c & \cancel{f} & i \end{pmatrix} & +\det\begin{pmatrix} a & \cancel{d} & g \\ \cancel{b} & \cancel{e} & \cancel{h} \\ c & \cancel{f} & i \end{pmatrix} & -\det\begin{pmatrix} a & \cancel{d} & g \\ b & \cancel{e} & h \\ \cancel{c} & \cancel{f} & \cancel{i} \end{pmatrix} \\ +\det\begin{pmatrix} \cancel{a} & \cancel{d} & \cancel{g} \\ b & e & \cancel{h} \\ c & f & \cancel{i} \end{pmatrix} & -\det\begin{pmatrix} a & d & \cancel{g} \\ \cancel{b} & \cancel{e} & \cancel{h} \\ c & f & \cancel{i} \end{pmatrix} & +\det\begin{pmatrix} a & d & \cancel{g} \\ b & e & \cancel{h} \\ \cancel{c} & \cancel{f} & \cancel{i} \end{pmatrix} \end{pmatrix}}{\det\begin{pmatrix} a & b & c \\ d & e & f \\ g & h & i \end{pmatrix}}$$

Fig. 1. Calculating the inverse of a matrix

```
instance  Field a => Field (Matrix a)  where
   inv m@(Mat xss)  =  ( Mat
                       . zippWith (<*>) altmat
                       . mapp ((</>(det m)).det.Mat)
                       . map (gaps.transpose)
                       . gaps
                       . transpose
                       ) xss
altmat   :: Ring a  => [[a]]
altmat   =  iterate tail altlist
```

The function `map(gaps.transpose).gaps` generates a matrix of matrices, where rows and columns are left out in all possible ways.

3.8 Polynomials

Polynomials are formal finite sums of terms, where each term is a value multiplied with a variable raised to a natural power. We will represent polynomials by lists of terms, where each term is a pair of a coefficient and an exponent:

```
type Term a  =  (a,Int)
data Poly a  =  Poly [Term a]
```

some auxiliary functions manipulate terms and simple polynomials:

```
coef    :: Term a -> a
expo    :: Term a -> Int
psingle :: a -> Int -> Poly a
pconst  :: a -> Poly a
hdcoef  :: Poly a -> a
coef              =  fst
expo              =  snd
psingle a n       =  Poly [(a,n)]
pconst  a         =  psingle a 0
hdcoef (Poly xs)  =  coef (head xs)
```

We will assume that polynomials are always in *normal form*, that is: no terms have zero coefficient, all exponents are unique, and terms are sorted with decreasing exponent. The following function brings a polynomial in normal form. It uses addition of coefficients, and thus requires the coefficients to form a monoid:

```
pnorm :: Monoid a => [Term a] -> [Term a]
pnorm =  filter ((/=zzero).coef) . puniq . sort
  where sort           = foldr ins []
        ins x []       = [x]
        ins x (y:ys)   | expo x > expo y   = x:y:ys
                       | otherwise         = y:ins x ys
        puniq []       = []
        puniq [t]      = [t]
        puniq (x@(a,n):xs@((b,m):ys))
                       | n==m        =  puniq ((a<+>b,n):ys)
                       | otherwise   =  x : puniq xs
```

Terms can be compared, negated and multiplied, provided that the coefficients can be. Terms can not be added, however, and thus don't form a monoid.

```
teq  ::      Eq a => Term a -> Term a -> Bool
teq (a,n) (b,m ) =  n==m && a==b
tneg ::   Group a => Term a -> Term a
tneg (a,n)       =  (neg a, n)
tmul ::     Rng a => Term a -> Term a -> Term a
tmul (a,n) (b,m) =  (a<*>b, n+m)
```

Polynomials can be made instance of the same classes (eq, monoid, group, rng and ring) as their base type. Addition is done by concatenating all terms an normalizing the result, negation is done termwise, and multiplication is done by taking the cross product of all terms:

```
instance Eq a => Eq (Poly a) where
   Poly xs == Poly ys  =  length xs==length ys && and(zipWith teq xs ys)
instance Monoid a => Monoid (Poly a) where
   zzero               =  Poly []
   Poly xs <+> Poly ys =  Poly (pnorm (xs++ys))
instance Group a => Group (Poly a) where
   neg (Poly xs)       =  Poly (map tneg xs)
instance Rng a => Rng (Poly a) where
   Poly xs <*> Poly ys =  Poly (pnorm [ tmul x y | x<-xs, y<-ys])
instance Ring a => Ring (Poly a) where
   one                 =  pconst one
```

A more interesting instance is that polynomials can be made an Euclidean space, that is division and remainder can be defined, provided that the base type is a field. As 'degree' function we can take the highest exponent, and -1 for the zero polynomial. An example is the division:

$$\frac{2x^4 + 5x^3 + 4x^2 - 3x + 2}{x^2 + x + 1}$$

The quotient of this division $2x^2 + 3x - 1$, the remainder is $-5x + 3$. It can be calculated by a kind of 'long division':

$$
\begin{array}{l}
x^2{+}x{+}1/2x^4{+}5x^3{+}4x^2{-}3x{+}2\backslash 2x^2{+}3x{-}1 \\
\qquad\qquad \underline{2x^4{+}2x^3{+}2x^2} \\
\qquad\qquad\qquad 3x^3{+}2x^2{-}3x \\
\qquad\qquad\qquad \underline{3x^3{+}3x^2{+}3x} \\
\qquad\qquad\qquad\qquad -x^2{-}6x{+}2 \\
\qquad\qquad\qquad\qquad \underline{-x^2\ {-}x{-}1} \\
\qquad\qquad\qquad\qquad\qquad -5x{+}3
\end{array}
$$

To start with, the head term of the numerator ($2x^4$) and the head term of the denominator (x^2) are inspected. They are divided (this is why the base type needs to be a field), which results in the first term of the quotient ($2x^2$). This term is multiplied with the denominator (x^2+x+1). The product ($2x^4+2x^3+2x^2$) is subtracted from the numerator, and thus the term with the highest exponent ($2x^4$) vanishes. The process is repeated with the remaining part of the numerator ($3x^3+2x^2-3x+2$), which yields the second term of the quotient ($3x$). The recursion stops when the remaining numerator has lower degree than the denominator, which is required for the remainder. The algorithm is formalized in:

```
instance Field a => Euclid (Poly a) where
   degree (Poly [])           =  -1
   degree (Poly xs)           =  expo (head xs)
   f 'divide' g  | n<m        =  zzero
                 | otherwise  =  (f <-> h<*>g) 'divide' g <+> h
                        where    n = degree f
                                 m = degree g
                                 h = psingle (hdcoef f</>hdcoef g)(n-m)
```

Now with the derived function `gdDiv` from section 2.2 we can calculate the gcd of polynomials over an arbitrary field.

4 Parsers

We will make use of Gofer's constructor classes prelude and of a monadic parser library, inspired by Wadler [Wad95]. In that library, the type `Parser` is made instance of `Functor`, `Monad`, `MonadPlus` and `MonadZero`, so that monad comprehensions (see [Jon94]) can be used for defining parsers. In the library, some common parser combinators are defined, like

```
satisfy :: (Char->Bool) -> Parser Char
many    :: Parser a -> Parser [a]
option  :: Parser a -> Parser [a]
```

Using the library, a parser for a single digit can be defined using a monad comprehension:

```
digit :: Parser Int
digit = [ ord x - ord '0'
        | x <- satisfy isDigit
        ]
```

From this, a parser for the type Nat of (Peano-like) natural numbers can be defined as:

```
instance  Repr Nat  where
    parse    =  [ foldl f zzero ds | ds <- sequence digit ]
         where  f a b = a `natMul` g 10 <+> g b
                g n = iterate Suc zzero !! n
    unpars x =  shows (f x)
         where  f Zer = 0
                f (Suc n) = 1 + f n
```

More involved parsers can be build by combining parsers using combinators and monad comprehensions. Unparsers can be combined by functional composition. For example, integers are represented as:

```
instance  Repr Integ  where
    parse = [ if   n==Zer
              then Zero
              else (if null s then Pos else Neg) n
            | s <- option (symbol '-')
            , n <- parse
            ]
    unpars Zero    = showChar '0'
    unpars (Pos n) = unpars n
    unpars (Neg n) = showChar '-' . unpars n
```

Similarly, a parser for floating point numbers can be defined (see [Fok95]).

For the parameterized types, like Quot and Iadd, (un)parsers can be defined by calling the overloaded parse function for the base type.

```
instance  (Ring a,Repr a) => Repr (Quot a)  where
    parse = [ Quot (n, if null d then one else head d)
            | n <- parse
            , d <- option (second (symbol '/') parse)
            ]
    unpars (Quot (x,y))
           | y==one     = unpars x
           | otherwise = unpars x . showChar '/' . unpars y
```

A term of a polynomial can be represented by strings like 3x^2. This format (where the coefficient defaults to one, the exponent to 1, unless the x is missing, in which case it is 0) is parsed and generated by:

```
instance  (Ring a,Repr a) => Repr (Term a)  where
    parse = [  ( if null c then one else head c
               , if null e then 1   else head e
               )
            |  c <- option parse
            ,  x <- option(token "x")
            ,  e <- if   null x
                    then result [0]
                    else option (second (token "^") parse)
            ]
```

```
unpars (c,e)
      | e==0  =  unpars c
      | otherwise
        = (if c==one && e>0 then id else unpars c)
        . (if e==0 then id else showChar 'x')
        . (if e==1 then id else showChar '^' . unpars e)
```

Then, parsers for polynomials are easily constructed using the parser combinator `listOf`, and the dual unparser combinator `listify`:

```
instance  Repr (Term a) => Repr (Poly a)  where
    parse = [ Poly xs | xs <- listOf parse (token "+") ]
    unpars (Poly xs) = listify unpars (showString " + ") xs
```

where

```
listify :: (a -> ShowS) -> ShowS -> [a] -> ShowS
listify f s [] = id
listify f s [x] = f x
listify f s (x:xs) = f x . s . listify f s xs
listOf :: Parser a -> Parser () -> Parser [a]
listOf p s = [ a:as
             | a  <- p
             , as <- many [ c | _ <- s, c <- p ]
             ]
```

A parser for matrices can be constructed in a similar way.

Two auxiliary functions are defined for parsing and showing a single item, by making an initial call to the functions **parse** and **unpars**:

```
pars   ::  Repr a => String -> a
shw    ::  Repr a => a -> String
pars    =  head . just parse
shw x   =  unpars x ""
```

5 Applications

The construction of the quotient field over an arbitrary ring in section 3.4 was a generalization of the construction of the rational numbers. Therefore, the rational numbers can be defined as a special case of it:

```
type Rat          = Quot Int
```

Likewise, complex numbers can be defined as taking the closure of adding i to the floating point numbers

```
type Compl        = Iadd Float
```

By using `Iadd` over other base types, we get Gauss' integer numbers, or Hamilton's quaternions:

```
type Gauss        = Iadd Int
type Qi           = Iadd Rat
type Quaternion = Iadd Compl
type Octonion     = Iadd Quaternion
```

Using the parse functions, it is easy to apply the library to concrete problems. The example polynomial division from section 3.8 can be carried out by defining:

```
p1, p2 :: Poly Float
p1 = pars "2x^4 + 5x^3 + 4x^2 + -3x + 2"
p2 = pars "x^2 + x + 1"
```

In a session one could evaluate

```
? shw (p1 `divide` p2)
2.0x^2 + 3.0x + -1.0
```

Note that the type information that is given in enough for `pars`, `divide` and `shw` to choose the right instance. The polynomials have to be declared as `Float`, and not as `Int`, because for polynomial division the base type is required to be a field. Declaring `p1` as a `Poly Int` would result in an error message

```
*** Required instance : Euclid (Poly Int)
*** No subdictionary  : Field Int
```

This is the advantage of our careful distinction of the different classes, rather than to make all numeric values instance of `Num`, as in the standard prelude.

Another field that can be used as base type for polynomial division is the field of rational numbers. If we define:

```
p3, p4 :: Poly Rat
p3 = pars "1/3x^3 + 1/5x + -1/2"
p4 = pars "1/2x + 1"
```

We can calculate

```
? shw (p3 `divide` p4)
2/3x^2 + -4/3x + 46/15
```

A first experiment with matrices is calculating a simple inverse. After defining

```
m1 :: Matrix Float
m1 = pars "(1 0 2|0 1 -1|2 1 0)"
```

we can calculate

```
? shw (inv m1)
(-0.33 -0.67 0.67 | 0.67 1.3 -0.33 | 0.67 0.33 -0.33)
```

By just changing the type of the matrix to

```
m1 :: Matrix Rat
```

the result would be given as a matrix of rational numbers:

```
? shw (inv m1)
(1/-3 2/-3 -2/-3 | -2/-3 -4/-3 1/-3 | -2/-3 -1/-3 1/-3)
```

A more involved example uses matrices over the ring of polynomials. We will calculate the equation of which the solutions are the eigenvalues of the matrix. An eigenvalue of a matrix A is a scalar k, where $Ax = kx$ for every vector x. Put differently, $Ax - kx = 0$, or $(A - kI)x = 0$ or $\det(A - kI) = 0$. This can be immediately programmed in Gofer:

```
eigenPoly :: ( Ring (Matrix (Poly a)) , Ring (Poly a))
             =>  Matrix a -> Poly a
eigenPoly m =  det (   map pconst m
                   <-> scalemat k one
                   )
        where k = psingle one 1
```

For example, the eigenvalues of

```
m2 :: Matrix Int
m2 = pars  "(1 2 3 4|5 6 7 8|9 10 11 12|13 14 15 16)"
```

are solutions of

```
? shw (eigenPoly m2)
x^4 + -34x^3 + -80x^2
```

6 Conclusion

We have shown that structures from abstract algebra can be succesfully modelled as Gofer classes. By providing parsers for constructions that are instances of these classes, the algorithms can be applied immediately to practical problems.

This work could be extended in several directions, e.g.:

- Adding more classes, e.g. vector spaces and modules, or algebraically closed fields.
- Proving that the required laws hold for the implementations given, in the style of the induction proofs in [BW88].
- Adding more instances, e.g. lists as a monoid with `++` as addition and `[]` as zero, or Klein's 4-group as a group, or symbolic expressions as a field.
- Adding more derived operations for the classes that were defined. For example, find the solution of a polynomial. One could use the *abc* formula for polynomials of degree 2, and Cardano's formulas for degree 3 and 4 (making use of polynomials over complex numbers), or use special strategies (for polynomials over `Rat`, every solution has the form b/c, where b is a divisor of the last coefficient, and c is a divisor of the head coefficient). Or program algorithms for handling matrices, e.g. finding the Jordan normal form.

Appendix

A Functional Programming Education in Utrecht

The material treated in this article is part of a first course on functional programming for computer science students in Utrecht. This course assumes no previous programming experience, and is taught *in parallel* with a course on imperative/OO programming (putting an end to the debate which paradigm to teach first).

After this introductory cpurse, functional programming is used throughout the computer science curriculum (which takes 8 semesters). The course sequence is coordinated by Doaitse Swierstra. By using functional programming in teaching various subjects, the student's fluency in functional programming is maintained and deepened. At the same time, all these subjects benefit from the concise formulation of algorithms made possible through the use of functional languages.

All courses have lectures, tutorials and lab assignments for approximately two hours once a week, and last 10 to 15 weeks. Students are assessed by a written exam and by their lab works. The courses involved, with their workload in hours and the literature used, are:

course	semester	lecture	tutorial	lab	homew.	literature
Functional Programming	1	20	20	40	40	[Fok92]
Grammars and Parsing	2	30	30	40	60	[JDS94]
Implementation of Prog.Lang.	3	20	20	80	40	[Meij95]
Advanced Functional Progr.	6	30	0	60	30	[JM95]
Partial Evaluation	7	30	0	0	90	[JGS93]
Category Theory	7	30	0	0	90	[Mee95]

The specialization courses in semester 5–8 are optional. Furthermore, there is a connection with the course on User Interfaces (semester 6). Unfortunately, the course on Linear Algebra (semester 4) is not integrated in the course sequence. Also, mathematics students do not participate.

References

[BW88] R. Bird and P. Wadler, *Introduction to Functional Programming.* Prentice Hall, 1988.

[Fok92] Jeroen Fokker, *Functional programming.* Course notes, Department of Computer Science, Utrecht University, 1992. Also available as *Functioneel Programmeren* and as *Programación Funcional.* From http://www.cs.ruu.nl/~jeroen.

[Fok95] Jeroen Fokker, 'Functional parsers'. In [JM95], pp. 1–23. Also http://www.cs.ruu.nl/~jeroen.

[JDS94] Johan Jeurig, Luc Duponcheel and Doaitse Swierstra, *Grammars and Parsing.* Course notes, Department of Computer Science, Utrecht University, 1994. From http://www.cs.ruu.nl/~luc.

[JM95] Johan Jeuring and Erik Meijer (eds.), *Advanced functional programming.* Springer LNCS 925, 1995.

[Jon94] Mark Jones, *Gofer 2.30 release notes.* http://www.cs.nott.ac.uk/Department/Staff/mpj.

[JGS93] Neil Jones, Carsten Gomard and Peter Sestoft, *Partial evaluation and automatic program generation.* Prentice Hall, 1993.

[Lan70] Serge Lang, *Linear Algebra.* Addison-Wesley, 1970.

[Mee95] Lambert Meertens, *Category theory,* Course notes, Department of Computer Science, Utrecht University, 1995. Ask lambert@cs.ruu.nl.

[Meij95] Erik Meijer and Doaitse Swierstra, *Implementation of Programming Languages.* Course notes, Department of Computer Science, Utrecht University, 1995. From http://www.cs.ruu.nl/~erik.

[Wad95] Philip Wadler, 'Monads for functional programming'. In [JM95], pp. 24–52. Also: http://www.dcs.glasgow.ac.uk/~wadler.

Inducing Students to Induct

David Lester and Sava Mintchev

Department of Computer Science, Manchester University,
Oxford Road, Manchester M13 9PL, UK.
{dlester,smintchev}@cs.man.ac.uk

Abstract. One of the problems encountered with a formal approach to the teaching of functional programming is to encourage students to perform inductive proofs for recursively defined functions. In this paper we investigate the use of a theorem prover (written in Haskell) to help students gain confidence in their mathematical abilities.
As examples, we use the material that we have developed for an introductory functional programming module; and show how the theorem prover can be of assistance.

1 Introduction

Wouldn't it be nice if students studying functional programming could be persuaded that proof by induction was easy? The problem that we all have when teaching functional programming is how to teach recursion, especially to those not already familiar with it. In this paper we show how a theorem prover — originally developed for compiler correctness [7, 9] — may be adapted to encourage students towards the belief that induction is easy.

One approach to teaching functional programming — adopted by Bird and Wadler [1] — is to use higher-order functions for the initial exercises. This has its own set of problems, which arise when students start to think about what is going on. The problem of disorientation is then compounded for those already familiar with recursion, because the presentation in Bird and Wadler involves induction.

We feel that a presentation that omits discussion of the formal aspects of functional languages is missing some of the beauty of functional programming. The omission of formality is the approach taken in the undergraduate teaching at Manchester; however we have been experimenting with material presented to students on our Conversion Course MSc. This is a one year post-graduate course for students who already have a BSc. Our module is presented *after* the students have learnt *C*, and introduces them to their first non-standard language.

Reasoning about pure functional programs is relatively easy in comparison with reasoning about imperative programs. At the same time, modern functional language implementations are reasonably efficient, and have been used in a fair number of practical applications. So a pure functional language seems a good vehicle for all stages of program development, from specification through to implementation and verification. And functional languages have traditionally been associated with theorem proving — after all, ML, one of the most popular modern functional languages, originated as the meta–language for a theorem prover!

Virtually all textbooks on functional programming include sections on reasoning about programs. Induction proofs are dealt with at length in [1], introduced in [14] and [5], and mentioned in [13]. Fold/unfold and algebraic transformations are covered in [4].

Functional languages also have a special place in modern texts on programming language semantics. In [11], for example, operational and denotational semantic definitions have been written in a pure functional language. The students are given the opportunity to play with the definitions, and hence to understand them better.

Work on theorem provers for functional languages has been published (e.g. [3], [15]), but overall developments in theorem provers lag behind compilers and interpreters. The usefulness of a theorem prover in teaching functional programming has been argued in [15].

In this paper we demonstrate how a tool for reasoning about functional programs can be used in a course on functional programming. We believe that such a tool will complement the programming environment (e.g. Gofer) which is normally used in the process of teaching. The examples we give have been taken from a conversion course module for MSc students [8] at Manchester University.

2 Course background

The conversion course MSc at Manchester is a one year course in which the students attend lectures for two terms and then write a dissertation for the remaining six months. Students are accepted onto the programme provided that they have a reasonable BSc degree in a 'numerate' subject.

Because of the selection procedure applied to prospective students, we are unable to assume any specific computing or mathematical skills; but the selection procedure *does* permit us to attempt to teach a formal methods oriented module. This second term module consists of 9 half–days, each roughly split as 1.5 hour lectures, and 2.5 hour supervised laboratory.

The module broadly follows Bird and Wadler, but extends the algorithmic part to include a discussion of complexity classes and cryptography.

While the course evaluation questionnaires have rated the module 'taxing', it has also consistently scored highly as the most interesting of the modules available to the students on this course.

3 A theorem prover for functional programs

A detailed description of the theorem prover can be found in [10]; here we give just a brief overview.

The theorem proving tool accepts two kinds of input files: core Haskell program files, and theory files. A theory is a sequence of axioms and theorems. The syntax of a theorem (or axiom) is:

$$name:\ logic\_formula$$

The syntax of logic formulae is shown in Figure 1. The logic is a three–valued first–order predicate calculus. Atomic formulae are made of the truth values (TT, FF), the unknown value UU, and predicates for semantic equivalence and approximation of core Haskell expressions. Complex formulae are built up of conjunction, disjunction, implication and universal quantification. Existential quantifiers are not available.

	Haskell-style	Pretty-printed	
	`TT`	TT	true
	`FF`	FF	false
Atomic	`UU`	UU	undefined
formulae	*app* :== *e*	$app \equiv e$	equivalence
(p, q, r)	*app* :>> *e*	$app \sqsupseteq e$	greater than
	app :<< *e*	$app \sqsubseteq e$	less than
	P /\ Q	$P \wedge Q$	conjunction
Complex	P \/ Q	$P \vee Q$	disjunction
formulae	[p_1, p_2, $\cdots p_n$] ->> Q	$[p_1,\ p_2,\ \cdots p_n] \Rightarrow Q$	forward implication
(P, Q, R)	[P_1, P_2, $\cdots P_n$] -: Q	$[P_1,\ P_2,\ \cdots P_n] \Rightarrow Q$	backwards implication
	`All` (\\x -> P)	$\forall\ x.\ P$	universal quantification
	`Ind` (\\x -> P)	$\underline{\forall}\ x.\ P$	induction

Fig. 1. Syntax of logic formulae

The prover has a simple command–driven interface.
There is no separate language of tactics and tacticals for controlling the process of proof construction: all the information needed for guiding the proof is contained in the theorems themselves.

Here is an example — the simplest example we could think of that requires induction. The theorem *appNil* states that the empty list [] is a right identity for the append function (++): $appNil : \underline{\forall} as.\ (as \mathbin{+\!\!+} [\,]) \equiv as$ The prover produces the following trace in evidence that *appNil* is a true statement:

> *pg appNil App*

Proof by induction of: $\underline{\forall} as.\ (as \mathbin{+\!\!+} [\,]) \equiv as$

$\bot \mathbin{+\!\!+} [\,] \equiv \bot$

$[] ++ [] \equiv []$

$[(list_{1.2} ++ []) \equiv list_{1.2}] \Rightarrow list_{1.2} ++ [] \equiv list_{1.2}$

$[(list_{1.2} ++ []) \equiv list_{1.2}] \Rightarrow (a_{1.1} : list_{1.2}) ++ [] \equiv a_{1.1} : list_{1.2}$

Proof State:

The proof trace shows the sequence of intermediate incarnations of a goal during the course of a proof, and can be terse (as the one above) or verbose. The trace is followed by the final *Proof State* – a disjunction of goals which the prover has failed to prove. In the case of a successful proof (as above), the proof state is empty.

How does the prover work? Every logical formula from Figure 1 has a well defined operational interpretation. For example, equivalence ($app \equiv e$) is handled by alternating syntactic comparisons and reductions (to weak head normal form), until the two sides become syntactically equivalent or reach different head normal forms. An implication ($[P_1, P_2, \cdots P_n] \Rightarrow Q$) is proved by checking Q on the assumption that $P_1, P_2, \cdots P_n$ hold. A universally quantified formula ($\forall\ x.\ P$) is proved by proving P in which a fresh constant identifier has been substituted for x. A formula with an induction quantifier ($\underline{\forall}\ x.\ P$), where x is inferred to be of type *datatype*, is proved with the help of the internally generated structural induction axiom for *datatype*. Since induction is distinguished syntactically from universal quantification, the prover does not have to search heuristically for a suitable induction schema (unlike the Boyer–Moore system, for example [2]).

In the example above, the base cases of the induction, for a nonterminating expression ($\perp$) and and empty list $[]$, are obvious. In the induction step, the assertion is proved to hold for the nonempty list ($a_{1.1}{:}list_{1.2}$) on the assumption that it holds for the list $list_{1.2}$. The name '$list_{1.2}$' is generated internally from the data definition of lists, and subscripts are added to ensure its uniqueness.

There are many useful theorems about standard functions, which are proved automatically.

$$appAssoc : \underline{\forall} as.\ \forall bs.\ \forall cs.\quad ((as ++ bs) ++ cs) \equiv (as ++ (bs ++ cs))$$

$$foldrMap : \underline{\forall} xs.\ \forall a.\ \forall f.\ \forall g.\quad foldr\ f\ a\ (map\ g\ xs) \equiv foldr\ (f\ .\ g)\ a\ xs$$

$$mapMap : \underline{\forall} xs.\ \forall f.\ \forall g.\quad map\ f\ (map\ g\ xs) \equiv map\ (f\ .\ g)\ xs$$

$$foldlStr : \forall f.\ [\forall z.\ f\ \perp\ z\ \equiv \perp]\ \Rightarrow\ (\underline{\forall} xs.\ foldl\ f\ \perp\ xs\ \equiv \perp)$$

$$\begin{aligned} foldlApp : \forall f.\ & [foldlStr,\ \forall z.\ f\ \perp\ z\ \equiv \perp]\ \Rightarrow \\ & (\underline{\forall} as.\ \forall acc.\ \forall bs. \\ & \quad foldl\ f\ acc\ (as +\!\!+\ bs)\ \equiv\ foldl\ f\ (foldl\ f\ acc\ as)\ bs \\ &) \end{aligned}$$

$$\begin{aligned} foldrApp : & \underline{\forall} as.\ \forall acc.\ \forall bs.\ \forall f. \\ & \quad foldr\ f\ acc\ (as +\!\!+\ bs)\ \equiv\ foldr\ f\ (foldr\ f\ acc\ bs)\ as \end{aligned}$$

4 Proving the duality theorems

It is fairly easy to prove theorems which require just one structural induction, such as the ones we have seen so far. All the user has to do is to figure out which variable to do the induction on, and mark that variable with the **Ind** ($\underline{\forall}$) quantifier.

It is often necessary to prove a number of lemmas before we can prove a theorem. Without the lemmas the proof of the theorem will fail; and it will be very helpful if the prover can suggest the lemmas required.

We illustrate proof failure in the next example — the duality properties of the left and right fold functions on lists [1]. Informally, the first duality theorem asserts that left- and right- folding a list with an associative operation, and with the left- and right-identity of the operation as an initial accumulator, produce the same result.

$$\begin{aligned} dual1 : \forall \#.\ \forall unit.\ & [\forall a.\ \forall b.\ \forall c. \\ & \quad ((a \# b) \# c)\ \equiv\ (a \# (b \# c)) \\ & ,\ \forall x.\ (unit \# x)\ \equiv\ x,\ \forall y.\ (y \# unit)\ \equiv\ y]\ \Rightarrow \\ & (\underline{\forall} as.\ foldl\ (\#)\ unit\ as\ \equiv\ foldr\ (\#)\ unit\ as) \end{aligned}$$

The attempt to prove *dual*1 fails, producing a short trace:

Proof by induction of:
$\underline{\forall} as.\ foldl\ (\#_1)\ unit_2\ as\ \equiv\ foldr\ (\#_1)\ unit_2\ as$

$$\begin{aligned} & [(?y \#_1 unit_2)\ \equiv\ ?y, \\ & (unit_2 \#_1 ?x)\ \equiv\ ?x, \\ & ((?a \#_1 ?b) \#_1 ?c)\ \equiv\ (?a \#_1 (?b \#_1 ?c))]\ \Rightarrow \\ & foldl\ (\#_1)\ unit_2\ \perp\ \equiv\ foldr\ (\#_1)\ unit_2\ \perp \end{aligned}$$

$$\begin{aligned} & [(?y \#_1 unit_2)\ \equiv\ ?y, \\ & (unit_2 \#_1 ?x)\ \equiv\ ?x, \\ & ((?a \#_1 ?b) \#_1 ?c)\ \equiv\ (?a \#_1 (?b \#_1 ?c))]\ \Rightarrow \\ & foldl\ (\#_1)\ unit_2\ []\ \equiv\ foldr\ (\#_1)\ unit_2\ [] \end{aligned}$$

$[foldl\ (\#_1)\ unit_2\ list_{5.2}\ \equiv\ foldr\ (\#_1)\ unit_2\ list_{5.2},$
$(?y\ \#_1\ unit_2)\ \equiv ?y,$
$(unit_2\ \#_1\ ?x)\ \equiv ?x,$
$((?a\ \#_1\ ?b)\ \#_1\ ?c)\ \equiv\ (?a\ \#_1\ (?b\ \#_1\ ?c))$
$]\ \Rightarrow$
$foldl\ (\#_1)\ unit_2\ (a_{5.1} : list_{5.2})\ ??? \equiv\ foldr\ (\#_1)\ unit_2\ (a_{5.1} : list_{5.2})$

The first two steps of the proof establish the base cases — when the list *as* is non-terminating ($\perp$) or empty. However, the third step (the induction step) has failed. The symbol '??? $\equiv$' shows that the prover has established neither validity nor contradiction. In addition to the trace, the prover outputs a disjunction of goals which it has failed to prove, and which are possible alternative paths for continuing the proof. There are 3 different alternatives in this case, 2 of which are obvious dead ends (cannot be proved). The third one, however, is more helpful, and is the only one we show here:

Proof State:

$[foldl\ (\#_1)\ unit_2\ list_{5.2}\ \equiv\ foldr\ (\#_1)\ unit_2\ list_{5.2},$
$(?y\ \#_1\ unit_2)\ \equiv ?y,$
$(unit_2\ \#_1\ ?x)\ \equiv ?x,$
$((?a\ \#_1\ ?b)\ \#_1\ ?c)\ \equiv\ (?a\ \#_1\ (?b\ \#_1\ ?c))]\ \Rightarrow$
$(\mathtt{case}\ list_{5.2}\ \mathtt{of}$
$\quad []\ \rightarrow\ unit_2\ \#_1\ a_{5.1}$
$\quad y : ys\ \rightarrow\ foldl\ (\#_1)\ ((unit_2\ \#_1\ a_{5.1})\ \#_1\ y)\ ys$
$)$
$\equiv\ (a_{5.1}\ \#_1\ foldr\ (\#_1)\ unit_2\ list_{5.2})$

It is not hard to see that the *case* expression in the above goal is equivalent to $(foldl\ (\#_1)\ a_{5.1}\ list_{5.2})$, so we decide that the lemma required is:

$$\underline{\forall} as.\ \forall p.\ foldl\ (\#)\ p\ as\ \equiv\ (p\ \#\ foldr\ (\#)\ unit\ as) \qquad (1)$$

The attempt to prove this goal by list induction runs into further difficulty, this time in the base case for $\perp$:

Proof by induction of:
$\underline{\forall} as.\ \forall p.\ foldl\ (\#_1)\ p\ as\ \equiv\ (p\ \#_1\ foldr\ (\#_1)\ unit_2\ as)$

$[(?y\ \#_1\ unit_2)\ \equiv ?y,$
$(unit_2\ \#_1\ ?x)\ \equiv ?x,$
$((?a\ \#_1\ ?b)\ \#_1\ ?c)\ \equiv\ (?a\ \#_1\ (?b\ \#_1\ ?c))$
$]\ \Rightarrow$
$(foldl\ (\#_1)\ p_9\ \perp)\ ??? \equiv\ (p_9\ \#_1\ foldr\ (\#_1)\ unit_2\ \perp)$

Proof State:

$$[(?y \#_1 \ unit_2) \equiv ?y,$$
$$(unit_2 \#_1 ?x) \equiv ?x,$$
$$((?a \#_1 ?b) \#_1 ?c) \equiv (?a \#_1 (?b \#_1 ?c))] \Rightarrow$$
$$\bot \equiv (p_9 \#_1 \ foldr \ (\#_1) \ unit_2 \ \bot)$$

We have two ways of dealing with this problem. First, we can require that the list *as* be finite (as in [1]), and hence there will be no base case for $\bot$. Alternatively, since $(foldr\ (\#_1)\ unit_2\ \bot)$ is $\bot$, the above goal is clearly satisfied if we assume that the operation (#) is strict in its second argument. With this additional assumption, the proof of lemma (1) goes through.

We insert the assumption of strictness, as well as Lemma (1), into *dual*1 (of course we could also have chosen to give lemma (1) a name and include it as a separate theorem preceding *dual*1). The modified version of the duality theorem is:

$$\begin{array}{l} dual1 : \forall \#.\ \forall unit.\ [\forall a.\ \forall b.\ \forall c. \\ \qquad ((a \# b) \# c) \equiv (a \# (b \# c)) \\ \quad ,\ \forall z.\ (z \# \bot) \equiv \bot \\ \quad ,\ \forall x.\ (unit \# x) \equiv x,\ \forall y.\ (y \# unit) \equiv y] \Rightarrow \\ \quad ((\underline{\forall} as.\ \forall p.\ foldl\ (\#)\ p\ as \equiv (p \# foldr\ (\#)\ unit\ as)) \land \\ \quad (\forall as.\ foldl\ (\#)\ unit\ as \equiv foldr\ (\#)\ unit\ as) \\ \quad) \end{array}$$

Now the proof succeeds without a hitch. All the information necessary for guiding the proof is encoded in the theorem itself, and it isn't that much!

Here is the trace of the proof of *dual*1. The assumptions (of *unit* being a left and right identity of (#), of (#) being associative and strict in the second argument) are implicitly present at every stage of the proof. The first conjunct in the conclusion of the theorem is proved first:

Proof by induction of:
$\underline{\forall} as.\ \forall p.\ foldl\ (\#_1)\ p\ as \equiv (p \#_1\ foldr\ (\#_1)\ unit_2\ as)$

The base cases (for $\bot$ and []) are dealt with first:

$$foldl\ (\#_1)\ p_9\ \bot \equiv p_9 \#_1\ foldr\ (\#_1)\ unit_2\ \bot$$

$$foldl\ (\#_1)\ p_9\ [] \equiv p_9 \#_1\ foldr\ (\#_1)\ unit_2\ []$$

In the induction step, the statement is proved for the list $(a_{7.1} : list_{7.2})$, assuming that it holds for the list $list_{7.2}$.

$$[foldl\ (\#_1)\ ?p\ list_{7.2} \equiv (?p \#_1\ foldr\ (\#_1)\ unit_2\ list_{7.2})$$
$$] \Rightarrow$$
$$foldr\ (\#_1)\ unit_2\ list_{7.2} \equiv foldr\ (\#_1)\ unit_2\ list_{7.2}$$

$[foldl\ (\#_1)\ ?p\ list_{7.2}\ \equiv\ (?p\ \#_1\ foldr\ (\#_1)\ unit_2\ list_{7.2})$
$]\ \Rightarrow$
$(a_{7.1}\ \#_1\ foldr\ (\#_1)\ unit_2\ list_{7.2})\ \equiv\ (a_{7.1}\ \#_1\ foldr\ (\#_1)\ unit_2\ list_{7.2})$

$[foldl\ (\#_1)\ ?p\ list_{7.2}\ \equiv\ (?p\ \#_1\ foldr\ (\#_1)\ unit_2\ list_{7.2})$
$]\ \Rightarrow$
$(a_{7.1}\ \#_1\ foldr\ (\#_1)\ unit_2\ list_{7.2})\ \equiv\ (foldr\ (\#_1)\ unit_2\ (a_{7.1} : list_{7.2}))$

$[foldl\ (\#_1)\ ?p\ list_{7.2}\ \equiv\ (?p\ \#_1\ foldr\ (\#_1)\ unit_2\ list_{7.2})$
$]\ \Rightarrow$
$(p_9\ \#_1\ (a_{7.1}\ \#_1\ foldr\ (\#_1)\ unit_2\ list_{7.2}))$
$\equiv$
$(p_9\ \#_1\ foldr\ (\#_1)\ unit_2\ (a_{7.1} : list_{7.2}))$

$[foldl\ (\#_1)\ ?p\ list_{7.2}\ \equiv\ (?p\ \#_1\ foldr\ (\#_1)\ unit_2\ list_{7.2})$
$]\ \Rightarrow$
$(foldl\ (\#_1)\ p_9\ (a_{7.1} : list_{7.2}))\ \equiv\ (p_9\ \#_1\ foldr\ (\#_1)\ unit_2\ (a_{7.1} : list_{7.2}))$

Now it is time to prove the second conjunct. But it is just a special case of the first conjunct:

$[foldl\ (\#_1)\ ?p\ ?as\ \equiv\ (?p\ \#_1\ foldr\ (\#_1)\ unit_2\ ?as)$
$]\ \Rightarrow$
$foldr\ (\#_1)\ unit_2\ x_{12.2}\ \equiv\ foldr\ (\#_1)\ unit_2\ x_{12.2}$

$[foldl\ (\#_1)\ ?p\ ?as\ \equiv\ (?p\ \#_1\ foldr\ (\#_1)\ unit_2\ ?as)$
$]\ \Rightarrow$
$x_{12.1}\ \#_1\ foldr\ (\#_1)\ unit_2\ x_{12.2}\ \equiv\ x_{12.1}\ \#_1\ foldr\ (\#_1)\ unit_2\ x_{12.2}$

$[foldl\ (\#_1)\ ?p\ ?as\ \equiv\ (?p\ \#_1\ foldr\ (\#_1)\ unit_2\ ?as)$
$]\ \Rightarrow$
$foldl\ (\#_1)\ unit_2\ as_7\ \equiv\ foldr\ (\#_1)\ unit_2\ as_7$

Proof State:

– – – – – – – – – – –

The second duality theorem also requires an auxiliary result (the first one of the two conjuncts below), similarly to the first duality theorem.

$$
\begin{aligned}
&dual2 : \forall\#.\ \forall@.\ \forall unit.\\
&\qquad [\forall a.\ \forall b.\ \forall c.\\
&\qquad\quad ((a \# b) @ c) \equiv (a \# (b @ c))\\
&\qquad ,\ \forall z.\ (z \# \perp) \equiv \perp\\
&\qquad ,\ \forall x.\ (unit @ x) \equiv (x \# unit)] \Rightarrow\\
&\qquad ((\underline{\forall} xs.\ \forall p.\ \forall q.\\
&\qquad\quad foldl\ (@)\ (p \# q)\ xs \equiv (p \# foldl\ (@)\ q\ xs)\\
&\qquad) \wedge\\
&\qquad (\underline{\forall} xs.\ foldr\ (\#)\ unit\ xs \equiv foldl\ (@)\ unit\ xs)\\
&\qquad)
\end{aligned}
$$

The proof of the third duality theorem relies on lemma *foldlApp* from Section 3. Again, instead of stipulating that the function *f* be strict, we could have chosen to restrict the validity of the theorem to finite lists.

$$
\begin{aligned}
&dual3 : \forall f.\ [foldlApp,\ \forall z.\ f\ \perp\ z \equiv \perp] \Rightarrow\\
&\qquad (\underline{\forall} xs.\ \forall x.\ foldl\ f\ x\ (rev\ xs) \equiv\\
&\qquad foldr\ (flip\ f)\ x\ xs)
\end{aligned}
$$

5 Proving an optimization correct: fast reverse

When we face the task of explaining how list *reverse* works, we are most likely to choose a definition like the following:

$$
\begin{aligned}
rev\ =\ \lambda\, xs\ \rightarrow\ &\textbf{case}\ xs\ \textbf{of}\\
&x : xs \rightarrow rev\ xs +\!\!+ [x]\\
&[] \rightarrow []
\end{aligned}
$$

This definition is intuitively clear, but inefficient, so we will have to explain why a different definition is used in practice, e.g. the one from the Haskell Standard Prelude:

$$reverse\ =\ \lambda\, xs\ \rightarrow\ foldl\ (flip\ (:))\ []\ xs$$

Perhaps the best way of convincing students that the fast version of reverse does the same as the original version is to run it! However, we wish to be formal, so we run the theorem prover:

$$fastRev : (\forall xs.\ reverse\ xs \equiv rev\ xs)$$

The direct proof by induction will fail. Simply replacing *reverse* by $(foldl\ (flip\ (:))\ []\ xs)$ in the theorem will not help. What is required is the insight that the statement is not general enough for the induction step to go through. The generalized statement is:

$$
\begin{aligned}
&foldlRev : [foldlStr,\ appAssoc] \Rightarrow \\
&\qquad (\underline{\forall} xs.\ \forall as. \\
&\qquad\quad foldl\ (flip(:))\ as\ xs\ \equiv\ (rev\ xs\ +\!\!+\ as) \\
&\qquad)
\end{aligned}
$$

The theorem prover does not attempt to do generalization. It takes out the tedium of reduction of expressions and testing expressions for syntactic equivalence, while leaving the creative tasks, like generalization, to human intelligence.

The proof of *foldlRev* uses Theorems *foldlStr*, *appAssoc* and *appNil* from Section 3. As usual, the base cases of the induction are dealt with first:

Proof by induction of: $\underline{\forall} xs.\ \forall as.$
$foldl\ (flip(:))\ as\ xs\ \equiv\ (rev\ xs\ +\!\!+\ as)$

$$foldl\ (flip(:))\ as_4\ \perp \equiv\ rev\ \perp\ +\!\!+\ as_4$$

$$foldl\ (flip(:))\ as_4\ []\ \equiv\ rev\ []\ +\!\!+\ as_4$$

The induction step comes next. The statement is proved for a list $(a_{2.1} : list_{2.2})$ on the assumption that it holds for the list $list_{2.2}$:

$$
\begin{aligned}
&[foldl\ (flip(:))\ ?as\ list_{2.2}\ \equiv\ (rev\ list_{2.2}\ +\!\!+\ ?as)] \Rightarrow \\
&rev\ list_{2.2}\ \equiv\ rev\ list_{2.2}
\end{aligned}
$$

$$
\begin{aligned}
&[foldl\ (flip(:))\ ?as\ list_{2.2}\ \equiv\ (rev\ list_{2.2}\ +\!\!+\ ?as)] \Rightarrow \\
&as_4\ \equiv\ []\ +\!\!+\ as_4
\end{aligned}
$$

$$
\begin{aligned}
&[foldl\ (flip(:))\ ?as\ list_{2.2}\ \equiv\ (rev\ list_{2.2}\ +\!\!+\ ?as)] \Rightarrow \\
&flip(:)\ as_4\ a_{2.1}\ \equiv\ [a_{2.1}]\ +\!\!+\ as_4
\end{aligned}
$$

$$
\begin{aligned}
&[foldl\ (flip(:))\ ?as\ list_{2.2}\ \equiv\ (rev\ list_{2.2}\ +\!\!+\ ?as)] \Rightarrow \\
&as_4\ \equiv\ []\ +\!\!+\ as_4
\end{aligned}
$$

$$
\begin{aligned}
&[foldl\ (flip(:))\ ?as\ list_{2.2}\ \equiv\ (rev\ list_{2.2}\ +\!\!+\ ?as)] \Rightarrow \\
&flip(:)\ as_4\ a_{2.1}\ \equiv\ [a_{2.1}]\ +\!\!+\ as_4
\end{aligned}
$$

$$
\begin{aligned}
&[foldl\ (flip(:))\ ?as\ list_{2.2}\ \equiv\ (rev\ list_{2.2}\ +\!\!+\ ?as)] \Rightarrow \\
&x_{7.2}\ +\!\!+\ flip(:)\ as_4\ a_{2.1}\ \equiv\ x_{7.2}\ +\!\!+\ ([a_{2.1}]\ +\!\!+\ as_4)
\end{aligned}
$$

$$
\begin{aligned}
&[foldl\ (flip\ :)\ ?as\ list_{2.2}\ \equiv\ (rev\ list_{2.2}\ +\!\!+\ ?as)] \Rightarrow \\
&x_{7.1} : (x_{7.2}\ +\!\!+\ flip : as_4\ a_{2.1}) \\
&\equiv \\
&x_{7.1} : (x_{7.2}\ +\!\!+\ ([a_{2.1}]\ +\!\!+\ as_4))
\end{aligned}
$$

$[foldl\ (flip\ :)\ ?as\ list_{2.2}\ \equiv\ (rev\ list_{2.2}\ +\!\!+\ ?as)]\ \Rightarrow$
$\mathbf{case}\ rev\ list_{2.2}\ \mathbf{of}$
$[]\ \rightarrow\ flip : as_4\ a_{2.1}$
$y\ :\ ys\ \rightarrow\ y : (ys\ +\!\!+\ flip : as_4\ a_{2.1})$
$\equiv$
$\mathbf{case}\ rev\ list_{2.2}\ \mathbf{of}$
$[]\ \rightarrow\ [a_{2.1}]\ +\!\!+\ as_4$
$y\ :\ ys\ \rightarrow\ y : (ys\ +\!\!+\ ([a_{2.1}]\ +\!\!+\ as_4))$

$[foldl\ (flip(:))\ ?as\ list_{2.2}\ \equiv\ (rev\ list_{2.2}\ +\!\!+\ ?as)]\ \Rightarrow$
$foldl\ (flip(:))\ as_4\ (a_{2.1} : list_{2.2})$
$\equiv$
$rev\ (a_{2.1} : list_{2.2})\ +\!\!+\ as_4$

Proof State:

– – – – – – – – – – – –

The situation of having optimized functions which are harder to understand than the unoptimized versions is far from uncommon. A theorem prover makes the correctness of optimizations convincing.

6 Reasoning about interpreters

The beauty of functional languages comes from their semantic clarity. It is this quality that makes them particularly suitable for use as meta-languages for other programming languages.

Our next example, taken from [8], illustrates the utility of a pure functional language in illustrating concepts from the semantics and implementation of programming languages. We will show how the power of illustration can be enhanced by the theorem proving tool. In addition, in this section we show that the structural inductions are permitted over user–defined data types. This is a useful exercise for the students, and reinforces the links between functional and imperative programming languages.

The exercise given to students has two parts.

6.1 A language of arithmetic expressions

In the first part of the exercise on interpreters, an interpreter for a simple language of arithmetic expressions is defined. The same language is also compiled into a sequence of instructions for a stack–based evaluator, and the evaluator itself is defined. The equivalence of the stack–based implementation with the original interpreter must then be demonstrated.

The pretty–printed data definitions for the language of expressions are given below:

$$
\begin{array}{lcl}
Exp\ v & ::= & Expr\ (Exp\ v)\ (Op\ )\ (Exp\ v)\ | \\
 & & Num\ (Int\ )\ | \\
 & & Var\ v
\end{array}
$$

$$
Op\ ::=\ Add\ \ |\ Sub
$$

The denotational–style semantics of the language of expressions, when executed in Gofer or compiled with a Haskell compiler, provides an interpreter for the language:

```
evalExp = λ e store →
   case e of
   Num n → n
   Var v → store v
   Expr x op y → evalOp op (evalExp x store)
          (evalExp y store)
```

```
evalOp = λ op → case op of
                  Add → (+)
                  Sub → (−)
```

Next, the language of expressions is compiled into a stream of stack machine instructions.

$$
\begin{array}{lcl}
Instr\ v & ::= & Oper\ (Op\ )\ | \\
 & & ILookup\ v\ | \\
 & & Ipush\ (Int\ )
\end{array}
$$

```
comp = λ e →
   case e of
   Num n → [Ipush n]
   Var v → [ILookup v]
   Expr x op y → comp y ++ (comp x ++ [Oper op])
```

Finally, the compiled instruction stream is executed in the context of a stack of values and a store. (The presence of a store does not make the problem more interesting at this stage, but is essential to the second part of the exercise described in this section).

```
go = λ s code store → foldl (exec store) s code
exec = λ store s instr →
   case instr of
   ILookup v → store v : s
   Oper op →
          case s of
          a : as → case as of
                        b : st → evalOp op a b : st
   Ipush n → n : s
```

Now we show that the stack evaluator does the same thing as the original interpreter. The proof uses the fact that left–folding the concatenation of two lists is the same as folding the second list with the result of folding the first list as the initial accumulator (Theorem *foldlApp* from Section 3). However, *foldlApp* requires that the function f be strict in its first argument. We want to apply the theorem with (*exec store*) substituted for f, and the trouble is that *exec* doesn't have that strictness property. There are two ways out of this difficulty: we can either make *exec* strict, or reformulate *foldlApp* so that it applies to any function f on a *finite* list. We choose the second option.

First we clarify what is meant by a 'finite list'. More precisely, we use lists of finite length:

```
spineL = λ xs → case xs of
                 [] → True
                 x : xs → spineL xs
```

We will use *spineL* to ensure that the instruction streams for the stack–based interpreter are always finite. But if the instruction streams are to be finite, then the arithmetic expressions that are compiled into those instructions must be finite too. The function *spineE* tests expressions for finiteness:

```
spineE = λ e →
   case e of
   Num i → True
   Var v → True
   Expr e1 op e2 → spineE e1 && spineE e2
```

We can now reformulate *foldlApp* for arbitrary functions and finite lists:

```
foldlApp : (∀a. [spineL a ≡ True] ⇒
           (∀acc. ∀b. ∀f.
              foldl f acc (a ++ b) ≡ foldl f (foldl f acc a) b
           ))
```

It is trivial to prove that the result of appending two finite lists is a finite list, in other words (++) terminates when given terminating arguments:

$$spineApp : \underline{\forall} as.\ \forall bs.\ [spineL\ bs\ \equiv\ True]\ \Rightarrow$$
$$(spineL\ (as +\!\!+\ bs)\ \equiv\ spineL\ as)$$

Knowing that append terminates, we can show that the compilation of a finite arithmetic expression results in a finite instruction stream:

$$spineComp : [spineApp]\ \Rightarrow$$
$$(\underline{\forall} e.\ [spineE\ e\ \equiv\ True]\ \Rightarrow\ (spineL\ (comp\ e)\ \equiv\ True)$$
$$)$$

Instantiating *foldlApp* with the function *exec* allows us to establish a fact about the stack–based evaluator (*go*) which will be needed in the proof of the main theorem.

$$goApp : [foldlApp]\ \Rightarrow$$
$$(\forall a.\ [spineL\ a\ \equiv\ True]\ \Rightarrow$$
$$(\forall b.\ \forall s.\ \forall store.\ go\ s\ (a +\!\!+\ b)\ store\ \equiv\ go\ (go\ s\ a\ store)\ b\ store$$
$$))$$

And finally, the correctness of stack–based evaluation is formally stated and proved.

$$evalGo : [spineComp,\ goApp]\ \Rightarrow$$
$$(\underline{\forall} e.\ [spineE\ e\ \equiv\ True]\ \Rightarrow$$
$$(\forall s.\ \forall store.\ go\ s\ (comp\ e)\ store\ \equiv\ (evalExp\ e\ store : s))$$
$$)$$

An aside: initially we had got the definition of the compiling function *comp* wrong, having accidentally swapped x and y in the expression ($Expr\ x\ op\ y$). The mistake became obvious from the trace of the failed proof of *evalGo*.

6.2 A small imperative language

The second part of the interpreter exercise involves a simple imperative programming language, *SImpL*. We already have a language of arithmetic expressions, which can be extended by students with new operations. All operations used in those expressions are, however, side–effect–free. To illustrate the concepts of imperative programming, the language is extended with *commands* which modify the store.

$$\begin{array}{lll} Command\ v & ::= & Skip\ \mid \\ & & Assign\ v\ (Exp\ v)\ \mid \\ & & Compose\ (Command\ v)\ (Command\ v)\ \mid \\ & & IfThenElse\ (Exp\ v)\ (Command\ v)\ (Command\ v)\ \mid \\ & & While\ (Exp\ v)\ (Command\ v) \end{array}$$

Commands are interpreted by the function *evalCmd*:

```
evalCmd = λ c store →
  case c of
  Skip → store
  Assign v e → assign v (evalExp e store) store
  Compose cmd0 cmd1 →
           (evalCmd cmd1 . evalCmd cmd0) store
  IfThenElse e cmd0 cmd1 →
              case evalExp e store > 0 of
              True → evalCmd cmd0 store
              False → evalCmd cmd1 store
  While e cmd →
        let f = λ store →
              case evalExp e store > 0 of
              True → (f . evalCmd cmd) store
              False → store
        in f store
```

It is the students' task to extend *evalCmd* to interpret other commands, e.g. *IfThen*, *Repeat*. More interestingly, students are required to show that the command interpreter possesses certain properties. For example, a *While* command can be unrolled using *IfThenElse* and *Compose*:

$$\begin{aligned}&\mathit{while} : \forall cmd.\ \forall e.\ \mathit{evalCmd}\ (\mathit{IfThenElse}\ e\\ &\qquad (\mathit{Compose}\ cmd\ (\mathit{While}\ e\ cmd))\ \mathit{Skip}) \equiv\\ &\quad \mathit{evalCmd}\ (\mathit{While}\ e\ cmd)\end{aligned}$$

This theorem poses no difficulty for the theorem prover. The proof involves case analysis on a boolean expression:

$$\mathit{IfThenElse}\ e_2\ (\mathit{Compose}\ cmd_1\ (\mathit{While}\ e_2\ cmd_1))\ \mathit{Skip}$$
$$\not\equiv$$
$$\mathit{While}\ e_2\ cmd_1$$

Case analysis on : $\mathit{evalExp}\ e_2\ store > 0$

$$[(\mathit{evalExp}\ e_2\ store > 0) \equiv \bot] \Rightarrow$$
$$\bot \equiv f\ store$$

$$[(\mathit{evalExp}\ e_2\ store > 0) \equiv \mathit{True}] \Rightarrow$$
$$\mathit{evalCmd}\ cmd_1 \equiv \mathit{evalCmd}\ cmd_1$$

$$[(\mathit{evalExp}\ e_2\ store > 0) \equiv \mathit{True}] \Rightarrow$$
$$(f\ .\ \mathit{evalCmd}\ cmd_1)\ store \equiv (f\ .\ \mathit{evalCmd}\ cmd_1)\ store$$

$[(evalExp\ e_2\ store > 0) \equiv True] \Rightarrow$
$f\ store \equiv (f\ .\ evalCmd\ cmd_1)\ store$

$[(evalExp\ e_2\ store > 0) \equiv True] \Rightarrow$
$evalCmd\ (While\ e_2\ cmd_1)$
$\equiv$
$(\lambda\ store \rightarrow$
case $evalExp\ e_2\ store > 0$ **of**
$True \rightarrow (f\ .\ evalCmd\ cmd_1)\ store$
$False \rightarrow store)$

$[(evalExp\ e_2\ store > 0) \equiv True] \Rightarrow$
$evalCmd\ (While\ e_2\ cmd_1) \equiv f$

$[(evalExp\ e_2\ store > 0) \equiv True] \Rightarrow$
$evalCmd\ cmd_1 \equiv evalCmd\ cmd_1$

$[(evalExp\ e_2\ store > 0) \equiv True] \Rightarrow$
$(evalCmd\ (While\ e_2\ cmd_1)\ .\ evalCmd\ cmd_1)\ store$
$\equiv$
$(f\ .\ evalCmd\ cmd_1)\ store$

$[(evalExp\ e_2\ store > 0) \equiv True] \Rightarrow$
$evalCmd\ (Compose\ cmd_1\ (While\ e_2\ cmd_1))\ store$
$\equiv$
$f\ store$

$[(evalExp\ e_2\ store > 0) \equiv False] \Rightarrow$
$evalCmd\ Skip\ store \equiv f\ store$

$evalCmd\ (IfThenElse\ e_2\ (Compose\ cmd_1\ (While\ e_2\ cmd_1))\ Skip)$
$\equiv$
$evalCmd\ (While\ e_2\ cmd_1)$

Proof State:

– – – – – – – – – –

This is where we stop with this example. In a course oriented towards programming language implementation we could continue by compiling commands into low-level instructions, and prove that the compiled code is correct. We could make life considerably harder by extending *Command* with jumps, procedures, local declarations, and so on.

7 Related work

The design of the theorem prover has been influenced by the classic Boyer–Moore system [2]. In comparison with Boyer–Moore, our theorem prover is less 'automatic': it does not attempt to generalize goals, for example, and it never applies induction of its own accord. On the other hand, delegating the responsibility for the more creative parts of a proof to the user results in a system that does not rely on heuristics, has a well–defined operational semantics, and is thus easily predictable. Unlike the Boyer–Moore system, our prover is targeted at a *non-strict* functional language, and consequently does not require that termination be proved for all function definitions.

The LCF prover and its heirs, and the Isabelle system [12] in particular, have had a major influence on the design of the theorem prover. Isabelle is a generic theorem prover, allowing various object logics to be used. Its meta–level inference mechanism is based on resolution with higher–order unification. In comparison with Isabelle, our prover is significantly less powerful, being restricted to one logic and object language; on the other hand, it is easier to control, and uses fast term rewriting for object language expressions.

The prover compares favourably with other specialized provers for functional languages. For example, it offers the expressiveness of a first–order logic, whereas [3] only has equational reasoning. The logic of the prover makes it more powerful than fold–unfold systems (e.g. [15]). It can be used to establish total correctness, while fold–unfold transformations do not in general guarantee that termination properties are preserved.

8 Further work and conclusion

The theorem prover we have used has a number of desirable features: it is compatible with Haskell; it has a fairly powerful logic, and theorems are not limited to equality of expressions, as e.g. in [3]; it is easy to control, and there is no separate language of tactics and tacticals. On the other hand, the prover has certain limitations: only Core Haskell is allowed; existential assertions cannot be proved; the proof trace doesn't say what theorems, axioms or definitions have been applied. Overcoming some of these limitations will be the subject of further work.

The reader will appreciate the importance of teaching students to reason about programs, and not just to program. We have tried to demonstrate that formal reasoning can be fun, if appropriate machine support is available.

A tool for theorem proving can be used in various ways, depending on the scope and level of the course. In an introductory course, it can just illustrate theorems by providing their proofs. In a more advanced course, students may be asked to 'fill in the gaps', e.g. to justify particular steps in a proof. Finally, students may be asked to prove theorems on their own.

A Course description

Title 'Algorithmics and Functions'.

Aims The aim of the course is to encourage students to: learn some simple functional programming, be able to prove simple properties about these programs, and to qualitatively understand the distinction between different complexity classes.

Students Students are accepted onto the MSc programme provided that they have a reasonable BSc degree in a 'numerate' subject.

Year Conversion course MSc.

Prerequisites Some exposure to imperative programming.

Textbooks For the part of the course we are here describing in this paper, the textbook is Bird and Wadler [1]. For the complexity aspects, we subsequently use Harel [6].

Timetable The course lasts nine weeks.

	number of times per week	duration per session	total duration per week
lecture hours	1	1.5	1.5
laboratories	1	2.5	2.5

Assessment The students are assessed by a two hour written examination (counting for 75% of the marks) and by four assessed practicals (counting for 25% of the marks).

References

1. R.J. Bird and P.L. Wadler. *An Introduction to Functional Programming.* Prentice-Hall Series in Computer Science. Prentice-Hall International (UK) Ltd., Hemel Hempstead, Hertfordshire, England, 1988.
2. Robert Boyer and J. S. Moore. *A Computational Logic Handbook.* Academic Press, 1988.
3. P.J. Brumfitt. Metamorph - a formal methods toolkit with application to the design of digital hardware. *Journal of Functional Programming,* 2(4):437–473, October 1992.
4. A.J. Field and P.G. Harrison. *Functional Programming.* Addison-Wesley International Computer Science Series, 1988.
5. H. Glaser, C. Hankin, and D. Till. *Principles of Functional Programming.* Prentice-Hall International, Inc., London, 1984.
6. D Harel. *Algorithmics: the Spirit of Computing.* Addison-Wesley, 1987.
7. D.R. Lester. *Combinator Graph Reduction: A Congruence and its Applications.* Dphil thesis, Oxford University, 1988. *Also* published as Technical Monograph PRG-73.
8. D.R. Lester. CS412 - Algorithmics and Functions. Course notes, University of Manchester, 1992.

9. D.R. Lester and S. Mintchev. Towards machine–checked compiler correctness for higher–order pure functional languages. In L. Pacholski and J. Tiuryn, editors, *Proceedings of the 1994 Annual Conference of the European Association for Computer Science Logic*, pages 369–381. Springer-Verlag LNCS 933, 1995.
10. S. Mintchev. Mechanized reasoning about functional programs. In K. Hammond, D.N. Turner, and P. Sansom, editors, *Functional Programming, Glasgow 1994*, pages 151–167. Springer-Verlag Workshops in Computing, 1994.
11. H.R. Nielson and F. Nielson. *Semantics with applications : a formal introduction.* Wiley, 1992.
12. L.C. Paulson. *Isabelle: A Generic Theorem Prover.* Springer-Verlag LNCS 828, 1994.
13. R. Plasmeijer and M. van Eekelen. *Functional Programming and Parallel Graph Rewriting.* Addison-Wesley, 1993.
14. C. Reade. *Elements of Functional Programming.* International Computer Science Series. Addison-Wesley, 1989.
15. C. Runciman, I. Toyn, and M. Firth. An incremental, exploratory and transformational environment for lazy functional programming. *Journal of Functional Programming*, 3(1):93–117, January 1993.

Conceptual Structures for Recursion

C T Peter Burton

Dept. of Computer Science,
Queen Mary and Westfield College (University of London),
Mile End Road, London E1 4NS, UK.
peterb@dcs.qmw.ac.uk

Abstract. Consideration will be given to the perplexity students experience with recursive function definitions. Certain conceptual structures will be suggested, which might provide a path through the thicket. In particular, emphasis will be placed on decisions that a programmer makes during the course of designing a recursive definition. By drawing attention to these decisions – by classifying them and making them explicit – it is possible to delineate the kind of "space" within which creativity operates. To vivify this, a rudimentary taxonomy of recursive function definitions will be sketched here. It will be illustrated in a particular application area, involving a family of simple string-processing tasks. This will highlight two different kinds of structure: (i) classification of different tasks within the family, (ii) classification of different approaches to a single task. Some of the points to be raised are not specific to recursion; accordingly, connections will be drawn here and there with certain more general pedagogical themes promulgated by Peter Landin in recent years.

1 Introduction

Recursion has a central place in any well-rounded curriculum, but can be one of the last topics with which students become comfortable. That it is seen to be "hard" is a matter of fairly routine observation: students tend to avoid using it (sometimes preferring bizarre alternative solutions); exam questions on recursion are shunned, or answered poorly in comparison to others.

There is also the evidence of direct student comments. The most frequent of all is along the lines of "we can see that it [a particular function definition] works, but we can't see where you got it from". This is a reminder that understanding the execution mechanism is, while obviously necessary, not remotely sufficient to grant skill in writing definitions. Sometimes, such remarks indicate that the speaker believes there is some way of eliminating the need for creativity altogether. This is a common student misconception, which becomes particularly acute in the case of recursion.

This paper advances two positions. The first (Sections 2 and 3) is that students sometimes find themselves having to internalise the concept of recursion in close conjunction with other concepts which might themselves be, as yet, imperfectly assimilated. The second, and more substantial of the two, is that there is value in making explicit the kind of choice-structure within which one operates when designing a recursive definition. Part of this "space of possibilities" can be illuminated by providing a broad taxonomy of different kinds of recursion – this is sketched rapidly in Sect. 4. Different, and finer-grained, "spaces" arise when considering the detail of a particular kind of recursion: a couple of such sub-taxonomies are indicated in Sect. 5. We then touch upon two other classification axes: different approaches to a single example (Sect. 6) and different examples linked by a common approach (Sect. 7). Some other themes in the teaching of recursion are mentioned briefly in Sect. 8.

The word "recursion" in the title is deliberately vague. This paper will mostly concern recursive *function* definitions. Functions are not the only kind of things amenable to this – the relations defined by a logic program are another obvious kind, which will not be discussed. Also, in non-strict languages, it is possible to write recursive definitions of infinite lists (and other infinite data-items): these will be discussed before we turn to functions themselves.

The observations made here are based on four years during which I have taught functional programming, in Miranda. The code in this paper is Miranda (or meant to be). Details of the course appear in the appendix. As a matter of assessment rather than teaching, I have had success with setting multiple-choice tests which probe students' ability to match perturbations of a simple definition (such as those in Sect. 5) with the corresponding results; the tests seem to be popular and well-answered.

2 Separation of Concerns

Ironically, it is the very convenience (of writing recursive definitions in functional languages) which seems to provide one of the initial obstacles to learning. Students are mystified by the fact that so much can be said in just a couple of lines. This discrepancy, between the depth of what is expressed and the amount of syntactic "stuff" needed to express it, makes students suspicious: "surely this can't be right", they think. The convenience of expression can make functional programming seem like a rather exclusive club, to which the rites of initiation are unclear.

This may derive from the fact that it is tempting to present a tightly integrated package of ideas which, while working with wonderful clockwork perfection together, would nevertheless pedagogically be better considered in isolation at first. One such package comprises the ideas of list-processing, recursion and pattern-matching. Each of these three is logically separate from the other two, and involves conceptual barriers of its own. It is profitable therefore to decompose the package into its three components.

List-processing is, admittedly, the most fertile of all soils for functional programming applications, and no-one will wish to linger over-long in the more arid realm of number-recursion. Even this realm, however, has its occasional oases: particularly when the temporary restriction to *recurse on numbers* is mitigated by allowing functions to *return lists.* This represents a worthwhile half-way house, suitable for an over-night stay at least: it is easier for students to understand list-processing when, for the moment, lists are being only *constructed* and not *traversed*. A whole family of such examples arises when generating "star-displays" of various sizes (the size being what is recursed on): see Sect. 8.

Admittedly again, there is one circumstance in which the ideas of recursion and pattern-matching sit well together right from the start, particularly with number recursion – namely, when presenting certain recursive definitions as mere *true statements* about arithmetic. As an obvious example, the statements

$$x \times 0 = 0$$
$$x \times (y + 1) = x + (x \times y)$$

transliterate into a Miranda definition of multiplication:

```
x $times 0 = 0
x $times (y+1) = x + (x $times y)
```

For such definitions, to drive a wedge between recursion and pattern-matching (i.e. to write a version with explicit conditionals) feels somewhat like cutting across the grain of the matter. Nevertheless, my current practice is to strip away from recursion, initially, both list-processing (so that discussion takes place within the familiar realm of arithmetic) and pattern-matching. Even after list-processing is introduced, it is still instructive (at the start) to make explicit the conditionals and head/tail operations which would otherwise be implicit in the pattern-matching.

3 Infinite Lists

We have mentioned setting lists and pattern-matching on one side, for a while. Later, when these concepts are re-admitted to the discussion, there are two other useful ways to limit the scope temporarily. One is to consider function definitions without conditionals at all (whether explicit or of the pattern-matching kind). The other is to consider recursively defined values which are not functions. Both these situations arise in connection with infinite lists – making essential the use of a "lazy" language.

The simplest infinite lists are those which consist of a single value repeated. Such a list, xs, is equal to its own tail:

```
xs = tl xs
```

Unlike those mentioned in the previous section, the above is a "true statement" which, despite mentioning xs on both sides, does not constitute a recursive definition. The following however does:

```
xs = 0 : xs
```

Here we have a recursive definition of a non-function value: an infinite list. As lists are easier to visualise than functions, this seems a good way of broaching the matter of recursion early on. Later, I sometimes follow this up by showing how, by a slightly more complicated recursive definition, again relying on laziness, it is possible to set up in effect a data-type of doubly-linked lists – even in a purely declarative language like Miranda.

The other special situation mentioned at the start of this section was that of "unconditionally recursive" function definitions. An example emerges smoothly from the discussion of xs above. As a preparatory step, let us generalise from 0 to an arbitrary value x; that leads to the following function definition:

```
repeat x = xs where xs=x:xs
```

This is in a sense the "mildest" possible way in which recursion might figure in a function definition: the definition of `repeat` itself is not recursive, but it involves a (non-function) recursion within its right-hand side. Equivalent to the above is the following:

```
repeat x = x : repeat x
```

This time the definition of `repeat` itself is recursive. This is still a very "mild" form of recursion, because the argument never changes. From here it is a short step to an example in which the argument does change – `natsFrom n` returns a list of all the natural numbers, starting from `n`, in order:

```
natsFrom n = n : natsFrom(n+1)
```

If it is desired to continue with the theme of "unconditionally recursive" definitions, there are many interesting functions which recurse down an infinite structure, returning an infinite structure.

4 Taxonomy

In the previous sections, various special cases of recursion arose. Because of their simplicity, they seem natural choices as nursery slopes. Let us now switch to the view from the peak. Perhaps the first division to catch to the eye is that between the following two broad families of recursive definition: (i) those which proceed by "steady descent", and (ii) those involving a "computed call", i.e. some non-trivial computation to yield the argument of the recursive call. In the case of list-recursion, (i) refers roughly to the kind which can be encapsulated by some kind of `foldr` combinator. Family (ii) is a rather wilder terrain – the guarantee of termination is not immediate in the way which it is for explicitly primitive recursive definitions. Some well-trodden paths, though, can be pointed out to the student-traveller, such as "descent by halving" (e.g. binary search, log-time exponentiation, mergesort and quicksort) or, even more prosaically, "uphill" recursions – such as the following:

```
f n = "", if n>31
    = cell ++ "\n" ++ f(n+1) , if n mod 7 = 0
    = cell ++ f(n+1), otherwise
      where cell = rjustify 3 (shownum n)
```

which forms a crude starting-point for developing a calendar-display program. If they can "picture" the recursion scanning through the calendar-display, the students are afforded yet another way to relate recursion to intuition.

Other bases for classification can be considered.

1. If there are two or more parameters, is the recursion on one parameter only – using the others as accumulators?
2. If the recursion involves more than one parameter, are they traversed "in step"? Is there one recursive call, or more than one?
3. If more than one, will only one be executed (as in binary search)?
4. Is the number of recursive calls fixed, or itself the outcome of some computation?
5. Regarding a particular recursive call, is it "tail-recursive"?
6. Is the argument to a recursive call itself obtained by invoking the same function (as in Ackermann)?

The point, of any such classification enterprise, is to provide a route-map, so that students can know what areas have been visited and what is still to come. On encountering, or planning, a new recursive definition, they should know where it belongs on the map – or whether a new part of the map needs to be drawn. They should have some feel for which areas are of everyday use, and which are comparatively recondite. One rather sparsely populated area is that of tail-recursive unaries. Indeed, if additionally constrained to "steady descent" it becomes totally uninhabited (by any non-trivial functions). Without this constraint however, there are some worthwhile examples, such as this:

```
f xs = xs, if xs = mkset xs
     = f(xs -- mkset xs), otherwise
```

which returns a list of those elements which have the greatest number of occurrences in `xs` (the Miranda function `mkset` discards duplicate occurrences, while `--` performs list-subtraction). I tend to use this as the starting-point for a series of applications which implement increasingly complicated kinds of "voting".

Let us return to number (i) of the two families mentioned at the start of this section – the family of "steady descent" definitions – in order to indicate some finer distinctions within those. Such definitions can be expressed by pattern-matching if desired – but this belongs to a rather different level of classification, concerning the manner of syntactic expression rather than the kind of recursive structure itself. More significantly, subdivisions arise according to the "rate" of descent: for example, a test for even/oddness naturally wants to take its argument two steps at a time. For any such function there is a choice of three styles of definition: a single n-step recursion; n single-step functions defined by mutual recursion; a single one-step function returning an n-tuple of results. The distinction, between these three styles, does not change the abstract structure of the recursion and yet can influence the run-time performance.

We now move to an even smaller-scale route-map. We shall focus on a simple kind of "steady descent", and make some distinctions within that.

5 Sub-taxonomies and Symmetries

The following function removes all spaces from a string – or, more generally, removes all characters satisfying predicate sp:

```
remSps "" = ""
remSps chs
     = remSps rest, if sp ch
     = ch : remSps rest, otherwise where ch:rest = chs
```

This can serve as a springboard for defining some new functions – again concerned with removing certain characters from a string. These function definitions will partly resemble remSps: the left-hand side patterns will be the same, but the right-hand sides different. The definition of remSps contains two recursive calls; of these, the first is tail-recursive and the second not (because of ch:). What happens if these features are systematically "perturbed"?

In particular, let us consider the effect of having a recursive call in just one of the two places. Independently, we can introduce variations in the issue of where (and whether) ch: occurs. As a rather incomplet summary, Fig. 1 shows a three-by-three table. The rows are labelled with three different possibilities for the right-hand side of the "if sp ch" equation; similarly the column-labels apply to the "otherwise" equation. The resulting nine functions, which in the table are all signified by the name f, happen to be describable using built-in Miranda combinators:

	ch : f rest	f rest	ch : rest
ch : f rest	id	filter sp	id
f : rest	filter (not.sp)	const ""	dropwhile sp
ch : rest	id	dropwhile (not.sp)	id

Fig. 1. Variants of remSps

Why ask this kind of question? It is intended to serve the general endeavour indicated in Sect. 1: that of finding ways of "inviting students in" to the activity of writing recursive definitions. "Where do you get it from?" is the constant enquiry. There are more direct ways of answering (see Sect. 8), but they are not fully satisfying, particularly in cases as simple as remSps. Instead, as an alternative and supplementary approach, I like to explore all the possible definitions that can be written, within a certain narrow range. This can also be presented in terms of *perturbing* a *given* definition and exploring the results. This can be more instructive than getting too mesmerised by the question of how the original definition came to be given.

For this "perturbation" activity to be successful, certain features are needed. One is that a clear game be perceived by the students: "change such-and-such to such-and-such", where the range of possibilities for "such-and-such" is clearly stated, finite (to enable a complete table to be drawn up), not huge (so that the investigation be feasible), and not too small (so that it be satisfying). Also the functions computed, by the various perturbed definitions, should be simple enough to be understandable; in the case of Fig. 1, for example, each of the nine functions (not all different of course) is readily describable either by a simple non-recursive Miranda expression, or in English (e.g. "remove leading spaces"). Finally, it is particularly satisfying if some symmetry is present; in this example, a glance at Fig. 1 is enough to observe a degree of symmetry in the nine versions.

Let us look at another example: this time there are eight versions and, instead of a three-by-three grid, they form a "cube". One corner of the cube is given by the following:

```
f 0 where
f i = [], if i>n
    = g i : f(i+1), otherwise
```

The function `f` calls `g` on each of the numbers `0` to `n`, and returns a list of the results: `[g 0, ..., g n]`. The following, with an accumulator parameter, returns the reversed list `[g n, ..., g 0]`:

```
f 0 [] where
f i xs = xs, if i>n
       = f(i+1) (g i : xs), otherwise
```

If it is desired to return the original list, using this accumulator method, then there are two ways to alter the code (other than by introducing an explicit `reverse`). One way is to use counting-down recursion instead of counting-up: such a version is obtained by swapping `0` and `n`, and changing `>` to `<`. The other way (inefficient, as it happens) is to accumulate at the other end of the list: changing `(g i :)` to `(++[g])`. Thus we have three axes of classification:

1. counting-up recursion or counting-down;
2. adding `g i` to the front or to the end;
3. adding `g i` to an accumulator parameter or to the result of the recursive call.

These give rise to eight versions, of which four return the reverse of what the other four return. We can think of there being three independently applicable *transformations* associated with the three "axes" listed above. Reversal depends on whether an odd or even number of the three transformations is applied. This is a symmetry of a rather banal kind, but pedagogically it serves to highlight the mutualy independence of the transformations and the fact that, in terms of the *denotation* of the function, any two of the transformations cancel each other out. Students may like to picture the mutually equivalent pairs of programs as being located at those pairs of corners which are *not* connected by an edge of the cube. If there are any who are familiar with groups, they might note that these three transformations generate $C_2 \times C_2 \times C_2$, while the passage from a function definition to its denotation is associated with a homomorphism from that group to C_2.

6 Enumerating Versions

In the examples of Sect. 5, we were in some sense making a complete enumeration of all possible recursive definitions within some small and tightly delineated space of possibilities. The points in this space were function-definitions for *different* functions, in general. An alternative kind of enumeration arises when one considers just *one* function, and proceeds to classify different approaches to defining it.

An example I find useful is that of "splitting a string into words". The classification of approaches to defining this function turns out to be interesting without being overwhelming. The approaches can be related to the various divisions of the taxonomy sketched in Sect. 4. For instance, the following belongs to the sub-taxonomy of "computed call" recursion, as the argument for the recursive call has to be computed by an auxiliary function `skipFirstWord`:

```
words "" = []
words (' ' : rest) = words(skipSpaces rest)
words chs  = getLeadingWord chs : words(skipLeadingWord chs)
```

The auxiliary functions are defined in the obvious way (and incidentally arise as further variants of the `remSps` of Sect. 5). A small side-step from here leads to a version which uses tupling in order to `get` and `skip` simultaneously:

```
words "" = []
words (' ' : rest) = words(skipSpaces rest)
words chs = w : words rest where
            (w,rest) = leadingWord_and_rest chs
```

These version embody a decision to make maximal use of auxiliary functions, in order to clarify the overall function. A quite different decision – to use no auxiliaries at all – leads to the following:

```
words [] = []
words (' ' : chs) = words chs
words [ch] = [[ch]]
words (ch : ' ' : chs) = [ch] : words chs
words (ch : chs) = (ch:w) : ws where w:ws = words chs
```

This uses pattern-matching *on the result of the recursive call*, in order to access the first word found by that call. A related strategy is to build up that word in an accumulator parameter `w`:

```
words chs = f "" chs where
            f "" "" = []
            f w  "" = [w]
            f "" (' ':rest) = f "" rest
            f w  (' ':rest) = w : f "" rest
            f w (ch:rest) = f (w++[ch]) rest
```

The strategy can be extended (just for the sake of illustration) to accumulate the list of words ws as well, giving tail-recursion:

```
words chs = f [] "" chs where
            f ws "" "" = ws
            f ws w  "" = ws ++ [w]
            f ws "" (' ':rest) = f ws "" rest
            f ws w  (' ':rest) = f (ws++[w]) "" rest
            f ws w (ch:rest) = f ws (w++[ch]) rest
```

These last three versions, while using some form of "steady descent", depart from the normal system of three cases: empty-string, space-first, non-space first. This trichotomy can be re-established, by defining two mutually recursive functions. Of these, words2 "knows" that that the previous character was a non-space, and is accordingly quite happy to produce the empty word, as this will be fleshed out to a non-empty word by the function which called words2:

```
words "" = []
words(' ':chs) = words chs
words(ch:chs) = (ch:w):ws where w:ws = words2 chs
words2 "" = [""]
words2(' ':chs) = "" : words chs
words2(ch:chs) = (ch:w):ws where w:ws = words2 chs
```

It is of interest to consider to what extent these approaches constitute *all* the "reasonable" recursive ones. Finally, the students' appreciation of recursion is enhanced by comparing such versions with non-recursive ones. The present example suggests a couple of direct approaches. One is to characterise the words in chs as those space-free segments which in which each end either meets a space or else is anchored to an extremity of the entire string:

```
[ seg a b chs
| a <- [1..#chs] ; a = 1     \/ chs $at (a-1) = ' '
; b <- [a..#chs] ; b = #chs \/ chs $at (b+1) = ' '
; ~ member (seg a b chs) ' '
]
```

The above is a Miranda list-comprehension which selects out precisely such segments (the auxiliary function seg returns the segment of chs from position a to position b inclusive). A contrasting non-recursive approach is to take all the non-empty segments of the original string (flanked by "sentinel" spaces) and pass this list of segments through a pipeline of filters and transformations:

```
words chs = ( filter (and . map (~=' '))
            . map (tl . init)
            . filter ((=' ') . hd)
            . filter ((=' ') . last)
            . filter ((>2) . (#))
            ) (ne_segments (" "++chs++" "))
```

None of these versions is advanced as an exemplar either of style or efficiency. The purpose is rather to illustrate, in a single example, a fairly wide range of strategies. As well giving rise to quite a rich space of possible definitions, this example has the advantage of being easily related to students' experience with word-processing and compiling, and supports certain "real life" applications which I like to introduce in the latter part of a functional programming course.

7 Dualities and Family Relationships

Next we return to the theme of "symmetries", but at a slightly less obvious level than the ones in Sect. 5, and moreover this time between definitions which embody different algorithms for a single problem. Recall the familiar "insertion-sort" and "selection-sort":

```
sSort [] = []
sSort xs = m : sSort(xs -- [m]) where m = min xs
iSort [] = []
iSort(x:xs) = insert x (iSort xs) where insert ...
```

– with the obvious definition of `insert`. In terms of the taxonomy sketched in Sect. 4, these two algorithms belong to quite different branches: `iSort` proceeds by simple descent, while `sSort` has a "computed call". Further thought however reveals quite a close relationship – indeed a kind of duality between them. To see this, consider Fig. 2.

The situation in the figure is that of sorting a five-element list s_1, whose sorted version is t_1. With selection-sort, the sorted list t_1 is equal to the list of x-values depicted in the middle of the diagram: $[x_1, x_2, x_3, x_4, x_5]$, while t_2 to t_5 are successive suffixes of t_1. With insertion-sort, by contrast, the list of x-values constitutes the *original* list s_1, while s_2 to s_5 are successive suffixes of s_1.

For both algorithms, the flow of control is as indicated. Thus f is a function of one argument (coming from the north-west) and two results, while g is a function of two arguments and one result (deliverted to the south-west). What f and g actually *do* depends on which of the two algorithms we are talking about. With selection-sort, f is the "selection" function – given s_i, this function delivers the two results x_i and s_{i+1}:

$$x_i = \texttt{min}\ s_i$$
$$s_{i+1} = s_i \texttt{ -- } [x_i]$$

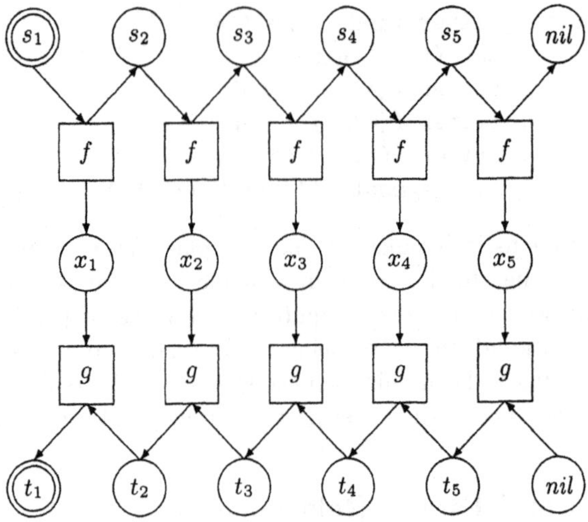

Fig. 2. Insertion/selection sorts

while g is the (two-argument, one-result) "cons" function:

$$t_i = x_i : t_{i+1}.$$

With insertion-sort, f is the "de-cons" function, which takes one argument and delivers the following two results:

$$x_i = \texttt{hd}\ s_i$$
$$s_{i+1} = \texttt{tl}\ s_i$$

while g is the (two-argument, one-result) "insert" function. Clearly "cons" and "de-cons" are the same three-place relation, P, used in different "directions". Also, the "select" and "insert" functions derive from sub-relations of a single three-place relation Q. Roughly speaking, the rôles of P and Q are interchanged, between insertion- and selection-sort.

Eschewing a more careful analysis of this "duality" here, let us merely note that it can be extended in a couple of ways. Firstly, there is a similar relationship between quicksort and merge-sort (of which, respectively, selection- and insertion-sort are obviously degenerate versions). Secondly, the relationships between all four of these sorting algorithms can be mirrored in four corresponding permutation-generation algorithms.

Observations such as these lead smoothly into certain areas of algorithmics and algorithm-classification. It is my practice (in an algorithms course, not the functional programming one) to use functional notation, where convenient, to expose the abstract structure. With algorithms such as those mentioned above, structural comparison is greatly enhanced by functional notation, notwithstanding the fact that the notation might in itself be inadequate to evince the intended run-time efficiency (the latter can be achieved separately, in a notation appropriate thereto).

We mentioned that the "insert/select" duality extends outside the area of sorting algorithms. This brings up the issue of cross-resemblences between algorithms for different tasks. Pointing these out is another way to heighten appreciation of strategies embodied in recursive definitions. For instance, the following function (which Miranda has built-in) transposes a list of lists (i.e. interchanges "columns" with "rows"):

```
transpose xss = [], if or(map (=[]) xss)
              = map hd xss : transpose(map tl xss)
```

A similar strategy can be applied to finding the breadth-first traversal of a tree:

```
breadthFirst t = f[t] where
                 f [] = []
                 f ts = map root ts ++ f(concat(map subs ts))
```

and there is furthermore a similarity, of a broader kind, with the first definition of `words` in Sect. 6 (the version with auxiliary functions).

8 Other Observations

Here I briefly mention some other policies, in teaching recursion, which seem to be successful and popular with students. The first is the plentiful provision of *reduction sequences* to illustrate program execution. This does not apply only to recursion, of course, but seems to be particularly welcome there. It highlights the fact that recursive evaluation proceeds in just the same way as any evaluation. It also allows different evaluation orders to be displayed: even though Miranda uses leftmost-outermost, it can be convenient, in understanding the recursion as a mere "true statement", to show a different order (such as call by value). Students seem enthusiastic about the game of writing down reduction sequences, and even respond by spontaneously devising their own notations to indicate the ways in which a sequence breaks naturally into sub-sequences.

Some other ideas are naturally linked to that of reduction sequences. A proof by induction involves similar steps; indeed, some features of the "recursion taxonomy" sketched here carry across to a similar taxonomy of inductive proofs. Again with similar steps, one can present fold/unfold derivations [3]. This, in simple cases, can come close to the philospher's stone which students seem to clamour for – although enthusiasm diminishes when they realise exactly what kind of "solution" this constitutes.

I have had better results with a kind of "synthesis by example". Suppose it is desired to define a "reverse" function `f`. For some typical `ch` and `rest`, write down (by oracle) `f(ch:rest)` and `f rest`. For instance, `f "abc"` is `"cba"`, while `f "bc"` is `"cb"`. By reduction (or rather unreduction) steps, rewrite `"cba"` as `"cb"++['a']`. Abstract from this to obtain `rest++[ch]`. This is circuitous, but its grounding in a particular instance seems to make it popular with students as a method (and, in fairness, it does become less risible when the example function is more substantial).

Also well received is the presentation of examples involving ASCII displays. These serve to dispel the idea that there is any inherent connection between functional programming and "mathematical" examples. The displays also have the advantage of allowing the computation structure, and in particular the recursive calls, to be visualised. Such "star-printing" examples were used extensively in [2], although its author attributes the idea in its original form to Landin. Particularly simple is the printing of a "lower-left" triangle:

```
triLL 0 = ""
triLL(n+1) = triLL n ++ rep (n+1) '*'
```

where there is a nesting of triangles inside each other, corresponding exactly to successive calls of `triLL`. By contrast, "right-handed" triangles call for something more. In the following method for lower-right triangles, successive calls can still be identified with successive sub-triangles, even though it is no longer the case that each call produces a contiguous portion of the final output:

```
triLR 0 = ""
triLR(n+1) = lay(map (' ':) (lines(triLR n)))
             ++ rep (n+1) '*'
```

As an example with two recursive calls, I am fond of using the following:

```
plant 0 = []
plant(n+1) = plant n ++ [rep(n+1)'*'] ++ plant n
```

The output is best viewed from the side (after being joined up). Alternatively, a function very similar to the `transpose` of Sect. 7 can be used to rotate the output, whereupon the following little shrub springs into view, which moreover has relationships to the Tower of Hanoi and to Gray codes:

```
               *
       *       *       *
   *   *   *   *   *   *   *
 * * * * * * * * * * * * * * *
*******************************
```

An alternative vision of the above is as a balanced, downward-growing tree. More productively, sideways-growing trees (in other words, pretty-printing of various kinds) provide a substantial family of ASCII-oriented examples, which serve a useful "real" purpose, and which can illustrate several branches of the taxonomy sketched earlier.

9 Conclusion

I can remember at an early age (which I shall not disclose) my reaction when a schoolteacher asked us to "multiply a number by itself". This has little to do with self-reference admittedly, but the phrase "by itself" triggered puzzlement (which was not shared by anyone else in the class). For me at the time, it was like being asked for the sound of one hand clapping. Perhaps (and this is a generous interpretation of my problem) I felt that, to square a number, I needed two "copies" of that number, and hence was not really multiplying it by "itself".

The point of this little anecdote is a conjecture: perhaps students are puzzled, unnecessarily, by the language (I refer to natural language here) with which we talk to them about recursion. Peter Landin[1] is fond of pointing out the numerous inconsistencies with which such language is riddled (the phrase "calls itself", for instance, probably elides all kinds of different semantic levels). An advantage of teaching via reduction sequences (mentioned in Sect. 8) is that it enables us to take the (natural) language out – just reduce, reduce, reduce (perhaps with the aid of a machine [5]).

In any case, language barriers account only for the "first stage" of perplexity: the *mechanism* of recursion. The second stage concerns the barriers in *creating* recursive definitions. This can seem, to students, to be a game which only their instructors can play. Playing a game requires, as a minimum, knowledge of the legal moves and what constitutes a win or a loss. To play well, in part, involves the ability to classify situations rather than working out each one from scratch. This, crudely, is my motivation in proposing classification structures. It also seems to provide students with a different kind of "game", arising from open-ended questions like the following: Are these *all* the significantly different approaches to defining this function? Can any of you think of another one? What about a more efficient one? What notion of "significantly different" is in operation?

In some ways recursion is the touchstone of functional programming. Admittedly, much can be done with combinators such as `foldr`, and Miranda's list-comprehension notation, avoiding recursion altogether. This is reflected in the order of topics in [1] for example. Nevertheless, I feel there is value in an explicitly recursive approach even when it is not necessary (and there are cases when it *is* necessary). It is here that students confront the issue of self-reference. Self-reference is what ignites the flame of infinity. Without this magic tinder-box, the material both of mathematics and of computing would be incombustible and unproductive indeed.

References

1. Bird, R. & Wadler, P.: *Introduction to Functional Programming*, Prentice Hall, 1988.
2. Bornat, R.: *Programming From First Principles*, Prentice Hall, 1986.
3. Burstall, R. & Darlington, J.: *A Transformation System for Developing Recursive Programs*, JACM 24 (1977).
4. Burton, C.T.P.: *An Introduction to Functional Programming and Miranda*, International Thomson Publishing, to appear January 1996.
5. Goldson, D., Hopkins, M., Reeves, S. & Bornat, R.: *A Symbolic Calculator for Non-Strict Functional Programs*, Computer Journal 37 (1994).

[1] Also of Landinesque origin, of the ideas in this paper, is the stress on perturbations and spaces of possibilities.

Appendix: Course Description

1) *Title:* "Functional Programming".
2) *Aims:* understanding of lists, trees, polymorphism, higher-order functions, recursion, pattern-matching, algebraic types, infinite data-structures, normal- and eager-order; familiarity with the syntax of Miranda; ability to produce reduction-sequences and type-derivations on paper; on-the-spot ability to code simple tasks; experience with developing one medium-sized program during the course.
3) *Student background:* mostly computer science specialists, with a smaller number pursuing a combination of maths and computer science.
4) *Year of study:* usually first (of three); sometimes a later year for combined-subject students.
5) *Prerequisites:* none.
6) *Book:* in the coming year, the book used will be [4].
7) *Duration:* eleven weeks, comprising the following each week:
- two or three lectures (each lasting one hour);
- half an hour small-group tutorial discussion;
- two hours supervised laboratory work;
- some additional (unsupervised) laboratory time, together with reading, is expected to be undertaken by each student, but not quantified.
8) *Assessment:* multiple-choice tests during the course, assessment of one programming project handed in at the end; final written examination.

Acknowledgement

I would like to thank Paul Boca and Farhad Esfandiari, for contributing to the smooth running of the course, and also for the many insights that have emerged in our conversations.

From Transistors to Computer Architecture: Teaching Functional Circuit Specification in Hydra

John O'Donnell

University of Glasgow

Abstract. Hydra is a set of methods and software tools for carrying out digital circuit design using Haskell. It has been used successfully for three years in the third-year course on Computer Architecture at the University of Glasgow, with plans to extend its use to the advanced fourth-year course. Some of its innovative features are: Signal type classes; support for CMOS and NMOS design; a large family of higher order combining forms; a set of tools for simulation; a language for expressing control algorithms; and automated tools for deriving control circuits from control algorithms. The system contains a rich library of circuits, ranging from low level implementations of logic gates using pass transistors to complete processor designs. The chief benefit of using functional circuit specification to teach computer architecture is that a complete computer system design can be presented, at all levels of abstraction, with no details omitted, giving students a genuine understanding of how computers work.

1 Introduction

A reasonable understanding of what computers are and how they work should be part of the cultural background of every computer scientist. Yet there is limited room in the curriculum for this large topic; it must be taught efficiently or not at all.

1.1 The problem

Without an effective method for presenting computer architecture, clarity and precision are incompatible with breadth and generality. If time is spent giving a detailed and thorough grounding in the basic components and their behaviors, no time is left to show how they are combined into useful systems. Conversely, if a course focuses on system organization, it easily degenerates into a miasma of vague diagrams. Most textbooks on computer architecture are either *detailed but narrow* or *broad but vague.*

A *detailed but narrow* course covers every type of flip flop, many types of 74xxnn integrated circuit, Karnaugh maps, and various other methods for minimizing logic gates. Such detail leaves no time for complex circuits or large-scale design methodology; only designs with about 100 components are covered (4 orders of magnitude less complex than modern computer architectures). Students learn how an adder works, but not a computer. This may be appropriate for students of electrical engineering, but computer science students do not need so much detail about the technology of the 1960s and 1970s.

A *broad but vague* course is about 'systems' in the worst sense of the word: a system is explained by showing how it consists of several smaller systems connected by some wires. Without understanding the subsystems, however, there is no hope of truly understanding the larger system.

The middle way between these two extremes is not necessarily better: some textbooks give a few random low-level details and some general, vague system diagrams, but fail to explain the connections.

All of these traditional approaches have one thing in common: students finish the course with the ability to regurgitate facts they will never use, but with no real understanding of how computers work.

Similar problems afflict the design of laboratory experiments to give students hands-on experience with digital hardware. A common laboratory exercise is to "design" and build a computer system using a CPU chip, some RAM chips and the like. This gives students the illusion that they understand computer architecture, yet all the interesting concepts and ideas are buried inside the chips. The only knowledge gained from such an exercise is the detailed usage of a set of chips that will be obsolete within a few years.

A much better course would give a precise, complete presentation of a simple computer architecture at all levels of abstraction, from the low-level behaviour of transistors all the way up to the operation of the datapath, control and memory, showing how they cooperate to execute machine language programs. Few textbooks and courses achieve this goal; one exception (almost) is Prosser and Winkel's text [13], which requires an intensive full year to cover. The fundamental reason the goal is normally unachievable is that traditional courses in computer hardware use wholly inadequate notations for specifying designs (typically schematic diagrams). A complete computer architecture design requires several hundred pages with conventional notation, and takes far too much time to present.

1.2 A solution

A solution to these problems is offered by Hydra, a computer hardware description language (CHDL) based on the standard functional language Haskell [2]. Hydra has been used successfully at the University of Glasgow for a third-year undergraduate course in digital circuits and computer architecture. It has succeeded because functional circuit specification is

- *natural:* circuits are black boxes that read inputs and produce outputs, just like functions.
- *concise:* typical building block circuits require only a few lines to specify, and a complete CPU circuit can be specified in just two or three pages.

- *general:* combining forms (higher order functions) clarify the deep structure of circuits, and allow circuits with size parameters that can be changed easily.
- *executable:* students can simulate their designs and see them working (or not working).
- *precise:* specifications are unambiguous and support the use of formal reasoning.

Hydra runs on Hugs (the Haskell-compatible version of gofer), the Glasgow Haskell Compiler, and hbc (the Chalmers compiler).

The aim of this paper is to give an overview of Hydra, describe a few of its interesting features, and explain its role in teaching computer architecture. The reader is assumed to know something of functional programming [1] and hardware [13], but does not need to be an expert in either area.

2 Organization of the course

In their second year, students at Glasgow are introduced to basic computer architecture at the level of assembly language, and they are also introduced to basic logic components. Hydra is used for teaching third year students. Since this course is under active development, details have changed every year.

1. *Title of the course:* Computer Architecture
2. *Aims of the course:* To give students a working understanding of how a computer system works, at each of the major levels of abstraction: transistors, logic components, basic circuits, state machines, datapath and control.
3. *Audience:* undergraduates with major subject in computing science
4. *Year of study:* third year (in a four year degree)
5. *Prerequisites:* Programming and introductory computer architecture.
6. *Textbook:* No existing textbook covers all the course material.
7. *Duration:* The course runs for 9 weeks. The following table shows the detailed allocation of time. During each week there is either a Tutorial (discussing exercises) or a Laboratory (where the students build simple circuits using prototyping boards in order to get a hands-on feel for hardware).

	sessions per week	duration per session	total per week
Lecture	2	× 50 min	= 2 hours
Either:			
Tutorial	1	× 50 min	= 1 hour
Laboratory	1	× 2 hours	= 2 hours
Homework	1	× 2 hours	= 2 hours
Total per week			= 5 hours

8. *Assessment:* 20% assessed exercises, 80% final examination.

The course topics are:

1. *Transistors and logic gates.* A brief introduction to semiconductors, MOS capacitors and pass transistors, and the implementation of CMOS logic gates.
2. *Circuit specification.* Components as functions; wires and signals; defining circuit functions; circuit types; the synchronous model; circuit simulation.
3. *Basic circuits.* Definition of basic building blocks, including multiplexors, adders, registers, register files, buses, etc.
4. *State machines.* Systematic methods for designing state machines. Examples: design of a sequential binary multiplier; design of a pocket calculator.
5. *Instruction set architecture.* A quick review of machine language and its representation. A very simple architecture is defined, and the aim of the rest of the course is to present its implementation in full.
6. *Datapath.* A state machine implementing a processor suitable for the Instruction Set Architecture. This contains an ALU, two operand buses, a result bus, a register file (for general registers available to the machine language programmer) and miscellaneous registers required for instruction execution (PC, IR, MAR, MDR).
7. *Control.* The concept of control algorithms is introduced, along with a functional language for expressing them. A method for deriving a control circuit from a control algorithm is explained, and used to derive a control algorithm for the Instruction Set Architecture presented earlier.
8. *Computer system.* The datapath, control and memory are combined to form a complete computer system design. This is a complete circuit specification—every last logic gate is included—yet it is readable, only a few pages long, and students can simulate it to see exactly what happens as the computer executes a program. The course finishes with an introduction to Input/Output and the interface to the Operating System.

3 Circuit specification

This work was inspired by Johnson's research on the use of first-order functional programs to model synchronous digital circuits [3, 4]. Hydra was developed gradually by adding various features, including libraries of intermediate level circuits, alternative semantic interpretations for circuits [7], higher order combining forms suitable for architecture designs [8, 9, 10] and various software tools. Sheeran developed a similar (though not identical) approach based on relational programming [11, 12].

It is important to cover both schematic diagrams and functional specification, since each form of specification offers valuable insight. The most successful approach is to teach these concurrently, stressing how to work out a functional specification given an arbitrary circuit diagram and vice versa. This works well in practice, and nearly all students have no difficulty with such translations. In their design exercises, students are required to write down both the diagram and the functional specification. (To save space, the diagrams are omitted in this paper).

3.1 Circuits as functions

A circuit is a function from its inputs to its outputs. Each port connected to a circuit must be clearly specified as either an input or an output, and inputs are usually curried. A 2-input And gate with inputs b and c, and output x, can be specified as

```
x = and2 b c
```

When there are several outputs, they are gathered into a tuple. The following equation uses a half adder that computes the carry and sum of two input bits a and b:

```
(c,s) = halfAdd a b
```

An equation defines a named signal; the equations above name three signals: x, c and s. There can also be *anonymous signals*, such as the signal that connects the output from the and2 gate to the input of the inverter in

```
x = inv (and2 a b)
```

Abstraction of circuit structure is provided by function definitions. The half adder is not a primitive component; it is a black box defined as a function, using the lower level logic gate functions.

```
halfAdd :: (Signal a) => a -> a -> (a,a)
halfAdd x y = (and2 x y, xor x y)
```

Each circuit specification consists of a type declaration and a function definition. Types are just as important for circuit design as for programming, and for the same reasons: writing down the type of a circuit entails understanding clearly what its inputs and outputs are, and how they are grouped together. In practice, most circuit design errors are type errors that are caught by the typechecker.

Abstraction allows complex designs to be expressed concisely using simpler building block circuits; as a result, Hydra specifications seldom become very large. A very small example is the definition of a full adder (which adds 3 bits together) using two half adders.

```
fullAdd :: (Signal a) => (a,a) -> a -> (a,a)

fullAdd (a,b) c = (or2 w y, z)
  where (w,x) = halfAdd a b
        (y,z) = halfAdd x c
```

Here the inputs are not curried; the first two are tupled together, making the full adder easier to use with the scan combining form (presented later).

3.2 Feedback

Feedback (loops or cycles within circuits, or, to use the terminology of graph theory, circuits that contain circuits!), is specified by recursive equations. Feedback is in a sense equivalent to memory, and a typical circuit with feedback is the 1-bit register with state **s**, data input **x** and store control input **sto**.

The register uses a D-type flip flop **dff** to hold the current state. On each clock cycle, if **sto** is 1 the register will store the data input **x** into the flip flop; otherwise it will retain its previous state **s**. The multiplexor (which is specified by another 2-line Haskell definition) makes this choice.

```
reg1 sto x = s
  where s = dff (mux1 sto s x)
```

The feedback results from the appearance of **s** on both sides of the equation. This is well defined, since Hydra requires circuits to be synchronous, and each loop in a circuit must go through a clocked flip flop. In the **reg1** circuit, the value of **s** during clock cycle 0 is the 'initial power up constant', and the circular equation defines the value of **s** during clock cycle $i + 1$ using the value it had during cycle i.

3.3 Functions and pictures

There is a simple correspondence between Hydra specifications and schematic diagrams. Functions correspond to black boxes; signals correspond to wires; names (on the left hand sides of equations) appear as labels on wires. There are some deeper connections, too.

- *Fanout* means that a signal driven by one source is read by several sinks; fanout always requires an equation to name the signal, and this name then appears more than once as an argument to a function.
- *Feedback* appears as a loop in a diagram, and it appears as a circular definition in the functional specification; for example, in **reg1**, the signal **s** appears on both the left and right sides of an equation.

Experience has shown that, in teaching Hydra, it is quite important to stress the relationship between functional and schematic specifications. After several exercises converting from functions to diagrams, and from diagrams to functions, most students have no difficulty at all with this relationship. The functional and schematic notations convey slightly different information, and they present different ways of viewing a circuit. Both are necessary.

4 Signal classes

A *signal* is an abstraction of the value carried by a wire. There are many useful concrete representations for a signal.

- If we define the Signal type to be `Bool` then the inverter has type `inv :: Bool -> Bool`, and it can be simulated by applying it to Boolean constants. This model is simple, perfectly adequate for basic combinational circuits, and provides a good practical way to introduce circuit simulation in a class.
- In order to handle CMOS and NMOS circuits it is necessary to represent undefined and inconsistently defined signals, as well as values that have been weakened by resistance. The `Bool` type cannot do this; a richer algebraic data type is required.
- Sequential circuits (that contain flip flops) require a way to represent signals that change over time. The standard way to do this uses streams, and it leads to a new set of types that can represent signals.

Because there are many ways to represent a signal, each component and circuit has many possible types. Some of the possible types for an inverter are

```
inv :: Bool -> Bool
inv :: Voltage -> Voltage
inv :: Bit -> Bit
inv :: Stream Bool -> Stream Bool
inv :: Stream Voltage -> Stream Voltage
inv :: Stream Bit -> Stream Bit
```

Each type gives a different semantic interpretation for the inverter.

The original version of Hydra contained a separate library of primitive function definitions for each signal type. The user could execute a circuit specification with various semantics by loading in the specification along with a suitable primitive library.

The type class mechanism of Haskell provides a much more elegant and robust way to keep track of the signal types. The class `Signal` consists of all types that are capable of representing a signal (ie.e a set of basic functions must be defined for such types). Thus the inverter has one general type:

```
inv :: (Signal a) => a -> a
```

This says, "for any type `a` that is capable of representing a Signal, `inv` has type `a -> a`".

4.1 The Signal class

Any signal type must have a set of functions and constant definitions. There are about 30 of them, falling into the following groups:

Utility functions. The functions `tt1` and `tt2` take representations of truth tables, and construct the corresponding functions. Additional functions read and show signal.

Component types. There are two constant values, `zero` and `one`, as well as a complete set of logic gates, including the inverter `inv`, the 2-input And gate `and2` and so on. (All possible logic functions with 0, 1 and 2 inputs are included, and the And/Or/Nand/Nor gates are also defined for 3 and 4 inputs.)

Default definitions. The component functions are defined by default using their corresponding truth tables. This provides suitable component definitions for the instances of Signal intended for simulation. Some instances, however, use signal representations intended for generating netlists or analyzing the circuit; these instance definitions must override the defaults.

```
class (Eq a, Text a) => Signal a where
  showSig       :: a -> String
  tt1           :: TT1 -> a -> a
  tt2           :: TT2 -> a -> a -> a

  zero, one     :: a
  inv, ...      :: a -> a
  and2, ...     :: a -> a -> a
  and3, ...     :: a -> a -> a -> a
  and4, ...     :: a -> a -> a -> a -> a

  inv           = tt1 tt_inv
  and2          = tt2 tt_and2
  and3 a b c    = and2 a (and2 b c)
  and4 a b c d = and2 (and2 a b) (and2 c d)
  ...
```

4.2 Boolean simulation

The simplest form of simulation, and the best one to introduce first to students, represents each signal with a Boolean value.

```
instance Signal Bool where
  showSig = show
  zero    = False
  one     = True
  tt1     = tt1Bool
  tt2     = tt2Bool
```

Given suitable definitions of the `and2` and `xor` logic gates and the half adder, we can simulate the half adder by applying it to Boolean data.

```
and2, xor :: Bool -> Bool -> Bool
halfAdd :: Bool -> Bool -> (Bool,Bool)

halfAdd True False  => (False,True)
```

4.3 The class hierarchy

All signal types are in the class Signal. The `Static` class contains representations that do *not* account for time, and there are functions for performing input/output on these types. A type in class **Lattice** has additional operations that support pass transistors and resistors; these are required to implement CMOS, NMOSs and three-state drivers. The **Dynamic** class uses a stream to represent the signal, and adds an orthogonal set of operations. The most commonly used class is **Sig**, which provides a stream-of-lattice representation. The following diagram illustrates the Signal class hierarchy.

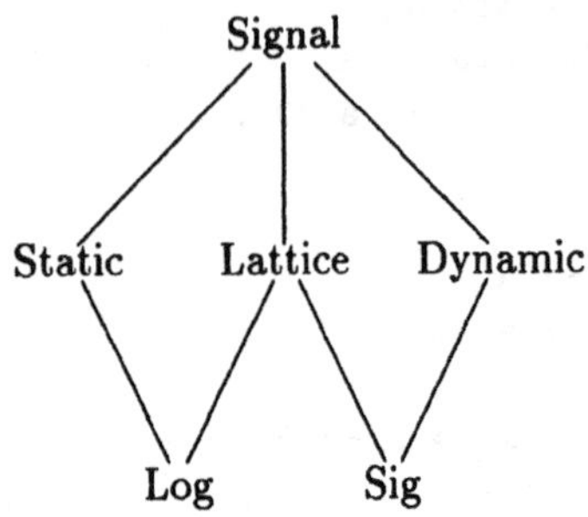

4.4 The Lattice class: behavior of transistors

The basic **Signal** class expresses some of the algebraic aspects of digital logic, but it misses most of the physical aspects. Further classes can be defined that introduce the operations needed for more precise hardware specification.

It might appear that functional hardware specification is feasible only for circuits that take well defined logic inputs and produce definite logic outputs. However, that is not the case; the Lattice class enables us to specify CMOS and NMOS circuits, as well as unusual components like three state drivers and open collector buffers.

The signal representation must include isolated values (bottom), short circuits (top) and both strong and weak representations of 0 and 1. There are two pass transistor functions, for N-channel and P-channel technology. Finally, there is a least upper bound function that defines what happens when any two signals from the Lattice are combined on a wire.

```
class (Signal a) => Lattice a where
  bot, top, weakZero, weakOne :: a
  weaken :: a -> a
  lub  :: a -> a -> a
  nchannel, pchannel :: a -> a -> a
```

In a real integrated circuit, a pass transistor has one input (the gate) and two ports **a** and **b** which are either connected or disconnected electrically according to the value on the gate. The **a** and **b** ports can be either inputs or outputs, and it is even possible to design a circuit where at times **a** is an input and **b** the output, and at other times the opposite is true.

Here we encounter a limitation of the functional model underlying Hydra. A Haskell function must clearly distinguish which are its inputs and which are its outputs. Consequently, some outlandish circuits are possible in VLSI but not expressible in Hydra. Fortunately, such bizarre examples are not often used in serious circuit design, where the emphasis is on controlling the complexity of large circuits rather than focusing on strange tiny examples.

The Hydra pass transistor functions `nchannel` and `pchannel` have two inputs, the gate `g` and the data input `a`, and they return a result on the output port `b`.

The specification of a CMOS inverter [6] illustrates how transistors can be used in Hydra. A CMOS logic gate connects the output directly to the High or to the Low power supply, depending on the input values:

$$\begin{aligned} output &= high, \quad &\textbf{if } not\ a \\ &= low, \quad &\textbf{if } a \end{aligned}$$

The circuit uses a P-channel transistor to connect the output to the constant on (i.e. the high power supply) if the inverter input is zero. The expression (pchannel a one) is one if a=zero, and it is bot if a=one. An N-channel transistor does the converse operation. Since the 'outputs' of both transistors are connected to each other, the signal value is defined to be their least upper bound.

```
cmosInv :: (Lattice a) => a -> a
cmosInv a = lub (pchannel a one) (nchannel a zero)
```

All the other combinational logic gates are designed using the same method; they offer scope for plenty of examples, plenty of exercises, and plenty of exam questions.

A three-state driver takes a data input `x` and a control input `put`. If `put` is 1 then the value of `x` is driven onto the output, but otherwise the three-state driver disconnects itself from the output. The name reflects three possible situations: the output is forced to 0, forced to 1, or there is no output at all. The purpose of this device is to provide distributed control for a bus. Pass transistors can be used to define the bus driver:

```
driver :: (Lattice a) => a -> a -> a
driver cs xs = nchannel cs xs
```

Now a three-state bus, one of the crucial subsystems in processor architecture, can be defined as the least upper bound of a set of driver outputs. This circuit appears to violate the functional paradigm, since each wire on a three-state bus is truly bidirectional. It can be expressed functionally because the value on each signal can be defined as a function applied to a set of inputs; this definition illustrates the flexibility of functional specification.

```
s3bus1 :: (Lattice a) => [(a,a)] -> a
s3bus1 xs = lubs (weakZero : map (\(c,a) -> driver c a) xs)
```

4.5 The Dynamic class

A `Dynamic` signal can support sequential circuits, which use the Delay flip flop, `dff`. We assume that when power is applied to the circuit, each flip flop stores the `initial` value (although no circuit design should rely on this).

```
class (Signal a) => Dynamic a where
  latch, dff :: a -> a
```

The essence of sequential circuits is their behavior through time, so dynamic signals are represented as streams of static values, representing the sequence of values on a signal, where the ith element of the stream is the value of the signal during clock cycle i.

It would be possible to use the ordinary Haskell list type to represent a stream, but there are two reasons for defining a completely separate type.

The main reason is that it is important to allow Haskell's typechecker to catch as many errors as possible at compile time and to give pertinent error messages. There is always a temptation to use lists to represent everything in sight, but that would allow some errors to look correct to the compiler. For example, suppose we represent a stream as a list and also represent a word as a list. Then `Stream (Word a)` and `Word (Stream a)` would both be represented by the type `[[a]]`, even though these types represent completely different objects! The compiler would not detect such errors, and the program would be likely to produce wrong answers or crash mysteriously. Therefore Hydra uses explicit abstract data types called `Stream` and `Word`.

The second reason for a separate Stream type stems from a subtle restriction having to do with type classes and modules in Haskell. It's convenient to make signals a subclass of Haskell's `Num` class. This allows us to use the conventional circuit design notation, where `a*b` is `and2 a b`, `a+b` is `or2 a b` and `(-a)` is `inv a`. The tricky bit arises for dynamic signals, where the instance declaration needs to be defined in the same module as the type constructor. Now the list type constructor is in the Haskell standard prelude, so it isn't possible to define a dynamic numeric signal instance using the list type. The problem can be avoided by defining Stream type constructors in the same module, rather than using lists.

A stream is defined just like a list, but it uses different constructors `Snil` and `Scons` that clearly identify that the object is a stream and not an ordinary list.

```
data Stream a = Snil | Scons a (Stream a)  deriving (Eq,Text)
```

Unfortunately, it now becomes necessary to define a few of the ordinary list functions for the Stream type, such as `shead`, `stail`, `snull`, `smap` and a few others.

4.6 Dynamic signals

A dynamic signal is represented as a Stream of values of type `a`, where `a` is a static signal type. This prevents someone from accidentally defining a stream of streams, which would be meaningless. The constants **zero** and **one** become streams of static signals, and the logic function builders use smap.

```
instance (Signal a, Static a) => Signal (Stream a) where
  zero = srepeat zero
  one  = srepeat one
  tt1  = smap . tt1
  tt2  = smap2 . tt2
```

The crucial sequential component is the Delay flip flop `dff`, which outputs its initial power up value during cycle 0, and subsequently outputs the value in cycle $i+1$ that was its input during cycle i.

```
instance (Signal a, Static a) => Dynamic (Stream a) where
  dff xs = Scons initial xs
```

It is straightforward to define streams of lattices, leading to a type `Bit` that represents the behaviour through time of a VLSI signal.

5 Basic circuits

The middle part of the course is devoted to building up a practical library of basic building blocks. A typical example is the multiplexor, the hardware equivalent of the if statement. A multiplexor takes a control input `a` and two data inputs; one of the data inputs becomes the output, and the choice is determined by the control.

```
mux1
  :: (Signal a)
  => a      -- control input
  -> a      -- data input case 0
  -> a      -- date input case 1
  -> a      -- output

mux1 a b c = or2 (and2 (inv a) b)
                 (and2 a c)
```

The heart of the design of a computer architecture is this systematic development of a good library. All the lessons students have learned about software engineering, structured design, documentation, testing etc. can be applied to hardware as well.

6 Combining forms

First order circuit specifications can become tedious. Here is a four-bit adder, where each full adder has an equation explicitly written out. The '?' operator extracts a bit from a word.

```
add4
  :: (Signal a)
  => Word (a,a)         -- word of in pairs
  -> a                  -- carry input
  -> (a, Word a)        -- (carry, sum)

add4 a b c = (c0, word [s0,s1,s2,s3])
  where (c0,s0) = fullAdd (a?0, b?0) c1
        (c1,s1) = fullAdd (a?1, b?1) c2
        (c2,s2) = fullAdd (a?2, b?2) c3
        (c3,s3) = fullAdd (a?3, b?3) c
```

As usual in functional programming, we should identify general patterns of circuits and specify those patterns abstractly using higher order functions. The adder propagates carry from the right to the left, and this can be specified easily using the standard **foldr** function.

```
foldr :: (a->b->b) -> b -> [a] -> b
foldr f a [] = a
foldr f a (x:xs) = f x (foldr f a xs)
```

This is a *combining form*: **foldr** expresses a common circuit pattern. The following diagram illustrates a specific case where the wordsize is 4.

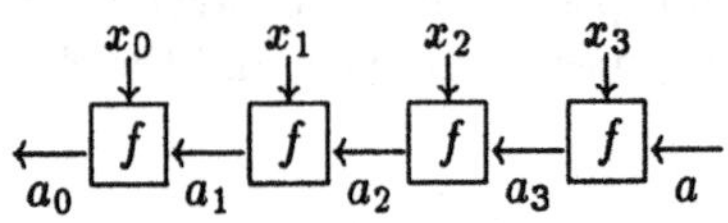

The following bidirectional fold function [10] is seldom used in programming, but it is ubiquitous in hardware design.

```
fold
  :: (a->b->c->(b,a)) -- fold circuit
  -> a                -- left input
  -> b                -- right input
  -> [c]              -- word input
  -> (b,a)            -- (left output, right output)

fold f a b [] = (b,a)
fold f a b (x:xs) = (b'',a'')
  where (b'',a') = f a b' x
        (b',a'') = fold f a' b xs
```

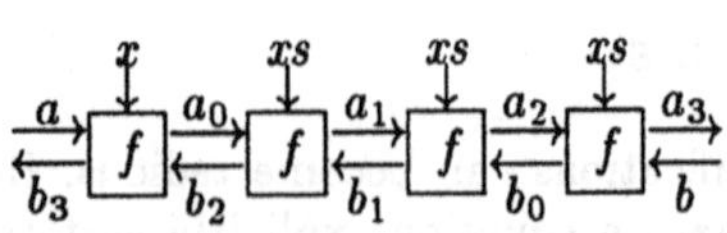

To specify the adder, we need a more general combining form: the mapping scan, which combines a map (to compute the sums) with a scan (to compute the word of partial carry propagations). The easiest way to understand the definition of **mscanr** is to compare the function with the following diagram.

```
mscanr :: (b->a->(a,c)) -> a -> [b] -> (a,[c])

mscanr f a [] = (a,[])
mscanr f a (x:xs) = (a'',y:ys)
  where (a'',y) = f x a'
        (a',ys) = mscanr f a xs
```

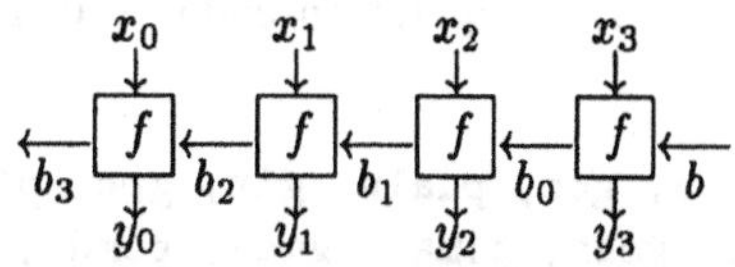

Now a general ripple carry adder of arbitrary size can be defined in one equation. This is a vivid illustration of the power of general combining forms to express circuits concisely. It is important to note that **ripAdd** defines the family of ripple carry adders for all wordsizes. In contrast, a schematic diagram would just define an adder for one fixed wordsize.

```
rippleAdd :: (Signal a) => Word (a,a) -> a -> (a, Word a)
rippleAdd = mscanr fullAdd
```

A critically important combining form is the bidirectional mapping scan, which is required for many circuits, including arithmetic-logic units (ALUs).

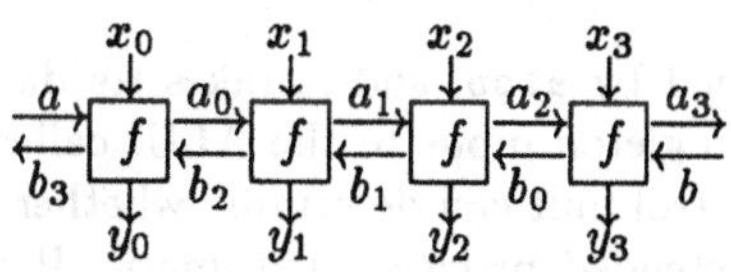

In addition to the map, fold and scan combining forms, there is a family of tree-structured functions. These are required to define general multiplexors, demultiplexors, register files and memories; in short, circuits that use addresses are usually specified using a tree combining form.

7 Datapath architecture

A processor datapath contains the ALU, registers and buses. The behaviours of all the subsystems are determined by control signals. For example, the ALU receives control signals telling it what to do (add, subtract, shift, ...) and each register receives a control signal telling it whether to load a new value or retain its previous value.

This section gives a complete datapath specification in Hydra. Although there is not enough space to explain fully all the details in this paper, all the details are here.

The inputs to the datapath are two words x_1 and x_2 which can be driven onto the buses; the memory input `mi` (which is used during memory fetches), and the collection of control inputs `ctl`. The outputs are *d* (the value on the destination bus), and the memory interface registers *mar* and *mdr*.

```
datapath x1 x2 mi ctl = (d,mar,mdr)  where
```

There are lots of control inputs, and we need to name them all within the datapath definition. This is done by a big pattern matching equation. One of the control inputs — **alop**, the ALU operation code — is a word, while the other inputs are all singletons.

```
[alop, p1x1, p2x2, a, gcc, pdalw, gir, gpc, p1pc,
 grf, p1rf1, p2rf2, gmar, p1mar, gmdr, p1mdr, pdmi]
= get_control ctl
```

The heart of the datapath definition is its collection of internal subsystems, each defined by an equation.

The datapath contains three buses: s_1 is the *source 1 bus*, s_2 is the *source 2 bus*, and *d* is the *destination bus*. The source buses carry two source inputs into the ALU, while the destination bus carries results to their destination.

```
s1 = s3bus k [(p1x1,x1), (p1rf1,rf1), (p1pc,pc),
              (p1mar,mar), (p1mdr,mdr)]
s2 = s3bus k [(p2x2,x2), (p2rf2,rf2)]
d  = s3bus k [(pdalw,aluw), (pdmi,mi)]
```

The ALU is controlled by **alop**, and it takes its data words from the two buses **s1** and **s2**. The singleton input to the ALU, called **a**, is a control input. This means that the control unit can determine whether the carry input is 0 or 1, which is useful for extended precision arithmetic. It also allows the control unit to specify the value that gets shifted in during a combinational shift.

```
(alub,aluw,alucc) = alu k alop s1 s2 a
```

The dual port register file takes 5-bit address inputs, so it has $2^5 = 32$ registers, all $k = 32$ bits wide. The destination address *da* determines which register will store the data input taken from the *d* bus. However, *reg*[*da*] will store the value on *d* only if the *grf* (get register file) control input is 1. If *grf* is 0 then *reg*[*da*] will remain unchanged. And, of course, all registers not addressed by *da* will remain unchanged. The register file is *dual port* because it takes two source addresses *sa1* and *sa2*, and it fetches and outputs the contents of both *reg*[*sa1*] and *reg*[*sa2*]. These outputs are names *rf1* and *rf2*.

```
(rf1,rf2) = dpRegFile k sa1 sa2 da grf d
```

The miscellaneous registers *mar*, *mdr*, *pc* and *ir* all take their data input from the *d* bus, and they all have a 'get' control signal that tells them whether to store the value on *d*.

```
mar = reg k gmar d
mdr = reg k gmdr d
pc  = reg k gpc d
ir  = reg k gir d
```

The instruction fields *opcode*, *da*, *sa1*, *sa2*, *immed* and *addr* are all defined by extracting fields from the *ir*, using the *ifields* specifier. This equation doesn't define any logic gates; it just names various groups of wires coming out of the *ir*.

```
[opcode,da,sa1,sa2,immed,addr] = split ifields ir
```

8 Control algorithms

A processor contains a control circuit that examines the state of the machine (primarily the Instruction register, which contains the instruction currently being executed) and generates control signals that command the subsystems in the datapath. Control is the most complex part of computer system design. There are several systematic methods for deriving control circuits, but even these systematic methods are usually presented in an informal, ad hoc and unsystematic manner.

A key concept in Hydra is the separation of control *algorithms* from control *circuits*. A control algorithm is an abstract function from system state to control signals. A control circuit is a collection of hardware components that realise a control algorithm.

The designer writes a control algorithm as a concise, readable function definition. Since the control algorithm is actually a Haskell function definition, it can be executed directly with the datapath specification in order to simulate the system. This enables a student to experiment with a datapath circuit working together with a control algorithm, without needing to provide the actual control circuit. Hydra also contains software tools that automatically derive control circuit specifications from a control function. There are several methods for doing this: delay elements, sequence counters, PLAs, etc.

9 Software tools for circuit simulation

Functional circuit specifications are executable. The meaning of a circuit depends on the meanings of its primitive components; thus by overloading the primitives, Hydra provides several alternative semantics for circuits. Some of these correspond to different forms of simulation, while others provide for the analysis of a circuit and the the extraction of its netlist [9]. The undergraduate course uses only the circuit simulation semantics.

It is very important for students to simulate their designs: it gives a great sense of satisfaction to see their circuits working (even if only in simulation). It would be even more satisfying to build the circuits with real hardware, but that is extremely time consuming and adds little fundamental understanding. The architecture course at Glasgow contains several simple laboratory exercises with real hardware, giving the course a valuable sense of reality, but most of the circuit designs are only simulated.

Hydra contains a variety of software tools to support circuit simulation. The most important of these is a set of functions that format input and output signals in various ways. For example, a processor requires a large number of control signal inputs, which would be very hard to read if written as sequences of zeros and ones. Therefore Hydra provides a simple mini-language for writing control signals concisely, along with functions to convert between the mini language and the actual control signals.

A useful technique for testing real circuits is to place a 'logic probe' on a wire, enabling the value of that signal to be read on an oscilloscope. (However, this technique cannot be used inside a chip, so it is most useful for obsolete technologies.) The advantages of functional circuit specification work against us here. A function specifies the circuit *exactly*; inserting a logic probe changes the circuit, so the functional specification must also be changed, in order to provide an additional output. Currently this must be done by hand, although it is planned to support Hydra logic probes via mechanized program transformation.

10 Formal methods

Possibly the most profound advantage of functional programming for hardware design is its excellent support for formal methods [5]. There has been ample published discussion about the costs and benefits of correctness proofs, correctness-preserving transformations and derivations from specifications. However, there is insufficient time for such topics in a short general course on computer architecture.

By far the most important formal method in teaching computer architecture is *clear, precise, unambiguous specification.* Obviously a precise specification language is required to do proofs, but the chief practical advantage for teaching computer architecture is that simulation requires a precise, formal specification, and simulation is the most valuable single technique for moving a student from a vague, woolly impression to a firm, clear understanding.

The third year course at Glasgow relies heavily on simulation, but it doesn't have enough time to introduce the other formal methods. There are plans to begin using formal derivations in Hydra for a fourth year module in advanced architecture.

11 Related work

Several alternative approaches achieve some of the goals of Hydra, and could be made the basis for a course on computer architecture.

Many courses on computer architecture use functional languages to specify the behavior of a computer at the 'instruction set architecture' level, expressing the architecture precisely as a state transition machine. This method can also be used to draw connections between architectures and programming languages.

Ruby [12] is a relational language with many similarities to Hydra. In particular, Ruby also makes heavy use of higher order combining forms to express regular circuit patterns. There are many differences of emphasis. For example, Hydra emphasises simulation more, while Ruby emphasises formal reasoning more, although each system supports both. Ruby has been applied to the design of signal processing chips, while Hydra has been applied to processor architecture design, resulting in quite different libraries of intermediate level circuits. Partly because of its emphasis on executable specifications and simulation, Hydra has always been built on top of an existing functional programming language (first Daisy, then Scheme, then LML, and now Haskell). The first working implementation of Hydra was in 1982. In contrast, Ruby is a distinct language in its own right, so implementing Ruby is a larger task.

Since they have so many similarities, and so many subtle differences, it would be very interesting to compare Hydra and Ruby in the context of a course on computer architecture.

Why not use the much more conventional industry standard language VHDL, instead of novel approaches like Hydra and Ruby? The reason is that VHDL is a far more complicated language; Hydra can be introduced gradually over a few lectures and tutorials, while VHDL requires much more time. VHDL certainly belongs in an engineering curriculum, where it can be covered in depth. However, the typical computer science curriculum allows only 20 or 30 lectures for computer architecture. If most of them are devoted to the design language, insufficient time is left for the actual content of the course.

12 Conclusions

Teaching architecture with functional circuit specification works! In the course of 18 lectures, it is possible to introduce the specification language and use it to give a clear, precise coverage of the spectrum of computer hardware, from transistors to processors. Traditional courses in computer architecture do not achieve this.

The greatest benefit of Hydra is that stronger students gain a thorough working understanding of computer architecture in just one academic term. Students who master all of the course material (and some of them do) come away with a real understanding of how computers work, not just a useless collection of facts about hardware.

All levels of computer hardware are presented precisely, from transistors to system architecture. Within each level, extraneous details are omitted. Just enough detail is presented to demonstrate the central ideas at each level, and to provide adequate tools for the next level up.

Each circuit presented can be simulated simply by executing the specification. Students can experiment with the complete system architecture; for example, there are practical exercises that require them to modify the datapath and control in order to install a new instruction into the machine language.

The computer architecture design is concise, compact, readable and precise. It corresponds directly to a schematic diagram. Size parameters (wordsize, number of registers, memory size, etc) can be modified just by changing a single equation, and the higher order combining forms automatically reconfigure the entire circuit. Circuit function types clarify the exact properties of the inputs and outputs to each circuit. Many (perhaps most) circuit design errors are caught by the Haskell typechecker.

Several important principles from computer science are demonstrated in the context of computer architecture and hardware engineering, including abstraction, systematic design, and the use of software tools (especially simulation). There is great scope for the application of formal methods.

In practice, the complexity of the Haskell type class mechanism turned out not to be a problem. The lecturer just needs to tell the class, "There are many versions of the primitive functions, one version for each signal type. When you apply a circuit specification to inputs, the computer examines the type of the inputs and automatically selects the corresponding versions of the functions." It should not be surprising that this explanation suffices: any experienced teacher of programming knows how prone students are to expect the machine to figure out what they mean!

The greatest problem with Hydra is that weak students often fail to distinguish between circuit specification and programming. For example, they occasionally use additional features in Haskell that do not correspond to any hardware component, thinking that if the Haskell program runs and produces correct outputs, their circuit specification must therefore be valid and correct. This confusion became apparent the first time Hydra was used in teaching architecture, and explicit attempts to overcome it were made in subsequent years with partial success. However, every time Hydra has been used to teach computer architecture, some students have been unable to understand the distinction.

Lest the reader become too despondent about using functional programming to teach hardware, we should note that in every class there are some students who fail to understand just about everything. The proper way to assess a fresh approach like Hydra is to see how far the strongest students go, and how much the average ones get out of the course. The weakest students will gain little or nothing from the course, regardless of what teaching methodology is used.

Unfortunately, there persists a slight degree of dogmatic opposition to functional programming. The reasons for this are unclear: no one objects to the application of techniques from software engineering, structured methodologies, human-computer interaction, and imperative programming languages to hardware. The one branch of computer science that seems to raise passionate opposition is functional programming.

It is important for the lecturer to focus on architecture, not on functional programming. The language presented should not be the *programming* language Haskell; it should be the *hardware description* language Hydra. The use of functional programming makes it possible to cover far more material about hardware, at a much deeper level, in a shorter amount of time.

References

1. R. Bird and P. Wadler, *Introduction to Functional Programming*, Prentice Hall (1988).
2. P. Hudak, S. Peyton Jones and P. Wadler (editors). Report on the Programming Language Haskell, A Nonstrict Purely Functional Language (Version 1.2), *ACM SIGPLAN Notices* **27**(5) (May 1992).
3. S. D. Johnson. *Synthesis of Digital Designs from Recursion Equations*, The MIT Press (1984).
4. S. D. Johnson. Applicative Programming and Digital Design, *11th ACM Symp. on Principles of Programming Languages (POPL)* (1984) 218–227.
5. A. Gupta, Formal Hardware Verification Methods: A Survey, *Formal Methods in System Design*, Vol. 1 No. 2/3 (1992) 151–238.
6. C. Mead and L. Conway, *Introduction to VLSI Systems*, Addison-Wesley (1980).
7. J. O'Donnell, Hardware description with recursion equations, *8th Int. Symp. on Computer Hardware Description Languages and their Applications (CHDL)*, North-Holland (1987) 363–382.
8. J. O'Donnell, Hydra: Hardware description in a functional language using recursion equations and high order combining forms, *The Fusion of Hardware Design and Verification*, G. J. Milne (ed), North-Holland (1988) 309–328.
9. J. O'Donnell, Generating netlists from executable circuit specifications in a pure functional language, *Functional Programming: Glasgow 1992*, Springer-Verlag Workshops in Computing (1993) 178–194.
10. J. O'Donnell, Bidirectional fold and scan, *Functional Programming: Glasgow 1993*, Springer (1994) 193–200.
11. M. Sheeran. muFP, A language for VLSI design, *Proc. ACM Symp. on Lisp and Functional Programming*, (1984) 104–112.
12. M. Sheeran. Designing regular array architectures using higher order functions, *Proc. Conf. Functional Programming Languages and Computer Architecture (FPCA)*, Springer-Verlag LNCS 201 (1985) 220–237.
13. F. P. Prosser and D. E. Winkel, *The Art of Digital Design*, Prentice-Hall International (1987).

Functional Programming in a Basic Database Course

Pieter Koopman, Vincent Zweije

Computer Science, Leiden University,

Niels Bohrweg 1, 2333 CA, Leiden, The Netherlands

email: pieter@wi.leidenuniv.nl

Abstract

This paper describes why and how a functional programming language was used in an introductory database course. The purpose of the programming exercises in this course is to give students a better understanding of the internal structure and use of databases and database management systems.

We used a functional language for its high level of abstraction and the automatic memory management which make writing a simple database management system considerably easier.

Although the students had no previous knowledge of functional programming, they were capable to obtain useful experience in the database field. In order to enable students to concentrate on the database aspects of the exercises and to make rather elaborated systems in a limited amount of time, we supplied skeletons of the programs to make. Only the parts that are the core of the exercise had to be written by the students.

The exercises appear to serve their purpose very well. The corresponding parts of the exams are made considerably better since the introduction of these exercises in the course. After some initial hesitation, the students indicate that they prefer a functional language for these exercises above the imperative languages they know.

1. Introduction

This paper describes how functional programming is used in an elementary database course and the experiences with this use. The database course is situated in the second year of the computer science curriculum of four years for university students. The goal of the course is to make students aware of the reasons of existence for database management systems and to give a firm introduction to relational databases. We treat the design of relational schemas including normal forms and the query languages relational calculus, relational algebra and SQL. Also the more old-fashioned hierarchical and network model are discussed briefly. See also appendix A for additional course description.

Programming exercises are used to make students familiar with the construction and use of ad hoc databases and simple database management systems. The reason for having programming exercises instead of using existing database systems is that it is an important goal of this course to given students a clear view of the background and internals of database management systems, this is explained in detail in section 2.

The students have one year experience in imperative programming (using Pascal and C) and no experience with functional programming. The high level of abstraction and the automatic memory management are the reasons to use a functional language in this course. Especially the excellent abilities to manipulate lists can be used extremely well for a simple implementation of relations. See also section 3. Details of the organisation and exercises are given in section 4 and 5. Section 6 gives some reactions of the students. Finally, there is a discussion in section 7.

2. Role of Programming in the Course

In previous instances of this basic database course the students did practical work with an existing relational database management system (INGRES). The exercises consisted of writing some queries on an existing database and changing the contents and structure of this database using SQL-commands.

Although these exercises taught the students to work in SQL, we were not satisfied with the skills and insight of the students. In particular the understanding of what is happening when an SQL-statement is executed was low. As a consequence they could not predict the cost of a given manipulation. Also the rationale behind many design decisions remained misty. Using a database system teaches students about the internals of the systems what the students of a Pascal course learn about compiler construction: basically nothing. These exercises also did not teach the students anything about writing queries in relational calculus or relational algebra. Neither is writing SQL-statements helpful for understanding the other data models treated in the database course.

To solve these problems we replaced the practical work with an existing relational database management system by exercises in which the students build a simple database management system (DBMS) themselves and use this system to manipulate some data. Other programming exercises broaden the field of topics covered by the practical work. The total amount of practical work for the students is increased by this change.

Although many important topics of the database course are covered by the programming exercises, there are also additional exercises for the student about the other issues of the course. Later on in the curriculum, the students can learn how a state of the art relational DBMS should be used.

3. Why Functional Programming

Once we had decided to replace the exercises with the relational DBMS with the implementation of some DBMSes we had to select a suitable programming language.

The two obvious candidates are the imperative languages familiar to the students: Turbo Pascal and C.

Especially the relational DBMS to construct requires the extensive use and dynamic creation of tables (relations). We want to prevent that the memory management involved attracts too much attention from the students. One option is to supply a package to store and manipulate relations in one of the imperative programming languages.

The lists which are standard available in functional programming languages are an excellent implementation of the relations used in our DBMS. In fact the list comprehensions in functional languages and the relational calculus share the same mathematical basis: Zermelo-Fraenkel set theory [Fraenkel 1922, Zermelo 1908]. No matter how sophisticated the relational package supplied with an imperative language is, it will be less usable and its syntax will always be inferior to the possibilities in a functional language. Together with the well known advantages of functional programming languages (they enable the construction of compact and understandable programs at a high level of abstraction that can be written fast) this is the reason to use a functional programming language in this course.

The Chosen Functional Language

After the decision to use a functional language we had to choose which language we were going to use. As indicated before, the students have no previous knowledge of functional programming. This means that we had free choice. However, since this is not a course in functional programming, a very simple and easy to explain yet powerful language is required. This makes an interpreter more suited than a compiler. Due to the extensive list manipulations that will be necessary the availability of list comprehensions (ZF-expressions) is a prerequisite. Speed is not considered to be of prime importance. Fancy type systems and other extensions are not required, nor wanted (they attract unnecessary attention).

Based on these requirements and the availability at our institute we have chosen Miranda[1].[Turner 85] Another good candidate was Gofer [Jones 94]. This language has a more powerful and hence more complex type system. An advantage of Gofer was its better availability, especially for students working at home on a PC. The reasons to select Miranda are the straightforward type system and simple, but sufficiently powerful, IO mechanism. Although we are satisfied with this choice, other functional languages can be used as an alternative.

4. Organisation of the Practical Work

The students are supposed to work in total four weeks full-time (about 160 hours) on this course. This time is spread over the semester of thirteen weeks. Each week there

[1]Miranda is a trade mark of Research Software Ltd.

are two lecture hours. These lectures cover parts I, II, III and IV of the textbook of Elmasri and Navathe [Elmasri 94]. In addition there is a session of two hours were students can work on all exercises of this course (both the programming exercises and the pen and paper exercises) under supervision and with direct support. The remaining time should be spent on studying the topics covered in the lectures, implementation of the exercises and making the other exercises. Students are expected to spend about 40 hours in total to each of these three parts. As documentation for functional programming we supply copies of overhead sheets and a copy of the paper [Turner 85]. The Miranda system has an on-line manual.

The primary goal of the practical work is not to teach students how functional programs must be constructed, but to teach them database topics. In order to enable the novice functional programmers to construct useful database programs without spending much time on problems with functional programming, we give them much support. This support consists of relevant examples and a partial solution of each exercise. The partial solution of an exercise is a program that contains all parts that are not considered as the crux of that exercise. The students are asked to make complete programs of these partial solutions. In order to enable the students to concentrate on database topics, we keep the program style simple and consistent over all exercises. We also supply data that can be used to test the constructed databases.

5. Contents of the Practical Work

The practical work is organised in five exercises. Some of these exercises are divided in a number of distinct parts. The main purpose of the first exercise is to get acquainted with functional programming. The next exercise is the construction of an ad hoc database. Due to the embedding of this exercise a relational model-like storage structure will be used by the students. The queries will be similar to relational calculus expressions. The third exercise is the construction of a relational DBMS with queries in relational algebra. In the fourth exercise this data model will be manipulated entirely by a subset of SQL. In the last exercise an existing interpreter for an imperative language is extended by commands to control a hierarchical database.

For each of these exercises we discuss the goal, the question, the given support and the structure of the solution in detail. We made the structure of all programs as consistent as possible. We also used similar applications of the developed DBMSes whenever possible.

Exercise 1: Introduction to Functional Programming

The main purpose of this exercise is to make students sufficiently acquainted with functional programming to make the database programs. We emphasis on IO, the meaning of list comprehensions and working with a program state.
After a large number of examples and simple programs constructed in interaction with the teacher we ask the students to write three small programs.

Part a: Interactive Palindrome Checker

The goal of this part is to make students familiar with simple list manipulations and IO, both as list of characters (`$-`) and as list of values (`$+`). The students should write two programs that check whether lines entered as input are palindromes. One of these programs accepts one list of characters as input. The other takes a list of lines, list of list of characters, as input.

Part b: Pythagorean Triangles.

This part is meant to make students aware of the meaning of ZF-expressions and the advantages of using them. The exercise consists of writing functions that yield the same list of Pythagorean triangles as the given list comprehension.

Students are encouraged to use list comprehensions as much as possible during this course. As an introduction many examples are developed together with the students on the blackboard.

Part c: Reverse Polish Notation Calculator.

The purpose of this part is to teach students to work with a program state, algebraic data types and formatted input (`$+` in Miranda). In order to do this, the students have to write an interpreter for a list of statements in reverse polish notation. We help the students by giving them appropriate data types and a description and the type of the functions to implement.

Exercise 2: Ad hoc Database

The topic of this exercise is the construction of a small ad hoc database to store information about books and their authors. The students have to define the state and a number of manipulation functions. We omit details of the attributes to store and manipulations to implement.

The database can be constructed along the same lines as a telephone database as specified in [Diller 94] shown as example. This guides students towards a tailor made relational model. We supply the types of the functions to implement, the command "loop" and data to fill and test the constructed database.

```
command == db -> (output, db)

bibl :: output
bibl = fst (interpret $+ emptydb)

interpret :: [command] -> command
interpret (c: cs) db
 = (out ++ outs, db2)
   where (out, db1)  = c db
         (outs, db2) = interpret cs db1
```

Using structuring primitives like Monads [Wadler 92, Jones 93] it is possible to define the function `interpret` a little more compact. We use the definition as shown to keep the function as simple as possible for the students.

The state can be defined as:

```
db     == ([author], [wrote], [book])
author == (ssn, name)
wrote  == (ssn, isbn)
book   == (isbn, title, sold)
ssn    == num
isbn   == num
sold   == num
name   == [char]
title  == [char]
```

We show two examples of database manipulations. First the function to add an author. This function checks the consistence of the SSN number as key. The second example is the query to find the authors of the book(s) with the given title.

```
addAuthor :: ssn -> name -> command
addAuthor ssn name db
 = ("Error: author exists", db ), if member ssns ssn
 = (""                    , db'), otherwise
   where (as, ws, bs) = db
         db'  = ((ssn, name): as, ws, bs)
         ssns = [ssn | (ssn, name) <- as]

findAuthors :: title -> command
findAuthors title db
 = (showAuthors as', db)
   where (as, ws, bs) = db
         as' = [(ssn, name)| (bisbn, btitle, bsold) <- bs;
                              btitle = title;
                              (wssn, wisbn) <- ws;
                              wisbn = bisbn;
                              (ssn, name) <- as;
                              ssn = wssn]
```

Note that the list comprehensions have many similarities with expressions in relational calculus. An important difference between relational calculus and ZF-expressions in Miranda is that calculus just gives a tuple definition and a predicate, while the list comprehensions are an algorithm to compute the tuples. All other manipulation functions have the same structure.

Exercise 3: Relational Algebra

In this exercise the students construct their first relational database management system. Instead of a fixed set of relations of known types, as in exercise 2, an arbitrary number of relations is used containing attributes not determined at compile-time. This requires an other approach to define the state. We supply the following definitions.

```
database  == [(tablename, table)]
tablename == [char]

table     == (schema,[tuple])
schema    == [attributename]
attributename == [char]

tuple     == [attribute]
attribute ::= String [char] | Num num | Bool bool | Null
```

Queries to this DBMS are written in relational algebra. The basic operators in algebra are the union, difference, cross product, selection of tuples and projection of attributes. In addition we define operators for the natural join, renaming of attributes, unique (to remove duplicates from the multi-set) and some aggregate functions. Queries are represented by an algebraic data type and contain the abstract syntax tree.

```
query     ::= Table      tablename             |
              Union      query      query      |
              Difference query      query      |
              Cross      query      query      |
              Project    schema     query      |
              Select     condition query       |
              Join       query      query      |
              Rename     [attributename] query |
              Unique     query                 |
              Aggregate  schema [(attributename, aggregate)] query

aggregate ::= Sum     attributename            |
              Product attributename            |
              Average attributename            |
              Min     attributename            |
              Max     attributename            |
              Count
```

Conditions come in a number of obvious forms.

```
condition ::= NOT condition                    |
              AND condition  condition         |
              OR  condition  condition         |
              LT  expression expression        |
              ...
```

For example, the query $\pi_{a,b}\,\sigma_{a=42}\,(R * T)$ is represented as the following data structure.

```
Project ["a", "b"] (Select (EQ (Attr "a") (Const (Num 42)))
                            (Join (Table "R") (Table "T")))
```

A query is interpreted by the function `retrieve`. This function recursively descends the data structure and calls the appropriate function.

```
retrieve :: query -> db -> table
retrieve query db =
 ret query
 where ret (Union q1 q2) = union (ret q1)(ret q2)
       ...
       ret (Unique q)           = unique (ret q)
       ret (Table t)            = lookup emptytable db t
       ret (Aggregate as f q) = groupby as f (ret q)
```

Students should implement the functions which define the semantics of the relational algebra operators:

```
cross      :: table  -> table -> table
difference :: table  -> table -> table
join       :: table  -> table -> table
project    :: schema -> table -> table
rename     :: schema -> table -> table
union      :: table  -> table -> table
unique     ::           table -> table
select     :: (schema- > tuple -> bool) -> table -> table
```

The implementation of these operators using list comprehensions is straightforward and very similar to the definition of the semantics of the operators in set theory. We show some examples (remember that each table consists of a Miranda tuple containing the list of attribute names and a list of database tuples):

```
cross (atts1, tuples1) (atts2, tuples2)
 = (atts1 ++ atts2, [t1 ++ t2 | t1 <- tuples1; t2 <- tuples2])

difference (atts1, tuples1) (atts2, tuples2)
 = (atts1, tuples1 -- tuples2)

select pred (atts, tuples)
 = (atts, [ t | t <- tuples; pred atts t])

union (atts1, tuples1) (atts2, tuples2)
 = (atts1, tuples1 ++ tuples2)
```

To practice writing queries in relational algebra the students should formulate a number of expressions. Since the students are familiar with the data structure to represent queries, a parser for relational algebra is omitted. The queries are written as Miranda data structure. This has as advantage that the database implementation remains simpler and the Miranda mechanisms for abstraction can be used. As example we show the query that yields a table containing the SSN-numbers and names of authors that wrote a book titled `t`. This title is supplied as argument to the command.

```
findAuthor :: title -> query
findAuthor t
 = (Proj ["ssn", "name"] (Sel c universal))
   where c = EQ (Attr "title") (Const (String t))
         universal = Join (Table "author")
                          (Join (Table "wrote") (Table "book"))
```

Exercise 4: Mini-SQL

The purpose of this exercise is to teach the semantics of SQL statements and to practise in writing these statements. To achieve this goal the algebra interface of the previous exercise is replaced by an SQL-interface. We supply the data types involved and the manipulations of the relations. The students should write a query interpreter and a number of SQL-statements.

Since SQL is an enormous large language (only the syntax definition of the core part of SQL2 in BNF takes 47 pages [Melton 93]), it is clear that we must impose severe restrictions here. It is possible to define a small sub-set of SQL, called mini-SQL, that introduces a large part of the features of SQL. We decided to include many possibilities to express queries and to omit the automatic constraint checking and many fancy attribute types.

The SQL based DBMS is constructed on the very same basis as the relational DBMS of the previous exercise. The entire DBMS state remains unchanged. The manipulation of this state will now be done by the following mini-SQL commands.

```
print       :: query -> command
createtable :: tablename -> schema -> command
droptable   :: tablename -> command
insertinto  :: tablename -> query -> command
inserttuple :: tablename -> tuple -> command
deletefrom  :: alias -> condition -> command
updatetable :: alias -> [(attributename, expression)]
                     -> condition -> command
```

The data structure to represent the syntax tree of SQL-queries is defined as:

```
query ::=
  Union  query query                                    |
  Except query query                                    |
  Select distinct [field] [alias] condition             |
  SelectGrouped distinct [(field, yield)] [alias] condition [field]

yield     ::= Copy | Collect bool aggregate

aggregate ::= Sum | Product | Average | Min | Max | Count

distinct  == bool
alias     == (tablename, tablename)
```

```
field      == (tablename, attributename)

condition ::= Not     condition                          |
              And     condition condition                |
              Or      condition condition                |
              Exists  query                              |
              In      [expression] query                 |
              Some    expression relation query          |
              All     expression relation query          |
              Compare expression relation expression

relation   ::= Lt | Le | Eq | Ge | Gt | Ne

expression ::= Plus   expression expression              |
               Times  expression expression              |
               Minus  expression expression              |
               Attr   field                              |
               Const  attribute
```

As example we show the command to remove all authors form the relation `author` that has not written any book. In SQL this can be written as:

```
DELETE FROM author a
   WHERE NOT (EXISTS (SELECT *
                      FROM wrote w
                      WHERE a.ssn = w.ssn))
```

This is represented by the following command:

```
deletefrom ("author","a")
   (Not (Exists (Select False []
                [("wrote","w")]
                (Compare (Attr ("a","ssn")) Eq (Attr ("w","ssn"))
```

We supply the implementation of the SQL-commands apart from the evaluation of queries. Students should write an interpretation function for the data type `query`. This can be done by a recursive descent of the data type `query` similar to the function retrieve in the previous exercise. We suggest to use a rather naive implementation of the queries. First all tables involved are combined to one table by making the cross product. From this table the tuples obeying the condition in the `WHERE` part are selected. Finally, the attributes listed after the keyword `SELECT` must be projected out.

The existence of sub-queries makes this exercise interesting. Students must be aware of the scope of variables and the semantics of the sub-queries in order to make a correct implementation.

Exercise 5: A Hierarchical DBMS

The topic of the final exercise is the hierarchical data model. This is a somewhat old-fashioned data model that is always manipulated with commands that are embedded in an imperative programming language. The data is logically structured in a strictly hierarchical tree. Physically the data is stored in the list by traversing this tree in pre-order. Via the database commands the user is aware of this physical organisation of the data. The hierarchical DBMS and the imperative program communicate by a number of shared variables. The imperative program controls the actions of the DBMS by executing the appropriate commands.

The purpose of this exercise is to teach the students how the data is organised and how it can be manipulated by embedded commands. This goal is achieved by a similar approach as the previous two exercises: we supply a storage structure for the data and an interpreter for a simple imperative language. The students have to extend this imperative language by retrieval commands for the database management system. This means that they define how the pointers in this linear list of records must be moved.

There are two commands that are used to retrieve information from the database: GET and GETPATH. Only the GETPATH command has to be implemented since the GET command can be treated as a special case of the GETPATH command. The nasty details of this exercise are omitted since they are not relevant for this paper. We show only the structure of program which is similar to the previous exercises.

```
state      == (database, memory)
command    == state -> (output, state)

memory     == [(identifier, value)]
identifier == [char]

database   == (schema, [record])
schema     ::= Recordtype recordtype [identifier] [schema]
recordtype == [char]
record     == (recordtype, [value])

cond :: expression -> [command] -> [command] -> command
cond e then else (database, memory)
 = exec then (database, memory), if result = Bool True
 = exec else (database, memory), if result = Bool False
 = (nobool, (database, memory)), otherwise
   where result = evaluate memory e
         nobool = "cond: " ++ show e ++ "not a boolean.\n"

while :: expression -> [command] -> command
while expr body (db, mem)
 = ("", (db, mem))                          , if result = Bool False
 = exec (body++[while expr body]) (db, mem), if result = Bool True
 = (nobool,(db, mem))                       , otherwise
   where result = evaluate mem expr

         nobool = "while: " ++ show result ++ "is not a boolean.\n"
```

As a next step the students write some imperative programs to obtain the some information from a database given as example. These programs can be interpreted by the Miranda program of the first part of this exercise.

6. Reactions of the Students

At the start of the course the students are rather sceptical about functional programming. A typical quote: "In Pascal I write an equivalent program in 10% of the time". During the course this attitude to functional programming changes completely. At the end of the course only a small minority (less than 10%) of the students indicates that they still prefer an imperative programming language for the kind of exercises in this course.

At the end of the course there is a wide spectrum of opinions on functional programming among the students. Some quotes are used to illustrate this:

- "Functional programming is too difficult for me. Too much is happening in one line."
- "After you have written some useful function it turns out to be in the standard environment."
- "Contrary to Pascal I have to think before I start programming."
- "Functional programming gives the practical part of this course additional value."
- "Why haven't you told this a long time ago?"

There opinion about Miranda is a bit ambivalent. On one hand they agree that it is a simple language with a nice and rather intuitive syntax. On the other hand they complain about the error messages (especially concerning type errors) and that it is slow. Another drawback is that they cannot run it on their PC at home.

7. Discussion

This paper shows how functional programming is used in an introductory database course. After writing a preliminary program in a functional language the students make four exercises related to databases: an ad-hoc database, an interpreter for relational algebra, an implementation of a sub-set of SQL and a hierarchical database. Some queries have to be written using each of these query languages.

The described approach is successful. The results on the topics of the programming exercises are much better in the exams. Especially the students' ability to write queries and the understanding of query evaluation is considerably improved. This is clearly visible in the parts of the written examination that test the students' ability to write queries in various languages. It is also clear that the students have a better understanding of the internal organisation of a DBMS.

Even for students who had no experience with functional programming it was possible to gain useful training in the database field by writing functional programs. As a matter of fact most of the students prefer the functional language in favour of the imperative languages they know.

A number of students have recorded the time spent on the exercises on a day by day basis. At an average they spent 40 hours to complete all implementation exercises. Considering that these are all newcomers in functional programming this shows that the students were able to do some useful work for a database course in a limited amount of time. It is important to mention that the students do not become full fledged functional programmers by making these exercises. We expect that the students will learn more about the database topics when they had some previous training in functional programming.

The given set of exercises has many possibilities for extensions. For example we can add query optimisation, automatic constraint control, efficient table access or a larger part of the SQL-language. Experienced functional programmers can implement a larger part of the programs themselves.

The given data types to represent queries serve as a clear definition of the border between the database system and the applications made with this system. The introduction of syntax and associated parser for the implemented query languages appears to be unnecessary and unwanted.

References

Diller, A.: Z, An Introduction to Formal Methods, Second edition, Wiley, ISBN 0-471-92973-0, 1994.

Elmasri, Navathe: Fundamentals of database systems, second edition, Benjamin Cummings, ISBN 0-8053-1748-1, 1994.

Fraenkel, A.A.: Zu den Grundlagen der Cantor-Zermeloschen Mengelehre. Mathematische annalen, **86**, pp 230-237, 1922.

Jones, M.P.: Gofer. 2.30 release notes, 1994.

Jones, M.P.: A system of constructor classes: overloading and implicit higher-order polymorphism. in: Proceedings FPCA 93, 1993.

Melton, J., Simon, A.R.: Understanding the new SQL: a complete guide. Morgan Kaufmann Publishers, ISBN 1-55860-245-3, 1993

Turner, D.A.: Miranda: a non-strict functional language with polymorphic types. LNCS **201**, pp 1-16, 1985.

Wadler, P.: The essence of functional programming. In: Proceedings of the 19th annual symposium on Principles of Programming Languages, pp 1-14, 1992.

Zermelo, E.: Untersuchungnen über die Grundlagen der Mengelehre. International Bibliography, Information and Documentation, **65**, pp 261-281, 1908.

Appendix A: Course Description

In order to ease the comparison of the courses discussed in this proceedings, we supply a course description in the format proposed by the program committee.

Title of the Course

Databases and File organisation.

Aims of the Course

The goal of the course is to make students aware of the reasons of existence for database management systems and to give a firm introduction to relational databases. We cover the range from high level modelling (ER, EER, OO) to file organisation. The design of relational schemas and the query languages algebra, calculus and SQL are treated. Also the hierarchical and network model are discussed briefly.

Intended kind of students.

The course is intended for second year computer science students. Usually there is also a small number of students from mathematics or physics visiting the course.

Prerequisites for the course

Students are expected to have some knowledge of imperative programming, data structures like B-trees and hash-functions. None of these topics are very heavily used. Imperative programming is used to show how embedded query languages look. We indicate that it might be very useful to use some tree or hash-function to find a specific record in a relation.

Text book used

For the database part of the course we use *Fundamentals of database systems* by Elmasri and Navathe [Elmasri 94]. As introduction in functional programming we use *Miranda: a non-strict functional language with polymorphic types* [Turner 85] and the Miranda on-line manual. We supply copies of the overhead sheets used as handout. These sheets contain many examples of the use of functional programming languages in a database context. In the current iteration of the course we supplied additional material about functional programming.

Duration of the course

The duration of this course is 12 weeks. The average student is expected to spend 160 hours in total on this course. In the current version of the curriculum this is increased to 200 hours.

There are two lecture hours and two hours of tutorial per week. The maximal time that can be spent on preparation for the examination is about 40 hours. This leaves at least six hours to be spent on home work. In the new curriculum this is nine hours.

Assessment of the students

Students are assessed by a written examination. In previous versions of this course a satisfactory mark of the programming exercises was a prerequisite. In the current version the lab assignments (programming exercises and ER-design etc.) determine 33% of the total assessment.

Using π–RED as a Teaching Tool for Functional Programming and Program Execution

Werner E. Kluge, Carsten Rathsack, Sven-Bodo Scholz

Christian-Albrechts-Universitaet Kiel, Institut fuer Informatik, D–24105 Kiel, Germany, E–mail: base@informatik.uni–kiel.d400.de

Abstract. *This paper describes an interactively controlled reduction system π–RED which may be employed to teach both basic concepts of functional programming and program execution at the undergraduate level, and advanced topics of computer science at the graduate level.*
π–RED supports the reduction languages KIR *- a sugared versions of an applied λ–calculus with a full-fledged (type-free) β-reduction. Functions (λ-abstractions) are truly treated as first class objects: they may be applied to other functions or to themselves, and λ-abstractions may be computed as function values. Name clashes are resolved by an indexing scheme similar to de Bruijn indices.*
Programs may be executed in a stepwise mode and intermediate programs may be displayed in high-level notation.
Special pattern matching constructs provide the means to directly specify in KIR *complex term rewrite systems. In conjunction with the stepwise execution mode, this feature has been extensively used, in lab courses accompanying graduate courses on computer architecture, to rapidly prototype and study various programming and (abstract) machine models, compilation schemes, type checkers, etc.*

1 Introduction

Functional or function-based programming languages such as MIRANDA, STANDARD ML, HASKELL or SCHEME [Turn86, HaMiTo88, HuWa88, AbSus85] have become increasingly popular in teaching basic programming concepts at the undergraduate level as well as advanced topics such as compiler construction, type systems, abstract machines, language interpreters etc. in graduate CS courses.

The functional paradigm derives its appeal primarily from its declarative programming style. Functional programs are pure algorithms which are generally simpler and faster to design, more concise and less vulnerable to errors than their imperative counterparts, and can be understood without mentally executing them.

The underlying semantic models (either the λ-calculus or a combinatory calculus) define program execution as processes of meaning-preserving program transformations, i.e., program execution conceptually takes place entirely within the space of programs, not in a state space [Back78]. A computing machine which faithfully implements this concept can be made to execute, under interactive control, programs step by step, and to display intermediate programs in the same notation in which the original program was specified. Moreover, the focus of control may be freely moved about initial and intermediate programs to select other than top-level redexes for evaluation, without causing side-effects in other program parts (referential transparency).

The benefits of using such a machine in CS education are manifold. Beyond learning an elegant programming style, students can be expected to develop very quickly a conceptual understanding of how computations are actually taking place at a level of abstraction very similar to algebraic formula manipulations. All that there is visible (and relevant) at this level, and can therefore be studied in a clean setting, are the program transformations effected by the rewrite (reduction) rules of the underlying calculus, the control discipline which drives computations step by step ahead, and the operational discipline which supplies operators with operands, e.g., instantiates functions with arguments. Moving step by step through a sequence of intermediate programs also facilitates program validation and the detection of logical errors (high-level debugging). To some extent, it may even substitute for inductive proofs on program correctness, rather than doing them by tedious paper-and-pencil work.

Additional advantages from an educational point of view come with a full λ-calculus. The β-reduction rule provides a versatile mechanism for the substitution of variables by λ-terms which maintains static binding structures (scopes) even in the presence of naming conflicts. This mechanism is absolutely essential for simple symbolic computations involving free variables, and specifically for supporting higher-order functions in the sense that functions (λ-abstractions) may be freely applied to other functions (and to themselves), and that functions may be returned as function values.

Teaching an applied λ-calculus as a programming language is the key to fully understanding elementary properties of operators, their application to operands, the role of variables as place-holders, the dual roles of functions (abstractions) as operators and operands, and the systematic construction of complex operators from simpler ones. Visualizing β-reductions step by step introduces students to the intricacies of λ-calculus and of the mechanical evaluation of λ-terms far more effectively than textbook or blackboard explanations.

Another important concept of functional programming is pattern matching - a mechanism which extracts substructures from given structural contexts and substitutes them for variables in other structural contexts. It is the key to teaching a number of advanced topics in computer science as it allows one to specify in a very concise form term rewrite systems. They may prototype compilers, type checkers, data base (expert) systems, abstract or concrete computing machines etc., or generally systems whose dynamic behavior can be described (or approximated) by discrete rule-based state changes.

The design of complex term rewrite systems benefits considerably from a stepwise execution mode. This is particularly true in education where students need to develop quickly some basic understanding of how abstract concepts or models actually work. The effects of (sequences of) rule applications can immediately be visualized in high-level notation and checked for consistency, correctness and confluence (if so required). Logical (specification) errors may thus be detected and corrected at an early stage, and progress towards achieving a course's objectives can be made without getting lost in irrelevant, often frustating details of low-level programming.

The advantages of visualizing individual steps of program execution for educational purposes have been well recognized elsewhere. Goldson describes a system called MIRACALC [Gol94] which supports a stepwise execution mode for MIRANDA programs. He points out that students can be expected to benefit considerably from viewing functional computations as rule-based evaluation processes and to enhance their '... creativity in specifying, designing and reasoning about their programs by relieving them of the need to carry out pencil-and-paper calculations ...'. Another similar system concept is described in [RuToFi93].

Unfortunately, almost all functional systems proposed and implemented to date do not support stepwise program execution [Turn76, John83, Car83, Plas93, Pey92]. Functions (abstractions) are usually compiled to code of some abstract or real machine which constructs and reduces graph representations of the program terms to be evaluated. Since intermediate states of program execution are distributed over program counters, stacks, registers and heap locations which render de-compilation into equivalent high-level programs an intractable problem, the code must run to completion to produce meaningful results.

Compilation to code to some extent also separates the world of functions from the world of objects they operate on: function code must be supplied with full sets of arguments to execute correctly, and the code itself cannot be modified, i.e., there is no direct way of computing new functions. Partial applications are wrapped up in closure until the missing arguments can be picked up. If the computation terminates with a closure, the user is simply notified of the fact that the result is a function, but it cannot be made visible in high-level notation. Further restrictions come with the type systems of these languages. They rule out certain higher-order functions, especially self-applications, as they cannot unify recursive types.

In this paper, we will give an outline of the reduction system π–RED which fully complies with the features of a good teaching tool as outlined above. It supports an interactively controlled execution mode for a syntactically sugared version of an applied λ-calculus called KIR (for Kiel Reduction Language), which also includes sophisticated pattern matching facilities. Rather than discussing the internal workings of this system (which is described elsewhere [GaKl94]), we will here concentrate on what the programmer can see of and how he / she can work with π–RED at the user interface, and on typical programming and program execution exercises that can be done with this system.

In the sequel we will first introduce, in section 2, a kernel of KIR , the basic idea of editing KIR programs in a syntax-directed fashion, and the means to control their stepwise execution. In section 3 we demonstrate, by means of selected examples, how stepwise execution works on λ-terms, how new abstractions can be computed from existing ones, and how naming conflicts are resolved in the course of β-reductions. In section 4 we introduce the pattern matching constructs provided by KIR , particularly those that are necessary to specify term rewrite systems on a KIR platform, and in section 5 we present, as a typical application, an interpreter for the SECD machine. In section 6 we summarize some of our experiences in using π–RED as a vehicle for teaching functional programming and language implementations in a graduate lab course.

2 The Programming Environment of π–RED

π–RED is a complex software system of about 2 MBytes C-code which can be installed on all UNIX-based workstations. It supports the reduction language KIR – a sugared version of an applied, type-free λ-calculus with an applicative order semantics [Klu94]. The basic concept has been adopted from Berkling's string reduction machinery developed as early as 1975 [Berk75]. The system version that is currently available for distribution reduces graphs by interpretation of abstract machine code. On average, it is about ten times slower than functional languages compiled to executable code [GaKl94]. A more recent version which compiles abstract machine code to C and thus is faster by factors ranging from 3 to 10 is presently in the testing phase.

Both programming and program execution are in π–RED supported as fully interactive processes. The system provides a syntax-directed editor which allows to construct KIR programs either top-down or bottom-up by systematically inserting expressions into place-holder positions of other expressions, or by replacing expressions with others. Program execution is realized as a sequence of meaning-preserving program transformations based on a fixed set of rewrite rules, of which the most important one is a full-fledged β-reduction. Programs may either run to completion or be reduced in a stepwise mode, with intermediate programs being displayed to the user for inspection and modification.

With a few minor exceptions, the syntax of KIR resembles that of most other functional languages. The following is a kernel of KIR :

```
e = v | c | pf
  | ( e_0 e_1 .. e_n )
  | IF e_0 THEN e_1 ELSE e_2
  | LAMBDA x_1..x_n IN e
  | LET .. x = x_e .. IN e
  | LETREC .. f x_1 .. x_n = f_e .. IN s_e
  | < e_1..e_n >
```

As a courtesy to people used to more popular languages, this syntax includes a few modifications of KIR as it is actually implemented, particularly w.r.t. the use of parentheses and keywords, It defines KIR programs as expressions composed of variables (denoted as `v`), constants (denoted as `c`), primitive functions (denoted as `pf`), applications of function expressions `e_0` to n argument expressions `e_1`, ..., `e_n`, `IF_THEN_ELSE` clauses as special applications, anonymous functions (`LAMBDA` abstractions), `LET` clauses which specify values for variables in some expression `e`, `LETREC` constructs which specify sets of mutually recursive functions, and lists (sequences) of expressions as a means to represent structured objects, respectively.

The set of primitive functions includes the familiar binary arithmetic, logical and relational operators, and some primitive structuring and predicate functions applicable to lists.

As a convention, KIR uses upper case letters to denote keywords such as **LETREC, IF ,THEN, IN** , etc., whereas all identifiers (variables) need to start with lower case letters.

KIR is an untyped language. Type compatibility checks between primitive functions and the operands to which they are actually applied are dynamically performed at run-time based on type-tags that are carried along with all objects of a program.

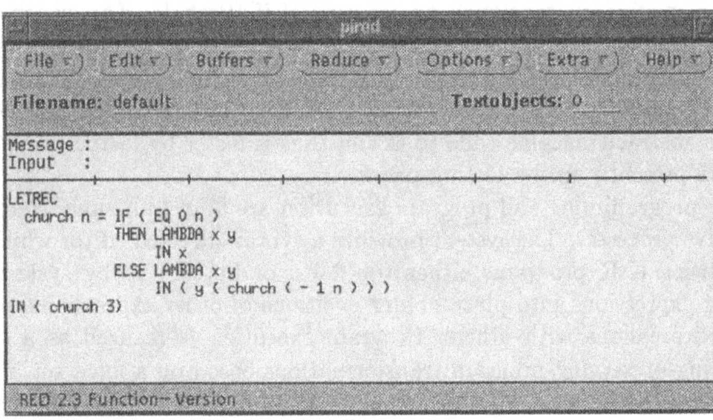

Fig. 1. X-Windows front-end of π–RED

Fig. 1 shows the screen layout of the user interface of π–RED. It consists of a window whose main part emulates an alphanumerical terminal on which programs may be edited and displayed. This terminal divides into two parts separated by a horizontal line. The upper part includes a message line and an input line, and the lower part displays the segment of the KIR program in which reductions are actually taking place (or constitutes the actual focus of control). This expression field is initialized with the symbol **#** which stands for an empty expressions.

In order to edit a program, the user may simply type some fragment of a legitimate KIR expression, say just the key word **IF**. It is immediately echoed on the input line, and the message line responds with **<expr>** , indicating that so far the input line contains a syntactically correct expression. Upon hitting the return key, both the message line and the input line will be cleared, and a syntactically complete **IF_THEN_ELSE** construct with as yet uninstantiated (or empty) components shows up in the expression field:

```
IF #
THEN #
ELSE #
```

The missing components may be specified in the same way, say, by typing as input the lines

```
( EQ 0 n ,
LAMBDA x y IN x ,
LAMBDA x y IN ( y ( church ( - 1 n ,
```

in this sequence, with the cursor automatically moving about the empty positions # from top to bottom. Note that only opening parentheses need be specified as input, the editor automatically adds the respective closing parentheses and returns in the expression field:

```
IF ( EQ 0 n )
THEN LAMBDA x y
     IN x
ELSE LAMBDA x y
     IN ( y ( church ( - 1 n ) ) )   .
```

All there remains to be done to turn this expression into the full program shown in fig. 1 is to type in the input line

```
LETREC church n = %  ( church 3 ,
```

where the % is taken as a place-holder for the entire expression that is already set up in the expression field. Upon entering this input, π–RED produces in the expression field

```
LETREC
  church n =
    IF ( EQ 0 n )
    THEN LAMBDA x y
         IN x
    ELSE LAMBDA x y
         IN ( y ( church ( - 1 n ) ) )
IN ( church 3 )     .
```

The layout of this program, which computes representations of natural numbers as Church numerals (in this particular case the Church numeral of 3), is exactly as produced by the editor. However, in the sequel we will occassionally change the editor layout by hand in order to make the programs fit the page format of this paper.

Syntactically incorrect input is immediately rejected by the editor, and some comment explaining the likely cause of the error appears in the message line. π–RED accepts for execution only programs which are syntactically correct and complete, i.e., do not contain empty components.

The window frame provides a number of menus which may be entered by clicking the respective buttons. Among them are the menus FILE which includes a number of file handling functions to store and retrieve KIR expressions, EDIT which provides editing functions such as **copy** and **paste**, and also access to a line-oriented editing mode, REDUCE which includes some functions to control reductions, e.g., a single step mode, modes which perform at most some pre-specified or unlimited numbers of reductions on the actual program term, and functions which move the cursor about the program to select other than top-level redexes for evaluation.

3 λ-Calculus and Stepwise Reductions

In this section we will work through a few programming exercises to show how π–RED may be used to teach an applied λ-calculus. In particular, we will demonstrate how functions (λ-abstractions) may be computed as results of function applications, and how naming conflicts are resolved by β-reductions which use a special indexing scheme to distinguish identically named variables that are bound in different scopes. By means of these programs we will also show how π–RED goes about reducing programs step by step.

π–RED may be set up, by means of the REDUCE controls, to perform on a given program some pre-specified number of reduction steps, after which it stops and returns in high-level notation the intermediate program reached at that point. Such shifts of reductions may be repeated, possibly with varying numbers of reduction steps, until the program is eventually reduced to its normal form, provided it exists. This stepwise execution mode may be used to move, say, through a sequence of recursive function calls in order to visualize the expansion of the program and the passage of parameters.

To see how this works, we set out with the program for Church numerals as edited in the preceding section, which computes closed λ-abstractions (or combinators) as results. The number of reduction steps necessary to complete in one shift a recursive call of `church` may be found out by first doing single step reductions and counting. After the first such shift, which in the particular case takes three steps, we get

```
LAMBDA x y
IN ( y LETREC
         church n =
           IF ( EQ 0 n )
           THEN LAMBDA x y
                IN x
           ELSE LAMBDA x y
                IN ( y ( church ( - 1 n ) ) )
       IN ( church 2 ) )     ,
```

i.e., the initial program is being replaced by the **ELSE**-clause of the function body of `church`, with the parameter `n` substituted by 3, with `church` substituted by the entire **LETREC**-construct, and evaluated to the point where nothing else is left to do but to reduce the function call `( church 2 )`. Another three shifts of three reduction steps (of which only two are used up by the last shift) returns the Church numeral of the value $n = 3$, which is the λ-abstraction

```
LAMBDA x y
IN ( y LAMBDA x y
       IN ( y LAMBDA x y
              IN ( y LAMBDA x y
                     IN x ) ) )        .
```

We may now make this λ-term the argument of a successor function applicable to Church numerals by typing as input

```
LET suc = LAMBDA z x y IN ( y z IN ( suc %          ,
```

which in the expression field returns as

```
LET suc = LAMBDA z x y
          IN ( y z )
IN ( suc LAMBDA x y
         IN ( y LAMBDA x y
                IN ( y LAMBDA x y
                       IN ( y LAMBDA x y
                              IN x ) ) ) ) .
```

Here we have an instance of a partial application of the function **suc** to the Church numeral of 3, which by means of one β-reduction transformes into the Church numeral of 4 by adding another line `IN ( y LAMBDA x y` .

The next program specifies a simple symbolic computation which also includes a self-application. It defines, under the **LET**-variable **y**, the Y-combinator of the λ-calculus as it must be used under the applicative order reduction regime supported by π–RED:

```
LET y = LAMBDA h
        IN LET a = LAMBDA x
                   IN ( h LAMBDA y
                          IN  ( x x y ) )
           IN ( a a )
IN ( ( y f ) r )    .
```

In the body of this **LET**-construct, the variable **y** is applied to the free variables **f** and **r** which fill in for some recursive abstraction and for some argument, respectively.

The first five β-reductions transform this program into

```
( f LAMBDA y
    IN ( f LAMBDA y
       |   IN ( LAMBDA x
       |          IN ( f LAMBDA y
       |                 IN ( x x y ) )
       |             LAMBDA x
       |             IN ( f LAMBDA y
       |                    IN ( x x y ) )
                 y ) y ) r ) .
```

Further β-reduction steps reproduce the self-application marked by the vertical bars, embedded in an application **(f LAMBDA y IN ... y)** . Thus, after one more step we get

```
( f LAMBDA y
    IN ( f LAMBDA y
           IN ( f LAMBDA y
                  IN ( LAMBDA x
                       IN ( f LAMBDA y
                              IN ( x x y ) )
                          LAMBDA x
                          IN ( f LAMBDA y
                                 IN ( x x y ) )
                       y ) y ) y ) r ) ,
```

and so on, which nicely visualizes the recursive expansion of the original program. As long as the variables `f` and `r` remain free, this expression would keep expanding without bounds.

However, in a subsequent editing step, the symbolic program thus obtained may be made the body of an abstraction of the two variables `f` and `r` and applied to two as yet unknown arguments by typing as input **(LAMBDA f r IN % # #** . This completes what is already in the expressions field to

```
( LAMBDA f r
  IN ( f LAMBDA y
         IN ( f LAMBDA y
                IN ( f LAMBDA y
                       IN ( LAMBDA x
                            IN ( f LAMBDA y
                                   IN ( x x y ) )
                               LAMBDA x
                               IN ( f LAMBDA y
                                      IN ( x x y ) )
                            y ) y ) y ) r ) # # ) .
```

The editor places the cursor automatically on the first of the two empty syntactical positions **#**. This position may now be replaced, say, by the abstraction

```
LAMBDA fac
IN LAMBDA n
   IN  IF ( GT 1 n )
       THEN ( * n ( fac ( - 1 n ) )
       ELSE 1
```

which computes factorial numbers. As described before, this abstraction may be edited in several steps, say, by typing and entering first the fragment **LAMBDA fac LAMBDA n** and then, again in several fragments, the (components of the) **IF_THEN_ELSE** clause. Having thus completed the abstraction, the editor then moves the cursor to the next of the above **#** which may be replaced by an argument value for the function `fac`, say 100.

The complete program, when run with unlimited reduction steps, eventually returns the factorial number of 100, which is

```
9332621544394415268169923885626670049071596826438162146859296389 5
21759999322991560894146397615651828625369792082722375825118521091
686400000000000000000000000
```

Termination of this program is enforced by the conditional included in the abstraction **fac**, which may even cut off superfluous expansions of the Y-combinator beyond the number of recursive calls required to compute a function value.

The programs discussed so far apply functions (λ-abstractions) to functions, and return functions as values. All β-reductions are in fact done naively, i.e., without regard for naming conflicts, since all abstractions other than the successor function **suc** are applied to full sets of argument terms, and all abstractions that are passed along as arguments are closed (or combinators).

Full β-reductions enter the game in cases of naming conflicts between free and bound variable occurrences. Rather than renaming in such situations the bound variables involved in the conflicts, as the classical definition of the β-reduction rule demands, π–RED uses an indexing scheme similar to deBruijn indices [Brui72, BeFe82b] to distinguish different binding scopes of identically named variables: a variable occurrence, say **x**, may be preceded by some n backslashes \ which offset (or protect it against) the innermost n binders **LAMBDA x**. For instance, in an abstraction

```
LAMBDA x
IN LAMBDA x
   IN ( x ( \x \\x ) )
```

the **x** is bound to the innermost **LAMBDA x** , the **\x** is bound to the outermost **LAMBDA x** but protected against the innermost **LAMBDA x**, and the **\\x** is protected against both binders (or free in the entire term). β-reductions may add backslashes to free variables when inserting them into the scopes of binders to the same name, and may remove backshlashes when consuming binders against which they are protected.

This may be exemplified by the following program:

```
( LAMBDA x
  IN ( LAMBDA y
       IN ( LAMBDA y
            IN ( LAMBDA y
                 IN ( y x ) x ) x )
       x ) ( y z ) ) .
```

When β-reducing the outermost application, the argument term **(y z)**, in which both **y** and **z** occur free, is being substituted for free occurrences of **x** in the body of the abstraction **LAMBDA x IN (...)** . In doing this, the free variable **y** penetrates the scopes of three nested binders **LAMBDA y** and thus creates naming conflicts. The β-reduction rule as implemented in π–RED resolves them thus:

```
( LAMBDA y
  IN ( LAMBDA y
       IN ( LAMBDA y
            IN ( y ( \\\y z ) ) ( \\y z ) )
       ( \y z ) ) ( y z ) ) .
```

Here we find the variable **y**, which as part of the application `( y z )` has been substituted for free occurrences of **x**, preceded by three, two , one and no backslashes, according to the number of **LAMBDA y** it has crossed. The variable **z** remains as it is since there are no binders **LAMBDA z** whose scopes are being penetrated. None of these occurrences of **y** are bound to a **LAMBDA y**, i.e., they maintain their original status of being free in the entire expression. When performing further β-reductions from outermost to innermost, backslashes are taken away as binders **LAMBDA y** successively disappear.

Thus, another three β-reductions carried out step by step return

```
( LAMBDA y
  IN ( LAMBDA y
       IN ( y ( \\y z) ) ( \y z ) ) ( y z ) ) ,
```

followed by

```
( LAMBDA y
  IN ( y ( \y z ) ) ( y z ))   ,
```

and terminating with

```
( ( y z ) ( y z ) )   .
```

Using backslashes similar to de Bruijn indices to distinguish variable bindings in different scopes may be considered a low-level approach. However, it has the distinct advantage of maintaining the variable names as introduced by the programmer even in the presence of naming conflicts.

4 Pattern Matching

Pattern matching is an operation which extracts (sub-) structures of particular shapes and elements from given structural contexts and substitutes them for place-holders in other structural contexts. It is available in all modern functional languages [Turn86, Lavi87, HuWa88] and primarily used as an elegant way of defining functions as ordered sets of alternative equations. However, its full potential lies in complex rule-based modifications of structured objects.

Pattern matches are in KiR defined as so-called **WHEN**-clauses which have the syntactical form

```
WHEN pat_1 pat_2 ... pat_n GUARD guard DO p_e,
```

where **pat_i** denotes either a variable, a constant, or a (recursively nested) sequence of these items. The **WHEN** constructor, similar to **LAMBDA**, binds free occurrences of the pattern variables in the optional guard expression **guard** and in the body expression **p_e**. Applications of **WHEN**-clauses to n argument terms must be embedded in a **CASE**-construct (which in general may include several alternative **WHEN**-clauses):

```
( CASE
  WHEN pat_1 ... pat_n GUARD guard DO p_e
  END_CASE
  a_1 ... a_n )  .
```

If the syntactical structures of the patterns and of the corresponding (evaluated) argument terms match w.r.t. all pairs **pat_i | a_i** , then all free occurrences of the pattern variables in **guard** and **p_e** are substituted by the respective argument (sub-) structures. If, in addition, the guard expression thus instantiated evaluates to **TRUE**, then the entire application is replaced by the instantiated body **p_e**. Otherwise, the arguments are considered not within the domain of the pattern (or not of a compatible type), and the application remains as it is.

A simple example may help to convey how pattern matching is implemented in π–RED:

```
( CASE
  WHEN < u v > y 2
    GUARD ( NOT_EMPTY ( TAIL y ) )
    DO ( u y )
  END_CASE
    < REVERSE TAIL > < 1 2 3 4 > 2 ) .
```

Here the **WHEN**-clause specifies a list of two variables, a single variable and a constant value as simple patterns. The guard tests whether the argument substituted for the variable **y** is a list of at least two elements. Since the arguments are a list of primitive functions **< REVERSE TAIL >** in the first position, a list of four numbers in the second position, and the value 2 in the third position, π–RED returns after a first step

```
( CASE
  WHEN  . . .
    GUARD ( NOT_EMPTY ( TAIL < 1 2 3 4 > ) )
    DO ( REVERSE  < 1 2 3 4 > )
  OTHERWISE
    ( CASE
        WHEN < u v > y 2
          GUARD ( NOT_EMPTY ( TAIL y ) )
          DO ( x y )
      END_CASE
        < REVERSE TAIL > < 1 2 3 4 > 2 )
  END_CASE
    < REVERSE_TAIL > < 1 2 3 4 > 2 )    .
```

The patterns in the **WHEN**-clause are now replaced by dots, indicating that they did match the arguments, and all occurrences of the pattern variables in both the guard and the body are substituted, i.e., **u** by the function **REVERSE** and **y** by the list **< 1 2 3 4 >**. Moreover, the **CASE** construct has been extended by an **OTHERWISE** expression composed of the complete original application. This is the escape hatch for the case that the guard expression reduces to something other than the Boolean constant **TRUE**. However, in this particular case, another three reduction steps will evaluate the guard to **TRUE** and throw this alternative away, returning **(REVERSE < 1 2 3 4 >)** , which in one more step reduces to **< 4 3 2 1 >** .

In general, a **CASE**-expression may include several **WHEN**-clauses and an optional **OTHERWISE** expression. Applications of it have the general syntactical form

```
( CASE
    WHEN pat_11 ... pat_1n GUARD guard_1 DO p_e_1
      :
    WHEN pat_m1 ... pat_mn GUARD guard_m DO p_e_m
    OTHERWISE esc_e
  END_CASE
  a_1 ... a_n ) .
```

As usual, all patterns are tried in sequence from top to bottom. The first successful match, including a satisfiable guard, is reduced to its normal form which, by definition, is also the normal form of the entire **CASE** application. If none of the pattern | guard combinations matches, then the result is the normal form of the **OTHERWISE** expression if explicitely specified or, if this specification is missing, the **CASE** application itself in unreduced form.

Pattern matching is also applicable to structured objects made up from user-specified constructors. They enable the programmer to define on top of KiR meta-languages whose interpretation may be freely specified by sets of rewrite rules. This feature, among many other applications, may be used to prototype and test abstract machines, compilation schemes, type checkers etc. for other programming languages, imperative or declarative, or for KiR itself (in fact, this has been extensively done to prototype advanced versions of π–RED).

A meta-level expression has the syntactical form

```
constr{e_1 e_2 ... e_n} ,
```

where `constr` is a character string beginning with a letter which, in conjunction with the curly brackets { and } that enclose a sequence of some $n \geq 0$ KiR expressions `e_1,...,e_n`, is taken as an n-ary user-specified constructor. The expressions `e_1,...,e_n` may be meta-level expressions themselves.

A pattern that matches such an expression must feature the same constructor name and the same arity, and may have as components only variables, constants, and recursively non-atomic patterns.

5 A Case Study : the SECD Machine

Let us now look at an interpreter for Landin's SECD machine [Lan64] to demonstrate the expressive power of pattern matching. The SECD machine, in its simplest form, is an abstract applicative order evaluator for expressions of the pure λ-calculus. It derives its name from the four stacks it uses as a run-time environment:

- S holds evaluated λ-terms in essentially the order in which they are encountered during the traversal of the original λ-expression;
- E holds name/value pairs for instantiations of λ-bound variables;

- C is a control structure which accommodates the (part of the) expression that still needs to be processed;
- D serves as a dump for actual machine states that need to be saved when entering into the evaluation of another application.

The operation of this machine is specified in terms of a state transition function

$$\tau : (S\,E\,C\,D) \rightarrow (S'\,E'\,C'\,D')$$

which maps current into next machine states. To do so, the function τ must distinguish among six basic constellations on the stack-tops of components of λ-terms. These constellations can be readily expressed in terms of pattern matches collected in a `CASE` construct.

The λ-terms to be processed by this machine may be specified in the following meta-syntax in order to distinguish them from the λ-terms of KIR proper:

`term` → `var{x}` | `lambda{x term}` | `apply{term term}` .

Variables, abstractions and applications are in this syntax special constructor expressions. In addition we need closures of the general form `clos{e x term}` which define abstractions `lambda{x term}` as values in environments `e`.

The specification of the machine may be based on the representation of its state as a sequence of four subsequences, denoted as `< s e c d >`, which correspond to the four push-down stacks. The state transition function τ can then be implemented by means of a recursive function `secd` whose body is made up from a `CASE` construct, as shown in fig. 2. It is composed of seven pattern matches, of which the first one defines the terminal state, and the other six specify the state transition rules for λ-terms.

In this program, the function `secd` is applied to a concrete λ-term of the meta-language which is initially set up in the control structure C, with all other structures (stacks) empty. Variable names must be specified in this syntax as constants, i.e., as character strings embedded in quotation marks, otherwise they would become variables of KIR but not of the meta-language, and as such could get parasitically bound outside the intended context.

A rule application in this program generally takes three reduction steps, one each to perform a recursive call of `secd`, to successfully match one of the patterns against the new machine state passed along through the parameter `state`, and to produce the new state by evaluation of the body of the matching pattern. There is one exception though: evaluating the body of the third `WHEN`-clause usually takes several steps since it involves calling the recursive function `lookup` to locate in the environment E an entry for a variable appearing on top of the control structure C, and to substitute it by the term with which it is instantiated.

Fig.3 shows three typical intermediate programs (in which the function definition parts are abbreviated by question marks since they remain unchanged), and the final machine state resulting from the successful application of the first pattern match.

After five state transitions of three reduction steps each π–RED returns the KIR program depicted in fig. 3(a). It shows the situation immediately before

```
LETREC
  secd state =
   ( CASE
     WHEN < s e <> <> >
       DO  < < s e <> <> > 'done' >
     WHEN < < w s > e <> < ss se sc sd > >
       DO ( secd < < x ss > se sc sd > )
     WHEN < s e < var{x} c > d >
       DO ( secd < < ( lookup x e ) s > e c d > )
     WHEN < s e < lambda{x term} c > d >
       DO ( secd < < clos{e x term} s > e c d > )
     WHEN < s e < apply{e_1 e_2} c > d >
       DO ( secd < s e < e_2 < e_1 < ap{ } c > > > d > )
     WHEN < < clos{e x term} < arg s > > e < ap{ } c > d >
       DO ( secd < <> < < x arg > e > < term <> > < s e c d > > )
     WHEN < < fun < arg s > > e < ap{ } c > d >
       DO ( secd < < apply{fun < arg >} s > e c d > )
     OTHERWISE < state 'irregular state' >
     END_CASE state )
  lookup var env =
   ( CASE
     WHEN <> DO var{var}
     WHEN < < x e > z > GUARD ( EQ var x ) DO e
     WHEN < x z > DO ( lookup var z )
     OTHERWISE < env 'erroneous environment' >
     END_CASE env )
IN ( secd < <> <> < apply{apply{lambda{'u'
                                         lambda{'v' apply{var{'u'} var{'v'}}}}
                                   lambda{'x' var{'x'}}} var{'w' }} <> > <> > )
```

Fig. 2. KIR specification of an SECD machine

reducing the first application of the meta-language λ-term, with two applicators set up on stack C, and with the two abstractions set up as closures on stack S (followed by the free variable **var{'w'}**). The next state transition step returns with the program of fig. 3(b) in which the application is actually reduced, with the instantiation of the variable **'u'** set up in stack E, with the abstraction **lambda{'v' ...}** set up on C, and with the remaining components of the enclosing application moved to the dump D.

The KIR program shown in fig. 3(c) describes the situation right before reducing the second redex of the meta-language term. After having reduced the innermost meta-term redex, the program terminates as expected with the expression of fig. 3(d).

It should be noted at this point that specifying the SECD machine in any other of the established functional languages, due to the availability of pattern matches, is equally straightforward and concise. What is missing, however, is

```
LETREC
      ?
      ?
IN ( secd
     < < clos{<> 'u'
              lambda{'v' apply{var{'u'} var{'v'}}}}
       < clos{<> 'x' var{'x'}} < var{'w'} <> > > >
     <>
     < ap{ } < ap{ } <> > >
     <> > ) ,                                              (a)
```

⇓

```
LETREC
      ?
      ?
IN ( secd < <>
         < < 'u' clos{<> 'x' var{'x'}} > <> >
         < lambda{'v' apply{var{'u'} var{'v'}}} <> >
         < < var{'w'} <> > <> < ap{ } <> > <> > > ) ,     (b)
```

⇓

```
LETREC
      ?
      ?
IN ( secd < < clos{<> 'x' var{'x'}}
               < var{'w'} <> > >
         < < 'v' var{'w'} >
           < < 'u' clos{<> 'x' var{'x'}} > <> > >
         < ap{ } <> >
         < <> <> <> <> > > )  .                            (c)
```

⇓

```
< < < var{'w'} <> >
        < < 'v' var{'w'} >
          < < 'u' clos{<> 'x' var{'x'}} > <> > >
        <>
        < <> <> <> <> > > 'done' > .                       (d)
```

Fig. 3. Sequence of state transitions of the SECD machine

the stepwise execution mode which enables the programmer to follow up on and study individual state transition steps.

6 Teaching Experiences

π–RED has been extensively used over the last five years in a graduate lab course which complements classroom teaching on various topics of functional programming and related computer architectures. The course is primarily attended by 3rd and 4th year CS students. Prerequisites are the successful completion of undergraduate studies in CS (which in Germany take 2 years) with oral exams, programming experience with some imperative language, and enrollment in the afore-mentioned computer architecture course. Recommended literature are a user and programming guide for π–RED [Klu94] and two complementary textbooks on the implementation of functional and reduction languages [Pey87, Klu92].

The course stretches over two terms (semesters) of 14 weeks each. It splits up into two hours of lecturing / tutoring and 4 hours of lab work (programming) per week. Students are also expected to spend some time on small homework assignents.

Course evaluation is based on continuous assessment, i.e., on progress made with programming assignments and term projects, and on a final (oral) exam.

To get aquainted with the language KiR , particularly with the expressive power that comes with a full-fledged λ-calculus and with pattern matching, but also to familiarize with the syntax-directed editor, with the stepwise execution mode and with other π–RED controls, the course always sets out with some light exercises in functional programming. They emphazise recursive programming techniques, the scoping of variables, simple symbolic computations, the use of higher-order functions, and rule-based programming.

The larger part of the course includes term projects in which students sofar have implemented

- several variants of SECD-machines for an applied λ-calculus (including δ-reduction rules for arithmetic | logic | relational and list processing functions) to study the effects of applicative order, normal order and lazy evaluation regimes on λ-terms, e.g., on different versions of the Y-combinator;
- an emulator for the G-machine, including a λ-lifter and an adaption of the G-compilation scheme as outlined in [John83] to the needs of compiling KiR to G-code;
- a compiler for KiR to C-code (which reqires some small C-routine to transform KiR output into C proper by removing quotation marks, KiR constructors, etc.);
- a language-independent parser which expects as actual parameters both the specification of a language-specific grammar and of the program to be parsed;
- prototypes of compilers, de-compilers and interpreters for advanced versions of π–RED based on several variants of abstract stack machines.

It turned out that, after some short time (usually not exceeding two supervised sessions of four hours) of getting used to the intricacies of syntax-directed programming and of using stepwise execution as a means to debug and validate programs, students became highly productive in writing fairly large programs (more than 100 kBytes of KiR code).

With respect to correct program design it was considered very helpful that

- syntactically incorrect input is immediately rejected by the editor;

- incompletely specified constructs are completed by place-holders for terms to be inserted later on, which considerably facilitates top-down programming;
- in the process of debugging / validating programs, other than top level redexes can be selected for evaluation;
- the λ-calculus allows for symbolic computations with free variables, which is essential for doing reductions in selected subterms in which variables that are bound in larger contexts occur locally free.

Pattern matching in conjunction with higher-order functions as supported by the λ-calculus, after having developed some expertise in using these concepts, were effectively employed in writing very concise, comprehensible and well-structured programs. A good example in kind was the design of the above-mentioned language-independent parser. It has been specified as a complex function of two parameters (whose body includes large sets of term rewrite rules implemented as pattern matches) which, when partially applied to just some syntax specification, reduces to the normal form of a unary function (λ-abstraction) which realizes a language-specific parser. In contrast to other implementations of functional languages, this function can be made visible as a high-level KIR program.

Criticism on π–RED in general and on the language KIR in particular primarily centered around lacking support for modularization. It made life sometimes difficult when it came to composing large programs and to understanding the effects of stepwise reductions, even when done in fairly local contexts. Occassionally, lacking interaction with a state was also felt to be a deficiency. Some difficulties were also encountered with the syntax-oriented editor, specifically with searching for and replacing multiple occurrences of certain subterms, and with some degree of randomness in introducing abbreviations that are necessary to make programs returning after shifts of reductions fit into the available window space. To overcome some of these problems, a more recent version of π–RED allows to switch to a line-oriented editing mode (vi) and to exercise a little more control over program layout.

We are presently also working on the implementation of KIR -compatible modules and of I/O operations.

Acknowledgement

We wish to express our gratitude to Dr. Harald Bloedorn who introduced and shaped the format of the lab course outlined in the preceding section and considerably contributed to its technical contents.

References

[AbSus85] Abelson, H.; Sussmann, G.J.: *Structure and Interpretation of Computer Programs*, MIT Press, McGraw-Hill, New York, NY, 1985

[Back78] Backus, J.: *Can Programming Be Liberated from the von Neumann Style? A Functional Style and Its Algebra of Programs*, Communications of the ACM, Vol. 21, No. 8, 1978, pp. 613–641

[Berk75] Berkling, K.J.: *Reduction Languages for Reduction Machines*, Proceedings of the 2nd Annual Symposium on Computer Architecture, 1975, ACM/IEEE 75CH0916-7C, pp. 133–140

[BeFe82b] Berkling, K.J.; Fehr, E.: *A Consistent Extension of the Lambda-Calculus as a Base for Functional Programming Languages*, Information and Control, Academic Press, Vol. 55, Nos. 1–3, October/November/December 1982

[Car83] Cardelli, L.; McQueen, D.: *The Functional Abstract Machine* The ML/LCF/HOPE Newsletter, AT&T, Bell Labs, Murray Hill NJ, 1983

[Brui72] DeBruijn, N.G.: *Lambda-Calculus Notation with Nameless Dummies. A Tool for Automatic Formula Manipulation with Application to the Church-Rosser-Theorem*, Indagationes Mathematicae, Vol. 34, 1972, pp. 381–392

[GaKl94] Gaertner, D., Kluge, W.E.: π-RED^{+}*: An Interactive Compiling Graph Reduction System for an Applied* λ*-Calculus*, to be published in JFP

[Gol94] Goldson, D.: *A Symbolic Calculator for Non-Strict Functional Programs* The Computer Journal, Vol. 37, No. 3, 1994, pp. 177 - 187

[HaMiTo88] Harper, R.; Milner, R.; Tofte, M.: *The Definition of Standard ML Version 3*, Laboratory for Foundations of Computer Science, University of Edinburgh, May 1989

[HuWa88] Hudak, P.; Wadler, P. (Editors) et al.: *Report on the Functional Programming Language : Haskell*, Draft Proposed Standard, December 1988, Yale University

[John83] Johnsson, T.: *Efficient Compilation of Lazy Evaluation* SIGPLAN Compiler Construction Conference, Montreal Queb., 1984

[Klu92] Kluge, W.E.: *The Organization of Reduction, Data Flow, and Control Flow Systems*, MIT Press, Cambridge, Mass., 1992

[Klu94] Kluge, W.E.: *A User's Guide for the Reduction System* π-RED, Int. Report, No. 9419, Inst. f. Informatik, CAU Kiel, 1994,

[Lan64] Landin, P.J.: *The Mechanical Evaluation of Expressions*, The Computer Journal, Vol. 6, No. 4, 1964, pp. 308–320

[Lavi87] Laville, A.: *Lazy Pattern Matching in the ML Language*, INRIA Rapporte de Recherche, No. 664, 1987

[Plas93] Plasmeijer, R., van Eekelen, M.: *Functional Programming and Parallel Graph Rewriting*, Addison Wesley, 1993

[Pey87] Peyton–Jones, S.L.: *The Implementation of Functional Programming Languages*, Prentice Hall, Englewood Cliffs, NJ, 1987

[Pey92] Peyton–Jones, S.L.: *Implementing Lazy Functional Languages on Stock Hardware: The Spineless Tagless G-Machine*, Journal of Functional Programming, Vo. 2, No. 2, 1992, pp. 127 - 202

[RuToFi93] Runciman, C.; Toyn, I.; Firth, M.: *An Incremental, Exploratory and Transformational Environment for Lazy Functional Languages*, Journal of Functional Programming, Vol. 3, No. 1, 1993, pp. 93 - 115

[Turn76] Turner, D.A.: *A New Implementation Technique for Applicative Languages* Software Practice and Experience, Vol. 9, No. 1,1979, pp. 31-49

[Turn86] Turner, D.A.: *An Overview of Miranda*, SIGPLAN Notices, Vol. 21, No. 12, 1986, pp. 158–166

Compiler Construction Using Scheme

Erik Hilsdale J. Michael Ashley
R. Kent Dybvig Daniel P. Friedman

Indiana University Computer Science Department
Lindley Hall 215
Bloomington, Indiana 47405
{*ehilsdal,jashley,dyb,dfried*}*@cs.indiana.edu*

Abstract

This paper describes a course in compiler design that focuses on the Scheme implementation of a Scheme compiler that generates native assembly code for a real architecture. The course is suitable for advanced undergraduate and beginning graduate students. It is intended both to provide a general knowledge about compiler design and implementation and to serve as a springboard to more advanced courses. Although this paper concentrates on the implementation of a compiler, an outline for an advanced topics course that builds upon the compiler is also presented.

1 Introduction

A good course in compiler construction is hard to design. The main problem is time. Many courses assume C or some similarly low-level language as both the source and implementation language. This assumption leads in one of two directions. Either a rich source language is defined and the compiler is not completed, or the source and target languages are drastically simplified in order to finish the compiler.

Neither solution is particularly satisfying. If the compiler is not completed, the course cannot be considered a success: some topics are left untaught, and the students are left unsatisfied. If the compiler is completed with an oversimplified source language, the compiler is unrealistic on theoretical grounds since the semantics of the language are weak, and if the compiler generates code for a simplified target language, the compiler is unrealistic on practical grounds since the emitted code does not run on real hardware.

An alternative approach is to abandon the assumption that a low-level language be used and switch to a high-level language. Switching to a high-level language as the implementation language has the benefit that the compiler takes less time to implement and debug. Furthermore, using a simple high-level language as the source confers the benefits of a small language without a loss of

Title	Compilers I
Goal	To provide a general knowledge of compiler design and implementation and to serve as a springboard to more advanced courses.
Students	Advanced undergraduates and beginning graduate students in Computer Science.
Duration	One fifteen-week semester with two 75-minute lectures per week.
Grading	Five projects, one midterm exam, and one final exam.

Figure 1: Course information

semantic power. The combination makes it possible to generate code for a real architecture and to complete the compiler within the bounds of a one-semester course.

Scheme is a good choice for both a high-level implementation and source language. It is an extremely expressive language, and the core language is very small.

This paper presents a one-semester course in which a Scheme compiler is constructed using Scheme as the implementation language (see Figure 1). While the paper focuses on the compiler constructed during the course, an advanced course in language implementation is outlined that uses the constructed compiler as a testbed.

The paper is organized as follows. Section 2 describes the compiler. Section 3 discusses issues affecting the design of the compiler and the course. Section 4 outlines an advanced topics course that uses the compiler. Section 5 gives our conclusions.

2 The Compiler

The compiler accepts a subset of legal Scheme programs as defined in the Revised^4 Report [7], a subset strong enough to compile itself.

- the language is syntactically restricted so that the only numbers accepted are integers in a bounded range,
- all **lambda** expressions have a fixed arity, *i.e.*, no rest arguments.
- programs cannot have free variables other than references to primitives in operator position,

- symbols cannot be interned at runtime,
- first-class continuations and I/O are not supported,
- derived syntax is not directly supported,
- garbage-collection is not provided, and
- the runtime library is minimal.

These omissions are not detrimental. A primitive can be treated as a value through an inverse-eta transformation [5, page 63] by putting it in a lambda expression that accepts arguments that are in turn passed to the primitive. Derived syntax is not supported directly, but the compiler can macro expand its input as a first step because the compiler is itself written in Scheme and the host programming environment makes a macro expander available. First-class continuations, I/O, and the ability to intern symbols dynamically are important (and are covered in lectures), but they are not pedagogically essential.

The compiler is described below, back to front. The run-time execution model is described first. The representation of the environment and control fixes the target of the compiler and motivates the structure of the compiler's intermediate language. The code generator generates its assembly code from the intermediate language, and the front end translates core Scheme programs to intermediate programs.

2.1 The Run-time Model

The run-time execution model is given in Figure 2. Control is stack-based, with the *fp* register pointing to the base of the current frame. A frame consists of a return address, the arguments to the active procedure, and temporary values. The *cp* register points to the closure of the active procedure, and the closure holds the values of the procedure's free variables. The *ap* register points to the next free location in the heap. An accumulator register *ac0* and three temporary registers *t0*, *t1*, and *t2* are used for intermediate values.

The procedure call convention for non-tail calls is as follows. The caller first saves the closure pointer at the top of its frame. The callee's frame is then built by pushing a return address and then evaluating each argument and pushing its value. The operator is evaluated last, and its value is placed in the *cp* register. Finally, the frame pointer is incremented to point to the base of the callee's frame and control is transferred by a jump indirect through the closure pointer. On return, the callee places the return value in the accumulator *ac0* and jumps to the return address at the base of its frame. The caller restores the frame pointer to its old position and reloads the *cp* register with its old value.

The calling convention is simpler for tail calls. The arguments are evaluated and pushed, and the operator is then evaluated and stored in the *cp* register. The arguments are moved downwards to overwrite arguments of the caller's frame, and control is transferred to the callee. The frame pointer does not move.

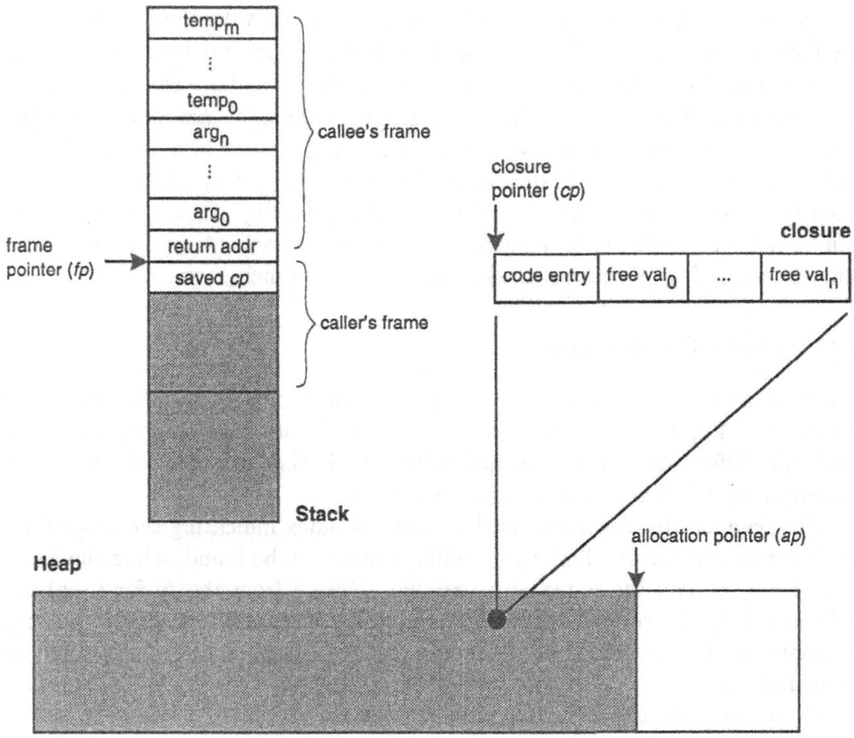

Figure 2: The run-time model is stack based, and a display closure is used to access variables free in the active procedure. Heap allocation is performed by incrementing a dedicated allocation pointer.

$$
\begin{array}{rcl}
E & = & i \mid R \mid (\textbf{begin}\ E\ E) \mid (\textbf{if}\ E\ E\ E) \mid (E\ E\ \ldots) \mid \\
 & & (P\ E\ \ldots) \mid (\textbf{closure}\ (v\ \ldots)\ (R\ \ldots)\ E) \mid \\
 & & (\textbf{let}\ ((v\ E)\ \ldots)\ E) \\
R & = & (\textbf{free}\ n\ v) \mid (\textbf{bound}\ n\ v) \mid (\textbf{local}\ v) \\
P & \in & \textit{Primitives} \\
i & \in & \textit{Immediates} \\
v & \in & \textit{Variables} \\
n & \in & \mathbf{N}
\end{array}
$$

Figure 3: The intermediate language

Values are represented using 64-bit tagged pointers with the low three bits used for tag information [23]. Four of the nine data-types, booleans, characters, fixnums, and the empty list, are immediate data-types and are encoded directly in the pointer. Vectors, pairs, closures, strings, and symbols are allocated in the heap. Since the low three bits are used for the tag, allocation must proceed on eight-byte boundaries. A heap allocated object is tagged by subtracting eight from the pointer to the object and then adding the tag. Fields of the object can be referenced efficiently using a displacement operand. A type check is also efficient, requiring at worst a mask, compare, and branch.

2.2 Code Generation

The code generator produces code for the run-time model from the intermediate language of Figure 3. The language is similar to core Scheme despite several syntactic differences. The principal difference is that variable references are subsumed by the **free**, **bound**, and **local** forms.

The **free** and **bound** forms each include an index indicating the offset from the *cp* or *fp* register at which the variable's value can be found, while the **local** form includes only the name of a variable. Offsets from the *fp* for **local** are determined by the code generator. The **closure** form is like **lambda**, but the locations of the free variables are made explicit. Constants are restricted to immediate values.

As an example, the following Scheme program

```
(let ((f (lambda (x)
           (let ((y (+ x 1)))
             (lambda (z)
               (cons y (cons z (quote (1 2)))))))))
  ((f 4) 5))
```

is written as follows in the intermediate language.

```
(let ((t (cons 1 (cons 2 '()))))
  (let ((f (closure (x) ((local t))
             (let ((y (+ (bound 0 x) 1)))
               (closure (z) ((local y) (free 0 t))
                 (cons (free 0 y)
                       (cons (bound 0 z)
                             (free 1 t)))))))))
    (((local f) 4) 5)))
```

Assignment is not part of the intermediate language, since variable assignment cannot be directly supported using the chosen run-time model. Closure formation copies the values of the free variables into the closure data structure. Therefore, a variable's value can occupy more than one location. For example, in the above program the value of y occupies a **local** location in a stack frame and a **free** location in a closure. Allowing multiple locations precludes direct

$$
\begin{array}{lcl}
E & = & (\textbf{quote } \mathrm{c}) \mid v \mid (\textbf{set! } v\ E) \mid (\textbf{begin } E\ E) \mid \\
 & & (\textbf{if } E\ E\ E) \mid (E\ E \ldots) \mid (P\ E \ldots) \mid \\
 & & (\textbf{lambda } (v \ldots)\ E) \\
c & \in & \mathit{Constants} \\
v & \in & \mathit{Variables} \\
P & \in & \mathit{Primitives}
\end{array}
$$

Figure 4: Grammar for regularized Scheme

assignment to those locations. Because variable assignment cannot be directly supported, variable assignments in the source language are converted to structure mutations by a source-to-source transformation discussed in Section 2.3.2.

Assembly code can be generated from intermediate programs in one pass. Code is generated bottom-up with the invariant that the result of evaluating a subexpression is left in the accumulator *ac0*. Arguments to primitives are stored in temporary locations on the stack, and code for primitives is generated inline. The code generated for primitives is unsafe, *i.e.*, no type checking is performed.

Offsets for **free** and **bound** references are provided. Computing frame offsets for **local** references requires a lexical environment to be passed downwards. The environment maps local variable names to frame offsets. The environment is necessary since temporary locations used for primitive and procedure applications can be interspersed with local bindings.

After code generation, the resulting assembly code is assembled using the system assembler `as` and linked against a C and assembly code stub using `ld`. The C stub obtains memory from the operating system for the stack and heap. The assembly code stub initializes the registers and places a return address back to C at the base of the stack. Upon return to C, the value left in the accumulator *ac0* is printed by a simple C-coded printer.

2.3 Compiling to Intermediate Code

The front-end of the compiler consists conceptually of three parts: a scanner and parser, a sequence of source-to-source translations, and a transformation that assigns locations to variables.

2.3.1 Scanning and Parsing

The scanner is specified as a Deterministic Finite Automaton (DFA). Most Scheme tokens are recognized. The exception is that the only legal numbers are exact integers without base prefixes, *i.e.*, the nonterminal `<number>` is redefined to be `<sign><digit>`$^+$. The scanner also incorporates a symbol table by forgoing the host system's implementation of *string->symbol* and uses a private implementation instead.

The parser uses a recursive descent algorithm. It takes a sequence of Scheme tokens and returns a Scheme datum.

2.3.2 Code Transformation

Three source-to-source transformations are performed on the forms the parser produces. The first transformation invokes the host system macro expander to expand the input program and then regularizes the expanded program. The second transformation eliminates **set!** forms. The third transformation eliminates complex quoted data.

Regularization. The first transformation is a one-pass traversal over the input form. The pass

- checks for syntax errors and flags unbound variables, *i.e.*, variables that are neither **lambda**-bound nor the name of an inlined primitive,
- ensures that primitives are used only in operator position,
- wraps unquoted constants in **quote** expressions,
- transforms the bodies of multiple-bodied **lambda** expressions into **begin** expressions, and
- makes **begin** expressions take two sub-expressions.

The output of this pass is a Scheme program in the language defined by the grammar given in Figure 4.

Assignment Elimination. Scheme's variable assignment form, **set!**, is eliminated from the language in the second transformation. A variable x that is the subject of a **set!** expression is shadowed by another variable x that is bound to a vector whose single element is the value of the first x. A reference to x then becomes a vector reference, and an assignment to x becomes a vector update. As an example, the following program

```
(lambda (x y)
  (begin
    (set! x (quote 3))
    (+ x y)))
```

is transformed into

```
(lambda (x y)
  ((lambda (x)
     (begin
       (vector-set! x (quote 0) (quote 3))
       (+ (vector-ref x (quote 0)) y)))
   (vector x)))
```

$$
\begin{array}{rcl}
E & = & i \mid v \mid (\textbf{begin}\ E\ E) \mid (\textbf{if}\ E\ E\ E) \mid \\
 & & (E\ E \ldots) \mid (P\ E \ldots) \mid \\
 & & (\textbf{lambda}\ (v \ldots)\ E) \\
i & \in & \textit{Immediates} \\
v & \in & \textit{Variables} \\
P & \in & \textit{Primitives}
\end{array}
$$

Figure 5: Grammar for simplified Scheme

Complex Quote Elimination. The third transformation eliminates complex quoted constants from the program. A complex quoted constant is a quoted symbol, vector, string, or list. An instance of such a constant is replaced by a reference to a fresh variable, and the variable is bound in a lexical scope surrounding the whole program. Symbols are treated specially since multiple occurrences of the same symbol must be commonized. Since symbols can occur in other complex quoted constants, symbols are created and bound in a lexical scope outside the scope in which other quoted data is created. For example,

(vector (**quote** (3 ab)) (**quote** ab))

becomes

((**lambda** (t_0)
   ((**lambda** (t_1)
      (vector t_1 t_0))
    (cons 3 (cons t_0 '()))))
 (make-symbol (string #\a #\b)))

The output of this pass is a Scheme program in the language defined by the grammar given in Figure 5.

2.3.3 Variable Addressing

The last transformation before code generation assigns locations to variables and transforms the simplified Scheme program into the intermediate language. One analysis pass determines the free variables of each **lambda** expression. A second pass rewrites the program. Each bound and free variable reference is converted into a **bound** and **free** form respectively, and **lambda** expressions are converted into **closure** expressions. Also, expressions of the form

((**lambda** (v_0 ... v_n) E)
 E_0 ... E_n)

are rewritten as **let** expressions, and **let**-bound variables are converted into **local** forms. The output is in the language defined by the grammar in Figure 3.

Project	Weeks
Scanning and Parsing Scheme	3
Parsing Algol-like Syntax	3
Code Transformation	3
Allocation of Variable Locations	2
Code Generation	4
	15

Figure 6: Projects

3 The Course

Each student implements the compiler in one semester. The implementation is divided into five projects, most requiring close to three weeks of class-time (see Figure 6).

For the first project the students implement the scanner and parser for Scheme syntax described in Section 2.3.1. They specify a DFA for the scanner and use one of two macro packages, **declare-table** or **state-case**, to convert the DFA into a runnable scanner. The **declare-table** and **state-case** macros are supplied so that students can spend time learning enough theory to write a DFA rather than spending all their time on the scanner's implementation details. Extra time is devoted to this fairly simple project to allow those without prior Scheme experience to become more familiar with the language.

Because parsing Scheme data is a trivial exercise, a second project is assigned to write a parser for an Algol-like language with complex precedence and associativity rules for its prefix, suffix, and infix operators. The students write an LL(1) grammar for the new syntax and implement a parser that recognizes expressions in the language specified in Figure 7. The parser returns an equivalent Scheme datum that can be fed to the rest of the compiler. Although traditional parsing techniques are taught [1], a more functional approach [21] might be an attractive alternative.

The third and fourth assignments involve implementing the transformations described in Sections 2.3.2 and 2.3.3. In order to ease the handling of such forms as the **let** form of the intermediate language, a macro package, **synlambda**, is made available to the students that extends Scheme with pattern-matching capabilities. Pattern matching over S-expressions does cause some execution overhead that can be avoided by first transforming the input into records. The source-to-source nature of the transformations can be obscured, however, if performed on records.

The last project is the implementation of the code generator described in Section 2.2. Students use the *Alpha Architecture Reference Manual* [20] for information on the general form of the assembly code generated. Object code for a working code generator is also made available for comparison.

⟨*expression*⟩ = **proc** (⟨*formals*⟩) ⟨*expression*⟩
| **let** ⟨*variable*⟩ ⟨*bindings*⟩ **in** ⟨*expression*⟩
| **let** ⟨*bindings*⟩ **in** ⟨*expression*⟩
| **if** ⟨*expression*⟩ **then** ⟨*expression*⟩ **else** ⟨*expression*⟩
| **if** ⟨*expression*⟩ **then** ⟨*expression*⟩
| ⟨*variable*⟩ ! ⟨*expression*⟩
| ⟨*expression*⟩ ? ⟨*expression*⟩
| ⟨*expression*⟩ . ⟨*expression*⟩
| ?⟨*expression*⟩
| ⟨*expression*⟩ **hd**
| ⟨*expression*⟩ **tl**
| ⟨*expression*⟩ (⟨*actuals*⟩)
| (⟨*expression list*⟩)
| ⟨*variable*⟩
| ⟨*literal*⟩

⟨*formals*⟩ = ϵ | ⟨*variable list*⟩

⟨*variable list*⟩ = ⟨*variable*⟩ | ⟨*variable*⟩ , ⟨*variable list*⟩

⟨*bindings*⟩ = ϵ | ⟨*binding list*⟩

⟨*binding list*⟩ = ⟨*binding*⟩ | ⟨*binding*⟩ , ⟨*binding list*⟩

⟨*binding*⟩ = ⟨*variable*⟩ <- ⟨*expression*⟩

⟨*actuals*⟩ = ϵ | ⟨*expression*⟩

⟨*expression list*⟩ = ⟨*expression*⟩ | ⟨*expression*⟩ , ⟨*expression list*⟩

⟨*literal*⟩ = ⟨*boolean*⟩ | ⟨*number*⟩ | ⟨*character*⟩ | ⟨*string*⟩

Figure 7: Grammar for an Algol-like language

The compiler is designed to balance pedagogy and reality. On one hand, the compiler should be straightforward so that it can be fully implemented by an undergraduate in one semester. On the other hand, it should not be a toy compiler; it should generate reasonably efficient code in a native assembly language. The compiler presented in Section 2 is well balanced between these two goals.

If necessary, the compiler could be simplified by macro expanding **begin** forms and not recognizing **let** expressions when assigning locations to variables. The generated code would be much less efficient, however. **begin** expressions can be macro expanded into **let** expressions. For example, (**begin** E_0 E_1) would become (**let** ((t E_0)) E_1), where t does not occur free in E_1. The cost of such an expansion is that a frame location is used unnecessarily to store the unreferenced variable t. If **let** expressions were not recognized, then a **let** expression would be treated as a full procedure call, which clearly has a higher run-time cost than binding the variables locally in the current stack frame.

If time is a premium, *e.g.*, in a ten-week quarter system, The Scheme 48 compiler [17] may be simpler to implement, though it sacrifices our goal of targeting genuine hardware. For another exploration of a simple Scheme compiler see Clinger and Hansen [8]. Additional background reading emphasizing proof of correctness of a Scheme compiler, with an extensive bibliography, can be found in [13].

It is notable that our compiler does not convert its input to continuation-passing style (CPS). Such a transformation simplifies the regularized language and is a transformation employed by some compilers for (mostly) functional languages [2, 18, 22]. While simplifying the regularized language is appealing, converting to CPS would not simplify the compiler used in this course. Pedagogically, converting to CPS requires an extra pass and obscures the correlation between the intermediate program and its source-level counterpart. This hinders debugging.

An alternative to converting to CPS is to A-normalize [12] the source program. An A-normalized program names all complex intermediate expressions and fixes the order of evaluation. It is similar to CPS, but the representation of control is not made explicit at the source level. Like conversion to CPS, A-normalization simplifies the source language and is an appropriate move in some contexts, *e.g.*, for the static analysis of programs [11]. It is inappropriate, however, for a one-semester course in compiler construction. Assigning a temporary location to every intermediate value, *e.g.*, the test part of a conditional, is unnecessary and results in the generation of poor code unless the pass that assigns locations to variables is made more sophisticated. Assigning locations and generating code can be done more simply and more directly when the program is in direct style.

We have chosen to use a stack rather than a heap model. While abandoning a stack discipline and using closures to represent continuations makes *call-with-current-continuation* trivial to implement, procedure calls are more expensive [3] unless some effort is taken to share continuation closures [19]. In addition, because heap allocation of continuation frames obviates many traditional problems of stack management, a compiler based around a heap discipline would not be appropriate for a course on general compiler design and implementation.

4 Advanced Coursework

Topics courses in advanced language implementation have been built on top of the first course. Such courses are intended for graduate students who have completed the first semester course. The students use their compilers from the first semester to implement the compiler optimizations, run-time system extensions, and language features discussed in lecture. The topics can be broadly classified as either compile-time or run-time.

4.1 Compile-time Topics

The following compile-time topics have been successfully covered in a follow-up course:

- macro expansion [9],
- destination-driven code generation [10],
- copy propagation and constant folding [1],
- register allocation [6], and
- type check elimination by abstract interpretation [16, 4].

With the exception of macro expansion, the compile-time topics are about compiler optimizations. To motivate them, an assignment is given early in which the students are told to hand-optimize a program that solves the eight queens problem. There is no constraint on the optimizations that may be applied, and optimizations to both the source and target code are allowed. Students typically perform procedure integration, constant folding, peephole optimization, and register allocation.

Some of the optimizations done by hand are covered in class and then implemented. The compiler's code generator is rewritten to use destination-driven code generation, which is a one-pass code generation technique that achieves most of the benefits of peephole optimization. For register allocation, traditional techniques are covered in lecture, including register assignment and save/restore placement. The students implement a three-pass algorithm that uses caller-save registers and does a good job of save/restore placement. The algorithm does not, however, try to optimize register assignment. The discussion of copy propagation, procedure integration, and constant folding leads to (on-line) partial evaluation. The students implement their own compiler passes to perform these transformations with the constraint that the passes must terminate.

4.2 Run-time Topics

Run-time topics are treated like their compile-time counterparts: theory and possible implementation strategies for each topic are discussed in class and a particular strategy is chosen for implementation. Some of the topics covered in a past course have been:

- separate compilation,
- buffered I/O,
- first-class continuations [14], and
- garbage collection.

The bulk of the run-time support code is written in Scheme using a set of low-level primitives supported by the compiler's code generator. One strategy for including the support code with user code is to simply wrap the support code (such as a definition of *string->symbol* or a garbage-collection routine) around the user code using a **let** expression and input the combination to the compiler as one monolithic program. While simple, this approach has the drawback that it is difficult to debug the compiler since even small programs are combined with a substantial amount of run-time support code.

An alternative strategy is to use a separate compilation facility. Run-time support code is separately compiled to produce a library. User code input to the compiler is then compiled and linked against the library to produce stand-alone assembly code as before. An early project in the semester is to implement a simple separate compilation facility that supports this model of program development. The details of the implementation can be found in the extended version of this paper [15].

With a separate compilation facility in hand, it is possible to implement substantial projects to enhance the run-time system. One possible set of topics is first-class continuations, garbage collection, and input/output. While others are possible, this choice allows students to bootstrap their compiler by the end of the semester.

To support first-class continuations, the stack model is generalized to a series of linked stack segments. The model supports stack overflow gracefully by treating overflow as an implicit continuation capture in which a new stack is allocated and linked to the overflowed segment.

First-class continuations simplify memory management techniques. In lecture, various types of memory management are presented, including mark-sweep, reference counting, copying, and generational. The students implement a copying collector in Scheme as a procedure of no arguments that immediately reifies its current continuation. Since registers are caller-save and the collector is a procedure of no arguments, the continuation is the root of the collection. The collector is an iterative Scheme program that performs a bounded amount of allocation. To detect when a garbage collection must occur, heap overflow checks are inserted by the compiler before each allocation.

Buffered I/O is a straightforward topic. The implementation requires code in the C stub to interface to the operating system as well as primitives supported by the code generator that call the C routines in the stub.

4.3 Discussion

The second semester can be taught with varying degrees of depth and breadth. If many topics are covered, the course has a "concepts" feel to it. For such a course, the time needed to implement the projects limits the number of topics that can be covered. Six or seven serious projects can be completed in a semester, but there is enough lecture time to cover more topics.

Regardless, six or seven projects is an ambitious undertaking for one semester. The fact that the students can complete this many projects is due to the framework developed in the first semester: the compiler is simple but realistic, and it is written in Scheme and developed in an incremental programming environment. The projects would take much longer if the compiler or any of the run-time support code, *e.g.*, the garbage collector, were implemented in a lower-level language like C.

As an experiment to further reduce debugging time, a simulator for an appropriate subset of symbolic Alpha assembly code has been recently introduced. The simulator is embedded in Scheme and thus allows for the intermixing of Scheme expressions and Alpha code to provide a more robust debugging environment than gdb. Whether the simulator actually reduced debugging time, however, has not been studied.

In the past, compile-time topics have been discussed first, followed by run-time topics. Perhaps a better organization would be to address run-time topics first, particularly if a goal is to have the students bootstrap their compilers.

When compilers are bootstrapped, students can use their own compilers as a non-trivial test of their systems. This makes the benefits of compiler optimizations later in the course much more dramatic. Furthermore, students learn first-hand the tradeoffs between the cost of compile-time optimizations versus their benefits. For example, adding a register allocator might add three passes to the compiler, but it still speeds up the bootstrapped compiler since it is compiled using register allocation.

5 Conclusions

This paper outlines a course in compiler construction. The implementation and source language is Scheme, and the target language is assembly code. This choice of languages allows a direct-style, stack-based compiler to be implemented by an undergraduate in one semester that touches on more aspects of compilation than a student is likely to see in a compiler course for more traditional languages. Furthermore, expressiveness is barely sacrificed; the compiler can be bootstrapped provided there is enough run-time support.

Besides covering basic compilation issues, the course yields an implemented compiler that can serve as a testbed for advanced coursework in language implementation. The compiler has been used, for example, to study advanced topics such as the implementation of first-class continuations and register allocation.

A technical report [15] giving more details is in preparation. The report describes the implementation of the compiler in considerably more detail. Furthermore, curricular materials such as the Alpha simulator and the **synlambda**, **declare-table**, and **state-case** macros are also described.

Acknowledgments

Carl Bruggeman, Robert Hieb and Suresh Srinivas helped design the Scheme subset used in this course. Chris Haynes provided useful feedback on various aspects of the course.

References

[1] Alfred D. Aho, Ravi Sethi, and Jeffrey D. Ullman. *Compilers Principles, Techniques and Tools.* Addison-Wesley, 1986.

[2] Andrew W. Appel. *Compiling with Continuations.* Cambridge University Press, 1992.

[3] Andrew W. Appell and Zhong Shao. An empirical and analytic study of stack vs. heap cost for languages with closures. To appear in *Journal of Functional Programming.*

[4] J. Michael Ashley. A practical and flexible flow analysis for higher-order languages. To appear in *Proceedings of the ACM Symposium on Principles of Programming Languages, 1996.*

[5] Henk P. Barendregt. *The Lambda Calculus: Its Syntax and Semantics.* Number 103 in Studies in Logic and the Foundations of Mathematics. North-Holland, 1984.

[6] Robert G. Burger, Oscar Waddell, and R. Kent Dybvig. Register allocation using lazy saves, eager restores, and greedy shuffling. In *Proceedings of the ACM SIGPLAN '95 Conference on Programming Language Design and Implementation*, pages 130–138, 1995.

[7] William Clinger and Jonathan Rees (editors). Revised^4 report on the algorithmic language Scheme. *Lisp Pointers*, 5(3):1–55, July-September 1991.

[8] William D. Clinger and Lars Thomas Hansen. Lambda, the ultimate label, or a simple optimizing compiler for scheme. In *Proceedings of the 1994 ACM Conference on LISP and Functional Programming*, pages 128–139, 1994.

[9] R. Kent Dybvig, Daniel P. Friedman, and Christopher T. Haynes. Expansion-passing style: A general macro mechanism. *Lisp and Symbolic Computation*, 1(1):53–75, 1988.

[10] R. Kent Dybvig, Robert Hieb, and Tom Butler. Destination-driven code generation. Technical Report 302, Indiana University, February 1990.

[11] Cormac Flanagan and Matthias Felleisen. The semantics of future and its use in program optimization. In *Proceedings of the ACM Symposium on Principles of Programming Languages*, pages 209–220, 1995.

[12] Cormac Flanagan, Amr Sabry, Bruce F. Duba, and Matthias Felleisen. The essence of compiling with continuations. In *Proceedings of the ACM SIGPLAN '93 Conference on Programming Language Design and Implementation*, pages 237–247, 1993.

[13] Joshua D. Guttman and Mitchell Wand, editors. *VLISP: A Verified Implementation of Scheme.* Kluwer, Boston, 1995. Originally published as a special double issue of the journal *Lisp and Symbolic Computation* (Volume 8, Issue 1/2).

[14] Robert Hieb, R. Kent Dybvig, and Carl Bruggeman. Representing control in the presence of first-class continuations. In *Proceedings of the ACM SIGPLAN '90 Conference on Programming Language Design and Implementation*, pages 66–77, 1990.

[15] Erik Hilsdale and Daniel P. Friedman. A Scheme-based course on compiler construction. In Preparation.

[16] Suresh Jagannathan and Andrew Wright. Effective flow analysis for avoiding runtime checks. In *Proceedings of the 1995 International Static Analysis Symposium*, 1995.

[17] Richard A. Kelsey and Jonathan A. Rees. A tractable Scheme implementation. *Lisp and Symbolic Computation*, 7(4):315–335, 1994.

[18] David A. Kranz, Richard Kelsey, Jonathan A. Rees, Paul Hudak, J. Philbin, and Norman I. Adams. Orbit: an optimizing compiler for Scheme. *SIGPLAN Notices, ACM Symposium on Compiler Construction*, 21(7):219–233, 1986.

[19] Zhong Shao and Andrew W. Appel. Space-efficient closure representations. In *Proceedings of the 1994 ACM Conference on LISP and Functional Programming*, pages 130–161, 1994.

[20] Richard L. Sites, editor. *Alpha Architecture Reference Manual.* Digital Press, 1992.

[21] Michael Sperber and Peter Thiemann. The essence of LR parsing. In *Proceedings of the Symposium on Partial Evaluation and Semantics-Based Program Manipulation, PEPM '95*, pages 146–155, 1995.

[22] Guy L. Steele Jr. Rabbit: A compiler for Scheme. Master's thesis, M.I.T (A.I. LAB.), Massachusetts, U.S.A, 1978. Also available as MIT AI Memo 474.

[23] Peter A. Steenkiste. The implementation of tags and run-time type checking. In Peter Lee, editor, *Topics in Advanced Language Implementation*, pages 3–24. MIT Press, 1991.

Basic Proof Skills of Computer Science Students

Pieter H. Hartel[1], Bert van Es[1], Dick Tromp[2]

[1] Faculty of Mathematics and Computer Science, University of Amsterdam, Kruislaan 403, 1098 SJ Amsterdam, The Netherlands, {pieter,vanes}@fwi.uva.nl
[2] Dick Tromp Formerly at SCO-KIOO (Foundation Centre for Education Research at the University of Amsterdam)

Abstract. Computer science students need mathematical proof skills. At our University, these skills are being taught as part of various mathematics and computer science courses. To test the skills of our students, we have asked them to work out a number of exercises. We found that our students are not as well trained in basic proof skills as we would have hoped. The main reason is that proof skills are not emphasized enough. Our findings are the result of a small experiment using a longitudinal measurement of skills. This method gives better insight in the skills of students than more traditional exam-based testing methods. Longitudinal measurement does not allow the students to specifically prepare themselves for particular questions. The measurements thus relate to skills that are retained for a longer period of time.
In our Department, fierce debates have been held in the past discussing such issues as "what proof skills do our students have?". An important aspect of our work is that it tries to find evidence to help answer to such questions. Research such as ours is rare in the field of teaching mathematics and computer science.

1 Introduction

Computer scientists must be able to study the foundations of their discipline. Discrete mathematics and mathematical logic are foundations of the core of Computer Science (CS) [14]. A computer scientist must therefore be skilled in the use of basic tools and techniques from discrete mathematics and logic. Continuous mathematics and other branches of mathematics are used more in applied CS subjects such as robotics and scientific computing. Mathematical tools and techniques from such areas are also important but perhaps not quite as fundamental. We will therefore concentrate on discrete mathematics and logic.

The development of skills in mathematical manipulation should also be an integral part of the programming activity. Gries, on the occasion of receiving the annual SIGCSE award for outstanding contributions to CS education, made it clear that such skills are essential to be able to manipulate large complex structures [3]. Parnas, another well known computer scientist subscribes to this view: "CS programs must return to a classical engineering approach that emphasizes fundamentals" [10].

It is thus rather unfortunate that mathematics is mostly taught to CS students as a separate activity. When the necessary skills are being taught, they are not always perceived as related to programming. The powerful interpretation of 'proofs as programs' is then not seen as natural. Many algorithms can be viewed as a slightly different rendering of a proof; see Asch [15] for a number of examples.

For CS, mathematics is best taught as part of an integrated curriculum in which the relationships between programming and mathematics are exploited [20]. Declarative programming styles (functional and logic programming) facilitate this integration. Teaching mathematics and declarative programming in an integrated fashion has received attention in the literature [7, 19, 6], and many CS departments are considering such issues [4].

In the CS department at the Universiteit van Amsterdam (UvA) we have also been discussing these issues. Our present curriculum begins with a first programming course in Pascal using methodical problem solving methods [13] and separate courses in logic and discrete mathematics. Functional programming is offered as the option 'functional languages and architectures' during the 3rd/4th year. As of the academic year 1995/1996, the first programming language will be a functional language. The relationship between the logic course, the discrete mathematics course and the functional programming course will be strengthened: all three subjects will be taught in parallel, thus providing the opportunity for integrated teaching.

As a preparation for the transition, we were interested in the present level of proof skills that our students have, and also in the question: Does the study of functional programming have an effect on the acquisition of such skills? Here we look at specific but essential aspects of discrete mathematics as a first step towards exploring the full set of mathematical skills of our CS students.

The aspects that we consider are basic equational reasoning and induction. This represents a choice out of a vast range of mathematical tools and techniques. Equational reasoning is the basis of all program transformation methods and as such an essential tool for the computer scientist. Induction is the only tool that supports the manipulation of potentially infinite structures, such as often encountered in CS. Induction and equational reasoning are therefore important.

It is unusual to find experimental data relating the skills of CS students to what their teachers would have expected, other than straightforward examination results. In a previous study we looked at all issues of the ACM SIGCSE bulletin over the past seven years. This study revealed that precious little hard evidence can be found for statements about CS education [5]. A notable exception to this rule is formed by the CS department of the Technical University at Twente. A recent Ph.D. thesis contains a comprehensive investigation into the effects that various decisions about the CS curriculum have on student performance [17]. Our experiment is of course small compared to the Twente experiment. It is interesting to note that both experiments relate to functional programming.

In the next section we discuss the context of the exploration into the mathematical skills of our students. Section 3 describes the experiment that has been carried out to measure the skills. The exercises and the evaluation criteria used to mark the exercises are described in Sect. 4. Section 5 presents the experimental results. The final section gives the conclusions.

2 Curriculum

The CS curriculum at the UvA nominally takes 4 years. A year has three terms of 14 weeks each. During a term 2–4 different subjects are taught. The amount of effort required to study a subject is rated using a point system. Each point corresponds to one week (that is 38 hours) of effort. The total number of points available during one term is thus 14. Subjects may be rated at 3, 4 or 7 points, depending on the amount of effort required by a hypothetical 'average' student. The point rating of each subject should cover all activities related to mastering that particular subject, including lectures, laboratories, homework and the preparation of the test.

2.1 Tests

Students normally take tests in a subject at the end of the term. There is no obligation to take a test directly after the course; tests are scheduled regularly. Students are also allowed to take a test a number of times until the test has been passed.

During the first 7 terms, the UvA CS curriculum has a common programme. Then, a choice must be made out of three specialisations, each of which lasts for another 5 terms. The specialisations on offer are theoretical CS (emphasis on mathematical logic, complexity theory, data base theory and natural languages), programming methodology (emphasis on algebraic formal methods) and technical CS (emphasis on robotics, image processing and parallel computing). The last 6 months of the specialisation are devoted to the final year project. There is a large degree of freedom in selecting topics for the specialisation. Students are encouraged to take courses from the different specialisations on offer. They are also allowed to choose some subjects from other disciplines.

The organisation of the curriculum offers the student considerable freedom in planning the programme of study. Firstly, a student chooses a number of subjects and an order in which they are studied. The dependencies specified by the prerequisites of each course constrain the freedom somewhat. Secondly, once a course has been taken, the student may delay taking the test until sufficient knowledge, experience and confidence has been acquired.

The system makes it difficult both for the student and for the staff to have accurate information about the progress that is being made. The data that are presently available record the number of points earned and the selection of tests passed. In theory, this should be a good predictor for the progress made. In practice, this is not always the case, as the points are awarded on the basis of how much work an 'average' student is supposed to spend studying a subject.

Table 1. Subjects taught during the first 6 terms of the CS curriculum. The numbers represent the point rating of each subject. One point corresponds to one week of full time study.

term I		term II		term III	
Introduction CS	3			Relational data bases	4
Logic	4	Discrete Mathematics	4	Graph Theory	3
		Continuous Mathematics	3		
Programming	7	Data Structures	7	Computer organisation	7
term IV		**term V**		**term VI**	
				CS ethics; presentation skills	7
Automata &	7	Linear Algebra	4	Calculus	4
complexity theory		Probability & statistics	3	Algebraic Structures	3
Operating systems	7	Programming Environments	7		

Many students spend more time, especially on the more theoretically-oriented subjects.

As a consequence, few students manage to complete their studies within 4 years even though a delay has severe financial implications. There are also other factors that cause delays, such as the need for many students to supplement their income through part-time employment.

The main problem with the present system of student performance assessment is that it does not give clear early warnings. A student who feels ill at ease with a particular subject will perhaps postpone a thorough study of the subject and also delay taking the test. For the staff this is not easy to detect, as one would have to monitor what students are *not* doing. For the student, the implications of postponing study of a particular subject may not be obvious: it is often the case that an insufficient background makes the study of new subjects more difficult, even though the newly-experienced difficulties are not directly traceable to the earlier, explicit or implicit choice to delay the previous subject.

A system of progress tests, such as operated by the University of Limburg Medical school in Maastricht [12] might be considered as an alternative to the present assessment system or as a means to supplement the present system. The progress test as used in Maastricht uses a set of questions that is fixed for the entire programme of study. The set is very large so that students cannot prepare specifically for the tests.

2.2 Proof Skills

The present paper reports on a small experiment with a test designed to identify progress in the acquisition of skills of the CS students. The small scale of the experiment required us to concentrate on a few aspects of the curriculum that we find essential. These are the skill in giving a simple proof by equational reasoning, the skill in constructing a proof by induction and the skill in creating an inductive definition.

Table 1 gives an overview of the subjects taught during the first two years together with their point rating. The contents of most courses will probably be obvious; the programming environment course includes as one of its components the subject of compiler construction.

The basic proof skills required are explicitly taught during the first term and reinforced during later terms. Explicit teaching of a concept means that the concept is taught for its own sake. Most teaching activities involve several concepts of which one is taught explicitly. The other concepts involved will then be taught more or less implicitly.

The following subjects contribute explicitly to a mastery of basic proof skills:

Logic – term I As part of the Introductory course on Logic equational reasoning and the principle of induction are taught. These techniques are applied to inductive proofs and definitions. On page 15 of the text book [16], the concept of an inductive definition is first explained. This is followed by several examples (the first example is actually the same as Exercise 3 of Round 1 of our experiments). The students practice giving inductive definitions during the tutorials. The test includes an exercise that requires an inductive definition.

Proofs by induction are the main subject of chapter 5 (page 69–86) of the text [16]. Here properties of formulae are proved by structural induction over inductively defined formulae. The tutorials include several exercises. However, the test is designed such that students may pass if they decide to skip the inductive proof. Students often do not appreciate the power of the principle of induction and prefer simple arguments or even a 'proof by example'.

Discrete Mathematics – term II Both set theory and induction are taught as part of the discrete mathematics course. Many proofs are shown as examples. Students are advised to try some of the proofs at home but do not always follow the advice. The test includes an exercise that requires an inductive proof. The test results for this exercise show that there are two main categories of students: those that do well and those that fail; there are not many intermediate scores. In the discrete mathematics course, inductive proofs are used mostly to prove equalities. Students find it harder to prove an inequality instead. This indicates that at this stage of the curriculum, the full generality of the principle of induction is not appreciated by all students.

Graph Theory – term III The graph theory course makes use of the principle of induction, both for the purpose of giving inductive definitions and for proving properties of graphs and graph algorithms. The course is aimed specifically at CS students and therefore emphasizes algorithmic aspects more than proofs. The exam does not require the construction of inductive proofs.

Automata and Complexity theory – term IV Set theory is used in the course on automata and complexity theory. Inductive proofs are used here often. The students are given exercises that require inductive proofs; the exercises are discussed during tutorials. The test also includes an exercise that requires an inductive proof.

Algebraic structures – term V Set theory is heavily used in the course on algebraic structures, inductive proofs are rare in this course.

Towards the end of the first year, we would expect students to have acquired a reasonable level of proof skills. However, it is possible that students progress to this point without actually understanding the principle of induction. During the second year, the students should improve their basic proof skills to the point where one would expect all students to be able to carry out at least a simple inductive proof.

Inductive definitions do not play quite such an important role in the courses described, so one might expect the students to have difficulties creating an inductive definition.

3 Experiment

The aims of the experiment were, firstly, to investigate to what extent UvA CS students are able to construct simple proofs and, secondly, to investigate at what stage of the curriculum basic proof skills were mastered. More specifically, the second aim has been to measure progress from one year to another, and to measure progress within each year.

The experiment consisted of two rounds. During both rounds we asked the participants to work out a set of three exercises. The two sets were different, but comparable: they were designed to be of the same level of difficulty.

For the first-year students the exercises might have been hard; for the final year students they might have been easy; but all participants have been taught how to work out such exercises. Any difference in skills should thus be attributed to the experience that participants may have gained during their programme of study.

The first round was held at the beginning of term III of the academic year 1994/1995. The second round was held two months later, at the end of that same term. The participants were asked to supply their registration numbers, so that the progress made by participants who would cooperate on both occasions could be recorded accurately.

To keep the conditions during which the experiments were carried out the same, the exercises were completed during regular lecture or laboratory hours. On both rounds we allowed 20 minutes in total to allow for a reasonable amount of time to work out the exercises and at the same time to disrupt regular teaching as little as possible. The participants were not prepared in any way for the first round. After that they knew that the second round was coming, but not when it would come. The results or model answers were not communicated to the participants.

During the first round we asked 77 students to participate, of which only one refused. Five students refused to cooperate during the second round when we asked 60 students to take part. The participants were told in advance that the results would only be used for research purposes. They would thus not be disadvantaged by participating. As a small reward, six (CS) books were distributed amongst the participants.

The cohorts 1990 ... 1994 of UvA CS students all contain roughly the same number of students. For our two samples to be representative for the total population we would thus expect the numbers of students from these cohorts in the samples to be similar. This was found to be the case with one exception: the 1992 cohort on Round 1 contains twice as many students as expected. This gives a slight bias towards third year students on Round 1.

We have no indication that the skills of the students who did participate are not representative for the skills of the population as a whole. Both very able students and less able students sometimes do not go to class. The experiments were carried out towards the end of the year, when the student population that goes to class is relatively stable. Most students who drop out do so towards the beginning of the year. There is thus no indication that we may have worked with particularly skilled or particularly unskilled students. We could have investigated this matter further by using the exam-based results of our students. We decided against this to guarantee students that participating in the experiment would not be connected with their exam-based results.

Table 2. A fragment of the algebra of sets: A, B en C are subsets of a universal set U, the complement of a set A is written as A^c.

1a.	$A \cup B = B \cup A$	Commutativity
b.	$A \cap B = B \cap A$	
2a.	$A \cup (B \cap C) = (A \cup B) \cap (A \cup C)$	Distributivity
b.	$A \cap (B \cup C) = (A \cap B) \cup (A \cap C)$	
3a.	$A \cup \emptyset = A$	Identity
b.	$A \cup U = U$	
c.	$A \cap \emptyset = \emptyset$	
d.	$A \cap U = A$	
4a.	$A \cup A^c = U$	Complement
b.	$A \cap A^c = \emptyset$	
c.	$(A^c)^c = A$	
5a.	$A \cap B \subseteq A$	Inclusion
b.	$A \subseteq A \cup B$	

4 Exercises

In both rounds, the first exercise tested equational reasoning, the second tested the skill in constructing an inductive proof and the third exercise required the construction of an inductive definition.

We have tried to make all execises of the same level of difficulty. During the design of the exercises we consulted with a number of colleagues to make sure that the exercises would represent a good test of basic proof skills.

4.1 Exercise 1: Equational Reasoning

Equational reasoning is the basis of many proof systems. Set theory is an important part of discrete mathematics.

The first round required the participants to prove the inequality below, while using the axioms of Table 2:

$$(A \cup B) \cap A^c \subseteq B$$

The second round required the participants to prove the inequality:

$$B \subseteq (A^c \cap B) \cup A$$

These exercises are of the same level of difficulty. We give the model answer to the first:

$$\begin{array}{llll}
 & (A \cup B) \cap A^c & = A^c \cap (A \cup B) & \{1b\} \\
 & & = (A^c \cap A) \cup (A^c \cap B) & \{2b\} \\
 & & = (A \cap A^c) \cup (A^c \cap B) & \{1b\} \\
 & & = \emptyset \cup (A^c \cap B) & \{4b\} \\
 & & = (A^c \cap B) \cup \emptyset & \{1a\} \\
 & & = (A^c \cap B) & \{3a\} \\
 & & = (B \cap A^c) & \{1b\} \\
\text{and:} & (B \cap A^c) & \subseteq B & \{5a\} \\
\text{therefore:} & (A \cup B) \cap A^c & \subseteq B &
\end{array}$$

The model answer for Exercise 1 of the second round follows the same lines, taking basically the same steps in a slightly different order.

To construct the above proof, the student needs to be able to instantiate an axiom and to use the transitivity of equality. This tests only the very essentials of equational reasoning. The choice of the particular proof steps must be driven by intuition. All students should be thoroughly familiar with the axioms of set theory that we are using here. All should therefore have sufficient intuition to choose the appropriate proof steps. The danger of choosing a familiar domain to test basic equational reasoning skills is that some of the axioms may be viewed as trivial. The commutativity axioms are obvious examples. We decided to choose familiar axioms, as using unfamiliar ones would have disabled the intuition of the student. This would have made the exercise too difficult.

The individual steps in the proof above have been labelled with the number of the axiom used. This makes the proof easier to read. Annotating proof steps should therefore be considered good practice. This view is not universally held. Many mathematics texts will give long sequences of proof steps without annotations. Examples of computing books that do annotate proof steps and derivation steps are the books by Morgan [9] and Bird and Wadler [1].

All exercises were marked on a scale from 0=poor to 10=excellent. A pass mark is at least 5.5. A general criterion and some specific criteria were used to calculate the marks. The general criterion looks at whether the question has been answered at all and, if so, whether the answer is complete.

For Exercise 1, the full set of criteria and the percentages of the mark awarded are:

connectedness: 20% Have the individual proof steps been connected properly? Some participants write a number of formulae without a hint of how they are connected, so that there is no apparent logic in the reasoning.

explicitness: 40% Have all steps been made explicit? Many participants forget to note the use of the commutativity axiom. Most other axioms were used explicitly but not by every participant. Each of the seven steps above contributes 1/8 of 40%.

annotations: 20% Has each step been labelled with the name or the number of the axiom applied? Many participants leave it to the reader to guess which axioms have been applied. Each of the seven steps above contributes 1/8 of 20%.

general: 20% The general criterion for Exercise 1 accounts for 20% of the mark.

Some criteria are awarded 20% of the full mark. This indicates that an otherwise perfect answer that completely fails on just one such criterion would still result in a good mark. Completely failing on a criterion that is awarded with 40% yields a mark that is just sufficient. Explicitness falls into the 40% category as this criterion essentially captures whether students are able to instantiate the axioms properly.

4.2 Exercise 2 : Inductive Proof

The properties of some formal systems can be proved by simple induction over the natural numbers. Properties of many more formal systems can be proved by structural induction. To test the skill in proving a property by induction we have chosen to work in the domain that is most familiar to the students; the natural numbers. Other domains such as formal languages would have been unsuitable for the first-year students.

The first round required the participants to prove by induction that for all positive natural numbers n the following equality holds:

$$\sum_{k=1}^{n} k^2 = \frac{n(n+1)(2n+1)}{6}$$

The second round required the participants to prove that for all positive natural numbers n the following property is true:

$$n^3 - 4n + 6 \quad \text{is divisible by} \quad 3$$

Both proofs involve elementary algebra using cubic polynomials.

The hypothesis $\sum_{k=1}^{n} k^2 = \frac{n(n+1)(2n+1)}{6}$ is used to prove the first equation by induction over n:

Case 1: $\sum_{k=1}^{1} k^2 = 1$

$$= \frac{1(1+1)(2\times1+1)}{6}$$

Case (n+1):

$$\begin{aligned}
\sum_{k=1}^{n+1} k^2 &= \sum_{k=1}^{n} k^2 + (n+1)^2 \\
&= \frac{n(n+1)(2n+1)}{6} + (n+1)^2 \qquad \text{(hypothesis)} \\
&= \frac{n(n+1)(2n+1)+6(n+1)^2}{6} \\
&= \frac{(n+1)(n(2n+1)+6(n+1))}{6} \\
&= \frac{(n+1)(2n^2+n+6n+6)}{6} \\
&= \frac{(n+1)(n+2)(2n+3)}{6} \\
&= \frac{(n+1)((n+1)+1)(2(n+1)+1)}{6}
\end{aligned}$$

The proof of Exercise 2 from the second round follows the same lines.

The evaluation criteria for Exercise 2 are:

connectedness: 20% Have the individual proof steps been connected properly? (See under Exercise 1).

base case: 10% Is the base case present and has it been worked out properly? Some participants prove the base case for $n = 0$ instead of $n = 1$. The exercise explicitly states that the proof should apply to the *positive* natural numbers.

inductive case: 30% Is the inductive case properly worked out? Some participants start to work with $\sum_{k=1}^{n}(k+1)^2$.

annotations: 10% Has the use of the induction hypothesis been annotated? A useful sanity check when giving an inductive proof is to verify that the induction hypothesis has been used. Some participants leave it up to the reader to find out when the hypothesis has been used.

algebra: 10% Is the elementary high school algebra a problem? Many mistakes were made with the elementary algebra.

general: 20% The general criterion for Exercise 2 accounts for 20% of the mark.

Some criteria are awarded 10% of the mark. These represent relatively minor issues or elements of the proof that require little work. The inductive case represents a relatively large amount of work, which justifies its relatively large contribution to the mark.

4.3 Exercise 3 : Inductive Definition

Compositionality is the key to reasoning about complex structures in terms of their simpler components. An inductive definition can be given for a vast number of complex structures. The skill in producing such an inductive definition was the target of our third and last exercise.

Constructing inductive definitions is taught explicitly as part of the course on logic during the first term.

The first round required the participants to give an inductive definition of the formulae of propositional logic using the connectives $\vee$, $\wedge$, $\rightarrow$, $\leftrightarrow$ and $\neg$ and using as basis elements the variables p, q, r.

The model answer is:

Base case The variables p, q en r are formulae.

Inductive case Let P and Q be formulae, then $(P \vee Q)$, $(P \wedge Q)$, $(P \rightarrow Q)$, $(P \leftrightarrow Q)$ and $\neg P$ are formulae.

Closure No other terms than the ones mentioned under Base and Inductive case above are formulae.

The second round required the participants to give an inductive definition of the formulae of arithmetic, using the connectives $+$, $\times$, $>$, $=$, $-$ and the numbers 0, 1, 2 ... as basis elements.

Strictly speaking, this exercise does not test a proof skill, but rather a 'definition skill'. A more interesting test would have been to construct an inductive definition and its induction principle. Then, some property of the inductively defined structure could have been proved. Unfortunately, such an exercise would have been too time-consuming for the present constrained experiment.

The evaluation criteria for Exercise 3 are:

Base case: 20% Is the base case properly identified? Many participants forget to state which formulae are the basic elements.

Inductive case: 60% Has the inductive case been formulated? Participants either describe the inductive case properly or reproduce something completely different, such as the laws of boolean algebra (Round 1) or the Peano axioms (Round 2).

Closure: 20% Have other terms been explicitly excluded? Participants often forget to make it explicit that only the smallest class of formula is relevant. (The 'no junk' rule).

For this exercise the general criterion is subsumed by the inductive case. The inductive case has a weight of 60% as without it, the answer would be insufficient. A correct base case gives 20% of the mark, such that the ratio base case : inductive case = 1 : 3. This is the same ratio as for Exercise 2.

Table 3. Various sub-groups of the participants of Rounds 1 and 2. Here n= the number of participants; $\bar{x}$ = average mark (on a scale from 0=poor – 10=excellent; a pass mark is at least 5.5), *m.o.e.*= margin of error, s= standard deviation.

Sub-groups	round 1				round 2			
	n	$\bar{x}$	s	*m.o.e.*	n	$\bar{x}$	s	*m.o.e.*
difference	34	-0.6	1.5	0.5	34	+0.6	1.5	0.5
total	76	6.0	2.2	0.5	55	6.4	2.7	0.7

(a) Exercise 1 results of all participants

Sub-groups	round 1				round 2			
	n	$\bar{x}$	s	*m.o.e.*	n	$\bar{x}$	s	*m.o.e.*
difference	34	-0.4	3.9	1.3	34	+0.4	3.9	1.3
total	76	6.1	3.3	0.8	55	6.8	3.5	0.9

(b) Exercise 2 results of all participants

Sub-groups	round 1				round 2			
	n	$\bar{x}$	s	*m.o.e.*	n	$\bar{x}$	s	*m.o.e.*
difference	34	-1.4	3.4	1.1	34	+1.4	3.4	1.1
total	76	2.1	3.7	0.8	55	3.0	3.9	1.0

(c) Exercise 3 results of all participants

Sub-groups	round 1				round 2			
	n	$\bar{x}$	s	*m.o.e.*	n	$\bar{x}$	s	*m.o.e.*
1–7 common	21	4.1	2.0	0.8	15	4.9	2.5	1.2
8–14 common	22	5.0	1.4	0.6	14	4.7	1.8	0.9
common+theory	16	5.3	1.1	0.5	12	6.4	1.8	1.0
common+programming	20	5.6	1.8	0.8	17	6.8	1.8	0.9
common+technical	36	5.2	1.8	0.6	33	6.4	1.9	0.7
once	42	4.5	2.0	0.6	21	4.8	2.4	1.0
twice	34	5.0	1.9	0.6	34	5.8	2.2	0.7
twice (functional)	11	6.3	1.6	0.9	11	7.2	1.9	1.1
VU	14	5.4	1.1	0.6	7	6.3	2.0	1.5
UvA	62	4.6	2.1	0.5	48	5.3	2.4	0.7
total	76	4.7	2.0	0.4	55	5.4	2.3	0.6

(d) Overall results of all participants based on the average of Exercises 1, 2 and 3

5 Results

The total number of registered UvA CS students during the academic year 1994/1995 is 163. A number of these students do not go to class, in particular when they are working on their final year project. We could thus not reasonably expect the entire student population to participate. During the first round, 76 students took part and during the second round there were 55 participants. 34 participants cooperated in both rounds. We specifically handed out the exercises during laboratories and lectures scheduled for UvA CS students, but a fraction of the participants were not UvA CS students. On the first round 51 (of 76) were UvA CS students and on the second round 35 (of 55) were UvA CS students.

5.1 Student Groups

Table 3 presents various breakdowns of the group. Table 3-a, 3-b and 3-c apply to Exercises 1, 2 and 3 respectively. Table 3-d applies to the total test, based on the average of the three exercises. The exercises have equal weight.

The rows within the table correspond to certain sub-groups of the group of participants. Each row gives results obtained during the first and the second round of the experiment. The results are the number of participants (n), their average mark ($\bar{x}$), the margin of error of the average ($m.o.e.$) and the standard deviation of the average (s). (The margin of error is defined as $m.o.e. = 1.96s/n$). The number n varies from row to row because not all participants are part of each sub-group.

The sub-groups in Table 3 have been chosen partly such that progress in the acquisition of basic proof skills of the group as a whole is visible; partly to investigate whether students interested in one specialisation/subject have better proof skills than others.

The sub-group *1–7 common* has studied between 1 and 7 subjects from the list given by Table 1. These students may or may not have taken the tests for these first subjects. This sub-group has studied at most about one third of the common programme. The sub-group *8–14 common* has studied between 8 and 14 subjects (two thirds of the common programme). The sub-group *common+theory* has studied all or most of the common programme and at least one theoretical CS subject, which indicates that they may perhaps be more interested in theoretical issues than other students. Similarly, the sub-group *common+programming* has studied at least one programming methodology subject and the sub-group *common+technical* has studied at least one technical CS subject. Many students will study subjects from the different specialisations. There is thus some overlap between these five sub-groups.

The sub-group *once* has participated either in Round 1 or in Round 2 but not in both. The sub-group *twice* has participated in both Rounds 1 and 2. There is therefore no overlap between the sub-groups *once* and *twice*. The sub-group *difference* is the same as the sub-group *twice* except that for each student in the sub-group the difference between the marks awarded in Rounds 1 and 2 is calculated. The statistics given apply to these differences. A positive average in the column for Round 1 indicates that the marks in Round 1 were higher, a negative average in the same column indicates that higher marks were obtained in Round 2. The sub-group *twice (functional)* applies to students who participated on both rounds and who took the third year optional course functional languages and architectures.

An agreement between the UvA and the nearby Vrije Universiteit (VU) of Amsterdam makes it easy for CS students to take part in the courses of the neighbouring university. The sub-groups *UvA* and *VU* represent participants from the two universities in Amsterdam. These sub-groups do not overlap.

5.2 Student Performance

Table 3 shows that the average marks for Exercises 1 and 2 are sufficient. The marks for Round 1 are 6.0 and 6.1 for Exercises 1 and 2 respectively; for Round 2 they are 6.4 and 6.8. The marks cannot be qualified as good, which would require at least an 8. The participants are thus able to perform basic equational reasoning and to give a simple inductive proof, but one would suspect that more demanding proofs would give problems to many students.

The average marks for Exercise 3 (Table 3-c) are insufficient (2.1 for Round 1 and 3.0 for Round 2). About 10% of the participants noted explicitly on their forms that they had no idea what an 'inductive definition' might be. About 25% of the participants indicated that they needed more time for the three exercises. Exercise 3 was the last exercise, which makes it likely that time pressure has had a negative influence on the result for Exercise 3.

The low average marks for Exercise 3 apply to all participants. We had hoped that UvA CS students would do better than they did but this was not the case. Their averages are about the same as those found for the whole group of participants. This applies to all exercises, not just to Exercise 3. Clearly the concept of a inductive definition is being taught but not used often enough for all students to make it operational.

The rows marked *difference* for Exercises 1, 2 and 3 show an improvement in performance from Round 1 to Round 2 of +0.6, +0.4 and +1.4 respectively. The margins of error for Exercises 1 and 3 are just small enough (0.5 and 1.1 respectively) to suggest that the improvements may be significant. The margin of error is meaningful only if the data follow a normal distribution. This is not always the case here. We have applied Wilcoxon's non-parametric signed rank-test for paired data [8] to investigate this matter more closely. This test confirms that the participants have learned something that has helped them to improve their performance on Exercise 1. From the same test we could not conclude that something has been learned to improve the performance on the other two exercises.

We have also investigated what caused this improvement: Is it the learning effect that taking the tests on Round 1 has had on the results for Round 2? Or is it the result of the education during the two months that separate the two rounds? A Wilcoxon two sample test shows that the effect of participating on Round 1 on the performance during Round 2 is not significant. We have not handed out the model answers or discussed the results, so the learning effect of taking part in one of the rounds is minimal.

The variation in the performance of students at different stages of their programme of study is presented in Table 3-d. The rising averages from sub-group *1–7 common*, via *8–14 common* to either of the three sub-groups *common+...* suggest that students acquire proof skills as they progress towards the end of their programme of study. This is what one would expect. The averages for the sub-group *common+theory*, *common+programming* and *common+technical* are close, with largely overlapping margins of error. Again the distributions are not always normal, so reverting to a Wilcoxon-test we found that on Round 1 the improvement from *1–7 common* to *8–14 common* 1 is significant and that on Round 2 the improvement from *8–14 common* to any of *common+...* is significant.

The VU students seem to perform better than the UvA students: on round one the VU average mark was 5.4, the UvA mark 4.6; on round two the average marks were 6.3 and 5.4 respectively. These marks apply to relatively few VU students so it is not sensible to investigate this further on the basis of the available data. A firm conclusion can thus not be drawn. It would be reasonable to expect VU students to do better than UvA students: students who take courses at the neighbouring university might be more strongly motivated, have more initiative and are generally more resourceful than other students. The initiative is needed to overcome the problem that one university uses a semester system, whereas the other uses a trimester system. The time-tables for students who visit the neighbouring university are therefore complex.

The option functional languages and architectures is being taught during the third term, as a 7 point subject. The course consists of two parts. The first part follows Bird and Wadler [1] closely, with a strong emphasis on program transformation and on proving properties of functions using induction. The second part of the course uses Peyton Jones [11] to teach the principles of implementing functional languages. The emphasis is on the lambda calculus and various abstract machine models. Here equational reasoning and inductive proofs are also used, but to a lesser extent than in part 1. The functional languages and architectures course is accompanied by a laboratory where the students build a combinator parser [18] and a type checker [2, Ch. 7] for a simple functional language. See table 5 for a summary of the details of the course.

We found no indication that the study of functional programming as a separate subject has an effect on the acquisition of basic proof skills. Of the participants who took the option functional languages and architectures, a small group of 11 students participated on both rounds. Their results are shown in the row marked *twice (functional)* in Table 3-d. The improvement of their basic proof skills from Round 1 to Round 2 was found to be +0.9, which is basically the same as that found for the entire group of 26 UvA CS students, who participated in both rounds. The average mark of the participants who took functional languages and architectures is rather higher than the average mark of all other participant groups. This is the case both on Round 1 (average mark 6.3) and on Round 2 (average mark 7.2). We think that this indicates only that students who choose functional languages and architectures as an option are attracted to the more fundamental approach to programming.

Table 4. Opinions of the participants of Rounds 1 and 2. n= the number of participants; $\bar{x}$ = average mark (on a scale from 0=poor - 10=excellent; a pass mark is at least 5.5), *m.o.e.*= margin of error, s= standard deviation.

	round 1				round 2			
	n	$\bar{x}$	s	*m.o.e.*	n	$\bar{x}$	s	*m.o.e.*
I found this easy	29	5.9	1.6	0.6	13	7.0	1.7	0.9
I enjoyed doing this	20	6.2	1.6	0.7	11	6.9	2.2	1.3
I practised proofs too long ago	26	4.1	1.9	0.7	13	4.2	2.2	1.2
I needed more time	35	4.4	1.9	0.6	10	4.3	1.4	0.8
I could do this if I had a book	25	4.0	1.8	0.7	13	3.7	2.2	1.2

Table 5. Summary description of the course on functional languages and architectures.

Title of the course:	Functional languages and architectures
Aims of the course:	1) To acquire functional programming skills. 2) To acquire basic insights in the theory of functional programming. 3) To gain a thorough understanding of how functional languages are implemented.
Audience:	Mandatory for 3rd/4th year technical CS students, optional for other CS students.
Prerequisites:	Thorough knowledge of imperative programming and computer architecture.
Texts:	Textbooks [1, 11] and assignment booklet.
Duration:	10 weeks teaching plus 4 weeks exam preparation

		times per week		hours per session		total hours per week
Time table:	lecture hours	2	×	1.5	=	3
	laboratories	1	×	2	=	2
	home work					15
Assessment:	Two written examinations and six laboratory assignments.					

5.3 Student Opinions

The exercises were accompanied by a number of questionnaire items which enabled the participants to express their opinion on the exercises. There was a list of 21 options, with a blank space for the students to write their own. Table 4 shows which opinions were indicated as most appropriate, with the average mark, margin of error and standard deviation as calculated for the sub-group expressing that particular opinion.

Participants who had positive feelings ("I found this easy" and "I enjoyed doing this") did reasonably well. Participants who had negative feelings about their skills ("I practised proofs too long ago") did not so well, like the participants who felt that circumstantial effects were important ("I needed more time" and "I could do this if I had a book"). The option "I will never learn this" was not selected as appropriate by a single participant.

6 Conclusions

Our students are not as well trained in basic proof skills as we hoped. This is unfortunate, as the UvA CS curriculum does provide opportunity for training these skills: one of the first three subjects being taught in the curriculum is a course in mathematical logic. This should provide for a good start, but clearly not all students appreciate the importance of proofs. During the first two years of the curriculum proof techniques are not emphasized enough. Students may get the impression that proof skills are not as important as programming skills. After these two years, the students choose a specialisation which offers the possibility to choose either subjects that strongly emphasize proof techniques or subjects that do not. As a result, it is possible for CS students to graduate with limited proof skills.

From the experimental results we conclude that:

- A clear relation between the study of functional programming as a separate subject (i.e. not integrated with the mathematics teaching) and the acquisition of basic proof skills could not be found.
- There is some improvement in basic proof skills as the students progress from the first to the second and to later years.
- There is some improvement in basic proof skills as the students progress from the beginning to the end of the third term.
- The basic proof skills of the students should generally be improved.
- Students should not be permitted to skip exam questions that test proof skills. This gives them the impression that proof skills are unimportant.
- The training of basic proof skills should not be confined to a small set of mathematically-oriented subjects. Such concepts should appear throughout the curriculum.

We believe that the situation could be improved by teaching proof skills as an integral part of the programming subjects. At the UvA, the coming academic year will see a better integration of subjects during the first term. This represents a first and important step towards a more integrated approach. We are hopeful that this may soon be followed by more steps.

The methodology that we have used could be a first step towards a more comprehensive longitudinal measurement of skill. The results highlight certain problems that are not so evident from the results of the more traditional testing scheme.

7 Acknowledgements

We thank Natasha Alechina, Marcel Beemster, Johan van Benthem, Jan Bergstra, Mark van den Brand, Ben Bruidegom, Kees Doets, Edo Dooijes, Peter van Emde Boas, Theo Janssen, Paul Klint, Hugh McEvoy, Hans van der Meer, Jon Mountjoy, Cora Smit, Leen Torenvliet and Rob Veldman for their help with the experiments and for their comments on draft versions of the paper. The comments of the anonymous referees are gratefully acknowledged. The willingness of many of our students to participate was greatly appreciated.

References

1. R. S. Bird and P. L. Wadler. *Introduction to functional programming.* Prentice Hall, New York, 1988.
2. A. J. Field and P. G. Harrison. *Functional programming.* Addison Wesley, Reading, Massachusetts, 1988.
3. D. Gries. Improving the curriculum through the teaching of calculation and discrimination. *Education and computing,* 7(1,2), 1991.
4. R. Harrison. The use of functional programming languages in teaching computer science. *J. functional programming,* 3(1):67–75, Jan 1993.
5. P. H. Hartel and L. O. Hertzberger. Paradigms and laboratories in the core computer science curriculum: An overview. Technical report CS-95-03, Dept. of Comp. Sys, Univ. of Amsterdam, Jan 1995.
6. J. L. Hein. A declarative laboratory approach for discrete structures, logic and computability. *ACM SIGCSE bulletin,* 25(3):19–24, Sep 1993.
7. P. B. Henderson and F. J. Romero. Teaching recursion as a problem-solving tool using standard ML. In R. A. Barrett and M. J. Mansfield, editors, *20th Computer science education,* pages 27–31, Louisville, Kentucky, Feb 1989. ACM SIGCSE bulletin, 21(1).
8. E. L. Lehman. *Nonparametrics: Statistical methods based on ranks.* Holden & Day, San Francisco, Calofornia, 1975.
9. C. Morgan. *Programming from specifications.* Prentice Hall, Hemel Hempstead, England, 1990.
10. D. L. Parnas. Education for computing professionals. *Computer,* 23(1):17–22, Jan 1990.
11. S. L. Peyton Jones. *The implementation of functional programming languages.* Prentice Hall, Englewood Cliffs, New Jersey, 1987.
12. E. S. Tan. *A stochastic growth model for the longitudinal measurement of ability.* PhD thesis, Dept. of Maths. and Comp. Sys, Univ. of Amsterdam, Dec 1994.
13. Th. J. M. (Dick) Tromp. *The acquisition of expertise in computer programming.* PhD thesis, Dept. of Psychology, Univ. of Amsterdam, Sep 1989.

14. A. J. Turner. A summary of the ACM/IEEE-CS joint curriculum task force report: Computing curricula 1991. *CACM*, 34(6):69–84, Jun 1991.
15. A. G. van Asch. To prove, why and how? *Int. J. Mathematical education in science and technology*, 24(2):301–313, Mar 1993.
16. J. F. A. K. van Benthem, H. P. van Ditmarsch, J. Ketting, and W. P. M. Meyer-Viol. *Logica voor Informatici*. Addison-Wesley Nederland, Amsterdam, 1991.
17. K. van den Berg. *Software measurement and functional programming*. PhD thesis, Twente technical Univ., Jun 1995.
18. P. L. Wadler. How to replace failure by a list of successes, a method for exception handling, backtracking, and pattern matching in lazy functional languages. In J.-P. Jouannaud, editor, *2nd Functional programming languages and computer architecture, LNCS 201*, pages 113–128, Nancy, France, Sep 1985. Springer-Verlag, Berlin.
19. R. L. Wainwright. Introducing functional programming in discrete mathematics. In M. J. Mansfield, C. M. White, and J. Hartman, editors, *23rd Computer science education*, pages 147–152, Kansas, Missouri, Mar 1992. ACM SIGCSE bulletin, 24(1).
20. U. Wolz and E. Conjura. Integrating mathematics and programming into a three tiered model for computer science education. In D. Joyce, editor, *25th Computer science education*, pages 223–227, Phoenix, Arizona, Mar 1994. ACM SIGCSE bulletin, 26(1).

The Dys-Functional Student

Chris Clack[1] and Colin Myers[2]

[1] Dept. of Computer Science, University College London, London WC1E 6BT
Email: clack@cs.uc.ac.uk
[2] School of Computer Science, University of Westminster, London W1M 8JS
Email: colin@wmin.ac.uk

Abstract. Functional languages liberate students from complex syntax, complex semantics and complex memory allocation; allowing them to concentrate on problem-solving. However, functional programming is not a universal panacea. Students still have problems with language features, program concepts and the legacy of the imperative paradigm. This paper aims to assist the lecturer asked to teach a functional language for the first time. We present typical student mistakes, attempt to explain why these mistakes arise, and propose possible remedies.

1 Introduction

Functional languages have been taught for a number of years at both University College London (UCL) and the University of Westminster, covering undergraduate and postgraduate courses.

The proximity of UCL and Westminster has resulted in a close collaboration. In particular, we have jointly produced two functional programming text books [Mye93, Cla94], together with on-line support in the form of coursework questions (solutions emailed on request), past exam papers, etc. These can be accessed via the World Wide Web at: http://www.cs.ucl.ac.uk/staff/C.Clack/teaching.

Our combined experience has proven extremely positive. For example, UCL first year undergraduates (many of whom have never programmed before) undertake a large Miranda[3] project at the end of the first term, including substantial programming tasks such as chess end-games, the travelling salesman problem and cross-compilation (this benefit has also been reported by, for example, [Lam93]). Furthermore, many advanced programmers find the experience of using a functional language improves their ability to solve problems in imperative languages.

Nonetheless, students find programming difficult. The aim of this paper is to help answer the question "What mistakes do students make and what does this tell us about how students think?"

Section 2 outlines our approach to teaching functional languages (course details are provided in the Appendix); Section 3 presents a collection of typical student problems that arise from Miranda language features; Section 4 looks at general programming problems and Section 5 at issues arising from previous experience of imperative programming. Each section contains *recommendations* for the lecturer to help overcome student errors and improve programming style.

[3] Miranda is a trademark of Research Software Ltd.

1.1 Scope

Space does not permit us to cover all classes and kinds of student mistakes. The approach taken by [Mye93] and [Cla94] is to teach programming practice by means of both correct code (to show how to do it) and incorrect code (how not to do it — examples often taken from actual student errors). We do not replicate this work, nor the valuable observations of [App94, Joo93, Mol93].

Furthermore, our discussion is limited to "programming in the small"; consequently, there is little consideration of data abstraction, design or larger software engineering issues.

2 The Teaching Process

From 40% to 100% of our students have had some previous experience of programming (often BASIC, Pascal, C or some assembler) and they are loath to discard their current programming skills. Indeed, experienced programmers will often be hostile since they do not believe that functional languages are used "in the real world".

This problem is exemplified by [Mor82], who asks whether functional programs are like *haikus*, in that they can teach through their innate elegance, even though in practice, they are as useless as a formal poem; or more like *karate* in that they have both an innate elegance and are useful in a fight.

We tackle this problem head-on and emphasize to these students that functional programming is a higher-level process that will make them better imperative programmers.

Rather than teach "functional programming" in general, our approach is to teach programming skills in a particular language (either Standard ML or Miranda). This is used to develop problem-solving skills which can be transferred to other paradigms. We avoid the notion of "programming as a mathematical exercise" because few of our students have sufficient background in mathematics to appreciate such a concept. This does not mean that we avoid rigour; merely that we emphasize a pragmatic approach.

3 Language features

This section details student problems that can be traced back to the features of Miranda. This should *not* be interpreted as a criticism of the language features themselves; the intention is to highlight the student learning path and the points at which conceptual jumps must be taken.

3.1 Problems with types

Students are introduced to *types* at a very early stage. However, data typing is not a straightforward issue for the naïve student:

Booleans.

Whilst students are generally happy to categorize numbers separately from text, they are less sure about Booleans. Booleans are more abstract than numbers and text; students cannot see, hear, taste, smell or touch "truth". Furthermore, a message (text) may itself be true or false; this causes further confusion, which manifests itself in difficulties with treating Booleans as data values, and is the source of the following common errors.

1. Returning strings instead of Booleans:

```
>equals_six :: num -> [char]
>equals_six x = "true", if x = 6
>               = "false", otherwise
```

2. Including unnecessary tests:

```
>equals_six :: num -> bool
>equals_six x = True, if x = 6
>               = False, otherwise
```

The simple version of the `equals_six` function often comes as rather a surprise:

```
>equals_six :: num -> bool
>equals_six x = (x = 6)
```

Numbers and their representation.

Students often do not understand the difference between a number and its representation; in everyday use they rarely use anything other than base ten to represent numbers. Despite the fact that most students have learnt about different number bases at school, they have difficulty with the number-to-string conversion function `ntos`.

This function takes input of type `num` and returns its denary (base 10) representation as a string. Thus, `ntos 23` returns `"23"`. Many students either cannot grasp the difference between `23` and `"23"`, or cannot understand what is involved in the conversion from a number to a string. When questioned, students agree that a computer stores all numbers as binary, but point out that Miranda treats all numbers as denary (viz. `x = 23`). Until challenged, some students tacitly assume that Miranda stores numbers as strings (as given by the built-in function `show`).

This concept needs much care; it may help to start with a function that gives the octal (or any non-denary) representation of a number.

Functions and type messages.

Many students find it difficult to accept that a function's type is a *mapping* from one type to another. They prefer to think it is the target type. It is probably this more than anything that leads to errors in function definition.

We encourage students to provide function type declarations before function definitions. Sadly, with higher order functions and with complex data structures (such as lists of lists or user-defined types) students often omit the type declaration when they write the function; because it "generates errors".

Recommendations.

Types are not intuitive. In particular, it is not obvious that "truth" can be manipulated as a data value. The lecturer must motivate the manipulation of truth values and should spend some time explaining the meaning of types; further, it is important to insist on type declarations before function definitions. Indeed, it is a good specification exercise to ask students to provide function type declarations without the function code.

Type error messages.

Both [Lam93] and [Joo93] comment that Miranda's type error reporting is not particularly helpful to the student. [Joo93] observes that it is mainly used to highlight the error's textual position but not the nature of the error. This is also our experience. For example, consider the following:

```
>splitsen :: [char] -> [[char]]
>splitsen sen = sss (sen, "")
>
>sss :: ([char],[char]) -> [[char]]
>sss (x : xs, wac)
>  = wac : sss(xs, ""), if x = " "
>  = sss(xs, wac : x), otherwise
```

This program generates the following error messages (we have wrapped some lines):

```
type error in definition of sss
(line  6 of "script.m")
cannot unify ([[char]],[char])
with ([char],[char])
(line  7 of "script.m")
cannot unify ([[char]],[char])
with ([char],[char])
incorrect declaration
(line  4 of "script.m")
specified, sss::([char],[char])->[[char]]
inferred,  sss::([[char]],char)->[char]
```

This is clearly unintelligible for the average student. Perhaps something closer to SML's error reporting would be more appropriate.

3.2 Problems with recursion

Not recognizing terminating cases.

When introducing the principle of recursion it is normal to introduce the idea of a base case and a general case; for example, zero and non-zero integers or the empty and non-empty lists. Students find this template easy enough to grasp but often will not understand how to extend it to deal with many base cases or with multiple lists.

This is exemplified in an answer to an exercise to give the pairwise addition of two lists. The code is taken from an actual student.

```
>listadd :: [num] -> [num] -> [num]
>listadd [] []  = []
>listadd (x : xs) [] = x : listadd xs []
>listadd [] (y : ys) = y : listadd  [] ys
>listadd (x : xs) (y : ys)
> = (x + y) : listadd xs ys
```

In the above code the second and third patterns should be treated as terminating cases but the student has erroneously thought that both lists must be empty to satisfy a terminating case. Perhaps they have been misled by writing the second and third patterns in the format:

```
>listadd (x : xs) [] = ???
>listadd [] (y : ys) = ???
```

If they started from the assumption that an empty list *anywhere* might be a base case then they might have written these patterns as:

```
>listadd any [] = ???
>listadd [] any = ???
```

In this manner they may have been less tempted on the path of fruitless recursion.

Note that the alternative approach of considering the general case/s and letting the base cases "fall out" would *not* particularly help to remove this problem. The student can justifiably argue that the following patterns are general cases:

```
>listadd (x : xs) [] = ???
>listadd [] (y : ys) = ???
```

Too many base cases.

It is also worthwhile noting that most students who gave an operationally correct answer also gave three base cases:

```
>listadd [] [] = []
>listadd [] any = any
>listadd any [] = any
```

In fact, there is no need to identify the first (double empty list) pattern. When questioned why they have included it, most students have argued for "efficiency purposes"; so that processing could stop immediately if two empty lists were encountered! They fail to recognize that the second and third base cases are specialized enough and that the extra test can only introduce extra processing.

Recommendations.

Despite many claims that recursion is easier to understand than iterative control structures, there is still a need to emphasize how to identify base cases, especially when more than one parameter of recursion is involved. There is also a need for a tool to think about general cases; for this we recommend the use of structural induction, as described in [Cla94].

At some point, program efficiency may also be mentioned. Beginners are told to put more general patterns last (because they often use overlapping patterns); once students have gained some facility with non-overlapping patterns, they may be invited to think more carefully about operational semantics and efficiency. For example, with `listadd` it may be best to place the base cases after the general case because they are less likely to occur for any given pair of lists.

3.3 Accumulating trouble

As has been observed, many students find it difficult to identify an appropriate base case for the parameter of recursion: in other words they have difficult with *last things.* Sadly, many also have difficulty with *first things* especially where numbers or accumulators are concerned.

The following exercise is typically answered incorrectly by over half the students of any given level of experience:

Find the two largest numbers in a list of numbers.

This specification seems easy enough to read but it generates one or more of the following mistakes.

Inadequate error handling.

For example, not catering for lists with less than two numbers. Curiously, if students are asked to discover the largest number in a list of numbers they will normally deal with the empty list as an error or exception but *two* largest numbers somehow deadens their validation skills.

False assumptions about the data.

Many students assume that "numbers" means "natural numbers". One solution to this simple exercise is to invoke an auxiliary function with two accumulators representing the two largest numbers and alter these accumulators, as required, on each recursive application:

```
>largestaux [] max1 max2 = (max1, max2)
>largestaux (x : xs) max1 max2
> = largestaux xs max1 max2, if x < max1
> = largestaux xs max2 x, if x > max2
> = largestaux xs x max2, otherwise
```

The common student mistake is to invoke the function as follows:

```
>largest any = largestaux any 0 0
```

The possibility that numbers might include negative numbers is rarely recognized.

Overcomplication.

It seems a universal truth that students will chose the more complicated of any two options. The above **largestaux** function relies upon the simple fact that **max1** will never be larger than **max2**. This means that it must be suitably invoked:

```
>largest []
> = error "at least two items needed"
>largest (x : [])
> = error "at least two items needed"
>largest (x : y : rest)
> = largestaux rest x y, if x < y
> = largestaux rest y x, otherwise
```

A little time looking at accumulator initialization often saves subsequent extra programming effort. Many students invoke **largestaux** as follows:

```
>largest (x : y  : rest)
> = largestaux rest x y
```

If the accumulators are unordered then the function **largestaux** is obliged somehow to sort the current **x, max1** and max2 and discard the smallest.

Innocence.

Another student solution is to select the largest number from the list and then search the list for the next largest number. Those students choosing this method rarely deal with the possibility of the two largest numbers being the same size. When asked why they have chosen this method, they occasionally say that they did not realize that they could identify the first *two* numbers in a list.

This error probably arises because it is so common to introduce list processing in the form:

```
>listhandler [] = ???
>listhandler (x : xs) = ???
```

Some students blink and miss more extended examples such as **(x : y : rest)**. Similarly the more passive student will not see the legality or desirability of more than one accumulator.

Laziness.

One of the problems with teaching is that students sometimes listen. It is now reasonably accepted that programming is theft, i.e. lecturers encourage students to re-use proven, working code. In the above example, clever students have been known to sort the list, reverse the result and extract the first two elements via pattern matching. The mistake is for the lecturer to penalize a good example of code re-use: however, some comments on algorithmic efficiency might be appropriate.

Recommendations.

Firstly, students should be encouraged to consider whether their functions are partial or total. The evidence is that the more complex the algorithmic task the more neglected the validation (irrespective of its level of complexity or difficulty).

Secondly, students must identify what is meant by a "number". David Turner, in conversation with the authors, has indicated that if Miranda 2 ever gets written then it may have two numeric types: natural numbers and floating point numbers. This may well be a more natural reflection of how students actually think about numbers.

Thirdly, students must consider the initialization of accumulators very carefully: to avoid errors and save on programming effort.

Finally, lecturers must show that pattern matching can extract any given element from a list.

3.4 Trouble with lists

Weaker students encounter two basic problems with lists: list construction and empty lists.

List construction.

Students are given two syntactic constructs for list manipulation: *cons* (:) and *append* (++). Furthermore, *cons* can be used on either side of a function equation *for different purposes.*

Whilst students are attracted to the simplicity of pattern matching, they are confused by the two uses of *cons*: both within a pattern to deconstruct a list and, conversely, within a function body to construct a list. There is no simple recipe that they can follow that will always work. They must make a choice at an abstract level of program design, and this is difficult for the weaker students.

Empty lists.

Students often confuse `[]` with `[[]]`, and `[]` with `""`. In particular, they are unaware that `[]` and `""` have different types. They are confused that `[]` is an empty list of *anything.*

There is a compulsion to use `[[]]` as the terminating value in a stack recursion producing a list of lists — the fact that `[]` can also be an empty list of type `[[*]]` is mystifying to some students.

The above problems are illustrated by the following student solutions to list-processing questions.

Write a function that will take a list of names and "shuffle" them by interleaving them a given number of times. To interleave a list of names, the list should be cut into two halves and then put together by taking elements from each half alternately.

Here is one student's answer (note the comments):

```
The output from sshuffle should be a list but
Miranda will not accept me using the cons ":"
thingy so I've had to use append "++".

>shuffle :: [[char]] -> [char]
>shuffle [] = ""
>shuffle lst = sshuffle (0,(#l div 2),lst)

>sshuffle :: (num,num,[[char]]) -> [char]
>sshuffle (i,pos,lst) = [], if i = #lst
>sshuffle (i,pos,lst)
> = (lst ! (pos+i)) ++ (lst ! i)
>    ++ (sshuffle (i+1,pos,lst))
```

Ignore the fact that the function doesn't answer the question (it will only do a single interleave) and that it needs further attention to avoid list indexing problems. The important issue is the confusion over lists and the important error is that the return type is `[char]` instead of `[[char]]`.

First, the student uses `""` as a terminating value for `shuffle`; from this point, all is lost because `""` has type `[char]`. Of course, the student should have used `[]` which has type `[*]` and can therefore happily accommodate a return type of `[[char]]`.

Second, by the student's own admission, there is a confusion over the use of *cons* and *append*. After making the apparently reasonable choice to use *append*, they miss the requirement to put the first two elements inside list brackets:

```
>sshuffle (i,s,l)
> = [(l ! (s+i))] ++ [(l ! i)]
>   ++ (sshuffle (i+1,s,l))
```

With just these two changes, the type definitions could be altered to `[[char]] -> [[char]]` and everything would be type correct.

Another example:

Write a function which takes a string of characters and returns the list of all words in the sentence, by dividing the string up at the spaces.

```
>splitsen :: [char] -> [[char]]
>splitsen sen = sss (sen,"")
>
>sss :: ([char],[char]) -> [[char]]
>sss (x:xs,wac)
>  = wac : sss(xs,""), if x=" "
>  = sss(xs,wac:x), otherwise
```

There are three basic problems: Firstly, the guard confuses a string with a character; it should be `if x = ' '`. Next, the final line shows a deep confusion regarding *cons*: the types are the wrong way around. Finally, the following base case is missing:

```
>sss ([], wac) = [wac]
```

On questioning, the student explained that Miranda had produced multiple type errors that were seemingly unrelated to the program. It was therefore difficult to debug the program (see Section 3.1.5).

As a final example of list abuse:

Write a function to transpose matrices.

```
>ro_list :: [[*]] -> [[*]]
>ro_list [] = []
>ro_list l
>  = (map hd l) : (ro_list (map tl l))
```

Here, each list item is successively tailed until only `ro_list [ [], [], [], [], ..., [] ]` remains. Then `ro_list` calls `map hd ([]:rest)` causing a `hd []` error. On questioning, the student thought there was a problem with the language! In fact, the solution is to include the following pattern:

```
>ro_list ([]:rest) = ro_list rest
```

Recommendations

It is wise to constrain weaker students so that they do not lose confidence. One approach is that weak students should use *cons* only in patterns to deconstruct a list and use *append* in function bodies.

Type problems, and problems involving empty lists, can only really be countered by providing the students with plenty of simple exercises that have been carefully constructed to illustrate the differences. Again, it is helpful to ask students to think about "last things" — i.e. what happens as termination is approached — and to encourage them to *visualize* the changes being made to data. Visualization is particularly helpful when lists of lists are manipulated (for example, successively mapping `tl` over a list of lists).

3.5 Higher order dysfunctions

The joy of functional programming is really obtained with the ability to understand and use higher order functions (HOFs). Students readily accept and understand simple and explicit HOF usage yet, despite lecturer enthusiasm, students seldom understand their implicit usage and more rarely employ their full potential. Students make simple use **map** and **filter** but are less willing to explore the power of partial application and function composition. We now describe some of the more common student misgivings.

Parameter passing.

One problem lies with the partial application of curried functions. After much exposure students can understand and define functions in terms of partial applications:

```
>multiply x y = x * y
>mult3 = multiply 3
```

They are far less likely to use them as parameters to other HOFs. The following code is rare:

```
>mapmult3 = map (multiply 3)
```

Students are more likely to write:

```
>mapmult3 nlist = map mult3 nlist
>                 where
>                 mult3 = multiply 3
```

Notice the student code is more explicit. Everything that is needed is *visible* and is either a constant or has a name. Students know that a function translates from one domain to another and expect *to see* this throughout their code. What the code fails to demonstrate is a willingness to undertake abstraction in the form of partial parameterization.

Mistrusting HOFs.

It appears that students do not trust that HOF code can be so concise as to not require a base case. The following code is typical in adding a superfluous test for `[]`:

```
>cubesplusone [] = []
>cubesplusone ns = map cinc ns
>                  where
>                  cinc x = (x^3) + 1
```

Once again notice the fear of passing a partial application as a parameter. Here, there is the added complication that a function composition of sections would be required (`(+1).(^3)`).

Manipulating HOFs.

As observed by [Lam93], students do not take naturally to using general recursive functions such as **foldr**. We agree, and notice that students are only comfortable if **foldr**'s functional parameter is an operator such as + or ++, which is associative and possesses an obvious identity.

Without guidance, most students do not discover HOF equivalences. For example, here is a typical answer to generate the sum of the squares of a number list:

```
>sumofsqrs xlist = sumlist (map square xlist)
>                  where sumlist = foldr (+) 0
>                        square x = x * x
```

A more concise (perhaps more efficient) answer is:

```
>sumofsqrs = foldr ((+) . (^2)) 0
```

This exploits the equivalence:

```
foldr f def (map g x) = foldr (f . g) def x
```

It is likely that students miss the equivalence because they have broken the problem into manageable chunks, i.e. firstly squaring each list item to create a new list, and then summing that list.

Overstretching the student.

Some HOF exercises are just too hard, although they can be simply expressed and have an elegant solution which may demonstrate many important points. Setting such questions actively discourages students. Examples include generating a powerset (depending on the student background), manipulating combinators and rewriting **filter** in terms of **foldr**.

Here is the best student answer we have seen to meet this last requirement:

```
>ffilter fun alist
> = foldr ((++) . auxr fun) [] alist
>   where
>   auxr fun elem = [elem], if fun elem
>                 = [], otherwise
```

This was a very good attempt; it needs an imaginative leap to represent an excluded item as **[]**, and hence to use **++** to combine the remaining items. Notice, however, that **auxr** did not require **fun** which was already in scope, and that mentioning **alist** was superfluous.

Recommendations.

Firstly, HO abstraction should be illustrated by means of textual substitutions [Cla94]. For example (where ==> represents a substitution step):

```
    mapmult3 [5]
==> map (multiply 3) [5]
==> ((multiply 3) 5) : map (multiply 3) []
==> (multiply 3 5) : map (multiply 3) []
==> 15 : map (multiply 3) []
==> 15 : []
```

Secondly, lecturers should emphasize that HOFs such as map, filter, foldr and foldl encapsulate *both the general case and the base case* of list recursion.

Furthermore, lecturers should control their enthusiasm for HOFs and avoid setting "clever" questions just for the sake of the question.

4 Programming problems

It is seductive to believe that using a functional language will somehow cause all the normal problems associated with programming to go away. This is not the case. However, the use of a functional language does facilitate the diagnosis of programming problems (often if only because the programs are shorter than the equivalent imperative programs).

4.1 Assumptions and comments

One of the major problems that students appear to have is to make assumptions when not required and not to make them when required.

It is by now well-established that it is difficult to provide an accurate natural language specification of even the simplest of problems. This makes setting student exercises a potentially hazardous business, relying upon a tacit understanding, by both lecturer and student, of what is required from the student at any given stage in their course.

To help resolve such ambiguity, it is not uncommon to precede exercises with a request such as:

> *Remember to add appropriate comments and assumptions. If any specification is vague then ask for clarification.*

Given that most students only attempt coursework twenty-four hours (at best) before the deadline, it is a rare event for a lecturer to be asked for clarification, *even if the original question is highly ambiguous.* Instead the better student will tend to resolve any ambiguity in the same way as the lecturer *and often not bother to explain the ambiguity.* Their answer will generally be accepted as correct and given full credit, despite the absence of clarifying comments.

Weaker students often fail to see the question's ambiguity and so either make no assumptions and hence provide a good answer to a simpler problem; or leap to some wild "resolution" of the ambiguity, also not bothering to state their assumptions. For both cases students lose marks and hence lose some confidence in their own ability.

The following amplifies the first of these points:

> *Write a function which takes a character and returns the next letter in the alphabet (make it return 'a' if given 'z').*

This exercise is horrid in that it allows the confusion of ASCII characters with lowercase alphabetic letters. What should be returned by `'Z'`? What about digits and other non-alphabetic characters?

Typically, only 10% of students will actually state their full assumptions. Of the rest, about half will assume that the input was alphabetic and catered for both `'z'` (as explicitly requested) and `'Z'` (as was perhaps was implied). Thus they answer a simpler question than intended.

The other half will decide (quite reasonably) that all non-alphabetic characters should raise an error (though will not comment that this was their assumption). Here, they should be given full credit for making a reasonable assumption; it would be churlish to act otherwise. However, apart from the code itself, there will be no visible indication that they have really thought through the problem.

Misunderstanding the question.

It is surprisingly easy for students to misunderstand a seemingly innocuous question:

> *Write a function to test if two lists have the same elements, regardless of their order.*

The simple answer uses the list difference operator:

```
>testlist :: [*] -> [*] -> bool
>testlist xs ys = ((xs -- ys) = [])
>                 & ((ys -- xs) = [])
```

However, consider this student answer:

```
>testlist :: [*] -> [*] -> bool
>testlist a b = True, if #(a--(a--b)) > 0
>             = False, otherwise
```

At first sight this could be either a misunderstanding of how the list difference operator works, or just poor reasoning. On further analysis, it becomes clear that the student is testing whether *two lists have any elements the same* rather than whether they have the same elements!

Here is another common misunderstanding of the above question:

```
>testlist :: [*]->[*]->bool
>testlist xs ys = ~ notsame xs ys


>notsame :: [*]->[*]->bool
>notsame xs ys
>     = (member (isinxs xs ys) False)
>       \/ (member (isinys ys xs) False)

>isinys = isinxs
>isinxs xs ys = map (member xs) ys
```

Here, the student has extended the question so that the function tests for the same elements *irrespective of repetition.* Some students did this deliberately; they stated their assumptions in their comments, thereby acknowledging that they were answering a different question. Others seemed not to realize that they were ignoring repetitions:

```
>testlist l1 l2 = and (same_test l1 l2)

>same_test (x : xs) list2
>       = others ++ test
>         where
>         test = ((member list2 x) : [])
>         others = (same_test xs list2)
```

The problem of misunderstanding the question often arises because there is a cultural gap between the lecturer and the students. The lecturer believes that it is "obvious" that the question cannot possibly have more than one interpretation, whereas the students think that a different interpretation is perfectly reasonable.

Students are often bewildered by questions because of naïvety, preconceptions, different schooling and different nationalities. They have to learn the culture of the university and the lecturer's expectations.

Recommendations.

Firstly, the ambiguity of natural language makes it hard to set even the simplest of unambiguous exercises. However, this is not necessarily a bad thing as it will often yield a good indication of which students are willing to think around a problem; which students passively take the path of least resistance; and which students are extra-terrestrials.

Secondly, notwithstanding the fact that ambiguity can be useful, we should endeavour to provide more precise questions *illustrated with examples.*

Thirdly, students should be obliged to use sensible comments even for apparently simple exercises. Of course, this begs the question 'what is a sensible comment?'.

4.2 Analysis and testing

Many students find analysis very hard. They find it so difficult to find an answer that works at all for just one simple test case, that they cannot face analyzing the problem further to provide a full solution. Testing is often viewed as pure drudgery; students often feel that they have found an answer to the question and that is good enough. Analysis and testing are, of course, key skills of programming and it is very important that students are trained to be thorough in both.

Here are two examples based on the previous `testlist` exercise. `testlist1` uses the test `(x=y)` instead of `(#x = #y)` (showing a lack of testing), whereas `testlist2` neglects to check for `((y -- x) = [])` (showing a lack of analysis).

```
>
>testlist1 :: [*] -> [*] -> bool
>testlist1 x y = (same x y = #x) & (x=y)
>
>same :: [*] -> [*] -> num
>same [] any = 0
>same (x:xs) ys
>  = 1 + same xs ys, if member ys x
>  = same xs ys, otherwise
>
>testlist2 :: [*] -> [*] -> bool
>testlist2 x y = ((x -- y) = [])
>
```

Recommendations.

Oblige students to provide a test plan, test data and test results.

4.3 Basic skills

Finally, some students still require help with their basic programming skills. The first example is from a student who is over-eager to give error messages (the function should actually return True for two empty lists) and over-eager to use **where** blocks.

```
>testlist :: [*]->[*]->bool
>testlist [] [] = error "Both lists empty"
>testlist [] any = error "One list empty"
>testlist any [] = error "One list empty"
>testlist l1 l2 = and (same_test l1 l2)
>
>same_test :: [*]->[*]->[bool]
>same_test (x : []) l2
>           = test
>             where
>             test = ((member l2 x) : [])
>same_test (x : xs) l2
>           = others ++ test
>             where
>             test = ((member l2 x) : [])
>             others = (same_test xs l2)
```

The second example is from a student who has forgotten that the base cases might be called immediately rather than at the end of the recursion (the function could be called as `testlist [] [1,2,3]` or as `testlist [] []`, both of which would provide the wrong answer). Furthermore, they have clearly failed to find a solution, as evidenced by the recursive call which seems to display a certain desperation!

```
>testlist :: ([*],[*])->bool
>testlist ([],anylist) = True
>testlist (anylist,[]) = False
>testlist (a:b,c:d)
>       = ((a=c) & testlist (b,d))
>         \/ testlist ((a:b),d)
```

5 The Grasp of the Imperative

Once a student has learnt to program using an imperative language, they find it difficult to escape its grasp. The converse is not true — students who first learn with a functional language go on to become good imperative programmers.

5.1 Pattern matching and guards

For the purposes of this section the term *pattern matching* will be used to describe the matching of a pattern to one of several alternative function patterns, e.g. the following function `cstylenot` has two patterns:

```
>cstylenot True = 0
>cstylenot False = 1
```

Using "guards" there are two possible versions:

```
>cstylenot1 x = 0, if x = True
>             = 1, otherwise
>
>cstylenot2 x = 0, if x = True
>             = 1, if x = False
```

The received wisdom is that pattern matching is probably better where discrete cases can be identified (as above). This corresponds more naturally to mapping the possible cases of input to their desired output: an observation that has proven useful from Jackson Structured Programming onwards. Yet at least half of final year BSc students and non-conversion MSc students chose the guard approach to solve similar simple problems or subproblems.

This is probably because students who can program fluently in a procedural language such as C, C++ or Modula-2 find it difficult to think in terms of functions. They find the transition to mathematical functions rather than imperative language "functions" hard. They eventually cope with definitions such as `f x = x + x` and that `f` can be treated as a value rather than some computation: however, they find it alien to have more than one definition of `f`, such as with pattern matching.

By contrast, students who learn a functional language as their first serious programming language can readily accept the idea of alternative patterns for a function. This leads more naturally to an appreciation of looking at the nature of input rather than fretting about operational expediency.

Given that most professional programmers do not use a functional language, it is not unreasonable to ask what advantages students gain from a pattern matching approach. The first advantage has been stated above: input awareness. The second is that imperative language **case**, **switch** or **evaluate** commands are really forms of pattern matching. The functional programmer should have no difficulty converting to a good imperative language style. The converse is not necessarily true.

5.2 Variables

Control.

The controlling of recursion can come as a nasty shock to experienced programmers. The more stubborn students (especially part-timers who earn their living from programming) will attempt to use external variables to achieve iteration rather than accept parameters of recursion. This is typical:

```
>x = 1
>loop y = y, if x = 3
>       = loop x + y, otherwise
```

Of course, this kind of error is a consequence of the students' imperative programming legacy and can easily be overcome within a function definition. However, many students cling to the procedural model which encourages them to use variable assignment and global state to solve problems; they are particularly puzzled by the functional language approach to file input-output and interaction.

Name redefinition.

Miranda enforces referential transparency by refusing to allow the re-use of any name already bound by the programmer in the script file or by the standard environment. Given the large number of names within the latter, this can lead to programmer frustration and, more importantly, to hidden errors if the programmer fails to alter all references to an offending redefinition.

5.3 Formal methods

One of the strongest arguments for the use of functional programming languages is that they have a sound mathematical basis. Consequently students who have a good grasp of discrete mathematics should become good functional programmers.

Its difficult to say whether this observation really holds for students who have already been swallowed by the imperative programming paradigm. The following student-generated code for writing the set membership function is typical:

```
>member []  x = False
>member (y : rest) x
>       = True, if x = y
>       = member rest x, otherwise
```

Students initially fail to see that the second pattern is better written as a disjunction:

```
>member (front :: rest) x
>       = (x = front) \/ (member rest x)
```

Instead they believe that a conditional must be used, and used in the manner of a control statement rather than a selector. This is probably a result of too much imperative programming.

Notice that Miranda permits an elegant pattern matching solution for this particular problem:

```
>member []  x = False
>member (x : rest) x = True
>member (y : rest) x = member rest x
```

Recommendations.

The imperative paradigm is hard to break once established. It is recommended to teach a functional language before an imperative language, *in conjunction with* teaching "formal methods". The above example only needs an understanding of simple propositional calculus. Similar formalisms can help to understand the ordering of expressions, the nature of functions and so on.

The semantics and functionality of file input-output and interaction have been the subject of much recent research; however, little work has been done on the provision of friendly syntax.

6 Summary

The issues discussed in this paper are widely neglected in the literature, yet there is a need to support lecturers who teach functional programming.

Based on our experience of using functional languages to teach programming skills, we have analyzed a range of student problems and provided recommendations for solving them. Of course, space has not permitted a complete list of student mistakes and their analysis, nor have our recommendations been exhaustive. We believe that there is still much useful work to be done in this area, to support the development of new teaching strategies and to guide the development of teaching-related language features.

Acknowledgments

We thank Mark d'Inverno for his constructive comments on earlier drafts of this paper.

References

[App94] A. Appel. *A critique of Standard ML. JFP*, 3:391–429, 1993.

[Cla94] C. Clack, C. Myers & E. Poon. *Programming with Miranda.* Prentice Hall, 1994.

[Joo93] S. Joosten, K. van der Berg & G. ven der Hoeven. Teaching functional programming to first-year students. *JFP*, 3:49–65, 1993.

[Lam93] T. Lambert, P.Lindsay & K. Robinson. Using Miranda as a first programming language. *JFP*, 3:5–34, 1993.

[Mol93] P. Molyneux. Functional programming for business students. *JFP*, 3:35–48, 1993.

[Mor82] J. Morris. Real Programming in Functional Languages, in J. Darlington P. Henderson & D. Turner *Functional Programming and its Applications*, CUP, 1982.

[Mye93] C. Myers, C. Clack & E. Poon. *Programming with Standard ML.* Prentice Hall, 1993.

Appendix

Courses at the University of Westminster

1. **Title**
   (a) Functional Programming.
   (b) Functional and Application Techniques.
2. **Aims**
   (a) A specialist course for final year undergraduates. It introduces the functional programming paradigm, and contrasts this with the imperative programming paradigm. The course has a heavy practical emphasis.
   A similar but lower level course has also been taught to Information Systems students, who generally only have first year programming skills.
   (b) An advanced MSc course. In addition to the objectives in (a), it compares the major functional styles and offers some theoretical underpinning.
3. **Audience**
   Both courses are aimed at Computer Scientists and Software Engineers.
4. **Level**
   (a) Final year undergraduates.
   (b) Advanced MSc students.
5. **Prerequisites**
   (a) A good foundation in imperative programming, data structures and data abstraction together with an introductory course in formal methods.
   (b) An honours degree or equivalent in Computing or a related discipline.
6. **Recommended Textbook**
   C. Clack, C. Myers & E. Poon [Cla94].
7. **Duration**
   Both courses are 12 weeks, with 3 lectures and one tutorial class per week.
8. **Assessment:**
   Both courses: 30% coursework, 70% examination.

Courses at University College London

1. **Title**
   (a) Introductory Programming.
   (b) Functional Programming.
2. **Aims**
   (a) Foundation first-term first-year undergraduate course. It aims to provide a solid introduction to problem-solving and the expression of solutions in algorithmic terms. The course has a heavy practical emphasis.
   (b) Second-term option for conversion MSc students. It provides an alternative programming paradigm, improving problem-solving and programming skills. It also introduces implementation methods.
3. **Audience**
   (a) Taken by students on the following undergraduate degrees: Computer Science ("CS"), Maths & CS, CS & Electronic Engineering. In the past, also by CS and Cognitive Science, and some affiliate students.
   (b) Taken by students with a non-CS first degree. These students have a variety of backgrounds, ranging from Fine Arts to Physics.
4. **Level**
   (a) First year undergraduates.
   (b) Conversion MSc students.
5. **Prerequisites**
   (a) None. ('A' Level Maths and some trigonometry preferred).
   (b) A non-CS honours degree. Reasonable facility in Maths and capacity for abstract thought.
6. **Recommended Textbook**
   (a) C. Clack, C. Myers & E. Poon [Cla94].
   (b) C. Myers, C. Clack & E. Poon [Mye93].
7. **Duration**
   Both courses are 11 weeks (in a 12-week term), with 3 lectures per week. The BSc course also provides one tutorial and one laboratory class per week.
8. **Assessment**
   (a) 20% coursework, 30% project, 50% examination.
   (b) 25% coursework, 75% examination.

Springer-Verlag and the Environment

We at Springer-Verlag firmly believe that an international science publisher has a special obligation to the environment, and our corporate policies consistently reflect this conviction.

We also expect our business partners – paper mills, printers, packaging manufacturers, etc. – to commit themselves to using environmentally friendly materials and production processes.

The paper in this book is made from low- or no-chlorine pulp and is acid free, in conformance with international standards for paper permanency.

Lecture Notes in Computer Science

For information about Vols. 1–945

please contact your bookseller or Springer-Verlag

Vol. 946: C. Froidevaux, J. Kohlas (Eds.), Symbolic and Quantitative Approaches to Reasoning and Uncertainty. Proceedings, 1995. X, 420 pages. 1995. (Subseries LNAI).

Vol. 947: B. Möller (Ed.), Mathematics of Program Construction. Proceedings, 1995. VIII, 472 pages. 1995.

Vol. 948: G. Cohen, M. Giusti, T. Mora (Eds.), Applied Algebra, Algebraic Algorithms and Error-Correcting Codes. Proceedings, 1995. XI, 485 pages. 1995.

Vol. 949: D.G. Feitelson, L. Rudolph (Eds.), Job Scheduling Strategies for Parallel Processing. Proceedings, 1995. VIII, 361 pages. 1995.

Vol. 950: A. De Santis (Ed.), Advances in Cryptology - EUROCRYPT '94. Proceedings, 1994. XIII, 473 pages. 1995.

Vol. 951: M.J. Egenhofer, J.R. Herring (Eds.), Advances in Spatial Databases. Proceedings, 1995. XI, 405 pages. 1995.

Vol. 952: W. Olthoff (Ed.), ECOOP '95 - Object-Oriented Programming. Proceedings, 1995. XI, 471 pages. 1995.

Vol. 953: D. Pitt, D.E. Rydeheard, P. Johnstone (Eds.), Category Theory and Computer Science. Proceedings, 1995. VII, 252 pages. 1995.

Vol. 954: G. Ellis, R. Levinson, W. Rich. J.F. Sowa (Eds.), Conceptual Structures: Applications, Implementation and Theory. Proceedings, 1995. IX, 353 pages. 1995. (Subseries LNAI).

VOL. 955: S.G. Akl, F. Dehne, J.-R. Sack, N. Santoro (Eds.), Algorithms and Data Structures. Proceedings, 1995. IX, 519 pages. 1995.

Vol. 956: X. Yao (Ed.), Progress in Evolutionary Computation. Proceedings, 1993, 1994. VIII, 314 pages. 1995. (Subseries LNAI).

Vol. 957: C. Castelfranchi, J.-P. Müller (Eds.), From Reaction to Cognition. Proceedings, 1993. VI, 252 pages. 1995. (Subseries LNAI).

Vol. 958: J. Calmet, J.A. Campbell (Eds.), Integrating Symbolic Mathematical Computation and Artificial Intelligence. Proceedings, 1994. X, 275 pages. 1995.

Vol. 959: D.-Z. Du, M. Li (Eds.), Computing and Combinatorics. Proceedings, 1995. XIII, 654 pages. 1995.

Vol. 960: D. Leivant (Ed.), Logic and Computational Complexity. Proceedings, 1994. VIII, 514 pages. 1995.

Vol. 961: K.P. Jantke, S. Lange (Eds.), Algorithmic Learning for Knowledge-Based Systems. X, 511 pages. 1995. (Subseries LNAI).

Vol. 962: I. Lee, S.A. Smolka (Eds.), CONCUR '95: Concurrency Theory. Proceedings, 1995. X, 547 pages. 1995.

Vol. 963: D. Coppersmith (Ed.), Advances in Cryptology - CRYPTO '95. Proceedings, 1995. XII, 467 pages. 1995.

Vol. 964: V. Malyshkin (Ed.), Parallel Computing Technologies. Proceedings, 1995. XII, 497 pages. 1995.

Vol. 965: H. Reichel (Ed.), Fundamentals of Computation Theory. Proceedings, 1995. IX, 433 pages. 1995.

Vol. 966: S. Haridi, K. Ali, P. Magnusson (Eds.), EURO-PAR '95 Parallel Processing. Proceedings, 1995. XV, 734 pages. 1995.

Vol. 967: J.P. Bowen, M.G. Hinchey (Eds.), ZUM '95: The Z Formal Specification Notation. Proceedings, 1995. XI, 571 pages. 1995.

Vol. 968: N. Dershowitz, N. Lindenstrauss (Eds.), Conditional and Typed Rewriting Systems. Proceedings, 1994. VIII, 375 pages. 1995.

Vol. 969: J. Wiedermann, P. Hájek (Eds.), Mathematical Foundations of Computer Science 1995. Proceedings, 1995. XIII, 588 pages. 1995.

Vol. 970: V. Hlaváč, R. Šára (Eds.), Computer Analysis of Images and Patterns. Proceedings, 1995. XVIII, 960 pages. 1995.

Vol. 971: E.T. Schubert, P.J. Windley, J. Alves-Foss (Eds.), Higher Order Logic Theorem Proving and Its Applications. Proceedings, 1995. VIII, 400 pages. 1995.

Vol. 972: J.-M. Hélary, M. Raynal (Eds.), Distributed Algorithms. Proceedings, 1995. XI, 333 pages. 1995.

Vol. 973: H.H. Adelsberger, J. Lažanský, V. Mařík (Eds.), Information Management in Computer Integrated Manufacturing. IX, 665 pages. 1995.

Vol. 974: C. Braccini, L. DeFloriani, G. Vernazza (Eds.), Image Analysis and Processing. Proceedings, 1995. XIX, 757 pages. 1995.

Vol. 975: W. Moore, W. Luk (Eds.), Field-Programmable Logic and Applications. Proceedings, 1995. XI, 448 pages. 1995.

Vol. 976: U. Montanari, F. Rossi (Eds.), Principles and Practice of Constraint Programming — CP '95. Proceedings, 1995. XIII, 651 pages. 1995.

Vol. 977: H. Beilner, F. Bause (Eds.), Quantitative Evaluation of Computing and Communication Systems. Proceedings, 1995. X, 415 pages. 1995.

Vol. 978: N. Revell, A M. Tjoa (Eds.), Database and Expert Systems Applications. Proceedings, 1995. XV, 654 pages. 1995.

Vol. 979: P. Spirakis (Ed.), Algorithms — ESA '95. Proceedings, 1995. XII, 598 pages. 1995.

Vol. 980: A. Ferreira, J. Rolim (Eds.), Parallel Algorithms for Irregularly Structured Problems. Proceedings, 1995. IX, 409 pages. 1995.

Vol. 981: I. Wachsmuth, C.-R. Rollinger, W. Brauer (Eds.), KI-95: Advances in Artificial Intelligence. Proceedings, 1995. XII, 269 pages. (Subseries LNAI).

Vol. 982: S. Doaitse Swierstra, M. Hermenegildo (Eds.), Programming Languages: Implementations, Logics and Programs. Proceedings, 1995. XI, 467 pages. 1995.

Vol. 983: A. Mycroft (Ed.), Static Analysis. Proceedings, 1995. VIII, 423 pages. 1995.

Vol. 984: J.-M. Haton, M. Keane, M. Manago (Eds.), Advances in Case-Based Reasoning. Proceedings, 1994. VIII, 307 pages. 1995.

Vol. 985: T. Sellis (Ed.), Rules in Database Systems. Proceedings, 1995. VIII, 373 pages. 1995.

Vol. 986: Henry G. Baker (Ed.), Memory Management. Proceedings, 1995. XII, 417 pages. 1995.

Vol. 987: P.E. Camurati, H. Eveking (Eds.), Correct Hardware Design and Verification Methods. Proceedings, 1995. VIII, 342 pages. 1995.

Vol. 988: A.U. Frank, W. Kuhn (Eds.), Spatial Information Theory. Proceedings, 1995. XIII, 571 pages. 1995.

Vol. 989: W. Schäfer, P. Botella (Eds.), Software Engineering — ESEC '95. Proceedings, 1995. XII, 519 pages. 1995.

Vol. 990: C. Pinto-Ferreira, N.J. Mamede (Eds.), Progress in Artificial Intelligence. Proceedings, 1995. XIV, 487 pages. 1995. (Subseries LNAI).

Vol. 991: J. Wainer, A. Carvalho (Eds.), Advances in Artificial Intelligence. Proceedings, 1995. XII, 342 pages. 1995. (Subseries LNAI).

Vol. 992: M. Gori, G. Soda (Eds.), Topics in Artificial Intelligence. Proceedings, 1995. XII, 451 pages. 1995. (Subseries LNAI).

Vol. 993: T.C. Fogarty (Ed.), Evolutionary Computing. Proceedings, 1995. VIII, 264 pages. 1995.

Vol. 994: M. Hebert, J. Ponce, T. Boult, A. Gross (Eds.), Object Representation in Computer Vision. Proceedings, 1994. VIII, 359 pages. 1995.

Vol. 995: S.M. Müller, W.J. Paul, The Complexity of Simple Computer Architectures. XII, 270 pages. 1995.

Vol. 996: P. Dybjer, B. Nordström, J. Smith (Eds.), Types for Proofs and Programs. Proceedings, 1994. X, 202 pages. 1995.

Vol. 997: K.P. Jantke, T. Shinohara, T. Zeugmann (Eds.), Algorithmic Learning Theory. Proceedings, 1995. XV, 319 pages. 1995.

Vol. 998: A. Clarke, M. Campolargo, N. Karatzas (Eds.), Bringing Telecommunication Services to the People – IS&N '95. Proceedings, 1995. XII, 510 pages. 1995.

Vol. 999: P. Antsaklis, W. Kohn, A. Nerode, S. Sastry (Eds.), Hybrid Systems II. VIII, 569 pages. 1995.

Vol. 1000: J. van Leeuwen (Ed.), Computer Science Today. XIV, 643 pages. 1995.

Vol. 1002: J.J. Kistler, Disconnected Operation in a Distributed File System. XIX, 249 pages. 1995.

Vol. 1004: J. Staples, P. Eades, N. Katoh, A. Moffat (Eds.), Algorithms and Computation. Proceedings, 1995. XV, 440 pages. 1995.

Vol. 1005: J. Estublier (Ed.), Software Configuration Management. Proceedings, 1995. IX, 311 pages. 1995.

Vol. 1006: S. Bhalla (Ed.), Information Systems and Data Management. Proceedings, 1995. IX, 321 pages. 1995.

Vol. 1007: A. Bosselaers, B. Preneel (Eds.), Integrity Primitives for Secure Information Systems. VII, 239 pages. 1995.

Vol. 1008: B. Preneel (Ed.), Fast Software Encryption. Proceedings, 1994. VIII, 367 pages. 1995.

Vol. 1009: M. Broy, S. Jähnichen (Eds.), KORSO: Methods, Languages, and Tools for the Construction of Correct Software. X, 449 pages. 1995. Vol.

Vol. 1010: M. Veloso, A. Aamodt (Eds.), Case-Based Reasoning Research and Development. Proceedings, 1995. X, 576 pages. 1995. (Subseries LNAI).

Vol. 1011: T. Furuhashi (Ed.), Advances in Fuzzy Logic, Neural Networks and Genetic Algorithms. Proceedings, 1994. (Subseries LNAI).

Vol. 1012: M. Bartošek, J. Staudek, J. Wiedermann (Eds.), SOFSEM '95: Theory and Practice of Informatics. Proceedings, 1995. XI, 499 pages. 1995.

Vol. 1013: T.W. Ling, A.O. Mendelzon, L. Vieille (Eds.), Deductive and Object-Oriented Databases. Proceedings, 1995. XIV, 557 pages. 1995.

Vol. 1014: A.P. del Pobil, M.A. Serna, Spatial Representation and Motion Planning. XII, 242 pages. 1995.

Vol. 1015: B. Blumenthal, J. Gornostaev, C. Unger (Eds.), Human-Computer Interaction. Proceedings, 1995. VIII, 203 pages. 1995.

Vol. 1017: M. Nagl (Ed.), Graph-Theoretic Concepts in Computer Science. Proceedings, 1995. XI, 406 pages. 1995.

Vol. 1018: T. Little, R. Gusella (Eds.), Network and Operating Systems Support for Digital Audio and Video. Proceedings, 1995. XI, 357 pages. 1995.

Vol. 1019: E. Brinksma, W.R. Cleaveland, K.G. Larsen, T. Margaria, B. Steffen (Eds.), Tools and Algorithms for the Construction and Analysis of Systems. Selected Papers, 1995. VII, 291 pages. 1995.

Vol. 1020: I.D. Watson (Ed.), Progress in Case-Based Reasoning. Proceedings, 1995. VIII, 209 pages. 1995. (Subseries LNAI).

Vol. 1021: M.P. Papazoglou (Ed.), OOER '95: Object-Oriented and Entity-Relationship Modeling. Proceedings, 1995. XVII, 451 pages. 1995.

Vol. 1022: P.H. Hartel, R. Plasmeijer (Eds.), Functional Programming Languages in Education. Proceedings, 1995. X, 309 pages. 1995.

Vol. 1023: K. Kanchanasut, J.-J. Lévy (Eds.), Algorithms, Concurrency and Knowlwdge. Proceedings, 1995. X, 410 pages. 1995.

Vol. 1024: R.T. Chin, H.H.S. Ip, A.C. Naiman, T.-C. Pong (Eds.), Image Analysis Applications and Computer Graphics. Proceedings, 1995. XVI, 533 pages. 1995.

Vol. 1025: C. Boyd (Ed.), Cryptography and Coding. Proceedings, 1995. IX, 291 pages. 1995.